WINNING THE SECOND BATTLE:

Canadian Veterans and the Return to Civilian Life, 1915–1930

More than half a million Canadians served in the First World War. Their return to civilian life presented an enormous challenge to government and social institutions. The degree to which that challenge was met and the far-reaching implications of the veterans' politicization form the core of this study by two eminent Canadian historians.

Desmond Morton and Glenn Wright point out that Canada was a leader among its allies in devising plans for the retraining of disabled soldiers. Canada's pension rates were the most generous in the world. From soldier settlement to returned soldiers' insurance, Ottawa had prepared for returning Canadian armies with a care and foresight that was virtually unique among belligerents. In those carefully laid plans, and in the veterans' organization and struggle to create their own version of civil re-establishment, were the roots of the modern welfare state.

But in the end, the momentum of the veterans' political drive was slowed by diminishing government support and dwindling resources, and veterans ultimately lost their 'Second Battle.' The story of that defeat, never told until now, reveals a great deal about Canadian government, pressure groups, and politics in the interwar period.

Desmond Morton is professor of history at the University of Toronto and principal of Erindale College. He is the author of *Ministers and Generals: Politics and the Canadian Militia, 1868–1904, A Peculiar Kind of Politics: Canada's Overseas Ministry in the First World War, A Military History of Canada, Bloody Victory: Canadians and the D-Day Campaign* (with J.L. Granatstein), and numerous other books.

Glenn Wright is a specialist in military and veterans' records with the Public Archives of Canada.

... it is the hardest battle that most of our boys have ever had to fight – to drive out the invading spirit of weakness and indecision, to recover the lost ground, the lost spirit of energy and independence; and he has to fight it alone, unless you fight it with him.

Invalided Soldiers Commission, 1918

Desmond Morton and
Glenn Wright

from the author

Winning the Second Battle: Canadian Veterans and the Return to Civilian Life

1915–1930

Thanks for the book. on how the Americans became a nation *Dr M.*

UNIVERSITY OF TORONTO PRESS

Toronto Buffalo London

© University of Toronto Press 1987
Toronto Buffalo London
Printed in Canada

ISBN 0-8020-5705-5 (cloth)
ISBN 0-8020-6634-8 (paper)

Printed on acid-free paper

Canadian Cataloguing in Publication Data

Morton, Desmond, 1937–
  Winning the second battle

  Bibliography: p.
  Includes index.
  ISBN 0-8020-5705-5 (bound). – ISBN 0-8020-6634-8 (pbk.)

  1. Veterans – Canada. 2. Veterans, Disabled – Canada.
  I. Wright, Glenn T. II. Title.

  UB359.C3M67 1987   355.1′15   C87-093263-2

This book has been published with the help of grants from the Social
Science Federation of Canada, using funds provided by the Social
Sciences and Humanities Research Council of Canada, and from the
Canada Council and the Ontario Arts Council under their block grant
programs. Publication has also been assisted by a grant from the
University of Western Ontario.

Part of the material in this book was delivered
by Desmond Morton as the 1985 Joanne Goodman Lectures,
established by Joanne's family and friends to perpetuate
the memory of her blithe spirit, her quest for knowledge,
and the rewarding years she spent at the
University of Western Ontario.

Contents

Preface

The demobilization of large citizen armies is one of the great social processes of our century. Among social scientists, it is one of the most ignored. Historians examine the formation of navies, armies, and air forces; their dissolution is an unwritten epilogue. Whether or not old soldiers fade away, their armies simply vanish.

From 1914 to 1919, Canada created and then dissolved her first modern army. Of the country's male population of military age, at least one-third put on uniform. Out of about 8 million Canadians, roughly 600,000 men and women served with the Canadian Expeditionary Force; another 50,000 joined the British forces or served in the ranks of allied armies. Close to 450,000 Canadians went overseas and, from the CEF alone, 60,000 never returned. The suffering and the sacrifices did not end with the Armistice in November 1918; more than 70,000 Canadians came home with disabilities that would torture them for the rest of their lives. The war dead left behind more than 30,000 widows, children, and parents dependent on public bounty for their survival.

The European nation-states, with their tradition of mass conscript armies, had at least some experience of restoring large numbers of young men to civil life. Military service was a *rite de passage* prolonged and complicated by war but possessing its own firm precedents and institutions. Canada and her two chief exemplars, Great Britain and the United States, had no such experience. All three depended on small professional armed forces recruited for the most part from the lowest ranks of society and supplemented by large and ill-trained voluntary reserves.

Because military service was part of citizenship, European states could blur the distinction between soldier and civilian. The poor physiques of German conscripts became a potent factor in persuading Bismarck to launch a panoply of health and welfare programs in the 1880s. One result of these measures was the elimination of many of the practical distinctions between Germany's war-disabled and the casualties of her modern industries. Even in Britain the appalling physical condition of would-be volunteers for the South African War helped justify Lloyd George's pioneering health insurance scheme in 1908. The Atlantic proved an effective barrier against such innovations. Moreover, there was no shortage of fit volunteers to fight Spain in 1898 or the Boers in 1899. Even in 1914 patriotism and recession combined to produce a far larger flood of volunteers than the Canadian government had expected or wanted for a war that would be over by Christmas. As with so much else in the Great War, the true dimensions of Canada's citizens' army and its impact on civil society took months and even years to reveal themselves.

In a democratic society, what is the claim of the veteran on the community for which he has risked life and limb? How far must the state support those who suffer in its service and what is its obligation to the dependants of those who die? These questions are easier to answer with rhetoric than with regulations. Is the obligation altered if death or disability is due to ailments to which all flesh is heir? Soldiers of the victorious North, marching home through Washington after the Civil War, passed under a huge banner proclaiming: 'The debt we owe the soldier is one the Nation can never repay.' Cynical veterans would later insist that the United States had never had much intention of trying. Critics of the notorious pension raids on the American treasury might respond that veterans had had a passkey to the national coffers. Canadians, sensitive to both tendencies in the neighbouring democracy, could only vow to avoid extremes without knowing where justice lay.

The veterans' claim is not merely financial. Does the state owe a special deference to the ideas of those who have fought for its defence, or are they on an equal footing with citizens who have profited from the war or opposed it or ignored it? Do veterans who have saved the nation from external enemies have the right or even the obligation to purge it of 'subversives,' 'aliens,' and other alleged internal enemies? If, like Cincinnatus, veterans return to the plough, how do they respond when politicians and old comrades insist – as they usually do – that the old cause is in peril again? Do veterans embody the soul of the nation they have served? There will be no lack of demagogues to tell them so. Do veterans have a special responsibility for the disabled and dependent victims of the war? Is there a limit to their responsibility or should the rallying slogan of the Canadian Legion apply: 'They Were Faithful until Death, Why Not You?'

These were questions Canadians scarcely had to consider before the Great War of 1914–18. There were no easy and obvious precedents for coping with thousands of disabled soldiers or for welcoming a vast array of soldiers-turned-stranger during the long years overseas. Canada's sole tradition for coping with disbanded soldiers was to distribute further tracts of land torn from a seemingly limitless acreage. By 1914 those limits had been reached and overreached. Nor was Canada's normal military mentor an appropriate model. Despite the elegance of the Royal Hospital at Chelsea, visitors to Britain remembered bemedalled veterans begging on street corners. Mendicancy for common soldiers and generosity to aristocratic officers were unacceptable in Canada. The American experience was, if possible, more horrifying. The Grand Army of the Republic, deathbed marriages, claims agents, and other features of what American reformers termed 'the pension evil' ranked high among the democratic excesses that influential Canadians preferred to avoid.

Veterans and their re-establishment presented Canadians with problems they must also solve eclectically and on their own. It has been customary to assume that Canadians avoided the challenge or failed to meet it in some characteristic fashion that no contemporary and no historian could be bothered to explain. In fact, the truth is more complex, impressive, and encouraging. A small number of imaginative and clear-sighted Canadians, virtually unknown to their contemporaries and wholly unknown to posterity, created effective institutions and policies.

Another group, almost equally unknown, organized veterans, formulated complementary and sometimes contradictory policies and goals, and began, from 1917, to wage that 'second battle' which is the title and theme of this book. Like most battles, it left the soldiers who fought in it very little to show for their struggle and pain. The real beneficiaries would be the children born in those inter-war years who, as veterans in their own right and as civilians, would benefit from the social innovations the ex-servicemen and women of 1914–18 had helped establish.

The task of historians is to record and explain experience and to connect it with issues and problems of their own time. Canadians know too little of the origins of our social structure; most will be surprised to discover the central role of veterans in launching some of the institutions that define and distinguish Canadian society.

This book is no more than a preface. Often we have had to restrain ourselves from explorations that might have filled more years of fascinating research and a further acre of print. The 1920s in Canada, like Canada's veterans, remain underdeveloped territory. We are all the more grateful for the few explorers who have provided us with landmarks: Robert England, Katherine McCuaig, Udo Sautter, Jim Struthers, and John Herd Thompson. Each journey begins with a first step. We hope that this book will establish veterans and their era as worthy of study. In future, passing references to ex-servicemen and women may be better informed. We are certain, too, that our findings will be challenged and improved. A first step must not be the last.

Acknowledgments

In one way or another, this book has engaged one or both of us since the 1960s. It is impossible now to recall all those who have offered encouragement, useful advice, and practical assistance. They are legion.

The Canada Council's Killam Fellowship allowed one of us two years of uninterrupted research and writing; without that time, the book could never have been completed. The dominion archivist made a comparable contribution by granting research time to the other. Funds from Labour Canada, the Ontario Arts Council, and the Social Sciences and Humanities Research Council have all assisted in the work.

We have been helped by our colleagues, students, and families, and by the many veterans who shared memories, letters, and diaries with us. If some of them search in vain for the evidence, they must take comfort in knowing that they helped us to begin to set the record straight, and that their contributions have been preserved so that others may set it even straighter.

We owe particular thanks to Craig Brown and Barbara Wilson for their specialized knowledge of the period, to Margaret McCallum for the legal and historial expertise she brought to our understanding of pension legislation, and to Malcolm Davidson for many insights drawn from his vast reading. Dr Norman Hillmer and his colleagues from the Directorate of History, Department of National Defence, have been unfailingly helpful. We have also profited from the resources of many university, provincial, and private archives as well as from the massive holdings of the Public Archives of Canada. Among many who helped us, we particularly remember Jane Dewar, the former editor of the *Legion*, the publication of the Royal Canadian Legion.

Though the audience may not recognize the result, this book evolved through the Goodman Lectures at the University of Western Ontario in

1985, and its publication has been assisted by the fund established in memory of Joanne Goodman. It seems fitting that her father, a gallant soldier and a distinguished veteran of the Second World War, should be associated with this commemoration of an earlier war and its aftermath.

Seemingly endless versions of the manuscript were typed by the swift and astonishingly cheerful Clara Stewart. In turn, the final version was patiently edited by Kathy Johnson. She and Gerry Hallowell made a manuscript into a book.

Most of the members of our families have watched our work unfold in varying states of bemused indifference. The topic, after all, does not instantly appeal to the young. Our wives are different. Both Jan and Sandra have conquered the pain and frustration of physical disability. Their courage and their constant sympathy have been a reminder of others who, more than seventy years ago, brought their own valour to a lonely 'second battle.'

Desmond Morton and Glenn Wright
8 January 1987

Abbreviations

ANV   Army and Navy Veterans in Canada
BESL British Empire Service League
BPC   Board of Pension Commissioners
CAMC Canadian Army Medical Corps
CEF   Canadian Expeditionary Force
CPC   Canadian Pension Commission
DPNH Department of Pensions and National Health
DSCR Department of Soldiers' Civil Re-establishment
DVA   Dominion Veterans' Alliance
FAB   Federal Appeal Board
GAUV Grand Army of United Veterans
GWVA Great War Veterans' Association
IVC   Imperial Veterans in Canada
MCH Military Convalescent Hospital
MHC Military Hospitals Commission
RSA   Returned Soldiers' Association
RSC   Returned Soldiers' Commission
RSI   Returned Soldiers' Insurance
SAC   Soldiers' Aid Commission (Ontario)
SSB   Soldier Settlement Board
TVA   Tuberculous Veterans' Association
UVL   United Veterans League

Everyone is determined to make every sacrifice to bring the war to a successful conclusion but the people are not so united in their intention to bring about the solution of the 'after the war' problem, because, while they realize that money must be used unstintingly to bring the war to an end, they have different ideas when it comes to providing for returning the soldier to civil life.

H.W. Hart,
Returned Soldiers' Association,
Victoria, 1917

The policy and object kept steadily in view has been to secure and provide economically but not parsimoniously, for the invalid soldier the best possible care and treatment upon the most modern lines, and so to fit him in the speediest way for return to duty; or, where that is impossible, for his discharge at the earliest possible moment, after treatment has attained finality, and the highest possibility of fitness secured.

Memorandum to Parliament from
the Board of Medical Consultants, 1918

There are so many malingerers that it is mighty difficult. The trouble is not with the average man who comes back, glad to get back and get on his feet again and get to work; it is with the man who has not an intention of doing another tap of work again; that is the trouble.

Colonel McGillvray
Board of Pension Commissioners, 1918

There seems to me to be a disposition to leave our ordinary common sense behind when we come to deal with the men who went to the front.

Sen. L.G. Power, 1920

A sick man returning to this country after doing his bit wants more freedom, he is an invalid, and should be treated as such, instead of being annoyed with military discipline and restraint.

Pte H.W. Hart to the Special
Parliamentary Committee,
1917

Toronto veterans gather for the unveiling of the city's Fenian Raid memorial, renovated after years of neglect. Until the First World War, veterans and their pensions seldom, if ever, troubled Canadians save as a worrisome example of American democratic excess. Veterans such as these, with memories ranging back to the Crimea, helped to cement imperial ties and recall past glories.

An American cartoon deploring the 'Pension Evil' was a warning to Canadians
that their post-war burden might far exceed anything their wealthy neighbour
faced – unless the pension system was tightly regulated and kept free of political
influence.

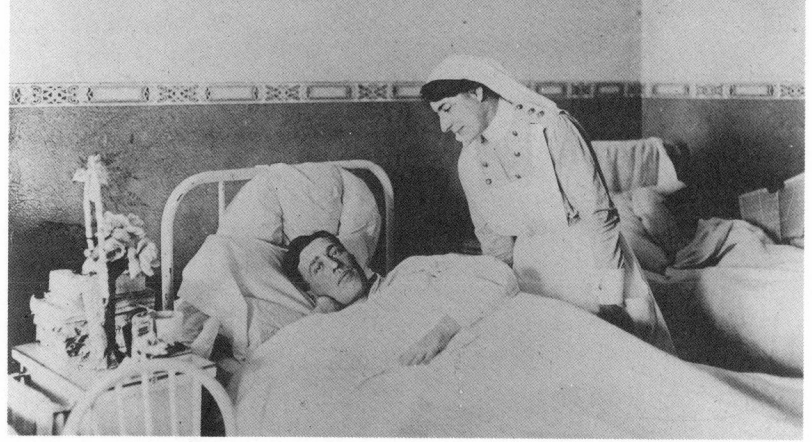

The popular image of the suffering soldier and his guardian-angel nurse captivated civilians and troubled MHC officials. Stirring such men into renewed activity and early self-sufficiency was the only antidote to idleness and enormous pension claims.

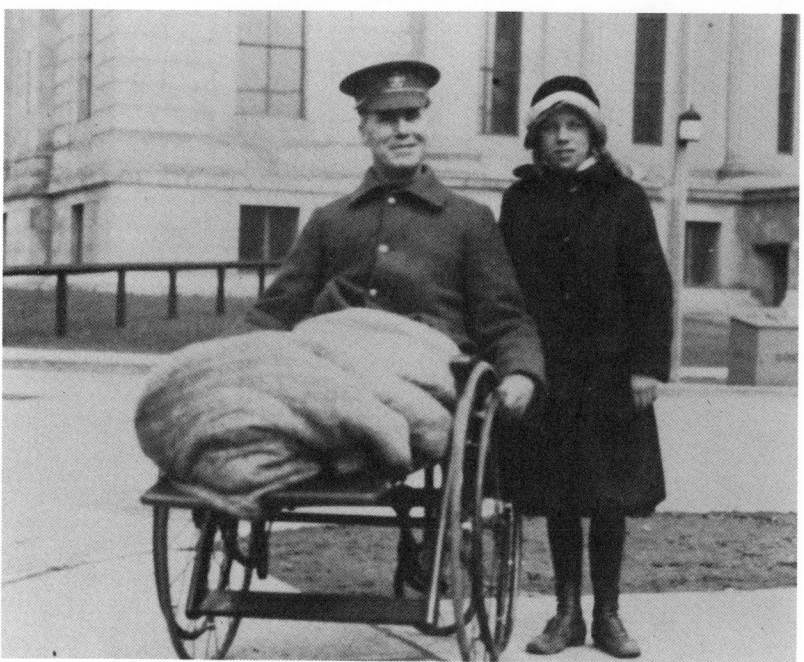

A legless soldier sets out, with a little help, to test his new wheelchair. After earlier wars, such men would have become beggars, dependent on family, friends, or public charity. The Military Hospitals Commission recognized at once that neither Canadians nor their veterans would tolerate such a fate. That was a small but real social revolution.

The Military Hospitals Commission meets the tuberculosis consultants in 1917. Among the more significant figures were Sir James Lougheed (hatless, with a cane, in the front row), Maj. John Todd (in uniform, in the front row), and Ernest Scammell (relegated to second from the left in the third row).

By films, lectures, and magic-lantern shows, the Military Hospitals Commission did its best to persuade Canadians that disabled soldiers could be trained and restored to self-sufficiency. It was a radical message.

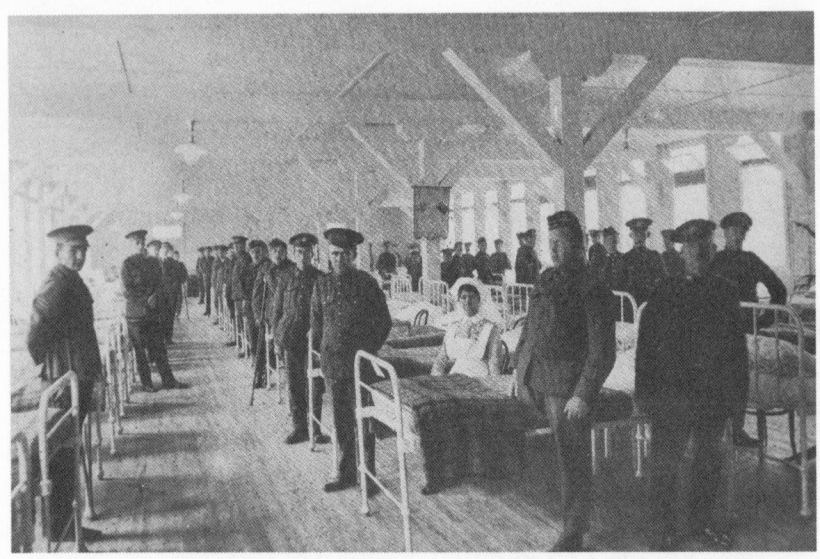

A ward in the MHC's orthopaedic hospital at Davisville. A product of wartime 'quick-build' methods, the Davisville hospital housed the commission's own artificial-limb factory.

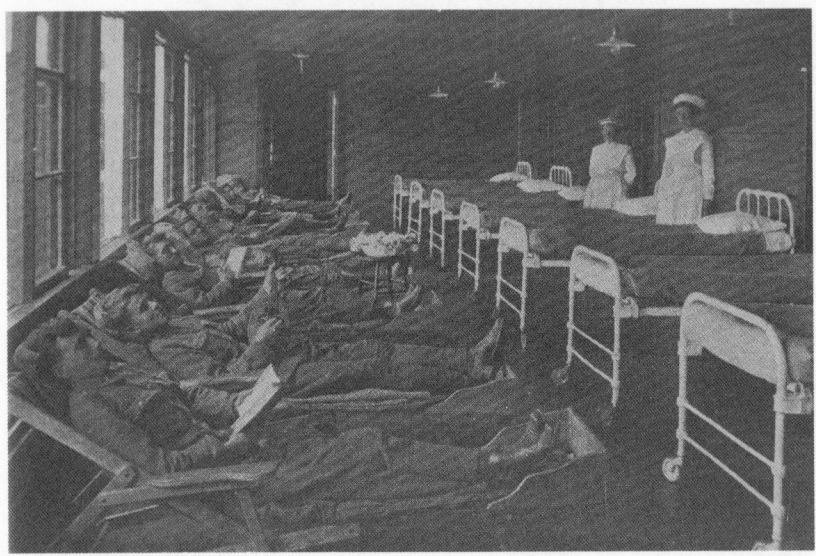

Compulsory rest periods at an MHC tuberculosis sanatorium. While the presence of nurses (and a photographer) ensured proper behaviour by these sufferers, army discipline was no guarantee that TB sufferers would put up with the rigorous discipline prescribed by medical science. Indeed, rebelliousness was said to be a symptom of the disease.

Cap firmly in place, with smiling nurses in attendance, an MHC patient stoically enters one of the specially designed hospital cars that the commission began to acquire in 1917. Canadians needed conspicuous reassurance that 'their boys' would be well treated.

Training in massage at Hart House, University of Toronto. One of several new therapies borrowed from the French, who were experts in military medicine, massage was a skill largely reserved for women and for blinded soldiers.

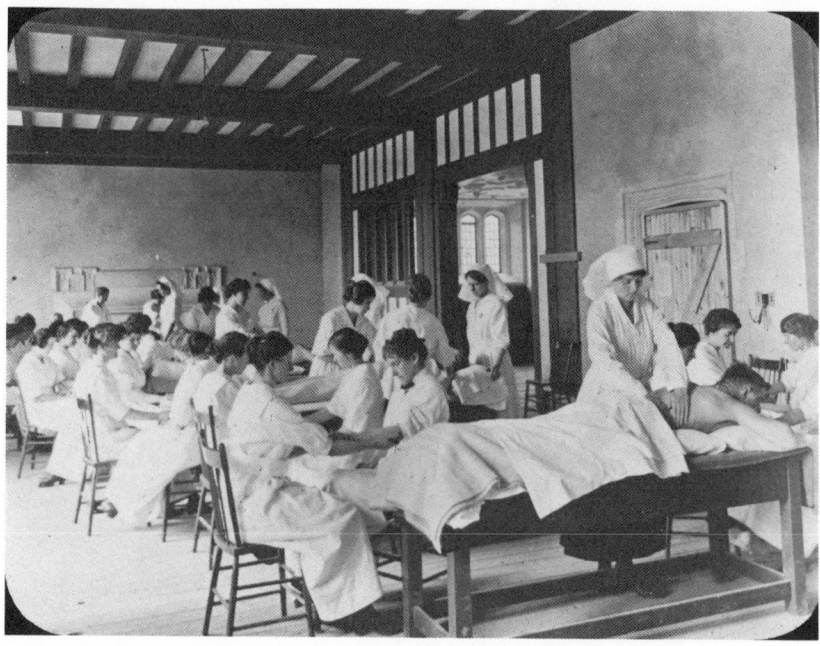

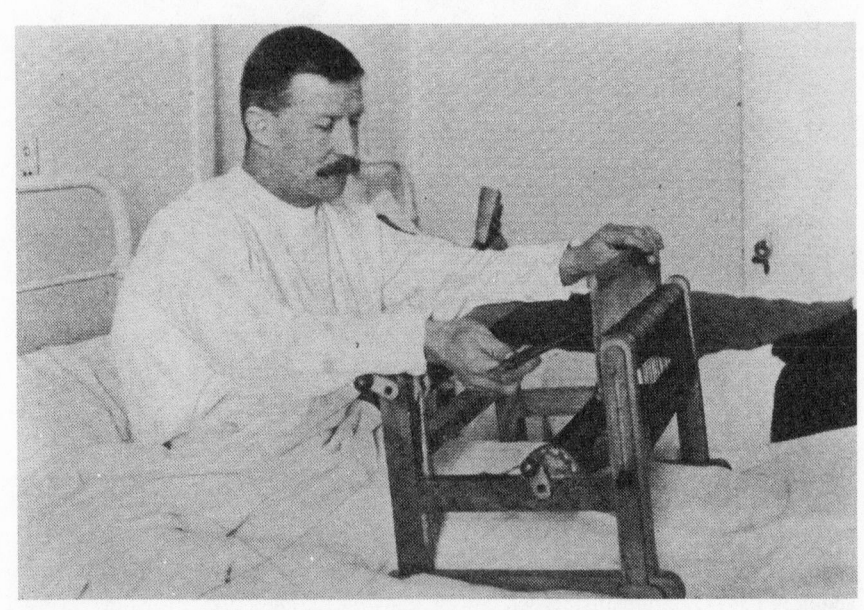

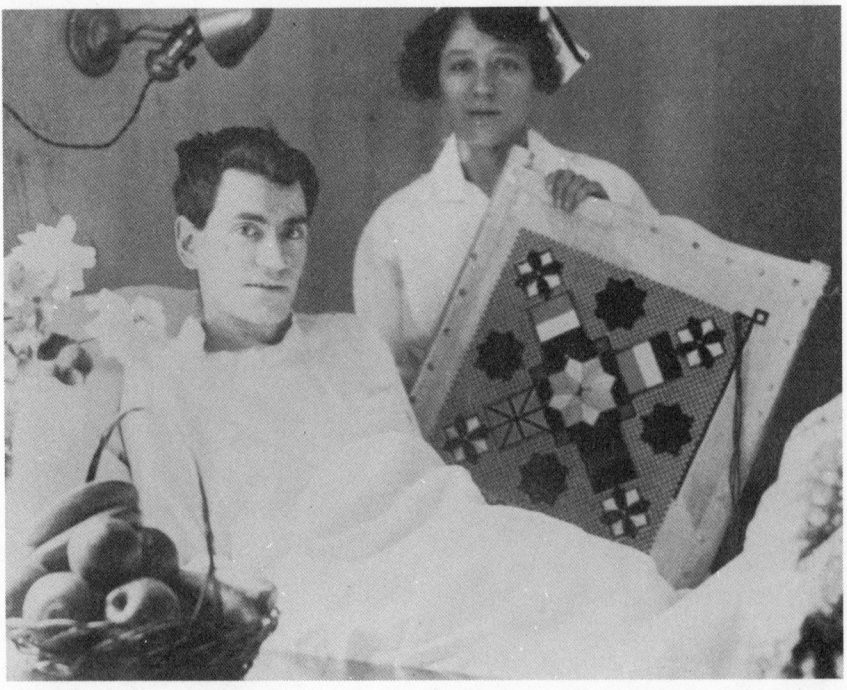

A wounded soldier practises his 'curative skills' on a hand loom. Occupational therapy was another wartime innovation, at least in Canada. Encouraging soldiers to learn weaving, knitting, and other domestic skills demanded all the persuasiveness of specially trained 'ward aides' backed by army discipline.

A bedridden soldier and his nurse take public pride in some painfully executed needlepoint incorporating the flags of the major allies. Ward occupations eased the monotony of endless months of recovery in an age before antibiotics.

Basket-making, embroidery, and needlepoint at a Winnipeg convalescent home. 'Ward occupations' might provoke ribald comments from soldier-patients, but they were part of a deliberate strategy to combat idleness and revive workplace discipline.

Teaching woodworking skills to MHC patients. Once soldiers reached a convalescent stage, the commission proposed to introduce them to 'curative workshops'
where they would begin to regain rusty skills and self-sufficient attitudes. Hard
experience taught the MHC that serious retraining had to wait until after
discharge.

A disabled Alberta veteran displays a wheelbarrow full of the crops he has harvested. While the MHC did its best to prepare its charges to return to the land, experience soon proved that few men with disabilities could endure the rigours of farm life.

"A LITTLE CHAT WITH PRIVATE PAT"

The Soldier's Return

From "DOWN and OUT" to "UP and IN AGAIN"

DEDICATED TO PRIVATE PAT AND ALL HIS COMRADES OF THE CANADIAN EXPEDITIONARY FORCE.

PRIVATE PAT ARRIVES. "I'm no returned soldier," said Private Pat, after hopping down the gangway from the hospital ship. "It's only a half-returned soldier I am,—or half a returned soldier, if you like,"—pointing down to his empty trouser leg.

He must always have his little joke, but he was more than half serious now.

"I mean, I've only got back to Canada," he said. "I'll be a proper returned soldier when I've got back to work. And the sooner the better; no loafing for me!

PEOPLE DON'T KNOW THE FACTS. "From the way my old father writes, and my wife too, they seem to think there's nothing for me to do but some kid's job, like peddling pins, or bobbing up and down with an elevator; or else tramping around after odd jobs, like the old soldier in the fairy tale, with may-be a bit of a pension to keep body and soul together.

"I'll take whatever pension my old leg's worth, but blamed if I want to LIVE on one, and RUST away the rest of my life. I want to be a man again as I was before, and make my own living, not sponge on other people...... How's it going to be done? Tell me all about it."

*   *   *   *

WONDERS OF MODERN SURGERY. "Well," said I, "to begin with, every man is carefully examined by doctors here, and then taken to the hospital where his trouble can be dealt with best. In your case, it will be the orthopaedic centre, where they'll fit you out with a good walkable leg.

"All the resources of modern science are brought into play; and you know what wonderful progress the art of healing has made in the last few years."

"You don't need to tell me that," said Private Pat. 'The doctoring's been a strong point with the army in this war."

*   *   *   *

"Yes," said I, "surgeons nowadays can take a human wreck and make him an active man again, in a way that would have been thought miraculous a few years ago.

"And surgery is not all of it, or nearly all. There are the physical exercises, massage, baths, diet, rest and occupations for the body and mind, all carefully regulated to suit each man's case.

THE BEST OF TONICS. "These exercises and occupations are the best of tonics,—they brace a man up as no drugs can."

*   *   *

Private Pat thought a minute. Then he said,—"And it makes a power of difference if a man WANTS to be braced up."

THE MAN HIMSELF. "You're right. If he uses his force of will, and puts his heart into the work of getting well again, he recovers much faster than the man who lets himself stay limp and makes no effort to help himself. The man himself is his own best doctor after all."

*   *   *

"Those occupations you were talking about," said Pat, "what are they, now?"

OCCUPATIONS IN HOSPITAL. "There are a lot; and they vary in different places. There is carpentry, for instance; that's always popular. Different kinds of leather and metal work; and motor engineering has come to the front. Mechanical drawing goes along with these. Of course there are typewriting, bookkeeping and other commercial subjects, for men going into offices.

"But not for me," said Private Pat with energy. "You would have to take off my other leg, before you could stuff me into an office and keep me scratching paper for my living. Don't they let you work outdoors!"

However returned men saw themselves, 'Private Pat' was the kind of veteran the Military Hospitals Commission wanted to welcome – cheerful, resourceful, and properly deferential. Reality, as usual, was more imaginative than prophecy.

Disabled veterans facing the struggle for re-establishment. Veterans, on the whole, were older and less visibly disabled than their fellow citizens had expected, and not all of their disabilities were easily catalogued by a pension examiner.

Maj.-Gen. S.C. Mewburn, Sir Robert Borden, and Sir Edward Kemp in London in 1918. As minister of militia in the Union government, Mewburn completed the campaign Kemp had begun: the Military Hospitals Commission was no more.

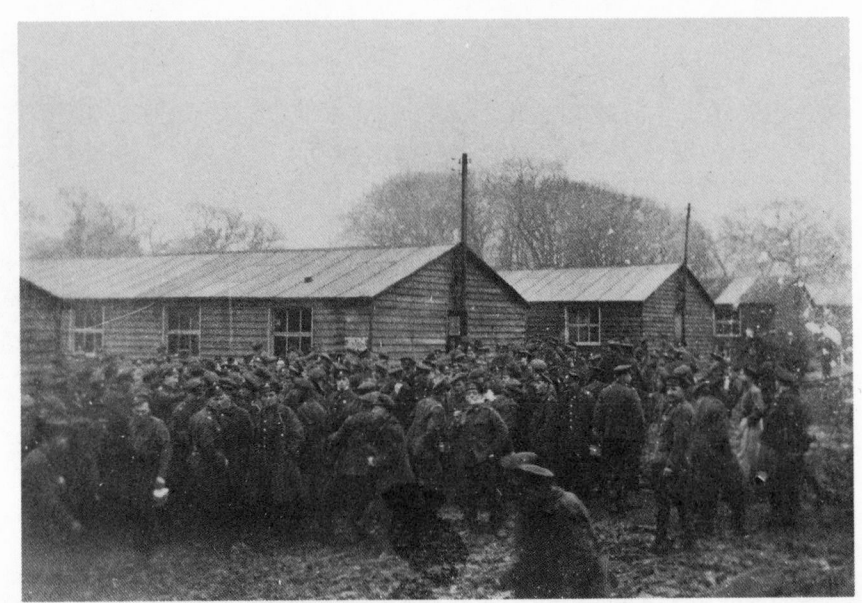

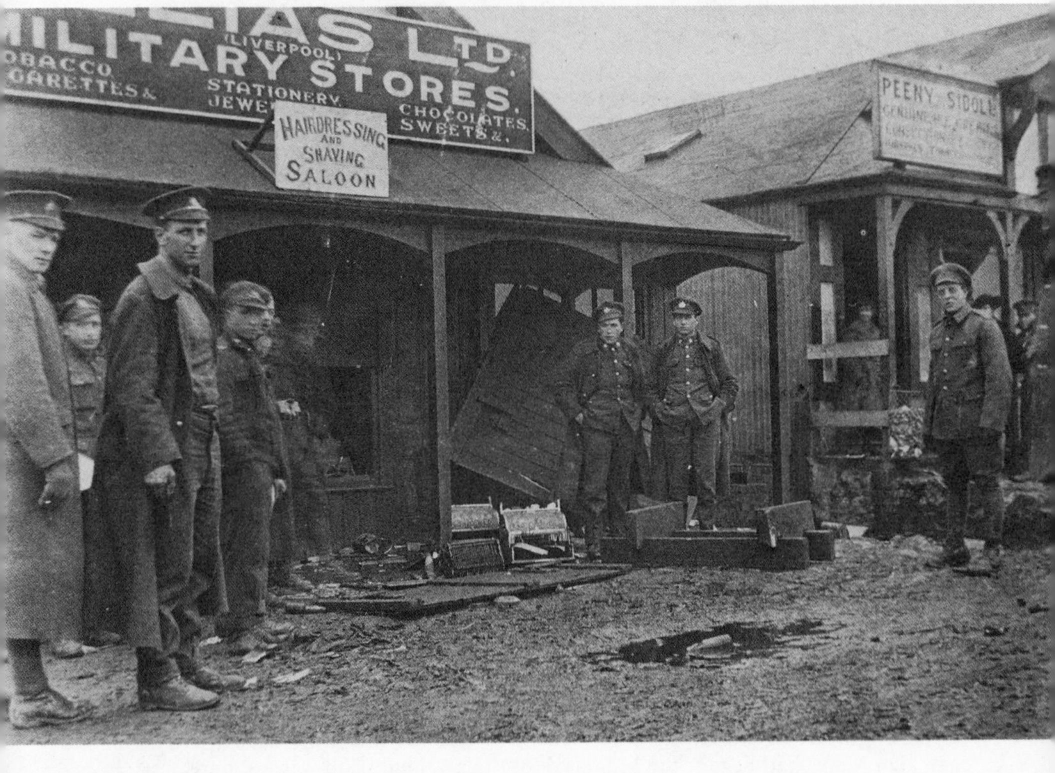
LTD.
(LIVERPOOL)
ITARY STORES.
OBACCO.
STATIONERY.
JEWE
CHOCOLATES.
SWEETS &.
HAIRDRESSING
AND
SHAVING
SALOON
PEENY

The Kinmel mutiny was a real tragedy: the frustration of good intentions.

The morning after at Kinmel's 'Tin Town.' In the first stage of a day-long rampage, soldiers crossed the road to demolish a row of shops which they felt had profiteered at their expense.

After ransacking Tin Town, Kinmel rioters proceeded to attack the central canteen stores in the centre of the sprawling Kinmel camp. A few officers drove them back at first, but the soldiers completed the task after lights went out. These snapshots were taken on the next day, before order was restored. Most participants remember 'hanging around, waiting for something to happen.'

Men of the 3rd Battalion wait to embark on the SS *Olympic* in April 1919. Sir Arthur Currie had complicated Canadian demobilization to preserve CEF battalions in the name of discipline.

Veterans smile dutifully for the camera as they wait to disembark at Halifax. Canadians wondered and worried about what army life and active service had done to the character of sons and husbands. They would soon find out.

The SS *Olympic*, one of the 'monster ships,' berthed at Halifax. One practical benefit of the Kinmel riot and other disturbances was to persuade the British to make their biggest and best liners available to hurry Canadians home. The real bottleneck, however, was not shipping, but Canada's worn-out railway system.

At Saint John discharged soldiers wait for their last pay; upstairs, their war brides and children were inspected by Canadian immigration officials. (This is a public relations photograph.)

THAT FIRST CIVIE COLLAR.

Collars and ties were dress distinctions reserved for army officers. Those men in the ranks who returned to white-collar jobs had an old skill to relearn.

A suitable home for a soldier settler, built in Winnipeg on the grounds of the YMCA's Red Triangle Hut. The Soldier Settlement Board was determined to help its clients make the realistic choices that homesteading demanded. Torn between propaganda and reality, too few soldier settlers realized the tough prospects they faced or the high risk of failure.

IN THE NAME OF GOD.
WHAT IS THERE
FOR US TO BE
THANKFUL FOR?

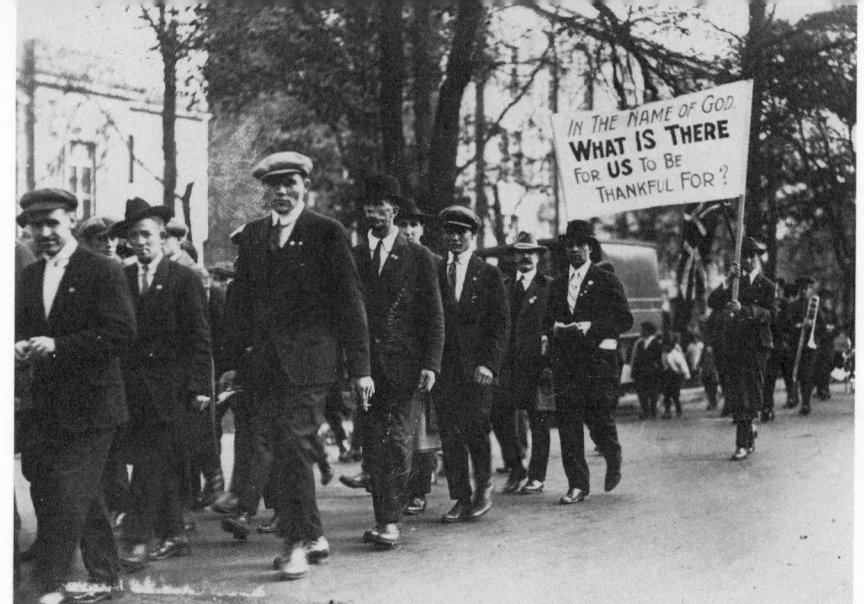

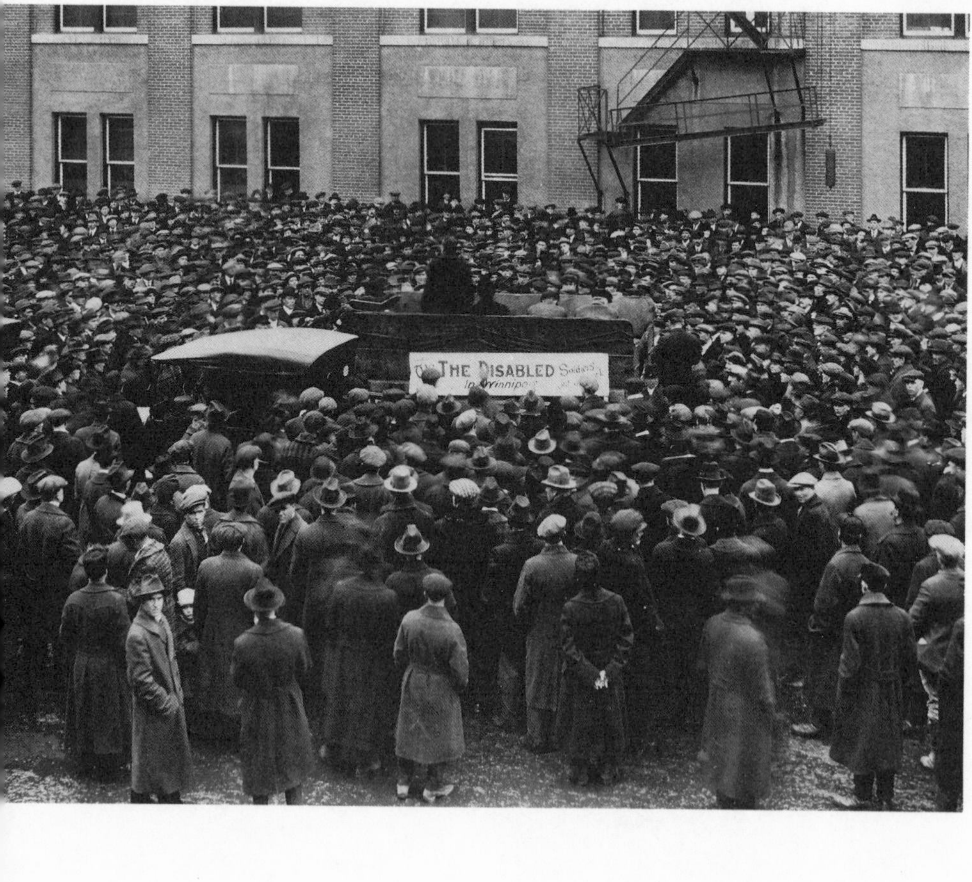
THE DISABLED

Toronto veterans on the march after the war. Fellow citizens had an inflated idea of their generosity to returned men – pensions, training, employment. Veterans were thought to be not suitably grateful.

A demonstration by unemployed veterans in Winnipeg on 2 April 1921. The 1921 depression was a blow to men who had found themselves a niche in the post-war economy. It was the economic disaster that undermined all the bold plans and hopeful forecasts.

Having lost a leg in France, Sidney Lambert was fitted with a limb and helped to complete his theological training. In turn, he became the cautious guiding spirit of the War Amputations Association.

2. VIMY. Le Mémorial Canadien.

The massive Vimy Memorial, completed and unveiled in 1936, symbolized the Canadians' greatest battle of the First World War. The Vimy pilgrimage marked the transformation of the veterans' movement from struggle to commemoration. The 'second battle' was finally over.

WINNING THE SECOND BATTLE

When this bloody war is over,
Oh how happy I will be,
When I get my civvy clothes on,
No more soldiering for me.

Anon.

1 Veterans

The Advent of War

By the summer of 1914, Canadians had lived through too many remote Balkan crises to take the latest one very seriously. The endless warnings of war from Sam Hughes, the minister of militia, or Hugh Graham, the proprietor of the Montreal *Star*, had grown boring.[1] If the crisis broke, the huge conscript armies of Europe would settle the issue long before men of the young dominion could get involved. Economists insisted that the modern world had grown too complex to survive a prolonged conflict: surely no one in his right mind would risk the destruction of Europe's glittering civilization. Newspapers reflected bland optimism.

A few thoughtful businessmen were worried: a war would postpone recovery from the acute depression that settled on the country late in 1913. If the winter of 1913–14 had been bad, a war would chill the investment climate, cancel orders, and make the coming winter even worse. No one knew exactly how many workers searched hopelessly for work that summer, but the municipal officials and charity officers who coped with Canada's destitute knew that their burden would grow when winter approached.[2]

Then, quite suddenly, on the evening of Tuesday, 4 August, Canadians discovered they were at war. As men scrawled reports on sheets of newsprint outside newspaper offices, crowds gathered. Militia sentries, posted on orders from Ottawa earlier in the civic holiday weekend to guard railway stations and bridges, felt a sudden glow of importance as civilians gawked and cheered. Gradually, word spread. From Temagami, an Indian guide plunged sixty miles through the bush to notify Maj. R.H. Labatt that he might be needed. The world was suddenly a small place. The empire was at war.[3]

Across Canada, three thousand British army reservists knew that they must rejoin their regiments. So did many hundreds of French and Belgian reservists and uncounted numbers of loyal Serbs, Russians, Germans, and Austrians. The Austrian consul at Montreal reminded Hapsburg subjects that the laws of the homeland reached across the Atlantic. [4]

On 6 August Canadians, too, heard the call. An excited Sam Hughes burst from a cabinet meeting to announce that twenty-five thousand young Canadians would be privileged to serve the empire. That evening, trainloads of workmen headed for Valcartier, a sandy plain near Quebec City, to begin building a military camp. [5] At armouries and drill halls across Canada, men in smart summer suits and rough work clothes jostled each other to enlist. Many were recent British immigrants, emotionally linked to their mother country, and often barred by long unemployment from any attachment to Canada. There were Canadian-born militiamen, too; why had they devoted evenings and summers to drill if not to answer the empire's call? [6]

Within the limits of their horizon, staff officers at militia headquarters had long since prepared for the great enterprise. With one angry shout, the minister scrapped their plans. [7] He deliberately created a swirling confusion at Valcartier, in which Col. Sam Hughes alone would be master. The 'miracle' of Valcartier was not due to Hughes; it was the slow triumph of military order and discipline over the sweaty, dusty disorder he had created. Somehow, staff officers formed battalions of infantry and batteries of artillery from the bewildered contingents deposited by a hundred railway trains. Rifles, guns, uniforms and equipment, wagons, limbers, and horses were distributed, lost, and found again. At Hughes's command, the men were vaccinated; the minister also insisted that soldiers could choose whether to be inoculated against the most deadly of war's killers, typhoid fever. [8] The chaos of Valcartier was then transported to the docks of Quebec. In early October an armada of thirty ships transferred thirty thousand Canadians to England. Recruiting for a Second Contingent could begin.

The hard consequences of war no more troubled military authorities than they worried the excited young men heading eastward for their great adventure. For example, no soldier could support a family, even at the Canadian Expeditionary Force rate of a dollar a day plus ten cents field pay. [9] Hughes insisted that married men must bring their wives' permission to enlist; almost four hundred shamefaced men were sent home for lack of domestic approval. Nor did men worry much about the meagre pensions Canada offered to war widows or to those who would return in the wrecks of minds or bodies. South Africa, with its handful of casualties, had bred no such fears. People burdened with such thoughts do not go to war.

Even a belligerent as inexperienced as Canada knew that some provision must be made for families, for the disabled, and for the comfort of the men themselves. These were not the exclusive responsibilities of the state. Rarely was the minimal role of Canadian government more apparent than in those first months of war. It was society's leaders who poured their energy and wealth into providing comforts, hospital supplies, food, and even a battery of quick-firing guns to defend Montreal from unnamed enemies. Toronto's municipal council promised one thousand dollars in life insurance to each citizen who volunteered. The risk seemed minimal, since the war would be so short.[10] Federal civil servants who enlisted would continue to draw their salaries for the duration of the war. Most provinces and several major employers followed Ottawa's lead.[11] Their employees, they were sure, would soon be back at work.

In 1812 Upper Canada had created its first Patriotic Fund, collecting £13,841 – chiefly from beyond the boundaries of the embattled colony – to support disabled militiamen and their families and to design a medal. The Crimean War brought a similar response: Canadians gathered £46,575 for the patriotic cause. In 1900, another Canadian Patriotic Fund was chartered under glittering patronage to support families left by volunteers for the South African War. Later, the fund supplemented the British pensions of widows, orphans, and crippled veterans of the war.[12]

When Canada's Parliament met in emergency wartime session in late August, there was no doubt that it would charter a new Patriotic Fund. On 20 August trustees of the old fund met to wind up its affairs and allocate an unspent balance of $76,000 to the needs of a new war.[13] By 22 August, when Parliament approved the charter, dozens of local funds had sprung into existence and the need for national co-ordination was urgent. Canada's leaders set an example. On 25 August the directors of the new fund held their first meeting. Seconded by Sir Wilfrid Laurier, leader of the opposition, Sir Robert Borden invited the governor-general to take the chair. Thomas White, the minister of finance, would be the honorary treasurer; the honorary secretary was Herbert Ames, a Montreal businessman and an MP with unique experience of philanthropy and the condition of the poor.[14]

That autumn, Canadians were deluged with patriotic appeals. The Red Cross, the YMCA, Belgian Relief, even the Overseas Club's Tobacco Fund – all pleaded their cases. The Canadian Patriotic Fund surpassed all. Cities vied with cities. Toronto, stronghold of imperialism, boasted of collecting $312,551 by the end of 1914, only to be humiliated by Montreal's total of $750,000. Toronto's revenge was a Fifty-Thousand Club, whose members pledged a dollar a month; Montreal answered with eighty-five thousand citizens, each committed to giving four days' pay a year.[15] For the fund's organizers it was no game. The alternative would be state intervention at double the cost. Privately, fund officials fumed at local inefficiency and the

gross discrepancies that allowed an average of $24.71 a month to a Sas-
katchewan soldier's family while a family on Prince Edward Island made do
with $9.70. Yet in public Ames and the fund's executive secretary, Philip
Morris, insisted that the fund's voluntarism permitted an economy and a
flexibility no government would be allowed. [16] Soldiers' families grumbled at
Patriotic Fund meddling and meanness, but Morris was more concerned
with charges by affluent subscribers that the CPF's generosity made it
impossible to find maidservants. It was never intended, Morris insisted, that
'when a man donned khaki, his wife should be expected to become a char-
woman.' [17] Indeed, if a soldier claimed her as a dependant, even an 'unmarried wife' became the fund's responsibility. [18]

Returned Men

Unlike its predecessors, the 1914–18 Canadian Patriotic Fund strictly
limited its responsibilities to soldiers' families. On 9 October 1914 the formidable Mrs Minden Cole of Montreal's Soldiers' Wives League had
tackled Ames about the problem of 'men who may return from active service abroad out of health and with no employment.' Ames and Sir Thomas
White were unmoved. The Patriotic Fund, Ames insisted, could do no
more. The CPF did extend its mandate to cover the families of British and
allied reservists. It would do nothing for soldiers who had yet to leave
Canada, or for those who had returned. [19]

The problem was not theoretical. No one had worried much about the
5,081 men rejected from the First Contingent, but close to 1,000 more
became invalids during the long, cold, wet months on Salisbury Plain. [20] The
Princess Patricia's Canadian Light Infantry, formed from British reservists
living in Canada, left for France in December. Almost at once the flow of
wounded casualties began. Christmas came, but the war did not abate.
Instead, the terrible pitch of commitment justified for a short war made a
compromise peace unthinkable. Optimists dreamed that victory might come
in 1915; realists knew better.

In March, as the 1st Canadian Division prepared to go to France, authorities in England made a special effort to send home the unwanted and the
unfit. [21] Private Harry Jennings, wounded with the PPCLI and still partially
paralysed, returned on the *Scandinavian* with a draft of 'undesirables,'
some of whom were insane. At Halifax, he was stripped of his British
uniform, handed a cheap suit of civilian clothes, and sent by day-coach to
Calgary. [22] C.H. King, crippled by frozen feet, returned in steerage on the
Missanabie, to be locked in a shed at Halifax with a single blanket while the
military authorities decided his fate. [23] W.A.R. Holmes à Court reported
that his draft, thirteen sick and eight 'undesirables,' had been confined in a

cheap lodging house in Liverpool before being shipped steerage class to Quebec. For his triumphal return to Battleford, Holmes à Court wore a $7.50 civilian suit without shirt, socks, or underwear. It was, he was told, according to the minister's orders. [24]

Such reports and more reached the prime minister. Perhaps such complaints were promoted by a 'butter-in, bent on giving trouble' but Sir Robert Borden knew very well how indignant Canadians would be at such treatment of their wounded heroes, to say nothing of the effect on recruiting. [25] In England, Col. John Wallace Carson, the minister's representative, issued orders for a rigid segregation of the unfit and the misfits. Complaints were 'exaggerated to the extreme,' Carson reassured Hughes. In Canada, a board of officers, headed by the director-general of engineer services, Lt-Col. G.S. Maunsell, met in April to plan for returning invalids and proposed a tented camp at Valcartier. Military districts, ordered to hunt for suitable convalescent homes, reported a flood of offers. The Red Cross, Maunsell suggested, could manage the homes, and the St John's Ambulance service might be persuaded to run the hospital at Valcartier and to escort convalescents to the homes. On 1 June the cabinet approved the arrangement. [26]

By then, the government and most Canadians had begun to shed the illusions of a brief, painless war. In a few terrible days at Ypres, from 22 to 26 April, the 1st Canadian Division suffered 6,036 casualties, a third of its fighting strength. Later in the same battle, the PPCLI lost 678 of its men. Thousands of maimed and crippled soldiers might soon return to Canada. Voters, reared on the legend of Florence Nightingale, would be harsh judges of military medical incompetence. Almost all the officers of Canada's tiny Permanent Army Medical Corps had gone overseas. Maj. J.L. Potter, too junior to impress his superiors at militia headquarters or influential medical colonels from the peacetime militia, was left in charge of medical arrangements in Canada. [27]

Late in May, Col. George Sterling Ryerson of the Canadian Red Cross offered the prime minister a glowing account of French efforts to fit their disabled soldiers for work. It was a matter, Borden gravely replied, that 'must immediately engage the attention of the Government as already some of our men are being invalided home and find themselves confronted with conditions in which the co-operation and possibly the aid of the Government will be necessary.' [28] Earlier the government had dealt with scandals in war contracts by creating a War Purchasing Commission. [29] Handing problems to businessmen had long struck Sir Robert Borden as an ideal alternative to government patronage and ineptitude. It was time for convalescent soldiers to feel the benefits of business management.

The Hospitals Commission, proclaimed by order in council on 30 June, would 'deal with the provision of hospital accommodation and convalescent homes for officers and men of the Canadian Expeditionary Force who return invalided from the Front.'[30] The ten men chosen for the commission represented a nationwide array of wealth and civic spirit, from the scholarly J.S. McLennan of the Dominion Coal Company to Sam Matson, proprietor of the Victoria *Colonist*. French Canada's sole representative, Sir Rodolphe Forget, was matched in wealth by the Montreal boot manufacturer Clarence Smith and Toronto's Sir Henry Pellatt. Apart from Major Potter, acting ex officio, medical expertise was limited to Dr Thomas Walker, a venerable practitioner from Saint John, New Brunswick.

Borden turned to the Conservative leader of the Senate to preside over the new commission. After his Brampton boyhood, James Lougheed had moved to Calgary, acquiring substantial wealth and an English accent in the process. Having married the daughter of Sen. William Hardisty, Lougheed had virtually inherited his father-in-law's Senate seat in 1889. Thanks to a civilized modus vivendi with his Liberal counterpart, Raoul Dandurand, Lougheed's Senate duties were not onerous and the Hospitals Commission might well keep him employed. Indeed, when Sam Hughes insisted on spending the summer of 1915 with 'his boys' overseas, Lougheed also became acting minister of militia.[31]

On 20 July 1915, the commission members met for the first time, discussed their duties, and adjusted their per diem to ten dollars plus 'reasonable expenses.' Voluntarism was already wearing a little thin. The commission also approved Lougheed's choice for secretary.[32] Ernest Henry Scammell was one of those officials a wise organization cherishes. Born in England in 1873, the son of a prominent Baptist minister, Scammell brought to Canada the smooth skills of a chartered-company secretary. In 1912, with joint backing from Sir Edmund Walker of the Bank of Commerce and William Lyon Mackenzie King, the former Liberal minister of labour, Scammell had gone to work as organizing secretary for the Canadian Peace Centenary Association, a quasi-official organization devised by the Borden government. British and American citizens, eager to celebrate a hundred years of peace since 1814, had left Canada out of their plans. The CPCA was Ottawa's hastily improvised means to get involved. The outbreak of war interrupted plans for the peace celebrations, and Scammell found temporary work in the Militia Department's censorship branch. His contacts and experience were too valuable to waste.[33]

By the time the commission met, furniture from the Peace Centenary Association had been shifted to the commission's new offices at 22 Vittoria Street and Scammell was at work. There was much to do. The wealthy benefactors who had offered their homes to Colonel Maunsell's committee had waited two months for an answer. If convalescent soldiers needed a quiet place for rest and rehabilitation, what would be better than a millionaire's summer home, or even a city mansion set in spacious grounds? Mrs J.K.L. Ross of Montreal offered her large house in Sydney, Cape Breton Island. Lorne McGibbon, a Montreal manufacturer, promised his Laurentide Inn at Ste-Agathe. In the First Division district alone there were dozens of offers, ranging from the McKeough home at Chatham to the bedroom vacated by a patriotic mother's soldier son. An MP offered his twenty-nine-year-old unmarried daughter.[34] All required answers; many demanded visits and decisions. Meanwhile, as Scammell discovered from a swift visit to Quebec, Maj. J.J. Sharples at the discharge depot was already receiving and dispatching one hundred invalid soldiers a week.[35]

The commission demanded more of its secretary than mere administration. Scammell wrestled with myriad housekeeping chores, from securing stationery from the government printer to fending off mattress contractors; he also formulated strategy. On 19 July he had provided Lougheed with a comprehensive report and recommendations on the problems inherited by the new commission. Civic committees, he suggested, should be formed to retrain veterans who were unable to return to former occupations and to find jobs for those who could. Such measures, Scammell thought, would be a powerful incentive for recruits.[36] When commission members met the next day, they commanded their secretary to prepare a full report on how Canada could provide employment 'not only for the disabled men but able-bodied as well' once the war was over.[37]

The Veteran Experience

It is common to claim that problems have no precedent. Canadians could easily assert that they were utterly inexperienced in coping with vast armies of veterans. In some vital respects, so were all nations. It was not the mass armies of 1914–18 that were new, or even the horrifying death tolls. Relatively, the wars of Napoleon a century before had taken as many lives. What was new was the remarkable proportion of sick and wounded who survived.[38] Modern medicine could claim no more than a stalemate in its attempts to heal the wounds from modern weapons, but it had conquered many of the diseases that once annihilated armies. In South Africa, typhoid alone killed far more British soldiers than Boer bullets.[39] In the 1914–18 war, only 3,825 Canadians in the CEF died from illness; 51,678 were killed in action or died of wounds. It was not that soldiers stayed healthy: in the CEF three times as many men were hospitalized for sickness as for wounds. The difference was that both the sick and the wounded came home.[40] Fifteen years after the war, 77,000 veterans collected disability pensions, while thousands more endured pain, debility, or premature aging without going through the sometimes humiliating ordeal of establishing a claim.[41]

The magnitude, not the nature, of the veteran experience made it seem new. Old soldiers were part of Canadian history. Veterans from the Carignan-Salières Regiment had been settled in the valley of the Richelieu as a bulwark against the Iroquois. Disbanded soldiers had populated Halifax in 1749. British, Hessian, and Loyalist regiments had been dropped on the shores of the Saint John River and along the upper St Lawrence in the aftermath of the American Revolution. Thousands of British veterans had been paid off in hundred-acre location tickets after the War of 1812. However discredited by experience, the distribution of public land as 'military bounty' became a recurrent evil after every war, including the South African campaigns of 1899–1902.[42]

Free land for ex-soldiers was one inherited Canadian experience; another was the military pension. Like much else in Canadian military history, pension practice dated from the War of 1812. Faced with the plight of maimed militiamen and their officers, the Loyal and Patriotic Society of Upper Canada borrowed its pension system from the British; the principles survived until the First World War.[43] Like other British military institutions, pensions reflected a society in which the gulf between officers and other ranks was almost unbridgeable. Officers were gentlemen whose status, even in adversity, must be sustained. Private soldiers had probably enlisted to avoid starvation. An officer deprived of an arm, a leg, or an eye in His Majesty's service was entitled to a year's pay as a gratuity, followed by half-pay for the rest of his life. A militiaman so disabled 'as to be rendered incapable of earning his livelihood' might be offered up to twenty pounds a year.[44] On the assumption that their families would care for them, most got far less. Colonial taxpayers assumed the burden of militia pensions from the Loyal and Patriotic Society, while British veterans drew their pensions from the British treasury by way of the Royal Hospital, Charles II's splendid monument in Chelsea.

In the nineteenth-century Canadian militia, boards of officers recommended pensions and the executive council weighed each case with appropriate political judgment. Such arrangements sufficed for the 1837 Rebellions, the Fenian Raids, and the intermittent illnesses and accidents of militia training.[45] The North-West Campaign of 1885 brought a modest Canadianization of the rules: unlike British soldiers, who were deemed celibate, Canadian militiamen obviously had families to support. Pension entitlement expanded accordingly. Otherwise the 1885 regulations remained faithful to their British model. Soldiers killed in action were more deserving than those felled by disease. Disabled officers were entitled to a full year's pay plus pensions that ranged from $2.80 a day for a lieutenant to $1,200 a year for a lieutenant-colonel. While hardly munificent, the sums protected officers from the penury that befell the lower ranks. A wholly disabled private could be pensioned at 30 to 55 cents a day if he needed no assistance, or at 45 to 60 cents a day if he did. [46] Since even a day labourer required a dollar a day to live, a helpless pensioner needed generous friends or wealthy relatives.

On rare occasions after 1885, pension issues intruded on Parliament, chiefly because recommendations from boards of officers were full of anomalies and cabinet approval was suspiciously political. Why else had parents of a dead lieutenant been awarded twice as much as the widowed mother of a dead captain? [47] If a sergeant had a higher pension because of higher previous earnings, it was a principle, warned a prominent Tory, that 'cannot fail to land the Government in no end of confusion.' [48] A few veterans brought their grievances to Ottawa. In 1890, a crippled sergeant vented his outrage from the gallery of the House of Commons. [49] Most cases were settled more discreetly. William Mulock, a Liberal, was spared embarrassment when he raised the claim of Maria Neely, the widow of an 1885 veteran. Toronto's police chief, Col. Henry Grasett, reminded the minister of militia that both Mrs Neely and her late husband had been bad characters and that at least some of her four children had been born out of wedlock. Widows' pensions, explained the minister, depended on good behaviour. [50]

They also depended on need and continued widowhood. Caroline McEachren, the widow of a young officer killed at Ridgeway in 1866, collected a meagre pension until she died in 1922. Mary French, widow of Capt. John French, who was killed in the assault on Batoche in 1885, received a gratuity of $2,397 and a pension of $342 a year for herself and $102.95 for each of her four children. When she married in 1887 she lost her pension, but her sons benefited until they were eighteen and her daughter until she was twenty-one. Mrs French was luckier than Mrs John F. Ryan, whose husband, a mere gunner, died of pleurisy after the 1885 campaign. Mrs Ryan and her infant daughter were left with a pension of $83.04. A more heroic death might have raised her pension to $109.36. [51]

Canada took no responsibility for its volunteers in South Africa. The few Canadians who depended on imperial pensions for wartime disabilities could repent their youthful adventure during a lifetime of poverty. A single exception demonstrated the potential and the limits of military charity. Lorne Mulloy, a young teacher in eastern Ontario, had postponed entering Queen's University to join the Canadian Mounted Rifles. A Boer bullet cost him his eyesight. He returned to Canada with a British pension of about two hundred dollars a year, but epic courage and financial backing allowed Mulloy to finish his BA at Queen's in 1907. Mulloy, who had been denied a Rhodes Scholarship because of his blindness, caught the attention of Sir Sandford Fleming. In response to Fleming's threats and bullying, the trustees of the Patriotic Fund grudgingly consented to finance Mulloy's further education at Oxford. The 'Blind Trooper' went on to teach military history at the Royal Military College and to adorn countless First World War recruiting platforms. Mulloy was also a reminder of the emotions a disabled veteran could arouse in a democratic society.[52]

Britain's pension tradition was essentially aristocratic. Even the private charities that eased its harshness – Capt. Edward Walter's Corps of Commissionaires or the workshops run by the Soldiers and Sailors Help Society – were firmly managed by lords, ladies, and retired generals. Canada had no counterpart, and, when visiting Canadians saw bemedalled amputees peddling pencils on English street corners, they found little to admire. Sentimental images of bronzed 'Soldiers of the Queen' contrasted brutally with the reality of ragged military mendicants.[53]

The democratic alternative was no improvement. The 'pension evil' ranked with Tammany Hall, elected judges, and lynchings as blots on the neighbouring republic. Lord Bryce, in his monumental pre-war study of democracy in the United States, insisted that American pensions were 'a source of infinite waste.'[54] The lessons for Canada were clear enough. 'The maimed veterans of the Union army,' wrote a Canadian army doctor, 'were received as heroes, banqueted and feted, provided with artificial limbs and all too soon permitted to drift into the almost hopeless battle for a livelihood in a world that promptly forgot their heroic deeds.'[55] Such a history might repeat itself in Canada.

So might the ensuing retribution. Contemporaries could blame the ensuing 'pension evil' on a late-blooming Civil War veterans' organization, the Grand Army of the Republic. Urging members to 'vote as you shot,' the GAR easily bullied politicians into drilling loopholes in pension laws. Claims agents and pension attorneys combed the land, pocketing a fee for each successful case. Compliant congressmen passed thousands of special bills for claimants who could not fit through the loopholes. In 1888, the GAR took credit for beating President Grover Cleveland. His successor, Benjamin Harrison, late of the 60th Indiana Regiment, presumably got the message. 'Be generous to the boys,' he allegedly advised his new pension commissioner, 'Corporal' James Tanner, a legless war hero. With his pledge to drive a six-mule team through the treasury and his cry of 'God help the surplus,' Tanner proved too great an embarrassment even for Harrison, but indignant conservatives never forgot the slogans. GAR strength was probably exaggerated, but images as potent as the 'pension evil' do not depend on exact measurement, and no one could deny that spending on veterans devoured one-fifth of U.S. federal spending by 1914.[56]

Canada was not immune to the example. The American decision in 1871 to grant a service pension to elderly survivors of the War of 1812 created pressures that even the frugal regime of Alexander Mackenzie could not ignore. Emboldened by estimates that only about six hundred men would apply, Mackenzie succumbed in 1875. In the event, more than three times that number qualified for the twenty dollars a year.[57] Still, the government refused to be profligate: it could not 'be expected to pay money indiscriminately to every man over 80 years of age who came and told them he was a veteran of 1812.'[58] Ottawa did not extend the pension to widows and dependants. Washington, less prudent, did so; the last American veteran of 1812 died in 1907, but Esther Ann Hill Morgan was still collecting her pension at the outset of the Korean War. She and her sisters came to symbolize another 'evil,' the 'pension widow' whose deathbed marriage had been contracted for the sake of a lifetime income.[59]

Not all Canadians feared prodigality to veterans. As the Conservative militia critic, Sam Hughes helped talk the Laurier government into the Volunteer Bounty Act of 1908, later described as 'military bounty in its worst form.'[60] Hughes's enthusiasm for recognizing Fenian Raid veterans had to wait for the Tory victory in 1911. A year later, about 6,000 aging citizens in Ontario, Quebec, and New Brunswick could thank the minister of militia for their hundred-dollar cheques. Unexpectedly, the legislation also benefited 11,160 Nova Scotians whose service in 1866 had been obligatory, nominal, and completely bloodless. Since the money was poured into the prime minister's native province on the eve of an expected federal election, the opposition cried foul.[61]

Pensions, bounty, and kindred issues hardly rippled the surface of Canadian life before 1914. Veterans' organizations barely existed. The martial mood of Winnipeg in 1885 had inspired British ex-servicemen to form an Army and Navy Veterans' Association, but it soon languished. Aging ex-militiamen in Toronto created the 'Grand Council of Canadian Militia Veterans' in 1912, but their chief purpose was to rededicate the city's monument to the battle of Ridgeway that had taken place forty-six years earlier.[62] In 1912 Canada's military pension burden was seventy thousand dollars, most of it paid as a retirement fund for ex-members of the tiny permanent force.[63] Militia training camps added a few beneficiaries each year – victims of riding and range accidents and, perhaps, of occasional camouflaged episodes of skylarking. In each case, a board of officers met to pore over the regulations until a member older or wiser than the rest proposed a settlement that allowed them all to retire to the mess for a drink. The system was not designed for a great war, but neither was the militia.

Adjusting to Crisis

Now Canada was in the greatest war of its history, and the past provided no more than rude warnings and inadequate precedents. Tradition taught Canadians that ex-soldiers would always be rewarded with land. The disabled would raise such a pressure for pensions that Canada's minimalist approach to public revenue might be jeopardized. Would Canadian veterans create their own version of a Grand Army of the Republic? Could fiscal conservatism be spared a Canadian 'Corporal' Tanner? If Canadian ex-soldiers avoided the example of a GAR, would they be tempted by the even more fearful spectre of trade unionism? [64]

Amid his endless chores in creating the Hospitals Commission, Ernest Scammell wrestled alone with such problems. Senator Lougheed appeared, if at all, in hurried transit between the Militia Department and his Calgary law office. If he had spare moments, Lougheed devoted them to his quixotic campaign to finance machine-guns for the CEF through private contributions. Though every available factory in Europe and the United States was jammed with government orders, it appealed to Lougheed's sense of fitness that the CEF should be armed by public subscription. In 1915 the national mood was one of fervid patriotism, and the Machine Gun Fund was popular. Schoolchildren, businessmen, and service clubs were caught up in the crusade to provide guns at a cost of a thousand dollars each. [65]

The machine-gun scheme ended abruptly when Borden and Hughes came home in September. Lougheed was forcefully reminded that his main responsibility was to the returned soldiers. While in England the prime minister had spent every spare moment visiting Canadian wounded. [66] The experience had moved Borden deeply, and he was in no mood to find a waiting pile of letters complaining of the treatment of invalided soldiers in Canada. From Toronto Sir Thomas White reported stirrings of complaint, even in the Tory stronghold of the Albany Club. The finance minister suggested that Lougheed's commission might also provide training for veterans too disabled to work; perhaps the government should create yet another commission. [67]

Commissions certainly were proliferating. Late in May 1915 a powerful delegation of mayors had invaded Ottawa complaining of the past winter's mass unemployment in their cities, demanding money, and claiming that the poor should somehow be moved back to the land. From Borden they got the usual sober words, no money, and the promise of an investigation into 'the whole economic condition of Canada.' Sir William Van Horne, the venerable builder of the Canadian Pacific Railway, volunteered to be chairman of the new 'Commission of Natural Resources,' but died on 11 September. Here was a fresh task for Senator Lougheed: like the Hospitals Commission, the Natural Resources Commission would be deeply enmeshed in the problems of a post-war Canada, and a single chairman made eminent good sense. [68]

Lougheed's personal and political preoccupations had left Scammell free from a meddling boss. Somehow through the summer he found time to absorb advice from an array of would-be experts, ranging from J.H. Sherrard, president of the Canadian Manufacturers' Association, to Ina Matthews of Sydney, Nova Scotia, a sister-in-law of the wealthy Mrs J.K.L. Ross. A more comprehensive Nova Scotia contribution came from Frederick Sexton, the province's American-born director of technical education. Sexton transformed Miss Matthews's ideas into a comprehensive brief on invalided veterans. 'The whole nation and the individual himself,' Sexton insisted, 'will be far better off if the disabled soldier is trained to earn a living than if he looks to public funds to maintain himself in idleness.' Modern industry, with its intricate division of labour, could find a place for virtually every category of disablement, from amputees to the blind. 'Proper, efficient training, thorough and advanced enough to put each man on his feet as an independent skilled or semi-skilled wage-earner would require from six months to a year at the outside. During this time the man should receive enough to pay his board, in the case of a married man enough to maintain his family. This may be expensive, but the facts must be faced.' [69]

By August 1915 France had absorbed a million casualties. An article by Dr Maurice Bourillon of the Asile national des invalides de St-Maurice gave Scammell the benefit of the French experience in training and job placement. As might be expected, the British experience was more influential. By 1915 the machinery of British voluntarism had virtually collapsed. A tradition that had left soldiers' and sailors' families, their widows and orphans, and the disabled men themselves to separate and competing charities was simply irrelevant for an army that had expanded to 2.4 million men and for citizen-soldiers who would no longer tolerate 'charity-mongering.' A British parliamentary select committee, headed by Sir George Murray, demonstrated how far Britain had been shoved from its traditional position on military charity: 'The care of the soldiers and sailors who have been disabled in the war is an obligation which should fall primarily upon the State: and the liability cannot be considered as having been extinguished by the award of a pension from public funds. We regard it as the duty of the State to see that the disabled man shall be, as far as possible, restored to health and that assistance shall be forthcoming to enable him to earn his living in the occupation best suited to his circumstances and physical condition.'[70]

Scammell was no radical. He fully echoed Lougheed's enthusiasm for financing services to the disabled from private charity if it could be managed. In Canada it was not possible for a single government to act without consultation. The Hospitals Commission's responsibilities, from medical care to retraining the disabled, belonged constitutionally to the provinces. In mid-September Scammell had consulted the premiers of Ontario and Nova Scotia. 'The result so far,' he reported to Col. C.W. Rowley, the commission's Winnipeg member, 'is that I shall have to prepare a revision which will certainly effect an improvement.' Provincial commissions would 'take charge of the question of employment and vocational education.'[71] The spirit of voluntarism was far from dead. In other respects Scammell's blueprint was more expansive than the British model. If Sir George Murray's committee accepted state responsibility for the medical and vocational needs of the disabled, Scammell was prepared to accept a commitment to the able-bodied as well. 'Definite machinery should be installed,' he urged in his report, 'whereby situations may be found for all able-bodied men at a remuneration as near to that which they were previously receiving as possible.'[72]

Scammell suggested that returning men be divided into four major categories. Some could return at once to jobs held open for them by patriotic employers. Others, whether physically fit or restored to health, would need active help to find jobs. A third group, too severely disabled to return to their former work, would need to be properly assessed, trained 'in the shortest possible time to a reasonable standard of productivity,' and found safe, stable employment. Finally, a few who were permanently incapacitated might need to be placed in special soldiers' homes. Each level of government and all sectors of the economy would be involved. The provincial commissions, with representatives of labour, employers, farmers, and technical educators, would organize the hunt for work. Municipalities must create employment bureaus; private citizens must scour the labour market for opportunities for the returning men. With Sherrard's encouragement, Scammell claimed that employers would increase their work forces by 5, 10, or even 20 per cent to absorb the thousands of returning soldiers. Military authorities could even improve morale by collecting information about soldiers' post-war employment expectations. To discourage rural depopulation, a recurrent problem of the era, Ottawa and the provinces must develop plans to encourage men to return to farming or market gardening.

Certainly, it would all cost money. While incorporating (with considerable personal enthusiasm) Lougheed's dream of a privately financed Disablement Fund, Scammell echoed Sir George Murray's principle: care of the disabled 'is an obligation which should fall primarily on the State, and this liability cannot be considered as being extinguished by the award of a pension from public funds.'[73] It was the federal government that must provide staff and facilities to retrain the disabled. It must even be prepared to subsidize the soldiers' clubs, which Scammell saw not only as valuable social centres for returned men but as places where grievances could be channelled to the proper officials.[74]

For all its implications of active government involvement, Scammell's report contained much to please Borden, Lougheed, and the businessmen-members of the commission. Retraining the disabled to make them self-sufficient, as Sexton had emphasized in his report, was obviously the right way to forestall an American-style clamour for pensions. Technical training in Canada might still be in its infancy, but that probably helped inflate expectations of its potential.[75] Nothing is as powerful as an untried idea. Funding soldiers' clubs made sense if any Canadian counterpart of the Grand Army of the Republic was to be kept under firm tutelage. Finally, amid conventional expressions of concern for returning soldiers, Scammell's firm, paternal tone reassured a government and a commission dominated by conservative employers: 'The soldier himself cannot be allowed to choose at will just what he prefers to do in the future if he cannot follow his previous vocation. His knowledge is not sufficient to enable him to judge perfectly. There must, of course, be nothing mandatory about the course he is to pursue, but he must have the wise counsel of someone who knows the whole problem better than he does himself. There must be a minimum of sentiment and a maximum of hard business sense concerning the future [sic] of the returned soldier to civil life.'[76]

Such a firm tone could best be maintained if the Hospitals Commission was independent of the state. Perhaps Lougheed's machine-gun fund could find another purpose. Among the backers had been 'Canada's Wheat King,' James Carruthers, a wealthy Montreal grain broker. Once satisfied that the soldiers would not suffer for lack of machine-guns, Carruthers was persuaded to make his $100,000 contribution the nucleus of a Disablement Fund. If the Patriotic Fund supported soldiers' families, surely patriotism could also support wounded heroes. Like the CPF, such a fund would also put businessmen, not politicians, firmly in charge of the disabled.[77]

A summer's experience, Scammell's draft report, provincial involvement, and the idea of a Disablement Fund all made it clear that the Hospitals Commission needed a new mandate. On 16 October 1915 a fresh order in council added five members to the commission, gave it authority to provide retraining and rehabilitation, and allowed it to accept patients who had yet to go overseas. A new title, 'The Military Hospitals and Convalescent Homes Commission,' was approved and, for good measure, Scammell's salary was set at $1,500.[78]

To launch the renewed commission, fourteen provincial premiers and ministers and the fourteen commission members gathered at the Château Laurier on Monday morning, 18 October, to be welcomed by Sir Robert Borden. Only British Columbia was unrepresented; its premier, Sir Richard McBride, had already pledged his full support. Other provinces could do no less. Late that afternoon, after a separate meeting, Ontario's Premier William Hearst emerged to report a unanimous agreement to establish provincial commissions to cope with the problems of returned men and to help find them work. For its part, Ottawa would take full responsibility for restoring and retraining the disabled. With their constitutional sensibilities at least partially anaesthetized by the war emergency, the provinces could congratulate themselves on avoiding a costly and potentially touchy problem. On Tuesday the premiers met again to debate a more urgent concern – the fear that returned soldiers might swell the flight from the countryside. Once again Ottawa was left with the task of planning for a soldiers' agricultural settlement program. A further conference would decide what to do when the entire CEF came home.[79]

Thanks to Scammell, Canada had an outline program for demobilization long before its allies. In looking beyond the immediate problem of providing beds for convalescent soldiers, Scammell had offered an alternative to the two old traditions, military mendicancy and the 'pension evil.' Cautiously, the Canadian state had assumed a responsibility for its disabled veterans that went beyond the tradition of 'military bounty.' It remained to be seen whether new principles would lead to new practices.

2 'A Motherly Touch'

Providing Enough Beds

The Military Hospitals Commission resumed life on 18 October with a clear long-term strategy for the demobilization of the Canadian Expeditionary Force and for restoring disabled veterans, at least, to some semblance of economic self-sufficiency. The interprovincial conference broke up on Tuesday evening, 19 October, in an unexpected mood of harmony and commitment. Jealous as they might be of their jurisdiction, the premiers were content to leave to Ottawa the task of coping with the sick and wounded. The chairmen of the provincial returned soldiers' commissions would at least be associate members of the MHC. The provinces would remain involved.[1]

Whatever its long-range plans, the MHC would be judged on its short-run performance in caring for soldiers. On 7 October the commission had eleven hospitals and convalescent homes in operation, with a total of 530 beds, serving about 600 in- and out-patients.[2] Probably the total was no more than the Militia Department could have mustered after a summer's work. Montreal's Khaki League had opened a home at Belmont Park for 46 patients in April 1915, even before the Militia Department became concerned; another home, for 57, was opened in August. Mrs Ross's house in Sydney, furnished for 33 patients, opened on 16 June. In Winnipeg, the Imperial Order of the Daughters of the Empire had started a hospital in February for men of the Second Contingent, using a run-down building loaned by the Hudson's Bay Company. When the troops left for overseas, the IODE eagerly promised 'a little bit of a motherly touch' to returning invalids. Beauvoir Manor, the Quebec home of Mrs W.M. Dobell, welcomed returning convalescents through the summer of 1915. Additional private homes in Kingston, Toronto, Hamilton, and London became available to convalescents in September and October, and the home of the late Sir Sandford Fleming in Ottawa was opened in December.[3]

A summer of protracted and often delicate negotiations had cooled Scammell's enthusiasm for voluntarist solutions. Recalling his experiences before the 1917 special parliamentary committee on re-establishment, he confessed that, 'generally speaking,' the arrangements had not been satisfactory.[4] Homes needed additions to the kitchens and the plumbing systems, and substantial repairs to the heating systems. The wives and daughters of the wealthy had often readied themselves by taking nursing courses with the St John's Ambulance Voluntary Aid Committees, but the training did not prepare them for the drudgery and monotony of real nursing. The 'bother-per-bed' was less when the commission could borrow the old naval hospital at Esquimalt from the Department of Naval Service or Savard Park, the Department of the Interior's immigration hospital at Quebec. Such institutions came properly staffed and equipped, and the doctors in charge at Savard Park were already in the militia.[5]

Scammell organized and negotiated on the run. In 1915 soldiers returned to Canada in numbers averaging a hundred a week, in whatever transportation the Canadian authorities in England could arrange. Unless they landed in Halifax, with destinations in the Maritimes, returning soldiers passed through the Militia Department's discharge depot set up in the huge barn-like immigration sheds at Quebec. The men underwent a final medical examination, collected whatever pay they were still owed, and tried on civilian clothing provided free for those who had served for six months or more. If they desired, they could take cash instead of the clothing – eight dollars in the summer, thirteen dollars in winter when an overcoat or reefer jacket was added to the free issue and, from February 1916, sixteen dollars if they lived west of Winnipeg, where a heavy coat was no luxury.[6] True to army tradition, the men also spent plenty of time waiting.

At the discharge depot, medical boards divided the returned men into three categories: those who could be discharged without further claims of any kind; those who required additional hospitalization; and those who could be sent home to await the ponderous proceedings of the Pensions and Claims Board. About one-quarter of the returned men left Quebec as civilians without further obligations or expectations.[7] In September Scammell visited the discharge depot and met its elderly commander, Maj. J.J. Sharples, a member of a well-connected Quebec City family. Scammell found crowding and delays. Sharples had little or no notification from overseas before drafts of invalids left England; it was often difficult to notify mayors and reeves across Canada so that welcoming committees could meet returning heroes. And, whatever the public might think, returning soldiers were not necessarily angels. Men spent their back pay and the money they collected in lieu of civilian clothes on drink, gambling, and other soldierly recreations. Then they came home destitute, blaming the authorities for their condition. W.M. Dobell, a new commission member from Quebec, spoke from a summer's experience when he demanded tighter discipline among convalescents. Beauvoir Manor was closed; the hospital at Savard Park could be more tightly run.[8]

The expanded commission met at Quebec on 10 November for its third session. After suitable refreshments and a conducted tour of the discharge depot, Lougheed and his colleagues reviewed the local arrangements. A crisis developed with word that the *Metagama*, packed with more than six hundred invalids, had sailed from Liverpool. Lack of co-ordination with Canadian officials in England, a problem since the spring, would become acute when six times the normal influx arrived on a single day. The commission ordered Beauvoir Manor reopened and authorized Sharples to double his staff. The incident underlined the need to persuade CEF staff officers overseas to give adequate notice of arrivals. The commission also dealt with other issues. Members agreed that artificial limbs should be purchased in Canada 'so far as compatible with efficiency and economy.' As usual, minor issues generated the most debate. Should invalids heading west be issued Pullman or tourist accommodation? The cheaper alternative won; 'many of the men would feel less at home in a Pullman.'[9]

When the *Metagama* docked on 15 November, the commission suffered its first public criticism. Despite additional staff and a few extra doctors from Montreal for the medical boards, delays exceeded even the army's tolerance. When the soldiers were finally cleared for discharge or hospitalization, the Intercolonial Railway could find nothing better for their transport than battered old colonist cars. Its more modern rolling stock was serving civilian passengers or delivering CEF battalions to Halifax. Rather than create a further delay, Sharples let the trains go. Across Canada unhappy soldiers poured forth their grievances over shipboard conditions, bad food, rude treatment, cheap clothing, and official incompetence.[10]

If invalids had been overcrowded on the *Metagama* or if their pay was held up, the fault, insisted Scammell, lay with the Militia Department. He rushed to Quebec, proclaimed that the controversial civilian clothing 'could not be matched for excellence anywhere in Canada,' and advised Sharples to fire his cook.[11] The lasting significance of the *Metagama* experience was reflected in the establishment of larger institutions and a tougher approach to the commission's clients. The original assumption, sarcastically described by Sir Herbert Ames, that 'kindly individuals would donate their homes and make everything lovely for a few soldiers,' had proved extravagant and inefficient. [12] True, voluntarism was far from over. 'We will go a long way and put up with some inconvenience in our adminis- tration,' Scammell admitted in 1917, 'rather than offend some of these people who are anxious to help us.' [13] But there would be limits.

Where they could, commission members took charge of local arrange- ments; some members had been added in October because of their potential contribution. Dr Thomas Walker, at seventy-five the MHC's oldest member, persuaded Louisa Parks to make her house available as Saint John's first convalescent home; the local Women's Canadian Club provided furniture and equipment. With only thirty-five beds available in the Parks Home, however, Walker also had to arrange accommodation in the local armouries. [14] In Winnipeg, the MHC member was C.W. Rowley, the manager of the local branch of the Bank of Commerce, a Boy Scout commissioner for Manitoba, and a recently promoted lieutenant-colonel in the pay corps. [15] Winnipeg was a hive of patriotic charity, from the IODE's hospital to the CPF. A Returned Soldiers' Association, formed by prominent citizens, sold voting memberships at five dollars. Volunteerism, Rowley reported, had its problems. The IODE resented criticism; the secretary of the Returned Soldiers' Association was angling for a job in Ottawa; and the secretary of Manitoba's returned soldiers' commission was, as Scammell put it, 'too slow for anything.' [16] The IODE hospital was a fire-trap and impossible to heat in winter, but the alternative, the dominion government's Immigration Hall, was on the wrong side of the tracks in downtown Winni- peg. Helped by a terminal case of frozen pipes and judicious intervention by the lieutenant-governor, Rowley managed the IODE ladies. [17] Next, he had to persuade Sir William Mackenzie's son Rod that his otherwise unprofitable Deer Lodge hotel would make an excellent convalescent home. By June Deer Lodge Hospital was in operation and an IODE take-over attempt had been firmly fended off. [18] In Vancouver F.W. Peters of the local Canadian Club earned his position on the Military Hospitals Commission by organiz- ing a successful club for returned soldiers. He also squelched Mrs W.J. Thomas, one of the more turbulent examples of the voluntarist urge, whose 'mania for putting her arms around returned soldiers and trying to impress them with the fact that she is the sole guardian of their future' caused much embarrassment. [19] The excesses of private enthusiasts increasingly exaspe- rated Scammell: 'It seems to be absurd that these women – and sometimes it is a case of men – will not read the newspapers and yet will hold meetings and issue reports from which it appears that the Government is utterly callous and is doing nothing to meet the situation. These busybodies do a great deal of harm.' [20]

The commission's main efforts were in Montreal and Toronto, the cities that had sent the largest contingents to the CEF. Thanks to the Khaki League and a three-hundred-bed wing of the Grey Nuns' Hospital, and the sisters' offer to provide food and bedding at seventy-five cents per patient per day, Montreal presented few immediate difficulties.[21] Toronto was another matter. Sir Henry Pellatt, a member of the original commission, insisted that he was in charge of activities. He recruited a local secretary, George I. Riddell, and rented him an office in the Trader's Bank Building.[22] Lougheed ignored Pellatt's pretensions. The real dynamo in Toronto was W.K. George, a successful manufacturer and ex-Liberal, who had organized the local Voluntary Aid Committee. He also managed to negotiate the loan of the former Bishop Strachan girls' school on College Street. 'Having to sit in the Council Chamber and listen to aldermanic oratory for four and a half solid hours,' George reported, was only part of the price a busy man had to pay.[23] With the influx of the *Metagama* men, the College Street site, with its potential 170 beds, was a welcome addition. The Knox College building at the head of Spadina Avenue was next on the MHC list.

On 15 December the commission held its fourth meeting at Pellatt's Toronto office, followed by a dinner and a concert by Boris Hambourg at Pellatt's mansion, Casa Loma.[24] Such lavish hospitality failed to win Pellatt the pre-eminence he expected, and he soon dropped out of active participation. Another ambitious Torontonian was Lt-Col. Frederick Marlow, a successful doctor who had accepted the wartime post of assistant director of medical services for Military District No. 2, covering Toronto and central Ontario. Commission members had been met by newspaper headlines demanding to know 'Who'll Run the Hospitals?' Marlow had an answer. While the prominent ladies and gentlemen of George's committee certainly felt a proprietorial claim, Marlow was determined that military hospitals would be a military responsibility. The colonel was forced to apologize for his blunt criticisms of the MHC at the time of the *Metagama* affair, but his determination to gain control had only been hardened by the embarrassment.[25]

The issue of authority had been casually overlooked when the Hospitals Commission was formed in June 1915. Like the Militia Department as a whole, the tiny permanent component of the Canadian Army Medical Corps had been preoccupied with mobilization and overseas service.[26] The Hospitals Commission had filled a vacuum but, beyond empowering it to call on other departments of government for aid, no one had clarified its authority over the Army Medical Corps or soldiers in general. As the exceedingly unmilitary acting minister of militia in the summer of 1915, Senator Lougheed had simply not recognized any problem.

If all returning soldiers had been discharged on arrival, the MHC could have dealt with its patients as civilians. That would have left them and their families destitute, as it did other ex-soldiers sent home that winter to await a pension decision.[27] Ames's Patriotic Fund was ruthless in cutting off families whose military head had returned from overseas, and the commission had no authority of its own to pay veterans. Instead, in late February 1916, the MHC won a battle to have 'prematurely' discharged men reinstated as soldiers, with pay and allowances, until their pension cheques arrived.[28] If the commission had been satisfied to organize and equip hospitals, leaving the CAMC and other militia organizations to manage them, its role might have been clear. That was much less than Scammell had proposed in October, and the importance of controlling the hospitals and their inmates became steadily more apparent as the weeks passed. Scammell and the commission found themselves increasingly enmeshed in the military administration of their charges and, indeed, of all returned soldiers. MHC officials were asked to decide such questions as whether discharged soldiers could be granted military funerals and who should pay for a soldier's trip home before he reported for treatment.[29]

Patients Deserving and Undeserving

The MHC soon discovered that many stereotypes of the war-wounded did not quite fit its patients. Popular images of armless, legless, eyeless men might dominate advertising and theatrical productions, but amputees and the blind were a tiny proportion of returning invalids. By the spring of 1917 the commission had admitted 13,862 patients; only 9 were blind, while 177 had suffered major amputations.[30] Illness always outweighed wounds as a military medical problem.[31] To commission members, and undoubtedly to eager volunteers in the homes and hospitals, this was slightly disillusioning. For soldiers and civilians alike the wounded had a heroic dimension that the sick could never attain.[32] Many of those sent back from England had never seen action; other MHC patients had never left Canada. The symptoms of pneumonia or rheumatism were the same, regardless of whether the illnesses were the result of months of trench warfare or of a winter of wet canvas, route marches, and pre-dawn physical training in Victoria, but commission members could hardly prevent themselves from distinguishing at least between 'overseas' and 'camp' men.[33]

In a third category were men who obviously never should have been allowed to join the army in the first place. Between June 1915 and May 1916 more than a quarter of a million men joined the CEF, making up almost half its volunteer intake. Cajoled by colonels, pressed by would-be privates, and urged on by their own patriotism, medical officers had more than a financial reason to overlook age or disability. Public opinion made heroes of youngsters who lied about their age and the 'thirty-niners' who cast off years to serve the imperial cause. When volunteering dried up in 1916, officers grew desperate to fill their battalions. Some communities never had been over-scrupulous about urging vagrants, paupers, and the feeble-minded to enlist. Anyone, so the ancient lore insisted, could be a soldier. Once accepted, some recruits got all the way to England despite physical or mental conditions that should have been visible to an untrained eye. In June 1916 a staff officer estimated that 18 to 20 per cent of Canadians arriving in England were physically deficient – usually over-age. In October 1916 a survey of the men who arrived in that month found that one in five was unfit for service. Among these were soldiers who lacked fingers, toes, part of a foot, and an entire forearm. One seventy-nine-year-old patriot from Guelph reached England in an advanced state of senility. Pte J.A. Couche, alcoholic, violent, and brain-damaged, enlisted five times in Montreal and twice went overseas.[34] Whatever the explanation, the medical problems of such men fell on the army and eventually on the Military Hospitals Commission. While Potter and the CAMC slowly created a distinct set of military hospitals in Canada to care for the thousands who flocked into the CEF battalions, invalided 'camp men' also passed to the MHC.

The most acute military medical problem was tuberculosis. To contemporaries, TB was a dreaded and highly contagious disease that was shameful because of its association with poverty. The public called it 'the white plague'; experts gravely discussed 'phthisiophobia,' the fear and horror other people felt at contact with the disease and its sufferers. No certain or easy treatment existed. Forty years earlier Dr Edward Trudeau had saved himself from the disease by fleeing to Saranac Lake in the Adirondacks; his apparent cure encouraged the sanatorium movement. In a remote and scenic location – some physicians attributed part of the benefit to pine trees or to high altitude – a patient's lungs would benefit from fresh air, absolute rest, careful diet, and rigorous control of germ-laden sputum. Most victims of tuberculosis were poor and could not afford such treatment. In Canada, existing sanatoria either depended heavily on charity or were under-financed speculative ventures. Some provinces provided modest subsidies; in the west, a couple had cautiously built their own facilities. Wealthy sufferers headed for the Trudeau Sanatorium at Saranac Lake. With dozens and then hundreds of tuberculosis cases on its hands, the MHC had to find beds closer to home.[35]

In retrospect one may wonder why the commission accepted cases that so obviously pre-dated enlistment. Scammell later complained that a simple three-dollar tuberculin test could have saved the government an average of five thousand dollars in pension and treatment for each sufferer. At the time, like most people and institutions, the MHC simply responded to a crisis. The causes and genesis of the disease were not matters of medical certainty. Discharging sick soldiers would cause an outcry. If men insisted that the symptoms were due to service, particularly if they had been overseas and subjected to poison gas, who could argue? The problem was finding sanatorium space. As a matter of policy the commission would offer its patients six months of care; after that the pension authorities could decide. [36]

In Quebec the space problem was easily solved. Lorne McGibbon was made a member of the commission largely on the strength of his offer of the Laurentide Inn in Ste-Agathe. With the Laurentian Sanatorium nearby to furnish treatment, the resort hotel could serve as a tuberculosis centre for Quebec and the Maritime provinces. [37] Kingston's Oliver Mowat Sanatorium offered space in eastern Ontario. The London Health Association offered to care for men from western counties. Tubercular soldiers in Toronto and central Ontario were admitted to the well-known National Free Sanatorium in Muskoka, but its autocratic president, the publisher W.J. Gage, drove a hard bargain, and military patients aggravated relations by defying the institution's strict rules. [38] In the crisis, the Minnewaska Sanatorium at Gravenhurst made an offer that seemed too good to be true: for a mere seven dollars a week for an incipient case (or twelve dollars for an advanced case) the institution would be delighted to accept sixty or seventy cases in each category. As the hyper-critical Colonel Marlow soon discovered, the offer *was* too good. Minnewaska promoters hoped that MHC patients would rescue a bad investment. Complaints from soldiers about poor food and lack of medical attention were easily confirmed. The commission eventually had to send its own doctor, assistants, and even food and drugs. Patients petitioned to be removed from the place. The MHC discovered too late that the president of the company had a notorious reputation, that nurses quit because they were never paid, and that patients were left to take their own temperatures, keep their own charts, and carry their own trays to bed. Scammell insisted that the commission needed its own buildings; but Minnewaska had to be used, over Marlow's protests, until the MHC could buy a small sanatorium near Kitchener and help another on Hamilton Mountain complete construction. [39]

Gradually, through 1916, the commission expanded its facilities for tubercular soldiers, from the Charles Dalton sanatorium on the highest point on Prince Edward Island (six hundred feet above sea level) to Tranquille outside Kamloops and the Kootenay Lake Hotel at Balfour in British Columbia. The MHC was often a partner and sometimes a reluctant proprietor, sharing the cost of building the open-air pavilions which contemporary wisdom dictated for tuberculosis sufferers, erecting kitchens and staff quarters, and contributing X-ray machines and other costly equipment. As the burden grew, commission officials could at least tell themselves that they were solving a health problem that even American states had thought to be beyond individual solution.[40]

Tuberculosis was the first of many medical problems to be dealt with. Mental illness was another special category. Once again, careless enlistment contributed more cases than battlefield conditions, but the combination caused added difficulties. Recruits who were obviously insane could be transferred to provincial asylums while the commission wrangled with provincial authorities about responsibility for the cost.[41] Soldiers home from the battlefield were another matter. Even if the real cause of the illness was tertiary syphilis or congenital feeble-mindedness, public opinion objected to sending soldiers to asylums. Heroes presumably driven mad by the horrors of war surely deserved more than the overcrowding, neglect, and stigma associated with mental institutions.[42] In July 1916, the Ontario government offered the MHC a relatively new mental hospital at Cobourg. Patients were promised competent doctors and attendants and the best modern 'electro-therapeutic and other apparatus.'[43]

A majority of the commission's patients remained in general treatment institutions. By the autumn of 1916 most of the original convalescent homes had been closed, though special circumstances and occasional political influence added others. Under relentless pressure, the Keefer Home at Port Arthur was opened in a house contributed by a former Lakehead mayor and managed by his wife. Local veterans, the commission was persuaded, needed a hospital of their own.[44] The Merritt home at St Catharines was another exception, justified because nearby sulphur springs could be used to treat rheumatic patients. The house was eventually used as a rest home for nurses. The Massey-Treble estate offered Euclid Hall in Toronto, complete with its splendid pipe-organ. After some misgivings, the commission took the mansion, painted the sombre woodwork, and declared that it would be a home for incurables. A local musician offered a weekly organ recital.

The commission struggled to find larger institutions. Once the Bishop Strachan School had become Toronto's Central Military Convalescent Hospital, work began on the former Knox College. By June 1916 it was ready for occupation at a cost of twelve thousand dollars. The commission rented the old Loyola College building in Montreal with the promise to restore it at war's end. The Calgary Brewing and Malting Company had offered its unprofitable Ogden Hotel to the Red Cross. The commission accepted both it and Red Cross management. In Regina, the Anglican diocese handed over its brand new girls' school, St Chad's. The Rocky

Mountain Sanatorium near Frank, Alberta, was accepted for 'a nominal rent.' Near Vancouver, another unprofitable speculation, the Resthaven Hotel at Sidney, was renovated and adapted for 160 soldier-patients.[45]

To manage the commission's growing medical empire, Lougheed turned to a parliamentary colleague. Alfred Thompson, a forty-seven-year-old Nova Scotia doctor, had joined the Klondike gold rush, managed the Dawson hospital, and promoted a series of companies, from a hardware store to a brewery, before his election in 1911 as member of parliament for the Yukon. Armed with the militia rank of lieutenant-colonel, Thompson took over his duties in time for the commission's meeting on 29 April. His plans, he explained modestly, were to get rid of volunteer nurses and improve the medical staff. On the whole, Thompson confessed, he was not a believer in change.[46]

Lt-Col. Thompson's appointment coincided with the commission's decision to follow its own path in the provision of artificial limbs. If amputees were far fewer than commission members had expected, they still constituted a significant and conspicious group, with the added status of having obviously suffered for their country. Since they would never again be fit for active service, it was also easier for authorities in England to send them home. Once in Canada, amputees and their families often failed to understand that it took several months for a 'green' stump to shrink sufficiently to be fitted with an artificial limb.[47] In some cases further amputations were necessary, particularly when front-line surgery had left nerve tissue caught in scar tissue, when bones grew spurs, or when, as commonly occurred, infection set in.

At Quebec in November 1915 MHC members had blithely agreed that artificial limbs should be procured in Canada. But the national industry consisted only of a scattering of individual craftsmen supplying crude appliances to victims of industrial accidents, together with sales agents from American firms using aggressive marketing tactics. Much of the high cost of artificial arms and legs was due to elaborate promotion and advertising.[48] The commission was a magnet for both parts of the industry. C.S. Chesley, a Hantsport limb-maker, reminded the prime minister that he was almost a neighbour. Surely Chesley would get the Nova Scotia business, particularly if he promised to train a returned man as an apprentice.[49] The Carnes Arm Company of Kansas City had a more sophisticated product and approach; 'The Carnes Arm,' it boasted, 'puts you on the payroll.' An agile demonstrator was available to prove the point. The cost per arm was a mere two hundred dollars.[50]

Prosthetics manufacturers may have assumed that Canada would follow the American example of giving war amputees an allowance to buy and maintain whatever limb they chose. The Hospitals Commission was more interested in British experience, and it sent Dobell, himself an amputee, to seek guidance. At Roehampton, Dobell found a vast depot where competing prosthetic devices were tested and improved and where amputees were fitted and trained by experts.[51] Dobell was immensely impressed, and urged his fellow commissioners to establish a similar depot in Canada. At its March meeting the MHC appointed a committee to pursue the matter. Centralization certainly created problems in so vast a country, but the total demand would obviously be small and standardization made sense. By running its own limb factory as a branch of government, the MHC could take advantage of all available patents and, like the Belgians, could retrain convalescents in a valuable skill. A futher argument, designed for Dobell's business-minded colleagues, was that 'the elimination of the question of profit would tend toward the securing of a better limb for each individual.'[52]

Ignoring politics and protocol, George Riddell was dispatched to visit Toronto's few prosthetics firms. He discovered that T.J. LeCras, the foreman at Authors & Cox, was the best in the business, and invited him to go to work for the MHC. Instead of the $3,000 a year LeCras demanded, Riddell offered $2,500 and a few hours a week to keep his old firm going.[53] The deal was struck. The experiment was controversial; Major Potter, for one, preferred to split the work among three regional firms. Lougheed insisted on a committee of experts drawn from the new field of orthopaedics to protect him from criticism. When they eventually met, two out of three, including Colonel Thompson, insisted that free enterprise was best. The third member, Dr W.E. Gallie, stoutly responded that a government-manufactured limb could combine the best features of every existing device. In any case, artificial legs were straightforward and functional, while no arm, including the costly and intricate Carnes device, was even remotely satisfactory. Col. Clarence Starr, a colleague of Gallie at the University of Toronto and Canada's leading orthopaedic surgeon, intervened to back Gallie's arguments, and the MHC was convinced. A limb factory was opened. But private enterprise was not easily fended off. In 1918 an order in council threatened a fine of one hundred dollars for any commercial competitor who disparaged government-made limbs.[54]

Dobell, Colonel Starr, and the British example of Roehampton persuaded the commission that patients who could benefit from the young specialty of orthopaedics should be concentrated at a single centre. Breaking with the rule of localism was at least as controversial as a government-run limb factory, but the efficiency of concentration easily took precedence over 'mere sentimentality.' The original Central Hospital on Toronto's College Street sufficed until the Salvation Army rented its Booth Memorial College in suburban Davisville to the MHC. Major renovations and expansion were completed in 1917.[55]

Among the first beneficiaries of the MHC's limb factory was an unexpected and poignant group of war victims, a shipload of Jamaicans from the 3rd Battalion, British West Indies Regiment, who had been caught in a savage winter storm during a North Atlantic crossing. More than one hundred casualties suffering from frostbite landed in Halifax in March 1916. Seventeen of them underwent major amputations. With charity and condescension, the chief of the general staff asked, 'What is the best we can do for our black brothers, victims of the Canadian winter?'[56] An answer soon emerged. A local merchant, W.J. Clayton, offered a house near the city's black district as a convalescent home for the Jamaicans. The MHC offered to fit artificial limbs and provide vocational training at a cost of seventy-three hundred dollars. Mrs F.H. Sexton, the wife of the Nova Scotia director of technical training, persuaded the local Red Cross to share the burden. Two visits by LeCras allowed at least a crude fitting of replacement limbs. In the late autumn of 1916 the Jamaicans took home a smattering of tailoring, shoemaking, tinsmithing, bookkeeping, and 'general subjects.' Another sub-Arctic winter was more than they could face.[57]

The war-blind represented a smaller but more difficult problem than amputees. Canada's few charities for the blind shared the traditional view that the sightless might master a few handicraft skills. They saw the war as an opportunity to gain funds for the entire blind community through public sympathy for sightless veterans. As early as November 1915 the Halifax School for the Blind offered its facilities to the MHC. A more modern approach was represented by Dr C.R. Dickson, a member of the Toronto-based Canadian Free Library for the Blind and a physician blinded by his own experiments with X-rays. Dickson was a crusader, critical of existing institutions for the blind, and convinced that adults who had lost their sight could do far more than basket-weaving. It was a viewpoint that had already taken practical shape in England. Sir Arthur Pearson had made a fortune satisfying the British appetite for a sensational press when his eyesight began to fail. The war gave the sightless publisher a new cause. At St Dunstan's Hostel in London's Regent Park, Pearson set out to prove that blind soldiers could become physically active, self-sufficient, productive, and even competitive. Sightless veterans found their way into London's busy streets, learned to type, and mastered a range of trades from woodworking to massage. Above all, as Pearson explained to admiring visitors, the blind learned how to be blind.[58]

To Dickson and to Sherman Swift, librarian of the Canadian Free

Library, St Dunstan's was the ideal place for Canada's blind soldiers. Rumours that the MHC might establish its own training centre at London, Ontario, provoked both men to angry protest. In July 1916 the commission assured Swift that all blind veterans were being referred to St Dunstan's to be retrained 'until their vocational re-education has been sufficiently finished to enable their returning to Canada and taking up some gainful occupations.' By any standard it was a happy decision. St Dunstan's Canadian alumni included Capt. E.A. Baker, a former engineer who became the guiding force behind the Canadian National Institute for the Blind, and Donald J. McDougall, a PPCLI private and a future professor of history at the University of Toronto. McDougall used his St Dunstan's training to place second in the annual British qualifying exams for masseurs.

Not all blind veterans wanted to go to St Dunstan's. Some wanted to go home at once; others responded to their personal disaster with drink, despair, and such a sense of futility that they could not be helped. Whatever Dickson and Swift might prefer, their rivals in charities for the blind, Frederick Fraser of Halifax and P.E. Layton, who ran a school for the blind in Montreal, had other ideas. They protested vehemently that a British institution had been favoured. Thanks to them, several blind soldiers were sent to Canadian institutions, though with unhappy results.[59] By the end of 1917 the MHC had succumbed to Pearson and his enthusiastic alumni; all future blind Canadian veterans would go to St Dunstan's, and those in Canada were allowed free transportation and escort across the Atlantic to try St Dunstan's for themselves. Late in 1918, Pearson Hall in Toronto became the centre for retraining and rehabilitation for blinded soldiers. Baker left a secretarial job with the Ontario Hydro-Electric Power Commission to take charge of programs for his blinded fellow veterans under the overall supervision of the 'Blind Trooper,' Col. Lorne Mulloy.[60]

Retraining amid Difficulties

Retraining and adjustment were not, of course, reserved for Jamaicans and the blind. From the outset, the innovative heart of Scammell's plan had been to restore disabled soldiers to economic independence. Experience only confirmed his determination. The very nature of most MHC patients helped. Among officials there ran an undercurrent of suspicion that the original philosophy of restful convalescence had been wasted on the undeserving. Medical care had always been a commodity rationed to those who could afford it. For soldiers, it was 'free.' The absence of antibiotics or other 'miracle' drugs to fight infection meant that wounds or sickness took a long time to cure. Patients spent months and even years in convalescence.

The result was a painful degree of institutionalization. When J.S. McLennan, the Cape Breton industrialist and publisher, was called to the Senate in February 1916, he decided to devote his time in Ottawa to the commission's programs of functional and vocational training.[61] In a personal report to the prime minister, McLennan explained past errors and future changes: 'The supply of comforts which in many cases were luxurious, the relaxation of discipline, the treating of men as one treats a civilian patient in the interval between illness and the resuming of ordinary occupation, which might do no harm if the experiment was to be counted in days, are more seriously detrimental to the best interests of the men when extended over the prolonged periods which have been found unavoidable. The first conception of the homes was that they were places of relaxation; the right one, which experience has taught us to realize, is that they are places of rehabilitation.'[62]

Scammell had foreseen the problem. 'Whatever is done,' he had warned in his 1915 report, 'should be done as soon after the return of the soldier from the front as possible. This is especially necessary in the case of invalided men who, unless some occupation is found for them, may deteriorate into unemployables.'[63] The idea of retraining was politely attributed to Ina Matthews, but it had been amplified by Nova Scotia's Frederick Sexton and reinforced by the French and Belgian examples.[64] A pre-war royal commission on technical education had underlined the primitive state of vocational training in Canada. Its application to the disabled was hardly more than a bright idea, but the field was still in the hands of enthusiasts such as Sexton and Ontario's John Seath and F.W. Merchant.[65] If disabled soldiers could break the tradition of becoming shiftless mendicants, Canada might ease its pension burden. 'There is no charity about this plan,' Sexton told the Women's Canadian Club in Saint John, '... nor is there any philanthrophy, but it is a great economic project. We don't want any pension orgy in this country as in the United States.' Sexton insisted that it would often be possible to increase the veterans' earning potential; few of the men had had any prior trades training and their ordinary education was poor enough.[66] However experimental, vocational training fitted a fashion in human engineering. 'The old sentimentality displayed towards disabled soldiers, which quickly expended itself and left the recipient with a depleted stock of moral stamina,' wrote Dr E.M. von Eberts, a Montreal surgeon, 'is giving place to the healthier and essentially more sympathetic view, that an incapacitated soldier can and must again become self-supporting, and that the state, in addition to giving him a pension, must provide the educational means for such an economic rehabilitation.'[67]

To manage the MHC's vocational training, Lougheed chose Thomas B.

Kidner, an Englishman who had spent more than a decade carrying the flame of vocational training through Nova Scotia and New Brunswick. In 1911 the city of Calgary had appointed him director of technical education, and Lougheed had observed his efforts to organize classes for returned soldiers.[68] As vocational secretary for the MHC from March 1916, Kidner faced the opportunities and difficulties of any pioneer. He had plenty of advice from Scammell, encouragement from Sexton, and opinions from the commission, but there were no precedents, instructors, policies, or funds. Lougheed's Disablement Fund had stopped growing after Sir Herbert Ames convinced the cabinet that Canadian generosity would stretch no further than the Patriotic Fund. Even the bulk of the Machine Gun Fund was retained by Sir Sam Hughes. Carruthers' contribution and some smaller gifts, notably from the Yukon Patriotic Fund, raised the Disablement Fund to $120,000; it rose no higher. The MHC won approval to spend public funds on its project; Carruthers' money was used to finance tiny loans and grants to 'needy cases.'[69]

With backing from Senator McLennan and most other members of the commission, Kidner soon developed an ambitious plan. Carefully chosen vocational officers would examine each man's disability, education, and job experience and fill out elaborate questionnaires. Fearful of extravagance, the commission insisted that training must be limited to men who could not resume their former occupations – and even then must lead them into a related skill or trade. Kidner accepted this rule; longer training, he agreed, also would deepen the men's existing 'institutionalization.' All the commission's patients needed a vigorous educational program to counteract the effects of their prolonged and demoralizing idleness. At each home and hospital a full-time instructor, aided by volunteers and a few part-time teachers, would run courses in mechanical drawing, woodworking, practical arithmetic, and other basic subjects. When the weather grew warmer, patients would move outside to work at gardening or poultry-raising. Experience among Calgary veterans persuaded Kidner that some of them also needed to learn English.[70]

As is usual in a pioneering field, theory was easier than practice. Suitable instructors were scarce. Kidner quickly realized that regular schoolteachers would have little value unless they were elderly or particularly proficient. Convalescent soldiers had a rich scorn for anyone, in or out of uniform, who qualified in their minds as a 'slacker.' Nor were they supportive of colleagues who chose to improve themselves. Apart from predictable ridicule, would-be students were warned by fellow patients that improved earning power would probably lead to a reduced pension. Kidner and the commission did their best to scotch that rumour.[71] It was not easy to organize courses; the dozens of convalescent homes were scattered across the countryside, and there was little space for classes or workshops. Classes at the Sandford Fleming home in Ottawa had to be taught in an unheated garage. At the Ross Home in Sydney, a covered squash-court was converted into a workroom and classroom for courses in carpentry, mechanical drawing, English, and furniture-making. The largest MHC institution, the Grey Nuns' Hospital in Montreal, offered a corner of its basement day-room, which was already crowded with patients smoking, chatting, and playing cards. [72] Everywhere training was interrupted by parades, medical treatment, leave, and eventual discharge. Within six weeks attendance had virtually collapsed. A Montreal teacher complained that of thirteen soldiers enrolled in his mechanical drawing class no more than one or two ever appeared. Similar reports from other centres convinced Sexton and Kidner that there could be no progress without compulsory attendance and some form of income so that trainees could support themselves and their families. [73]

Discharged veterans felt little incentive to endure Kidner's makeshift classes. By mid-1916 jobs were plentiful and well-paid, even for the disabled. Warnings that post-war Canada would be less hospitable and that disability would become an acute vocational liability fell on deaf ears. Backed by Senator McLennan, Kidner proposed a training allowance for faithful students, though action, as usual, was held up until Sir James Lougheed returned from one of his prolonged journeys to the West. On 29 June 1916 the government gave its approval: men in hospital who enrolled in a course could be paid eight dollars a month with an additional sixty cents a day for those who lived at home. Small additional payments supported a veteran's wife and family. [74] The amounts were meagre, but they were a first step in showing that the commission was serious. Gradually, Kidner found his vocational officers. Frederick Sexton, made available by the government of Nova Scotia, looked after Quebec and the Maritimes. Others were borrowed, part-time, from provincial departments of education. Using civilians was important. Whatever their experience, officers somehow failed to put other ranks at their ease. A key part of the instructor's role, Kidner felt, was gaining and building a trainee's confidence. [75]

Retraining invaded a provincial sphere. That had not been an issue at the interprovincial conference in October 1915, but second thoughts followed. Meeting in March 1916, the MHC had referred Kidner's plans to a committee made up of McLennan, the Honourable George Simard of the Quebec Soldiers' Employment Commission, and W.D. McPherson, chairman of Ontario's Soldiers' Aid Commission. [76] The recommendations were modest: there should be provincial 'advisory committees'; instead of relying on a single expert, men should be guided by a more formal 'Disabled Soldiers'

Training Board' with a medical officer and a provincial representative in addition to Kidner's vocational officer. Kidner spent most of April and all of May in the west promoting the training scheme, while Sexton toured the eastern provinces. Except for Prince Edward Island, which never got around to forming an advisory board, the arrangement seems to have satisfied all of the provinces but one.[77]

The exception was Ontario. Proud of its leadership in technical education and confident that it could manage the business better than any jerry-built federal organization, the Ontario government insisted that it would take full charge. To the dismay of his officials, Lougheed conceded the point. W.W. Nichol, a mathematics teacher and former principal who had pioneered a night school program in Ottawa, was appointed Ontario vocational officer at a salary of three thousand dollars, to be paid by the commission. He would use only provincially certified teachers. Other instructors, explained McPherson, might be illegal.[78]

Retraining, of course, prepared soldiers for civil self-sufficiency. Commission officials soon began to see military life itself, as well as prolonged hospitalization, as a threat to patients' morale and motivation. Kidner's own viewpoint reflected MHC thinking: 'In point of fact, the process of rehabilitation of a disabled soldier or sailor must include his demilitarization, so to speak. It is a necessity that as a soldier or sailor he shall sink his individuality and shall in all respects live under orders in all his doings throughout his military career. It is this very fact which has made the problem of the ex-soldier always a difficult one, and in my opinion just as soon as it is decided that a man is of no further use in military service, he should be discharged to the care of some civilian authority.'[79]

That, of course, had not been done. The MHC's patients remained soldiers; after February 1916, so did men waiting for pensions. Problems of discipline began almost as soon as Scammell was appointed as the commission's secretary.[80] They were compounded by confusion over pay and administration. The Militia Department might be at fault, but somehow the commission got the blame. When soldiers came home, drunk and disorderly, to confront embarrassed relatives and welcoming committees, it was 'officialdom' that was condemned. Scammell's problems in securing sanatorium accommodation were aggravated when soldier-patients ignored strict rules about rest or sputum cups, broke bounds to get a drink in a neighbouring village, and defied civilian medical superintendents. At Muskoka, W.J. Gage simply refused to have any more soldiers unless they came in civilian clothes; at the Laurentian Sanatorium, 15 per cent of the military patients were sent back to MHC institutions for disciplinary reasons.[81]

In a civilian hospital, recalcitrant or disorderly patients could easily be discharged; a military hospital had no such option. Lougheed might fulminate about stripping rowdy soldiers of their uniforms, but only the military authorities could do so. 'Many of these men are chronic troublemakers,' Lougheed complained.[82] One possible brake on soldiers' conduct was their final discharge document. Prolonged negotiations with militia headquarters led to soldiers' being reminded of 'the importance of their good conduct or otherwise subsequent to their return to Canada as affecting the character which will be given to them in their discharge certificate.'[83] McLennan believed that the men's pay should be withheld to teach them 'the magic of the bank book.' Hospital patients, he noted, had more money than wealthy men gave their sons as allowance; inevitably it was spent on liquor and tobacco.[84]

In the end, the commission retreated from 'civilianization' in favour of more effective military authority. The MHC's patients would become a 'casualty command,' a unit of the Canadian Expeditionary Force, suspended somewhere between the Militia Department and the commission.[85] Dobell's friend Major Sharples was promoted to take command, but the rest of his officers and NCOs would be returned soldiers, 'preference being given to those who had been distinguished for conduct and bravery.' At the end of July 1916 patients and staff in each military district became a unit of the new Military Hospitals Commission Command (MHCC). McLennan's faith in activity was evident in one paragraph of the order establishing the new oganization: 'The difficulty of maintaining discipline which has previously existed, may be minimised by the enforcement of such regulations in the hospitals and homes that a man will not be idle except insofar as repose is necessary to his restoration to health.'[86]

Henceforth, hospitalized soldiers would no longer enjoy the dangerous luxury of idleness; keeping them busy would be a matter of military regulation as well as civilian theory. Students were expected to work from 9:00 to 12:30 and from 2:00 to 4:15 each weekday, with a half-holiday on Saturdays. Physical exercise, at Kidner's insistence, was part of the program; free movies, even for instructional purposes, were not.[87]

The Year of Expansion

A full year after its October 1915 reconstitution, the MHC's resources had quadrupled to 2,193 beds in forty-seven institutions in every province and every major city. Kidner, Thompson, and Sharples had joined Scammell as senior officials of the commission and the offices at 22 Vittoria Street now swarmed with clerks and stenographers. The commission itself had languished. Meetings, initially scheduled for the third Monday of every month, grew further apart, ran out of steam in the summer of 1916, resumed in September, and then ceased altogether. Some MHC members – McLennan, Clarence Smith in Montreal, F.W. Peters in Vancouver – were now fully involved in local or central administration; others had lost interest or were too busy. As Scammell had hoped and planned, professionalism had taken over.[88]

In the second half of 1916, Canada's overseas organization had taken a similar path. For eighteen months Sir Sam Hughes had maintained personal control of the CEF operations in England by the simple device of creating such confusion in the command structure that only he could give a final order. However personally satisfying this might be, the results were costly, wasteful in manpower, and ultimately humiliating for Canada. In September 1916, as Hughes devised still newer ways of preserving his control, an exasperated prime minister ended the farce by giving his friend, Sir George Perley, the portfolio of the new Ministry of the Overseas Military Forces of Canada. The OMFC would in effect separate the CEF in France and Britain from the Militia Department in Canada.[89]

Among those caught in the change was Col. Herbert A. Bruce. Hughes had dispatched the aggressive, super-competent Toronto surgeon to review the overseas medical organization. When Bruce criticized Maj.-Gen. Guy Carleton Jones, the director of medical services, Hughes gave him Jones's job.[90] The appointment split the CAMC into bitter factions, and one of Perley's first tasks was to fire Bruce, reinstate Jones, and summon Maj.-Gen. G.L. Foster from the Canadian Corps to serve as a new broom. The ensuing storm reverberated inside and outside the medical corps for years.[91] The effects on the MHC were more immediate. Bruce claimed that Canadian casualties took an inordinate amount of time either to recover or to be sent home to Canada. Whatever the reasons, the claim was true and the problem had to be remedied. If further impetus was needed, it came with the terrible casualties that occurred when the Canadians joined the battle of the Somme in September. By the end of October the Canadian divisions had suffered 24,029 casualties, three-quarters of them wounded.[92]

Perhaps the MHC should have foreseen the crisis, but its expansion through 1916 had been cautious. Lougheed plainly feared that too many unused beds would bring charges of extravagance.[93] During the year the commission added only 1,208 beds to the 1,363 it had at the end of 1915. Yet the MHC's medical burden now had to reflect changes on the Western Front. In England, the deluge of wounded that began on the first day at the Somme, 1 July 1916, flooded every improvised hospital ward and convalescent home. In Ottawa, the MHC seems to have been caught unaware by a telegram from Perley on 16 November warning that three thousand casualties would be sent to Canada at once. Doctors and nursing sisters would accompany the wounded, but would have to return immediately. An MHC appeal to retain medical help was brusquely refused.[94] A staff officer sent from London warned that the total casualty evacuation might reach five thousand, half of them stretcher cases. In 1917 five hundred cases would be sent each month.[95]

Lougheed and his officials were dumbfounded. Apart from a windfall acquisition of the Strathcona Hospital south of Edmonton, the MHC had no active treatment facilities. The few cases requiring care had been placed in civilian hospitals. In the autumn, the commission had ordered ten 'hospital cars' from the Intercolonial and CPR shops, but they were not ready. Neither were the disembarkation facilities at Quebec or Halifax for stretcher cases. Worst of all, the news had coincided with the onset of winter, when both movement and fresh construction would be doubly difficult. The MHC faced a problem far worse than that of the half-forgotten *Metagama*.[96]

Perley's request could hardly be refused, though it might be delayed. Meanwhile, the commission would have to expand its facilities to dimensions so far unimagined. To handle the transformation, Lougheed appointed the MHC's first director. Samuel Armstrong was a forty-two-year-old Sarnia lawyer and railway promoter who had followed his mentor, W.J. Hanna, into Ontario's Conservative government. By 1909, he was Hanna's assistant provincial secretary, responsible for building the enormous new prison at Guelph in 1909 and a vast new hospital for the insane at Whitby in 1912. Armstrong was a man who knew how to get big projects underway. His Tory credentials and contacts with the Ontario government were no liability.[97]

In keeping with the army tradition of 'hurry up and wait,' it took far longer than Perley had forecast for masses of casualties to arrive from Britain. Shiploads of wounded began arriving early in 1917, but sailings were soon complicated by Germany's resumption of unrestricted submarine warfare. The flow was also limited by the capacity of the two hospital ships placed on the Canadian run.[98] Armstrong worked fast. If Scammell had thought in hundreds, the new director thought in thousands. His former colleagues made the Guelph reformatory and the Whitby hospital available, though on terms that would produce endless post-war bickering. In wartime, who cared? Factories and workshops intended to reform Guelph's convicts would be just as valuable to train veterans. The new oxy-acetylene process could slice away steel bars and doors, and a fresh coat of paint would turn a prison into a hospital. Whitby, with its innovative cottage wards, would easily absorb thousands of sick and wounded. Inmates and insane patients would have to yield to the patriotic need. At Winnipeg, Armstrong found another bonus. Manitoba's agricultural college had moved to a new site on the Red River and the old buildings at Tuxedo were suddenly available. Where better could treatment and retraining be combined, all to the benefit of a city that produced more soldiers per capita than any other?[99]

Existing buildings were not the only or even the best solution. The commission's architect, Capt. W.L. Symons, had managed the conversion of Knox College in Toronto and Loyola College in Montreal. He had even adapted Grant Hall at Queen's University, a building he had originally helped design. The experience was frustrating. College structures appeared to be well suited to hospital needs, but they always required costly structural and plumbing changes. It would be faster and cheaper to build from the ground up. At Halifax, Symons got his chance. Pine Hill, the Presbyterian seminary, made its building available; Dalhousie University first agreed, then dithered, and finally changed its collective mind. While Pier 2 was adaptable as a vast reception and transit hospital for over a thousand patients, Halifax needed more. The answer was Camp Hill, a new three-hundred-bed hospital started in the spring and fully in operation by the autumn – a triumph of the new 'quick construction' methods. While the commission continued to adapt schools and even a new YMCA building in Saskatoon, Camp Hill was the inspiration for similar structures at Kingston, Montreal, Whitby, and Vancouver's Shaughnessy Heights. The Salvation Army's Memorial Training College, offered to the MHC in November 1916 and adapted in 1917 as the MHC's main orthopaedic centre, gained two extra wings and a central services building, allowing beds for four hundred patients.[100] Symons's buildings were ugly, functional, and admirably inexpensive.

Increasing patient loads encouraged further specialization. Mixing all categories of insane persons, from psychopaths to the shell-shocked, in Cobourg raised growing protests from veterans, relatives, and politicians. In 1917 the Quakers offered their boys' school, Pickering College, to the commission. It was adapted at once as a hospital to classify the insane, sorting out those who might recover quickly from the hopeless cases who were to be sent to provincial asylums. Cobourg could then be reserved for the treatment of 'neurasthenia' and other apparent battlefield conditions.[101] Sanatoria presented further problems. Expansion projects in the West and the Maritimes, undertaken largely at commission expense, left only Ontario with a shortage of beds for tubercular patients.[102]

By expanding dramatically, the commission more than met demand. In mid-1917 it had 5,600 beds, and by the end of the year Armstrong could report 13,802 beds, including 1,428 in sanatoria. The patient population had grown from 2,610 to 11,981.[103] The original voluntary institutions were submerged in an organization that now boasted of its professionalism. Violet M. Ryley typified the change. As chief organizing dietitian, she was proud of her university-trained staff, who presided over the latest in kitchen equipment and nutritional expertise. Instead of motherly care, soldiers shared the brand-new experience of collecting their meals cafeteria-style. Ryley boasted that four hundred men at the Quebec discharge depot could be served in fifteen minutes. The savings, she maintained, were substantial.[104] Her pride typified the MHC's determination to publicize its methods and achievements. As a manager, Armstrong was politician enough to know that the commission's best defence against its inevitable critics was aggressive image-building. If Canadians believed that they were the best in the world at caring for their returned men, it would be harder for the commission's critics to get a hearing.[105]

Not everything was admirable. Retraining, Armstrong concluded, was a failure. In March 1917 there were 5,000 patients in MHC institutions, but only 638 had enrolled in Kidner's classes.[106] By July of 1917 the commission offered training for thirty-nine occupations, but over half of the candidates had chosen only four of them: commercial, civil service, motor mechanics, and gas and steam engineering. Thanks to Kidner's influence and the aggressive work of Howard Stutchbury, the secretary of Alberta's Returned Soldiers Commission, that province led the way with 141 of the 189 candidates approved for vocational training. Ontario was different: only 19 candidates had even bothered to apply.[107] The attempt to let the Soldiers Aid Commission and the province's education system handle the problem had failed; but W.D. McPherson, now provincial secretary as well as chairman of the Soldiers' Aid Commission, refused to accept the blame. The hospitals, he insisted, had not co-operated and the men had been almost deliberately discouraged.[108] Both charges may have been true, but Kidner had another view of the problem: 'The educational methods which are applicable to Soldiers are so entirely different from those applicable to school children that the men who occupy the position of Vocational Officer would be better qualified if [they] did not possess long experience in Technical and Public School methods.'[109]

The dig at W.W. Nichol, Ontario's choice, was obvious. So was the problem. Elsewhere, Armstrong broke barriers by enlisting the help of provincial universities. The University of Saskatchewan's president, Walter C. Murray, with his strong bent for practical education, made his institution the centre for MHC vocational training activity in his province. The University of British Columbia and Macdonald College, McGill's agricultural and vocational satellite, were eager participants.[110] Ontario institutions showed no such enthusiasm. The glimmer of a solution appeared in July, when Armstrong met with Toronto's Joint Committee of Technical Organizations. Its leading light, a mining engineer named Walter L. Segsworth, had a plain and practical approach to the problem. The MHC's vocational organization was too classroom-bound. A fear (brought back from France by Dobell) that employers would exploit disabled trainees was best met by supervision, not prevention. The place for industrial training, Segsworth felt, was in industry. Only there could the vast range of occupations be made accessible to trainees. Such refreshing realism was welcome. On 1 August Segsworth became the MHC's new director of vocational training.[111]

Not all of Segsworth's ideas were new. Kidner had also pressed for using ex-soldiers as instructors, for screening the disabled as potential trainees, and for a clearer distinction between 'curative' and 'vocational' training. With his aggressive confidence and Armstrong's full support, Segsworth made changes happen faster. To Sexton's annoyance, a district vocational officer, Capt. R.T. McKeen, displaced him in Montreal, and others were soon appointed in the Maritime provinces. A grander title, 'vocational officer for the eastern provinces,' only partially eased his disappointment. In the West, Segsworth persuaded the Alberta government to hand over the Calgary Institute of Technology, one of the few facilities west of Winnipeg available for mechanical training. A disturbance at Winnipeg's Tuxedo Home – promptly labelled a strike by the local press – underlined the need to separate different categories of 'students.' By September 1917 all MHC patients whose physical condition permitted it were obliged to work. 'Ward occupations' kept the bedridden busy with crafts ranging from basketry and embroidery to toy-making. Young women were trained at the University of Toronto's Hart House, provided with uniforms, and paid sixty to seventy-five dollars a month to work as 'ward aides' supervising the crafts. Ambulatory patients worked part of the day in 'curative workshops' or, in suitable weather, tended crops and poultry.[112]

Real vocational training began only after discharge. Segsworth endorsed Scammell's original notion that eligible candidates must be firmly guided into occupations close to their former experience. A few selected success stories indicated the possibilities. A construction carpenter with rheumatism became a cabinet-maker; a railway brakeman with a missing leg was trained as a telegrapher or station agent; even an illiterate disabled miner could learn to operate a concentrating table. Making use of experience cut costs and shortened the training period. It also prevented some ex-soldiers from postponing the grim discipline of civilian life. 'These men did not want to work before the war and they will not do so now if they can help it,' was Segsworth's cold judgment. 'They dislike taking upon themselves responsibility. A Vocational training course offers such an opportunity of putting off the evil day.'[113]

Segsworth's solution for the Ontario problem was equally blunt: the commission would proceed as if the province and its Soldiers' Aid Commission did not exist. His friend H.E.T. Haultain, the respected head of the University of Toronto's school of mining engineering, became the MHC's vocational officer for Ontario. As a power in the university, Haultain took over its facilities. In wartime few questions were asked. If Nichol and his staff co-operated, they would be heeded; if they did not, they would be ignored.[114]

Training the disabled, Segsworth realized, would be useless if they could not find jobs. As early as June 1917 Sexton had urged that the National Service Bureau, created to conduct the pre-conscription registration drive, be used to conduct industrial surveys. Without knowing the potential labour market, re-education could hardly proceed. Kidner replied that the idea had been 'under consideration' for some time. Segsworth acted. G.A. Boate, a Canadian who had been working in the United States, was brought back to organize the search for work that disabled veterans could perform. A team of visitors, recruited largely from travelling salesmen, interviewed employers and returned with detailed assessments of likely occupations. Segsworth's representative in Manitoba announced that he had persuaded industrialists in Winnipeg and in Brandon to organize their own surveys. With 133 graduates placed in jobs by January 1918, Segsworth organized follow-up surveys. Vocational officers checked on both the man and his employer to see that each was giving value. On Haultain's advice, Segsworth cautiously ventured into social service; families could exacerbate a man's disability by their own problems of adjustment. Social workers could help wives manage disabled men and their money. 'There was no attempt to extend this social service work on a paternal basis,' Segsworth explained, 'and investigations are not made unless the man is absent from his classes or for some reason unknown to the Department he is not making progress.'[115] At the outset of 1917, Kidner had reported 35 instructors and 523 students; by the year-end Segsworth had found 267 teachers for 3,143 trainees, excluding bedridden patients.[116]

It remained immensely tempting for men to choose wartime wages, even in a temporary or dead-end job, rather than commit themselves to a long-term investment in learning a skill. Segsworth and the commission worked hard to change their minds with posters, magic-lantern shows, a film, and pamphlets. Convincing the public was as important as convincing the soldiers themselves, since the idea that the disabled could earn a genuine living defied experience. The text of the MHC's presentation, designed to be given in church halls and service clubs, conveyed warnings as well as optimism and self-congratulation: 'Remember ... that the invalided man, after what he has undergone, often finds it very difficult to settle down to steady work. He has lost the habit of it, owing to the length of time spent in training camps and at the front. To make matters worse, his energy has been sapped by illness. His friends and fellow-citizens must help him, and can help him immensely by stimulating his ambition and self-respect, and by showing that they look to him for an example of the same grit and perseverance here that he showed so splendidly at the front.'[117]

Perhaps the MHC's most widely circulated pamphlet was 'The Soldier's Return,' an interview with a cheerful amputee named 'Private Pat' (or an identical French-Canadian counterpart, 'Poil-aux-Pattes'). Certainly Pat expressed all the right sentiments, from a determination to get back to work to his scorn for 'scratching paper for my living.' His goal, reflecting a strong underlying MHC preference, was to live an outdoor life, with no loafing and no more pension than his old leg was worth. 'I want to be a man again as I was before, and make my own living and not sponge on other people.' Whether his readers were civilians or fellow invalids, Private Pat had a stirring message: 'If we're down and out, help us to get up and in again. That's all right and that's what you're doing with your Military Hospitals Commission. Lend us a hand to get our legs again, real or artificial and you'll see if we don't keep our end up and make our own living like the rest of you! Believe me, we've got just as much pride and independence as any one else.'[118]

It might be fiction, but the commission certainly hoped that it would become true.

3 Avoiding the 'Pension Evil'

Pension Experience

Canadians are not a rashly innovative people. Restoring the war-disabled to productive, self-supporting labour may have been a new idea in Canada, but the example came from the French and the Belgians. In his overseas visit in the winter of 1915–16, William Dobell of the MHC was inspired by the French and even more impressed by their embattled neighbours. Expelled from all but a battered corner of their homeland, the Belgians had established factories in northern France. Any soldier too severely disabled to fight was patiently trained and put to work. Belgium's pre-war leadership in industrial rehabilitation proved to be a wartime asset.[1]

Canada's innovation was administrative: no other belligerent was as prompt in creating a single government agency to cope with the problems of re-establishing disabled soldiers. In France the task was handled by a host of competing charities and by municipal authorities of varying enterprise and resources. In Britain the workshops of the Sailors' and Soldiers' Help Society served no more than a small minority of the disabled. While Senator Lougheed might have preferred a Disablement Fund and volunteers, the MHC soon depended on a professional staff and the apparently bottomless resources of the war appropriation.[2]

In addition to a humane sense of obligations owed to suffering heroes, there was a powerful incentive to treat returned men properly. Recruiting the CEF would have become impossible long before mid-1916 if disabled veterans had been left to starve on pensions of twenty dollars a month.[3] The efficiency of the MHC and its provincial counterparts was vital to wartime morale. Premier Hearst was appropriately frank when he inaugurated Ontario's Soldiers' Aid Commission in 1915: 'If you only have that thought in mind – the securing of recruits for Overseas Service – nothing will help you more than to assure the men when they come back that the country will do its duty in caring for them.'[4] It was not likely that Canada's new army would tolerate the impoverished dependence of maimed comrades. J.G. Turriff warned his fellow parliamentarians that soldiers would constitute one-fifth to one-seventh of an all-male electorate, and no politician needed a detailed explanation of the significance of such a voting bloc.[5] 'I do not think there is a man in this House who would attempt to make capital out of the question of pensions,' claimed J.D. Hazen, the minister of marine and fisheries.[6] This was pious talk. If any politician was ignorant of the 'pension evil' or veterans' politics in the neighbouring republic, editors and fellow MPs helped complete his education.[7]

Lt-Col. J.G. Adami, professor of pathology at McGill and the CAMC's designated historian, journeyed to Washington in 1915 to document the American pension problem and ways to avoid it. 'The Pension Evil in the United States is notorious,' he reported; 'the burden placed upon the revenues of the country is scarcely believable.'[8] Civil War pensions alone had already cost Americans $4.2 billion, eight times Canada's national debt in 1914. Washington officials advised that fingerprinting and photographs would have discouraged some of the worst pension frauds, but even careful record-keeping would not avert political pressures.[9] Adami predicted: 'The main bulk of our troops will be relegated into private life; very many will find it difficult to return to their previous occupations; either their places will have been taken, or they will no longer be as capable or as adept as before; there will be an inevitable tendency to band together to improve their condition; [and] an equally inevitable tendency to claim support from public funds.'[10]

Canada's pension provisions in 1914 were little altered from the scheme Sir Adolphe Caron had pushed through cabinet in the wake of the North-West Rebellion. A widow or dependent mother qualified for a pension unless she 'subsequently proved unworthy of it,' or was or became wealthy.[11] A son might be supported until the age of fifteen and a daughter until the age of seventeen unless either became 'physically or mentally incapacitated to earn a living.' In that case, the pension continued until the child turned twenty-one, when the burden could be transferred to private or municipal charity.[12] Disability pensions were ranked in four categories. The highest level was for those 'rendered totally incapable of earning a living' as a result of wounds, injury, or disease suffered in the face of the enemy. The second category of pension, three-quarters of the maximum, was enough for a soldier 'rendered materially incapable' on active service or totally disabled during training or drill. A third-degree pension, one-half of the maximum, compensated a soldier made 'in a small degree incapable by a wound' or 'materially incapable' by training. The lowest pension, one-quarter of the maximum, was available to a man rendered 'in a small degree incapable' by a training mishap.[13]

Mobilization in 1914 cost the Pensions and Claims Board its two military members. In March 1915 the acting adjutant-general proposed reconstituting the board, but his file was lost in the chaos of militia headquarters and rediscovered only in June.[14] In late July the new members met: Col. J.S. Dunbar, a permanent-force veteran with legal training, Lt-Col. C.W. Belton from the Permanent Army Medical Corps, and the department secretary, Lt-Col. C.L. Panet.

The government had long since conceded that its pre-war pension rates would not do for the CEF.[15] Inspired by Australia's example – and heavily influenced by the Australian figures – pensions were substantially improved, particularly for the lower ranks.[16] A totally disabled private would have $264 a year, a lieutenant would have $480, and a lieutenant-colonel $1,200. A private's second-class pension would be $192, a third-class $132. A private's widow would have $22 a month and $5 for each child. A lieutenant-colonel's widow received $40 a month and $10 for each child.[17] Parliament offered no debate beyond a half-hearted suggestion from two Liberals that militia officers who had dropped their ranks to serve in the CEF should have the pension accompanying their previous rank. 'Something might be said on the other side,' the prime minister cautiously admitted, but not by him. If Borden could help it, pensions would not become a partisan issue.[18]

Parliament could congratulate itself. Canada's 1915 pension rates were higher than Australia's. In Britain, only officers fared better. The fact remained that a helpless veteran would have to support himself and perhaps his family on less than a day-labourer's wage. Was a disability less crippling because it was caused by a range accident at Niagara instead of in Flanders' fields? What incentive did a soldier have to retrain himself for a job if pensions were defined only by one's inability to work? What the Military Hospitals Commission endeavoured to do, the militia pension system might undo.[19]

Criticism, Reform, and J.L. Todd

As the casualties of 1915 funnelled back to their homes, the shocking inadequacy of their pensions filtered into public awareness. While most communities had a handful of pensioners, Toronto found itself with hundreds. The local Patriotic Fund refused them money but could not ignore their plight. Frank Darling, a prominent Anglican layman and one of Canada's leading architects, spearheaded a committee of concern that included Hume Blake, Archdeacon H.J. Cody, Bishop Neil McNeil, and President Robert Falconer of the University of Toronto. In its report, the committee found a pension of twenty-two dollars a month hopelessly inadequate for a totally disabled man and deplored an 'illogical and unreasonable' distinction between injuries suffered in camp and on the battlefield. Extra money for the lower ranks, the committee thought, might be taken from officers' pensions: 'There is little or no social distinction between many men serving as privates, and men serving as commissioned officers; all went to the front anxious only to do their duty in such positions as offered, the difference in rank being often merely an accident.'[20] Canada's pension system must be administered by a permanent board that was immune from politics. Nor was it tolerable that any part of the pension burden be carried by public philanthropy: 'For twenty, thirty, forty and, and in some cases, even fifty years, this support must be given, and it must be drawn from a source absolutely stable and secure. We owe our defenders no less than this. We must save them from both the humiliation and the uncertainty of public charity, and give them permanent and adequate security from want, paid them not as a favour but as a right, for it would be an unpardonable insult to a body of brave men if the payment of a pension carried with it the faintest trace of charity or the least suspicion of patronage.'[21]

Darling's coherent and powerfully argued report, backed by leading figures in Toronto society, could not be ignored. The prime minister had no trouble recognizing an issue whose time had come. He also knew that the existing system was unworkable. Even a restructured Pensions and Claims Board had to wrestle with outdated regulations. Recommendations still had to travel through the Treasury Board to an overworked cabinet. The whole system had to be changed. In the wake of the Darling report, Borden asked W.D. Hogg, a respected Ottawa lawyer, to examine the Pensions and Claims Board and recommend changes.[22]

In England a separate Canadian Pensions and Claims Board had been established in June 1915, disbanded, and then reconstituted on 21 September. The chairman, Sir Hugh Montagu Allan, was a Montreal sportsman, financier, and heir to the vast family fortune amassed by his shipowner father. Another member was Maj. W. Grant Morden, also a Montreal businessman and a close crony of Sam Hughes. The third was Maj. John Launcelot Todd, erstwhile professor of parasitology at McGill.[23]

Of the three, Todd was the most junior and most influential. Born outside Victoria in 1876, the young Todd was sent east to Upper Canada College and then to McGill. His graduate work at the new Liverpool School of Tropical Medicine led to long research expeditions to Gambia and the

Belgian Congo. When his superior died in the Congo, Todd stayed on; he finally succeeded in isolating parasitic trypanosomes as the cause of sleeping sickness. He returned to acclaim from the Belgian king, controversy with his fellow researchers, and control of the Liverpool School's research laboratories. In 1907 he came back to McGill. He married Marjory Clouston, the beautiful young daughter of Sir Edward Clouston, the general manager of the Bank of Montreal and Canada's most powerful financier. The war found Todd, like many in his profession, eager to enlist. Logically, so brilliant a researcher should have found plenty to do; but the CAMC wanted surgeons, not a thirty-nine-year old parasitologist with rusty medical skills.[24]

Todd was a passionate, ambitious man, devoted to his wife, fond of fast cars, utterly confident in his own wisdom. Oddly, the director of medical services, Maj. Gen. Guy Carleton Jones, assigned him to the seemingly dreary chore of organizing medical records. Accurate records were vital, Jones explained, if post-war pension claims were to be based on fact, not fantasy.[25] Todd was persuaded. Membership in the overseas Pensions and Claims Board was a logical next step. Friends, colleagues, and his own wife were dismayed at the waste of his talents. But Todd insisted, 'It's now that plans, acts, customs must be made, adopted and formed, if all sorts of evils are to be avoided.'[26] Certainly the personal strain was considerable. 'Montagu is very slow to grasp a point,' Todd reported of his chairman; 'it took me over an hour to get a simple proposition into his head.' Maj. Maurice Alexander, sent as legal adviser to the board, was remarkable for 'the extraordinary way in which he agreed with whomever is the biggest man present.'[27] Years in Africa, Todd complained to his mother, had made him incapable of handling 'thoroughbred horses and silly white men. ... I must school myself to hold my tongue and not roar at others' apparent errors so soon as they are made.'[28] Yet Todd believed that the worse his colleagues, the more important his mission. If pensions became 'a political plaything,' he warned, 'the bill paid by future Canadians will be a thing disgraceful and enormous.' In language designed to influence friends of the late Sir Edward Clouston, Todd explained to his wife: 'The biggest thing in Canada at the present time is the whole Pensions question. If it is not removed from politics and put into the hands of a small commission of about three men – like the railroad commission – we will have pensions trouble in Canada that – for our size – will make that of the U.S.A. look like a beginner.'[29]

Todd's notion of an independent three-member commission was sufficiently a reflection of current political fashion that it had also occurred to Frank Darling and to W.D. Hogg. Nothing was more characteristic of contemporary progressive thought than its faith in business methods carefully insulated from democracy. Robert Borden's ill-fated Halifax Programme of 1907 had been packed with such 'progressive' reforms, and the faith persisted. In Ontario a reform-minded Conservative government had pioneered a family of boards and commissions, begun by Sir Adam Beck's Hydro-Electric Power Commission and completed, in 1914, by a Workmen's Compensation Board. In Ottawa, Sir Robert Borden took pride in his 'scientific' Tariff Commission and the Board of Railway Commissioners, which Todd took as his inspiration, and he hoped to strengthen a Civil Service Commission inherited from the Liberals.[30]

Hogg's advice, offered on 7 December 1915, was that the members of the Pensions and Claims Board should serve on a full-time basis. He opposed any appeal from the board's decisions. Forbidding appeals, he suggested, 'would go a long way to prevent many of the abuses which were allowed to take root and grow in the pension system of [the] United States.'[31] Nor, Hogg urged, should the minister of militia continue to decide which widows were worthy of pension. Independently, on the far side of the Atlantic, Todd was eager to go much further. 'The disposal of ex-Soldiers in Canada should be placed entirely in the hands of a Commission consisting of three men,' he reported to General Jones. 'The members of the Commission would be appointed like the Judiciary for life, and would only be removable by impeachment; only in this way can the question be removed from Politics and only in this way can men of sufficient calibre be obtained.'[32] Every ex-soldier, disabled or otherwise, would come under Todd's all-powerful judicial body. With none of the inhibitions of a military professional, Todd enlisted political support from his late father-in-law's friends, including the dynamic Sir Adam Beck. What could a patriot do but involve others in a matter 'fraught with the gravest dangers for Canada'? If Americans had their 'Pension Evil,' he reminded Beck, there could be no immunity for Canada: 'Canadians, in their social organization and in their manner of thought are, in many districts, extremely like the citizens of the United States. Nothing can be more certain than that returned Canadian soldiers will, especially if they imagine they have cause for dissatisfaction, band themselves together in organizations of varying magnitude.'[33]

Canada now had an opportunity to make the right start. Instead of Britain's plethora of quarrelsome charities or the tradition-bound Chelsea Commissioners, a 'Supreme Board of Commisioners' could be the salvation of Canadian soldiers – and taxpayers. Canadians, Todd reminded Beck, 'are altogether too prone to consider the Government "fair game" ... At once a propaganda should be commenced in Press and Pulpit, in Parliament and in Picture Palaces, to make Canadians understand that *the Government is themselves* and that a Canadian Pension is something given by

Canadians to those of their fellows who have suffered an incapacity to earn their livelihood by reason of their service in the War so that they may compete with their fellows on equal terms'[34]

Creating an independent and even an all-powerful agency was meaningless, Todd recognized, unless it acted through coherent policies. By apparent coincidence, he had come to the same conclusion about re-establishment as Scammell. However important pensions might be in the eyes of disabled soldiers, they were no more than a modest compensation for whatever earning power a man might have lost, 'an advantage given to a man so long as he is unable, through disabilities contracted during service, to earn a full livelihood. It is nothing more than this, and it is not necessarily permanent.'[35]

Todd's views represented a radical synthesis of American, French, and British experience. Americans had provided the cautionary tale. Like Canadians, the British linked pension rates to earning ability and reduced payments for each few extra shillings earned. In France, Todd found, such folly was not tolerated. Instead, a persistent message assured sceptical *poilus* that pensions had nothing to do with earnings. That message – and probably the meagre amounts doled out by the French government – persuaded French invalids to get to work; their British counterparts had a logical argument for idleness. French pensions were issued for pure disability, not for loss of earning power. Disability tables, concocted with hard French logic, assessed the value of severed arms, legs, or hands and of damaged internal organs. From Britain's Chelsea Commissioners Todd acquired a general definition of disability. It would be impossible to have a simple policy if soldiers were judged by their former trades as watchmakers, lawyers, or hard-rock miners. The British had devised a delightfully economical definition of a soldier: each man, however skilled, educated, or highly paid, looked the same to the army:

Men enlisting for Active Service ... as privates bring to the service of their country a healthy body. The previous occupation of the recruit is not recognized as having any reference to the service which the soldier could give the State, unless it secures for him a higher rank than that of private, in which case the return made to him by the State in pay and pension is proportionately increased. The private soldier then is looked upon as offering merely a healthy mind and body to the public service. For practical purposes the market for healthy bodies is said to be the 'general market for untrained labour.'[36]

Within a few weeks Todd had developed a comprehensive pension policy; it remained to sell his ideas to his colleagues. It was, as he had expected, frustrating and difficult. Powerful friends and new contacts helped. Todd wrote exultantly to his mother that Loring Christie, 'the young lawyer of whom I have told you, who is Borden's secretary,' had spoken to the prime minister.[37] Sir Montagu Allan, he discovered, could be managed if the aging playboy could be persuaded that he had thought up the ideas himself. Some of Todd's ideas could not be accepted: there was no hope of supplanting the Military Hospitals Commission with a single all-powerful agency. In other matters he prevailed. There should be six degrees of pension, not merely four. If the totally disabled were to be guaranteed 'a decent livelihood' rates must be increased; but rates for junior officers did not have to be raised as much as for privates and it was not necessary 'to increase the rates for the higher ranks at all.'[38] By January 1916 Todd's basic work was done. While adjudicating fifty to one hundred cases a week, the overseas Pensions and Claims Board had found time to approve and forward an extensive report that bore Todd's imprint and Sir Montagu's signature. It was a fair division of labour. The weary major was finally free to take his wife and his bronchitis across the Channel to see for himself how the French managed their veterans.[39]

The overseas board's report reached Ottawa at an opportune moment. Todd had provided the government with a neat, detailed, carefully argued program just at the moment when Borden and his colleagues had fully recognized their need for a policy.[40] Powerful friends like Beck had helped. Admittedly, no government ever wishes to acknowledge that its past arrangements have been ineffective. The answer was to seize the initiative in Parliament, remind the opposition of how little they had said in 1915, praise all and sundry, and invite a special committee of the House of Commons to explore the topic. Any Liberal with enough interest in the pension problem was welcome to serve, with a balancing weight of government members and the Honourable J.D. Hazen to guide proceedings.[41]

The 1916 Special Committee was a model of non-partisan zeal. If some Liberals condemned the vast disparity in pensions offered to privates and officers, the Tory member from Kingston, W.F. Nickle, could more than match their egalitarian sentiments.[42] Well aware of the enormous political leverage that control of pensions might give a party in power, the Liberals were as eager as the Conservatives to create an independent, carefully insulated, quasi-judicial body. Both parties shared a horror of pension extravagance. Frank Darling, echoed by later witnesses, focused on meagre pension amounts, on the 'outrageous' distinction between injuries in barracks and those in the face of the enemy, and, above all, on the distinction between officers and men. 'Personally,' declared Darling, 'I am a Democrat and a Conservative also. I like the American system. I would make the curve in payments upwards from the private soldier nothing like as high as ours is at present.'[43] MPs were hurriedly reminded that, for all its abuses, the American army's pension system treated the leg of a private or a colonel with democratic impartiality. The MPs balanced their democratic convictions with a more profound principle – the sanctity of contract. While there might be no absolute legal obligation to leave officers' pensions as high as they were, changing them would be a breach of faith with those who had gone overseas. In any case, Canadian officers fared poorly by British standards even if they were a little better off than their Australian counterparts.[44]

The war had swept men of all income levels into the ranks, and the British had felt compelled to add special allowances for pre-war earning power to pensions that otherwise were geared to the wages of unskilled labour. Canadian politicians, armed with Todd's cold logic, allowed no such concession. Darling, the voice of business as well as compassion, warned of the dangers: 'You would discover that all the budding millionaires of this country had gone to the war.'[45] Scammell, Kidner, and Dobell provided the solution. Retraining and the labour market, insisted the MHC's witnesses, would more than restore any conscientious man's pre-war earning power. The totally disabled would be no more than a tragic but tiny minority.[46]

The Special Committee report, tabled on the final day of the 1916 session, was a sketchy document, virtually a summary of Todd's report. The MPs had bypassed long passages in the original that explained how pensions would be granted. Such matters would be left to an independent board of three commissioners appointed for ten-year terms and immune from appeal. Pensions would be determined solely by disability, without reference to prior occupation (or income).[47] A pensioner would not suffer 'owing to his having undertaken or perfected himself in some form of industry.'[48] Disabilities would be rated in six classes, not four, and some hints of the ratings were included in the report. Loss of both eyes would be a total dis-ability; a single eye or foot would rate as 40 per cent; a finger would rank below 20 per cent and would be paid off by a fifty-dollar gratuity.[49] A bipartisan majority had overruled the argument by Frank Oliver, an Edmonton Liberal, that a single soldier needed a smaller pension than a married man. As Frank Darling had argued, a bachelor veteran should not be condemned to 'celibacy and cheap boarding houses for the rest of his life.'[50]

The Special Committee was rather more generous on pension levels than the overseas Pension Board. Raising a single man's pension to the married man's rate gave higher pensions to all ranks without appearing to raise those for most officers, but there were substantial real increases for the lower ranks. A private's maximum pension rose from $264 to $480 a year; totally disabled pensioners up to the rank of lieutenant might be entitled to $250 to pay for attendants.[51] More senior ranks would pay such costs themselves. Child allowance was raised to $6 and the cut-off age for boys went from fifteen to sixteen; that for girls remained at seventeen. 'If there is one thing more than another that a child is entitled to whose bread-winner is taken away ...' declared W.F. Nickle, 'it is a fair chance in life.'[52]

Widows would have 80 per cent of the maximum pension for their late husband's rank unless they remarried; in that case a year's pension would serve as a kind of state dowry. 'Misbehaviour' would lead to suspension or cancellation, but wartime morality finally acknowledged, as had the Patriotic Fund, that an 'unmarried wife' might become a widow. The pension board must, of course, satisfy itself 'that the circumstances were such as to warrant the conclusion that the woman had at the time of enlistment and for a reasonable time, previously thereto, publicly been represented as the wife of said member of such Force.'[53]

Tabled hurriedly on the final day of a tempestuous session, the report allowed Tories and Liberals to congratulate themselves on their unanimity, generosity, and great good sense. Members from both parties made no secret of the temptations they were placing beyond their reach. The board's decision must be final, insisted Hazen, so 'that no impression shall be allowed to get abroad in the country that a man's claim to a pension can be influenced in the slightest degree by pull or influence of any kind.'[54] Seconding the report, E.M. Macdonald, a Cape Breton Liberal, sternly insisted that Canadian pensions would be exclusively for the disabled, not for 'every one who has gone across.' His only complaint was that there had been no time to translate principles into legislation as a further safeguard against the American example: 'As we pass through this war and the years succeeding it, proposals will no doubt be made from various sources in the direction of the extension of the liability of the country in regard to the pension system. What has occurred in the United States gives an illustration of what may be expected in this country in that particular, and hence it is that I regret that legislation has not been formulated so that a definite policy might be laid down by Parliament.'[55]

It was surely a minor caveat. So nearly unanimous a conclusion to so perplexing and potentially contentious an issue was too valuable to waste. Canadian pension administration would be lifted out of the realm of politics into the cool, clear light of objectivity. Darling, Hogg, and even Colonel Dunbar had all made a contribution, but the architect was John Launcelot Todd.

The Pension Commissioners

On 3 June 1916 a slightly tidied version of the Special Committee report was adopted by the cabinet, but three more months were needed before the

Board of Pension Commissioners could actually be announced.[56] Endless additional isues had to be resolved. How would pensions for insane soldiers be administered? What about non-commissioned officers who reverted to the rank of private when their battalions were dissolved? Should they or their relatives suffer? For some reason, the rank of sergeant had been missed from the pension schedule. Could they be placed with company sergeant-majors? So independent was the new board that no one had thought to assign it to a department. The Department of Finance was chosen in preference to the over-burdened Militia Department and in recognition of the vast sums the board would have to disburse.[57]

Finding appropriate commissioners was another formidable task. As chairman, Borden turned to Lt John Kenneth Leveson Ross, a Montreal millionaire, yachtsman, and philanthropist, and the son of the ruthless Scottish-born contractor who had built much of the Canadian Pacific Railway. Ross's pre-war patriotism had been made famous when, after the Senate turned back the Naval Aid Bill, he pledged half a million dollars of his own in the campaign to build a Canadian *Dreadnought*. When war broke out, Ross transferred the money to the government, contributed his yacht, *Albacore*, to the navy, and went to sea in command of HMCS *Grilse*, one of Canada's improvised warships. Clearly, Ross was not begging for a salary.[58] Nor was Col. R.H. Labatt, a customs broker from Hamilton, a younger member of the brewing family and a keen militia officer, whose career went back to the 1885 Rebellion. Labatt had taken the 4th Battalion overseas, but a duodenal ulcer and a sudden heart attack had robbed him of more than a few days of commanding his battalion in action. Back in Canada, Labatt poured his remaining energy into raising two battalions and almost a quarter-million dollars for Lougheed's Machine Gun Fund. His friend and former commanding officer, Col. Sydney Mewburn, urged him to reject the Ottawa appointment, but Labatt's sense of duty prevailed.[59]

The third appointment, professedly to his own surprise, fell to John L. Todd. 'I hardly reached home,' he recorded 'before the telephone commenced to ring and bring messages of friends whom I had not seen for twenty years, asking for employment.'[60] Todd, far better than his colleagues, knew what was required; he would be the most active member of the board. Ross kept an office, his business and sporting commitments, and his family in Montreal, and Labatt's health problems soon earned him a total disability pension. For six months in 1916 Todd had made himself master of everything he could learn in England and France about pensions and rehabilitation. Only he had the answers to such arcane questions as whether a disabled soldier could be compelled to undergo an operation or whether a soldier injured on leave could qualify for a pension.[61] Todd's logical mind shaped the board's procedures. Pension applicants would first be examined by a local medical board. Disabilities must be described and measured with scientific precision. Describing a heart condition as 'dyspnoea' or 'soldier's heart' would not do; 'it is necessary to describe the condition of the heart and exactly what it can do, its behaviour, rate, rhythm, when the soldier is excited, is at rest or is undergoing exercises of prescribed severity.'[62] That was all. According to a board memorandum, 'the responsibility of a Board of Medical Officers ends with the forming of an accurate report on the physical condition of a soldier.' Only at the BPC office in Ottawa would pension examiners, armed with a table of disabilities and the applicant's army medical records, determine the pension category.[63]

The 'Table of Incapacities' was close to the heart of Todd's system. The French original, encrusted with precedents dating back to a Pension Law of 1831, was, in Todd's view, 'absolutely absurd'; but the principle was not.[64] The board's version drew on the experience of workmen's compensation in Europe and North America after 'a large number of individuals, suffering from that disability ... have gone out in life and attempted to make their way in competition with their fellows.'[65] Loss of both eyes, legs, or hands, insanity, or acute heart disease certainly represented total disability in the manual labour force, but the bulk of disabilities rated far lower. Loss of a single leg or arm began as a 60 per cent loss, but Todd cut the rating to 40 per cent within a year. Total deafness was assessed at 40 per cent, but the loss of hearing in a single ear was worth no more than a gratuity of fifty dollars. Ailments ranging from urinary incontinence to varicose veins were ranked up and mostly down the scale as they affected one's capacity for physical labour. A rare infusion of sentimentality rated the loss of genital organs at 60 per cent.[66]

Such a system promised a sublime rationality. Pension examiners, immune from bias or sentiment, could administer swift justice regardless of an applicant's status or location. Medical practitioners were surely 'scientific' enough to describe what they saw. The three pension commissioners would hear appeals from decisions by their own officials, but essentially they would be free to administer the board and interpret the law.[67] Logic, of course, has its limitations. Physicians soon felt insulted by the board's precise instructions, and they were outraged when anonymous officials overruled their judgments. What right had men who had never seen the case to reach decisions on the basis of a few scraps of paper? Todd's rejoinder was uncompromising: if pensions had been wrongly assessed, it was the fault of those who had misdescribed the disability. More charitably, he reminded critics that complete medical records, available only at the BPC head office, sometimes disclosed details an applicant had forgotten or failed to reveal. Syphilis was a common example. 'There are very few among us,' Todd observed, 'who have not had an acquaintance who had died of locomotor ataxia and whom we never thought of as syphilitic.'[68]

The brisk logic of Todd's procedure obscured the most critical issue of pension policy, 'attributability.' Disability might be an objective medical question; how far the disability was 'attributable' to service was a matter of almost metaphysical complexity. As usual, Todd had an answer. The government 'must replace to the uttermost farthing every personal loss due to the war,' and the Board of Pension Commissioners would act as a trustee to see that the debt was paid.[69] Yet what, precisely, was 'due to the war'? Was an accident on leave or syphilis contracted by 'wilful misconduct' attributable to the unusual circumstances of army life? Could a soldier who had been certified fully fit at enlistment claim a pension for an infirmity he had slipped past a careless medical officer? Should a soldier who died of cancer be entitled to a military pension for his dependants? Todd had anticipated the question in 1915 and his reply, if prolix, was clear: such a man was 'pensionable in accordance with the extent to which his incapacity is the result of disability aggravated or created by his service as a Soldier,'[70] In slightly less wordy language, Todd had earlier spelled out the principle in what ostensibly was Sir Montagu Allan's report: 'Under Canadian social organization, private citizens must bear for themselves the risks of disabling illnesses or accident to which all human beings are subject. It is but fair when a private citizen is engaged on public service that, while he continue to bear his own risks, all risks resulting directly from disabilities which he incurs as a result of his public service, should be borne by the nation of which he is a member and for which he has served.'[71]

Like many crucial issues, 'attributability' was hardly discussed and probably never understood by the parliamentarians who established pension policy. In almost the only reference in the 1916 debate to the circumstances in which pensions would be paid, W.F. Nickle, a member of the special committee, declared that the new regulations allowed a pension to a man 'who may have been suffering from some complaint of which he was not aware or which escaped the watchful eye of the medical examiner.'[72] If that was so, it was not explicit in the committee's report or in the ensuing order in council, and it was certainly contrary to Todd's assumptions. Instead, the board and its scattered agents were left to make judgments that could not be reduced to the mechanical application of a Table of Incapacities. A gunshot wound or a battlefield amputation, Capt. E.A. Baker's sudden blindness or the lifelong ankylosis that Grant MacNeil brought home from the Battle of the Somme – these were easy to decide; but wounds afflicted only a minority of the men invalided home from France and England or released from the camps in Canada.[73] How far was rheumatism or tuberculosis part of the normal risks of life and to what extent had the illness been aggravated by the exposure, strain, and exhaustion of a soldier's life? By 1916 it was notorious that thousands had gone into the CEF suffering from disease, disability, and old age. To critics, Todd could only be blunt. 'My opinion is that Canadian military pensions should be Canadian military pensions. If you want them to be anything else than that, say so.' The alternative was simply a general insurance policy: 'If ... it is desired to make every detriment which appears in a man during his service pensionable, then let it be said, plainly, that the object of our pension legislation is not only to pension disabilities caused by war, but also to insure our soldiers and sailors against all the risks of existence during the time they are in the Canadian Expeditionary force.'[74]

To Todd, issues such as 'attributability' were tiresome minutiae in the overall task of rehabilitation. In England he had cursed his weakness in allowing his colleagues to send forward a report dealing solely with pensions.[75] The two months he spent in France in 1916, watching efforts to rehabilitate the war-disabled, had revived his analytical skill. The French were making mistakes – there were far too many agencies and too much confusion and waste – but on the principle they were absolutely right. No man had a right to be supported in 'effortless idleness.' 'Everyone must understand,' he wrote, 'that armless, legless men *can* become self-supporting.'[76] Back in Canada by the summer of 1916, he had been delighted to find that most of his suspicions of the amateurish MHC were groundless. Its work of rehabilitation, retraining, and re-employment would 'entirely dwarf pensions properly.'[77] If he could not be in charge, Todd could certainly be involved. The Pensions Commission, he maintained, was as much affected as the MHC by the provision for prostheses. He warned the MHC's Col. Alfred Thompson that failures would add to the pension burden. It was folly to allow men to choose their own artificial limbs. 'If anything of the sort is permitted here you will have firms bidding against one another, firms offering disabled men rake-offs if they will elect a special appliance, you will have all the difficulties of inspecting apparatus supplied by private firms.'[78] He urged that direct action be taken to pre-empt the need for soldiers' organizations 'serving their particular interests, as distinguished from those of the nation.' He had no doubt that the board would be a prime target for such organizations.[79]

Just as urgent, in Todd's view, was the need to educate Canadians – and Americans, when they entered the war in April 1917 – about how retraining and rehabilitation could out-flank both nations' risk of a 'pension evil.' The French and Canadian experiences would have to permeate both countries, for Canadians alone would never withstand the American example, good or bad. 'We are so close to them,' he wrote to his mother, 'that we are certain to be greatly influenced by them. It will be too bad if they do not fully benefit by our influence and our mistakes.'[80] Todd's own convictions were apparent: 'Disabled men who receive money alone and are not assured an occupation,' he told the Canadian Medical Association, 'almost always deteriorate and lose their social position.' Pensions and treatment were not enough for a veteran: 'To discharge its indebtedness to him, his countrymen must, in addition, make him employable, by appropriate re-educational training, if military service has deprived him of his occupation, and must help him find employment.'[81] The French and Canadian experiences sent a basic message: only through economic re-establishment would the war-disabled be made whole again. No pension system, by itself, could satisfy the needs and hopes of the disabled, though, under pressure from the profligate and irresponsible, it could threaten a national economy. John Todd saw himself as a trustee for all Canadians, not just invalid soldiers and sailors.

Growing Pains and Adjustments

It was John Todd who created the practice as well as the theory of Canadian pension administration. Ross was increasingly preoccupied by his racing stable; Labatt was loyal, but walking even a few hundred yards left him exhausted. Inevitably, the new organization built on the old. Colonel Belton was transferred from the Pensions and Claims Board to become the BPC's new medical director, and thirty staff provided continuity.[82] By February 1917 the board's offices in the United Bank Building were filled with 150 employees. Ross announced plans to open sixteen branch offices across Canada and a seventeenth in London for soldiers who took their discharge in Britain. Already the board was paying out a quarter of a million dollars a month to 12,654 pensioners.[83]

Having devised a system that relieved him and his fellow commissoners of the day-to-day adjudication of claims, Todd was free to look beyond pensions to the wider problems of returning soldiers. He had never abandoned his conviction that pensions should be no more than a small part of re-establishing the disabled and that his board should be the single agency for that broader purpose. The MHC's problems with its provincial counterparts, to say nothing of the emergence of private charities and returned soldiers' associations, reminded him of the unhappy side of the French experience. In Toronto, for example, a returned soldier might trudge a weary circle from the offices of the Hospitals Commission to the Soldiers' Aid Commission to the Pension Board, to say nothing of the military headquarters at the

Exhibition Grounds or such false leads as the Patriotic Fund, in order to have a single problem resolved.[84]

The case of William Laidlaw, a Winnipegger who had lost most of his left leg, illustrated both problems and solutions. Early in 1916, a medical board had recommended a 75 per cent pension and an artificial leg for Laidlaw. A second-class pension of $192 might have sufficed, along with an effective prothesis and a paying job, but Winnipeg doctors insisted that the luckless Laidlaw had too short a stump to fit a wooden leg. In the interim, Manitoba's Returned Soldiers Commission put him to work making toys and Laidlaw's case wandered from office to office. Attempts at retraining failed when Laidlaw's wound opened; he returned to hospital, and his training pay ceased. Efforts to find a limb-maker who was not German-born produced more delay. Laidlaw's luck changed only when he was discovered by an outspoken Liberal lawyer, T.S. Ewart. By cause or coincidence, Laidlaw and his family of five found their monthly pension suddenly raised from $16 to $50, and with an added $26 as an allowance for a renewed retraining course.[85]

Such problems and the risk of unfavourable publicity persuaded the prime minister to repeat the 1916 experiment of a parliamentary special committee. By opening the whole range of problems of returned soldiers to scrutiny, potentially explosive issues might be kept out of partisan debate. Sir Herbert Ames, full of experience with the Canadian Patriotic Fund, would serve as chairman, and most of the members of the 1916 committee returned. Amid the political turmoil of the 1917 session, the Special Committee on Returned Soldiers' Problems would be an island of tranquillity.

The real innovation of 1917 was the presence of veterans themselves, echoing grievances that ranged from resentment at the favoured treatment of officers to bitterness at civilian employers. Of the philosophy of re-establishment the returned men had no criticism. 'It is our hope,' said Willard Purney, their leading spokesman, 'it is our aim that we be more than careful to guard against the destruction or the weakening of the spirit of independence in our returned comrades.'[86] Achieving that goal was another matter. The disabled themselves were the first to wonder whether they would be allowed to compete in a post-war labour market undistorted by shortages and patriotism.

On the whole, the pension commissioners escaped criticism. A Vancouver pension applicant, reported Norman Knight, had made 'a very rude remark over the "phone" ' on learning that his pension file was mislaid.[87] Another complained that a doctor in civilian clothes had had the audacity to cut his pension. The hard edge of Todd's policy was sometimes visible. Pte Edward James had led his three sons into the CEF in 1914; soon after his own discharge in 1916, he complained that asthma, caused by poison gas, had left him helpless. Surely a man who had lost one of his sons on Vimy Ridge deserved better of his country? The board responded that James, aged fifty-six, had lied about his age on enlistment and that his records showed no basis for his claim.[88] Private Poirier of the 22nd Battalion had lost his post office job because of failing eyesight. For one eye, lost in action, Poirier had a 40 per cent pension; but he had no proof, the board held, that the other eye was a military responsibility. Perhaps he should have a 50 per cent pension, but Parliament had set rates of 40 or 60 per cent.[89] Another ex-soldier with failing eyesight forfeited his pension when evidence surfaced of a long history of vision problems. Surely, demanded an MP, it was not government policy to offer as little as it could. 'That,' replied Ames, 'is the policy of any and every Government, and always will be.'[90]

Todd easily handled his critics. If there were grounds for complaint, there would be an early re-examination of the case; but problems were usually due to a man's own reticence or to inadequate medical examinations. In other cases, Todd hinted, the disability might have more to do with syphilis than with the Germans. Surely politicians would not wish to subsidize immorality.[91] Veterans themselves, awkward and unbriefed, made unsympathetic witnesses. One elderly sergeant-major was typical. A German bullet through his wrist had ended his career as 'professor of physical culture' at a Toronto private school, but his pension would be only $136 a year. The committee members did not warm to his pretentious manner or to his view that the pension system favoured professionals and those in sedentary occupations – a fair summary of their own status.[92] In its report, the Special Committee urged higher pensions (inflation had devoured the 1916 increases) and a permanent Pension Act, but Todd's enthusiastic explanation of the justice and rationality of his system disarmed potential critics.[93]

It was the commissioners themselves who sought reforms in the autumn of 1917, when most Canadians were preoccupied by conscription, a new Union government, and an imminent general election. The shortage of pension categories, illustrated by the eyesight problems of Private Poirier, had persuaded the board to create twenty rates instead of six. Harsh experience also dictated regulations dealing with children abandoned by their mothers, revising the definition of 'remarriage' to include cohabitation, and denying pensions when the death or disability was 'occasioned by the intemperance or improper conduct of such member.'[94] Though Todd had reported that Canadian pensions were now the highest in the world, the pressure of inflation persuaded the government to add 40 per cent to pension rates up to the rank of lieutenant and to double the rate of helplessness allowance to $300.

Senior officers got nothing. Equalization had been the one unequivocal message from the returned-soldier witnesses.[95]

Todd had no complaints. How large pensions should be was Parliament's business; how pensions were distributed was the board's concern. Of fifteen hundred pensions issued between 22 March and 24 April, only forty had led to complaints. In twelve of those cases he or his colleagues had deemed action to be necessary; six had led to a readjustment.[96] Surely it was as excellent a system as could be devised. 'If we can get our way in everything,' Todd had written before he testified before the Special Committee, 'I think that we shall have a very perfect scheme for looking after men returned disabled.'[97] The Special Committee apparently agreed.

4 Voices from the Ranks

Returned Soldiers' Associations

Both Todd and Scammell had made their plans without consulting prospective clients. No veterans had been asked to give advice on disability tables, annual pension examinations, or vocational training. Paternalism had even extended to planning how returned men could preserve their wartime comradeship. Scammell wanted nothing left to chance: 'Soldiers' Clubs should be established in all the principal centres and in some of the smaller ones. These clubs would not only be places of recreation and education but would enable men who may have grievances to discuss them with others, and to submit them to the proper authorities. It would be necessary to prepare a model constitution for these clubs, which should be subsidised in proportion to their membership.'[1]

Subsidy purchased control. Clubs launched under the kindly patronage of the Hospitals Commission were less likely to evolve into a 'Grand Army of the Dominion'; grievances presented to the 'proper authorities' would not encourage agitators.

By mid-1915 individuals, groups, and communities had been organized to welcome men home. Halifax's Reception Committee accepted a national responsibility for the 250,000 men who eventually surged through Pier 2. The Red Cross, the Knights of Columbus, and the YMCA co-operated to provide soldiers with fruit, candy, cigarettes, and appropriate reading material. The Women's Christian Temperance Union issued its own welcoming card. Montreal's Khaki League had begun in December 1914 as a way of organizing a recreation room for a new CEF battalion. 'God bless you,' Sam Hughes told the league's president, Arthur Doble. 'Anything you can do for the boys will be acceptable.' The league soon expanded from recreation rooms to establishing Montreal's first convalescent homes. The roster of helpers included Molsons, Marlers, Cloustons, and Mrs Marjory Todd.[2] Kindred Khaki Clubs opened in Quebec City, Saint John, and Halifax.

In Ottawa the IODE provided a reading room and cheap meals. Around the corner, the Ontario Soldiers' Aid Commission opened an office to handle queries and help returned men find jobs.[3] In Saskatchewan the Returned Soldiers' Employment Commission boasted four hundred local branches of its Welcome and Aid League.[4] In Vancouver, as elsewhere, the Men's and Women's Canadian Clubs took the initiative. An unused school was refurbished as a Returned Soldiers' Club, and Lt-Col. Alfred Markham, who had lost one of his two sons overseas, was appointed secretary. The MHC paid the Vancouver club $175 a month to cover rent and Markham's salary.[5]

Winnipeg, with its flood of recruits and its civic pride, was more ambitious. From April 1915 the local Army and Navy Veterans ran a soldiers' club, but reports that a returned man had been forced to seek shelter in a boxcar prodded the city's élite to fresh efforts. Mayor R.D. Waugh created a Returned Soldiers' Association. Vigorous fundraising including the sale of memberships and books of stamps urging citizens to 'Be a Sticker,' amassed $65,000 between December 1915 and March 1917. In turn, the association disbursed $48,000 in loans and issued 130 tons of food, 500 cords of firewood, 150 suits of clothes, and 250 sets of underwear. Winnipeggers, as usual, could be proud of their generosity.[6]

If the hard-headed managers of Winnipeg's Returned Soldiers' Association could recognize need, it had to be real. Some soldiers were discharged with a few hundred dollars of back pay; more were penniless. 'A man likes to spend a little money immediately on his arrival home,' confessed an army paymaster; but, profligate or prudent, returned men had good reason to be hard up.[7] Weeks and even months passed before a pension was awarded, and the new pension commissioners were as cautious as the old board in acknowledging disability. Apart from issuing an enamelled discharge button, the CPF washed its hands of both veterans and their families after disembarkation.[8] Even on full pay and allowances few soldiers could support a wife and family, and a pension was only a fraction of army pay. Without a welcoming employer, a wealthy family, or personal savings, homecoming meant hard times.

To most Canadians, the logical solution was charity. Citizens 'did their bit' by welcoming soldiers at the railway station, lending a chauffeur and car to take a hero home in style, or helping personally, as did Mrs Denholm Molson ('Mother' Molson to journalists) at the Khaki Club. Those same Canadians forgot that a soldiers's poverty was no accident of war. A private soldier's pay, $1.10 a day, was half the rate for a day-labourer in 1915; even a sergeant received only $1.60. Below the barrier that separated commissioned officers and the other ranks, a private's status was symbolized by a coarse, ill-fitting uniform, unvarying food, and an utter lack of privacy.[9] In wartime Canada civilian wages rose dramatically, particularly during the inflation of 1917 and 1918; military pay was unaltered from 1914 to 1919. Because soldiers and their families were poor and grew poorer, they could be patronized, overseen, and instructed in the name of charity. The Patriotic Fund boasted of its 'Third Responsibility' – to teach its charges thrift and good housekeeping. Militia Department paymasters boasted of their efficiency in cancelling the separation allowances of allegedly immoral wives.[10]

Like the CPF, the MHC, and the Board of Pension Commissioners, local charities kept power in the hands of affluent men. Angus Hay, a Winnipeg veteran, asked if he had a vote in the local Returned Soldiers' Association. Certainly, he was told, if he purchased a five-dollar membership like everyone else.[11] For Hay, that represented two weeks of pension. The MHC emphasized the need to restore initiative and independence among veterans: 'Most of the men come back with sluggish mental action. They have been under military discipline so long, clothed, fed and ordered about that they have lost independence.'[12] 'In point of fact,' Thomas Kidner told Americans in 1918, 'the process of rehabilitation of a disabled soldier or sailor must include his demilitarization.'[13] In practice, the MHC found it easier to use military discipline than freedom. Control, as usual, was the instinctive response to the problems of poverty.[14]

There were men in the ranks of the CEF from the marginal class that traditionally preferred humiliation to starvation. They were a minority. For most soldiers, poverty was a painful and unexpected part of army life, endured because it was thought to be transitory. The men defined by Todd (and the Chelsea Commissioners) as unskilled labourers had very real skills, status, and expectations in their normal civilian existence. Disability, however, trapped its victims. Pensioners and their families would be poor not for 'the duration' but perhaps forever. Yet disabled veterans had a weapon other victims of the poverty trap lacked: a powerful sense of entitlement. Returned soldiers in Canada and elsewhere rejected charity because they had earned support at the cost of their own pain and blood.[15]

Entitlement could be established only by organization. Scammell and Todd had conceived of 'Soldiers' Clubs' as largely commemorative in purpose: members would gather to celebrate Ypres or St-Eloi as their father had met to dine on Paardeberg Day or to join the Battleford Column. In time the CEF would product its battalion and battery associations or the

Canadian Corps Association, but it would take years for the mists of nostalgia to gather. That was not the mood in 1917. The French historian Antoine Prost observed that the chance associations of a veterans' organization could never reproduce the comradeship of trench or dugout, however much that goal was sought. Whether their founders realized it or not, ex-service associations were and are economic organizations, created to fight a different kind of battle.[16]

Returned men had much in common. Veterans from overseas shared bitter stories of 'safety first' officers in Canada who demanded punctilious salutes from men who had seen months of fighting. A row of cells greeted convalescents at the MHC's Grey Nuns' Hospital in Montreal: a new commanding officer was determined to teach his charges discipline.[17] Ex-soldiers fell foul of the prohibition movement, using patriotism to make Canada dry.[18] The government gave veterans preference in the civil service, but the jobs in the post office and other departments were so humble and the wages so low that even a civil service commissioner wondered how anyone could survive on them.[19] There were comrades too crippled in mind or body to work, whatever the MHC or the pension commissioners might believe. Veterans had no illusion about idlers in their ranks, but then it was not for civilian 'slackers' to sit in judgment.

These were thoughts not easily articulated in IODE-run clubrooms by men unpractised in organization or argument. The initiative came from outside. William Douw Lighthall, a Montreal lawyer, traced his roots to New York patroons and British gentry. At fifty-seven he had written more than forty books and pamphlets on subjects ranging from ethnography to poetry. Most Canadians knew him as the ex-mayor of Westmount who had beaten the Montreal Light, Heat and Power Company. Lighthall called himself an 'independent Liberal'; an admirer described him as a 'practical idealist.' He had organized every kind of association, from the Zenana Foreign Mission to the Canadian Handicrafts Guild; but his major achievement was the Union of Canadian Municipalities, formed in 1901. He had also served in the militia, but his efforts to volunteer in 1914 failed. Instead, Lighthall turned his energies to the Khaki League and to creating a real Returned Soldiers' Association.[20]

In June 1915 Lighthall notified Henry Holcomb, adjutant-general of the Grand Army of the Republic, that 'we are proposing here the establishment of an Association resembling the G.A.R.'[21] Holcomb responded, recommending Robert Beath's massive authorized history of the organization; a GAR representative in Montreal furnished Lighthall with a copy of the Grand Army constitution. A preparatory meeting in his office on 27 September laid the groundwork for a full public meeting in the Khaki Club dining room at Belmont Park on 6 November. After three months of organization, on 13 February 1916, newspapers announced the formation of the Canadian Association of Returned Soldiers – 'independent of Governments, parties, politics, benefactors and all other outside influences.'[22]

Lighthall was no radical. To his friend, Col. C.F. Winter, currently Ottawa's chief censor, he sent reassurance that, despite apparent similarities, the new Returned Soldiers' Association would not be a GAR.[23] Col. Frank S. Meighen, president of Lake of the Woods Milling, took the chair at the public meeting, and Maj.-Gen. E.W. Wilson, the prosperous insurance agent who commanded the Montreal military district, was a conspicuous presence. The association, Lighthall assured him, 'will help recruiting and make the men feel that their future will be on a sound basis.' In wartime Montreal, any cause that might attract fresh soldiers was worth supporting. Lighthall was proud of his creation and excited by its potential. He was not dismayed when young ex-soldiers firmly took charge. They might know little of the complex lodge rituals that were second nature to a Canadian of Lighthall's vintage, but they had other unifying experiences.[24] Membership, they insisted, must be reserved for 'overseas men'; Lighthall himself was excluded. Undaunted, he continued to spread the word, writing to friends in Toronto and Ottawa, visiting the two cities in May and June, and persuading Ottawa veterans to become a branch of the association. By November 1916 Lighthall could describe the movement as 'booming solidly.' In a letter to the Sydney Bulletin, Lighthall even urged Australians to consider a 'Grand Army of the Empire.'[25]

In Toronto veterans faced a different situation. In contrast to most of Montreal's politicians, Toronto civic leaders were noisily committed to the war effort. The city's volunteers were guaranteed a thousand-dollar life insurance policy and first preference in municipal employment. Schoolchildren, for a time, were commanded to salute any returned veteran. Mayor Tommy Church was a shrewd practitioner of the local brand of Tory populism, and he was quick to recognize that Toronto's fifty thousand men in uniform would be the key to his own political future. 'The best that a city can give the soldiers,' he proclaimed to any audience that would listen, 'is none too good for them.'[26] Church personally bade farewell to each departing battalion and welcomed each returning soldier. When veterans wanted to form an organization, city funds were available. A subtle pressure persuaded them to base clubs in existing wards or in suburban communities, such as Parkdale, Brockton, or Riverdale, to which Torontonians bore allegiance. In April 1916, the Toronto Regiment – the CEF's 3rd Battalion – launched its own Returned Soldiers' Association.

Winnipeg sent more men to war, proportionately, than Toronto, but it had neither a Lighthall nor a Tommy Church. The idea of an independent organization arose spontaneously among veterans congregating at the city's hub, Portage and Main. Casual conversation led Fred Law to persuade some twenty-five fellow ex-soldiers to part with four dollars each to finance a charter. Robert Maxwell, a wounded Ulster-born veteran from the First Contingent, suggested the name, and on 18 October 1916 the Great War Veterans' Association was formed. Angus Hay, the young accountant with crippled feet who had been rebuffed by the respectable leaders of the RSA, was the first president. The legislature ordered the charter fee returned and the young association used the money to rent an entire floor in a downtown office building.[27]

All across Canada, local veterans' organizations took shape in 1916. In Calgary, the European War Veterans' Association limited its membership to returned men. The Saskatchewan Veterans' Society, faced with a population scattered in tiny hamlets, chose to take anyone who had served in any war. In Vancouver, a Returned Soldiers' Association emerged on friendly terms with the citizen-sponsored Returned Soldiers' Club.[28] Across the Georgia Strait, where the Legion of Frontiersmen controlled the Victoria Veterans' Club, returned men rebelled at having to join a bogus military organization to gain a voice in their own affairs. 'I think had I joined that association,' claimed a local veteran, 'I might have been a major-general by now.' Instead, despite obstruction from local MHC officials, Victoria veterans organized their own club. Eleven men appeared for the meeting in a dank, candle-lit basement room rented for ten dollars a month. They began, H.W. Hart recalled, with a moment of silence and continued by chipping in a dollar each. By December 1916 British Columbia veterans felt strong enough to hold a provincial convention in Vancouver.[29]

Even without Lighthall the objectives of many of the local returned men's associations would have borne a family resemblance to those of the most effective veteran's organization in the world, the GAR. Montreal members were committed to 'perpetuate the close and kindly ties of service in the great war,' to preserve the memory of those who had suffered and died, and to 'see to the erection of monuments to their valour and the establishment of an annual Memorial day.' They would also 'continually inculcate loyalty to Canada and the Empire and unstinted service in their interest.' Obviously, Beath's book had been on hand and open when those words were recorded. It was the Montrealers' third object that would disturb Ottawa officials: 'To ensure that provision is made for the due care of the sick, wounded and needy among those who have served, including reasonable pensions, employment for such as are capable, soldiers' homes, medical care, and proper provision for dependent families of enlisted men.'[30]

Returned men seized on GAR phraseology because they had yet to articulate their own concerns, but merely coming home to Canada reminded them of their sense of difference from the smug, insulated communities they had half forgotten. Organization was possible, too, because the veterans were becoming a significant minority. Between September 1916 and March 1917, ten thousand Canadian soldiers returned from overseas. They spread to every community in the country. In towns and cities there were now veterans enough to form their own organizations and to escape from the patronizing embrace of home-front patriots.

The Great War Veterans

Lighthall's activities and the emergence of veterans' associations worried Todd and Scammell. To Todd in particular, the GAR overtones were ominous. Any kind of organized 'private enterprise' could be a menace. 'The result will inevitably be that the soldiers will become banded together in Associations serving their particular interests, as distinguished from those of the Nation.'[31] In one of the many memos with which he bombarded Scammell, Todd urged that the provincial commissions be urged to do 'everything possible to make the formation of organizations of Returned Soldiers undesirable by leaving nothing, not even the holding of Annual dinners ... for them to do ... If the Military Hospitals Commission is to realize its responsibilities to the full it must be regarded by the Returned Soldiers as their father and mother, trustee and everything else that has but one end, and that is the interest of the returned soldiers.'[32]

Scammell dutifully urged the provincial commissions to consider Todd's advice and to watch for signs of a 'Dominion Soldiers' Association.' 'This organization,' he noted cautiously, 'can be of great service, or it may have a contrary effect.'[33] The outcome would depend on the leaders. Capt. Kenneth Macpherson, the junior civil servant who had started the Ottawa organization, was invited to Scammell's house. Macpherson proved to be a reasonable man. 'On the other hand,' Scammell acknowledged, 'there are men of the Sea Lawyer type who consider that anything which favours of [sic] Government is of necessity antagonistic to the ambition of the men.'[34]

Having created an organization, Macpherson applied for an Ontario charter. With more caution than Manitoba, the provincial secretary's office invited the dominion government to state whether 'the proposed name and objects are objectionable.' To Surgeon-General Eugène Fiset, deputy minister of militia, they were very objectionable indeed. Not only was such an organization utterly unnecessary, but it appeared 'to have been set on foot in a spirit of dissatisfaction' with what those in authority were doing. Moreover, Fiset insisted, it was undesirable that 'the Act of Incorporation, whether Provincial or Dominion, should permit the Association to deal with such objects as "reasonable pensions", "soldiers' homes", etc. which are provided by the Government at public expense – matters which should not in any way be interfered with by Associations or officials other than those appointed and controlled by the Government.'[35] This somewhat constrained view of democracy was given short shrift by Borden's minister of justice, C.J. Doherty: 'The purposes appear to me to be lawful and the reasons advanced in support of action restricting the formation of such associations do not seem to me to justify the conclusions reached.'[36]

By early February 1917, the Canadian Association of Returned Soldiers had branches in Montreal and Ottawa, while the B.C. Returned Soldiers' Association had attracted most veterans' groups on the lower mainland. Talk of a national association was in the air. In Parliament, Fred Pardee, a Liberal from Sarnia, launched a sharp attack on the government for financing its aid to returned men by door-to-door charitable appeals, blamed it because a returned man had suffered from frozen hands, and recommended that the Pensions Board ought to take charge of the disabled, as the French did, and teach them a trade.[37] The ensuing discussion, as well as the pension problems mentioned earlier, helped to persuade Borden that if the rest of the country was as ignorant as Pardee another special committee was needed. Under Sir Herbert Ames and Lougheed's law partner, R.B. Bennett, the 1917 special committee inaugurated an annual parliamentary ritual.[38]

In March the committee ventured forth to hold some of its twenty sessions in Montreal and Toronto. Among the hundred witnesses were veterans summoned from farther afield at public expense.[39] The result was an instructive and occasionally ill-tempered counterpoint to the bland self-congratulation of officers and government officials. Ex-soldier witnesses complained of everything from inferior accommodation on returning troop-ships – officers had the boat deck while troops were crowded below – to alleged medical experiments on helpless convalescents. Western veterans reminded MPs of the plight of returned settlers confronted by overdue taxes, homestead duties, and untended farms. Easterners complained of employers all too willing to cut wages even if disabled men could do a day's work. Warrant Officer Napoléon Marion reminded the committee that only three medical officers and one nurse in the MHC's Montreal hospitals could speak French.[40]

Assembling the veterans served as a catalyst for launching a national organization. Meeting in Toronto on 24 March, a day after they testified, western veterans encountered their Ontario and Quebec counterparts and began working out the details for a founding convention at Winnipeg. Experience before the special committee underlined the need for a common voice for ex-soldiers. Lighthall provided a draft of the association's aims. The vexed question of rank would be resolved GAR fashion: titles would be banned and members would address each other as 'comrade.'

When veteran-delegates gathered in Winnipeg on 10 April (having benefited from special half-fares on both national railway systems), the convention was overshadowed by the United States entry into the war and the Canadian capture of Vimy Ridge. Reservations about creating an association were temporarily forgotten while the lieutenant-governor opened proceedings at the Travellers' Building and Mayor Davidson received the delegates at a civic reception. With the confusion over returned soldiers' associations and clubs, the Winnipeggers' name, 'Great War Veterans,' seemed the best choice. Ottawa was chosen over Winnipeg (by eight votes) as headquarters. The harshest debate was over membership; to qualify, veterans had to have crossed the Atlantic; others could be non-voting associates. The Army and Navy Veterans were furious. Since 1885 that association had welcomed British ex-sailors and ex-soldiers to Winnipeg and the west. As the only pre-war veterans' organization at the convention, its delegates demanded a wider definition of membership. When the majority refused, the three ANV delegates walked out. It was the beginning of a lasting schism. [41]

Policy-making was less contentious. The pension resolution unanimously demanded twelve hundred dollars a year for the totally disabled 'equally for officers and men.' The pension commissioners were denounced for changing local recommendations without seeing the men or even explaining their decisions. Obviously, there must also be an appeal to some higher body. Another grievance was the miserly gratuity paid on discharge. Veterans' resentment boiled over at the Last Post Fund, a Montreal-based charity that provided funerals for indigent veterans. Surely the government could 'meet the cost of a decent interment.' Western delegates demanded a 320-acre grant and a minimum, two-thousand-dollar loan for each soldier who had been overseas and to widows, 'provided always that the title of the land be entrusted to a responsible trustee.' Acreage for this vast bounty, according to another unanimous resolution, would come by taking Indian reserves, unused railway land, and all other 'blanketed' grants. [42]

Delegates argued that they were mere trustees for men still in the fight. Echoing a growing demand, they urged that men of the First Contingent – the 'Old Originals' – be brought home for their first furlough in thirty months. To replace them, conscription was essential. Departments of government must be 'combed out.' Slackers and 'safety-first' officers in Canada must be replaced by returned men and sent overseas. Veterans, the elderly, and 'women, if need be' could replace fit male workers in industry. Western delegates led the new association further. Industries vital to the war effort must be taken over by government. To share the sacrifices, wealth, too, must be conscripted so that 'all incomes and wealth, in excess of the holder's reasonable needs, be placed at the disposal of the Government for the successful prosecution of the war and to meet the immense financial drain on the country; equitable retribution [*sic*] to be made as soon after the end of the war as possible so that the principle may be carried out that one citizen shall not give more than another, that all shall give their best for the preservation of the nation.'[43]

Capt. Ivan Finn of Prince Albert led the convention in a darker direction. Like other western soldiers, Finn had found the 'foreign-born' prospering while soldiers' farms went to weed. The simmering pre-war hostility to immigrants had been given respectability by the war. In 1916 Calgary veterans had rioted against German Canadians, and recruits in Berlin, Victoria, and other cities had tested their patriotic virility on German-owned businesses and clubs. Delegates found the mood infectious. Farms of German and Austrian settlers, declared an angry veteran, should be sold and the proceeds used to help prisoners in German camps. Instead, the convention voted to conscript all aliens, friendly or hostile, 'for any service the Government deems fit to use them for.' Saskatchewan was condemned for 'hiving' its soldiers into separate constituencies to benefit 'the enemy alien.' For good measure, the convention demanded an even higher head-tax on immigrants from an allied country, China.[44]

True to the GAR model, the Great War Veterans insisted that they were non-partisan and non-political. Maj. Willard Purney, elected president on the final day, was a Nova Scotia lawyer with Tory connections. Two vice-presidents, Sgt-Maj. James Robinson and J.J. Shanahan, represented Vancouver and Toronto respectively, while a crippled veteran from Windsor, Ontario, Norman Knight, agreed to serve as secretary-treasurer. For all the egalitarian and anti-officer rhetoric of the convention, five of the twelve members of the full executive were former CEF officers.[45]

Once launched, the Great War Veterans could build on a substructure of local veterans' clubs and organizations in most of the communities of Canada. Some were resentful rivals of civilian patriotic societies, others were grateful beneficiaries; but all could unite on a common agenda of grievances and claims. The GWVA was created by men from every province but Prince Edward Island, and, even without the official recognition it soon acquired, it became the national voice of the returned men.

Purney's first task was to reassure the GWVA's potential critics. The new association, he promised, would do nothing to embarrass veterans or the country.[46] On 5 June, as the special parliamentary committee wound up its hearings, Ames invited the entire GWVA executive to present its views and policies. Again, Purney and his colleagues sought to dispel fears of a Canadian GAR. With some statistical ingenuity, Captain Macpherson of the Ottawa branch managed to adjust the convention demand for a $1,200 pension to a more modest $840. Sergeant-Major Robinson admitted that the conscription resolutions, passed so enthusiastically at Winnipeg, 'are rather extreme.'[47] It was manpower conscription the GWVA really wanted, Purney explained; the extras would cheerfully be sacrificed. He assured the committee that 'the great body of the War Veterans of this country only ask that they be given reasonable consideration.' Their secretary, Norman Knight, went even further: 'We really think that the powers now are really trying to do for the returned soldier all they possibly can do, but we do not want the returned men to go about telling other people all their grievances. Let them come to us and we will take the matter up with the proper authorities.'[48]

What Knight, Purney, and their colleagues wanted was legitimacy. Meetings with Borden, Lougheed, and MHC officials and lunch with the finance minister were a gratifying beginning, but everything had yet to be done. GWVA officials had claimed to speak for 10,000 members, but most of those men had yet to join; the organization had begun with 3,884 members in twenty-seven branches. The convention had been promised a national publication, but staff and funds had to be found. Delegates agreed that the organization would be based on provincial commands and local branches, but all of that took money.[49] Almost by definition the GWVA's members had few dollars to spare: funds would have to come from the kind of public charity the association professed to deplore. To collect and safeguard funds, the GWVA needed both respectability and a charter. The veterans' bid for incorporation gave Lougheed and his officials an irresistible opportunity to reassert control. Certainly, Lougheed agreed, a charter was desirable, but the government was contemplating legislation for all war charities; the GWVA should wait. Perhaps it could be incorporated after amendments to the Dominion Companies Act had been passed. Seeking opinions was another delaying technique. Ontario's Premier William Hearst objected that the association's concern with education and hospitals surely invaded provincial jurisdiction. Knight tried to move Borden with the spectre of agitators invading GWVA branches 'with the idea of forming a Soldiers' and Workingmen's Party' with Soviet overtones. Borden settled Hearst's problem, but six months later, Knight was still vainly waiting for his charter.[50]

Even without a charter, the association grew. Thanks to a head start, British Columbia was the first provincial command to be organized. Ontario followed on 15 May, choosing an ex-chaplain from Brantford, the Reverend C.E. Jeakins, as president. William Turley, a former national champion bantamweight boxer and journalist, was elected secretary. On 2 November Saskatchewan veterans met in Regina and chose Maj. James McAra, the MHC's local purchasing agent, as president, and Grant Mac-Neil, a young ex-machine-gunner, as secretary. Provincial conventions proclaimed fresh policies. Ontario delegates declared that any surplus officer who refused to revert to the ranks should be dishonourably discharged. At Regina, veterans demanded ten thousand dollars from the provincial government, thundered against enemy aliens and demanded that soldiers' dependants be supported by the state, not by charity. Both gatherings echoed the call for conscription.[51]

By November 1917, conscription was also an issue in the national election. Despite Lougheed's suspicions, his colleagues needed the GWVA. The veterans too had little choice. Whatever they had suffered from a Conservative government, they could hardly support Laurier and the anti-conscription Liberals. The dénouement of the Military Service Act debate, the formation of a Union government, could hardly have been more convenient. Surely a 'Union' was not 'partisan' in the sense of the GWVA constitution. The new government helped by sending Purney overseas to run the election among Canadian troops in England and France.[52] The Unionist Manifesto offered soldiers glowing assurances: 'The men by whose sacrifice and endurance the free institutions of Canada will be preserved must be re-educated where necessary and re-established on the land or in such pursuits or vocations as they may desire to follow. The maimed and the broken will be protected, the widow and the orphan will be helped and cherished. Duty and decency demand that those who are saving democracy shall not find democracy a house of privilege, or a school of poverty and hardship.'[53]

Read carefully, the statement pledged no more than the government had been doing, but political platforms are not written like legal contracts. J.J. Shanahan, acting as president in Purney's absence, gave the Union government all the support it could have wished. 'It will behoove us,' he told GWVA branches, 'to bring all our forces to bear to secure the defeat of any candidate who is not prepared to do all in their [sic] power to secure the enforcement of Conscription.'[54] GWVA branches endorsed a variety of soldier candidates,' all of them officers. Only the Calgary branch emphasized the GWVA commitment to conscript wealth. In Toronto, Winnipeg, and Vancouver, ex-soldiers guided democracy by breaking up anti-conscription meetings. Capt. C.G. 'Chubby' Power, the sole pro-Laurier candidate among the soldiers, easily held the new seat of Quebec South. Twenty officers stood as pro-conscription candidates; sixteen won. Maj. G.W. Andrews, running as a Liberal-Unionist in Winnipeg Centre, collected a 20,930-vote majority, the biggest in the election.[55]

Veterans were not shy about claiming credit for the Unionist victory. The military vote, collected and counted separately (91.5 per cent for the government), added to the impression of a Borden landslide.[56] 'It has been urged by many,' Norman Knight reminded the prime minister, 'that the returned soldier and his loyal connection, our brave women folk, had quite as much to do with the return of the Union Government as any other force in Canada. All we ask in return is a little consideration.'[57] With conscription decided, the GWVA increasingly turned to its chosen enemy, the 'aliens.' Anit-immigrant feeling was part of most veterans' cultural milieu; returned men easily persuaded themselves that eliminating 'foreigners' would punish wartime enemies and smooth the way of their own re-establishment. Lively spirits in the GWVA's Hamilton and Toronto branches jeered Premier Hearst at Queen's Park when he refused to back their wilder demands, and proposed to bring their case to Parliament Hill. Signatures multiplied on a petition demanding suppression of enemy alien newspapers, compulsory badges for foreigners, and forced labour for German and Austrian men at the soldiers' rate of $1.10 a day.[58]

Caught, like many pressure-group leaders, between an angry membership and political realities, Knight needed government help. 'I with others have tried to stop this demonstration, counselling milder methods,' he explained to the prime minister. 'The best way to do it is by quiet and close conference. These men are in earnest and have reached the limit of their patience.'[59] Borden obliged. On 28 March GWVA leaders came to Ottawa at public expense and offered their views to a trio of ministers in the hallowed precincts of the Privy Council chamber. The immediate results were meagre: the government moved to register Russians as enemy aliens but more months passed before German-language newpapers were suppressed. For the moment that mattered less than the evidence that the GWVA had access to the very heart of Canada's government.[60]

The GWVA needed to look important, for by 1918 it was no longer the sole voice of veterans. The small defection at Winnipeg had had consequences. Alarmed at the GWVA's apparent radicalism and nervous about their own continuing influence over returned men, Winnipeg's civic leaders hurriedly secured a charter for the Army and Navy Veterans in the dying moments of the twelfth parliament. Such citizens as Maj.-Gen. H.N. Ruttan and Lt-Col. Sir Daniel Macmillan were not easily denied. In contrast to the activist objects of the Great War Veterans, the Army and Navy Veterans promised to be 'a body of retired soldiers and sailor veterans of a non-partisan and non-sectarian character, for purposes of good fellowship, mutual improvement and assistance, and patriotic endeavor and service to the Empire.'[61] In membership, the ANV proposed to be both more and less exclusive than the GWVA: the association would admit veterans with a service medal or six years' service in His Majesty's forces or who had served in France (but not if they had only gone to England 'unless they could prove it was through no fault of their own').

The ANV's founding convention, held at Winnipeg from 11 to 15 May 1918, summoned 63 delegates and claimed to represent 8,337 members, a quarter of them in Winnipeg, an impressive 1,710 in the old military town of Kingston, and most of the rest scattered in western cities. As at the GWVA convention, the sharpest debate was over membership. The restrictive approach prevailed; the GWVA, a Kingston delegate scornfully claimed, might 'take in a man if he has been in the army five minutes and had the clothes on,' but not the Army and Navy Veterans. Veterans' unity might be a fine principle, said a naval officer from Vancouver Island, but 'I am dead against any idea whereby the identity of the Army and Navy Veterans is to be eliminated through any process of amalgamation.'[62] The conservative tone of the new organization was confirmed by the election of Maj. W.J. Tupper, grandson of the former Conservative prime minister, as president and Capt. R. Crystal Irving as secretary. The headquarters would remain, with the officers, in Winnipeg. On that issue, westerners stood solid against the east.

Pensions and Re-establishment

However important conscription and enemy aliens might be in fuelling debate in veterans' clubs, the real test of the GWVA and its rivals was their practical success on behalf of their members. In 1918 no issue bothered returned men more than pensions. The GWVA had come too late to the 1917 Special Committee for any serious discussion of its proposals. The ensuing year had only aggravated the veterans' grievances. Inflation devoured the purchasing value of the maximum pension of six hundred dollars, and 90 per cent of pensioners were receiving nowhere near the maximum. Worst off were the 'functional' or 'shell-shock' cases. Whether doctors took them seriously or dismissed them as cowardly malingerers, the consequences were virtually identical. Such men had subconsciously willed themselves into a primitive state, explained Lt-Col. Colin K. Russell, the CEF's chief specialist in 'neurasthenic' diseases. To give them pensions only encouraged them: 'You have thrown away the four aces.'[63] This was small comfort to the sufferers or their families.

Veterans had other complaints, ranging from arrogant or offhand doctors on medical boards to the arbitrary and unexplained decisions of the Board of Pension Commissioners. A soldier considered perfectly fit in 1914 by a reputable insurance company was denied pension for a heart condition because, said the BPC, it 'pre-existed enlistment.'[64] Another man got only a 10 per cent pension, possibly because his medical board forgot to mention the shrapnel wounds that made his life an agony.[65] Few soldiers felt at ease in the military formality of a medical board or in wrestling with a remote bureaucracy. 'I would have tried to get pension while in the army,' explained a veteran with impaired vision and speech, 'but cannot talk very plain and was afraid of them laughing at me.'[66] Pte E.R.R. Mills, a young lawyer whose career now seemed hopeless because of his 'functional' disability, angrily complained: 'When you go before a medical board you are treated as a malingerer, if you are a private. They disgust [sic] you to start with, and in some cases I have heard them almost tell them to their faces that they were liars.'[67]

On 10 April 1918 the new House of Commons appointed its third special committee on veterans, this time to consider pensions, the new board, and its regulations. The Board of Pension Commissioners was pleased; it had plenty of reforms to suggest, and Todd rejoiced in any chance to publicize his ideas.[68] The 1918 committee was headed by Newton Rowell, one of the Union government's leading Liberals; its members, Liberal or Tory, felt little allegiance to past practices. Veterans who had come to the 1917 committee unbriefed and with little notice were better prepared this time. Knight had returned sick and exhausted from a cross-Canada tour in January, but his files bulged with grievances, and he had useful supporters in E.R.R. Mills and the Army and Navy Veterans' representative, Sgt Herbert Jarvis.

Politicians were in the mood for reform, and the veterans took the offensive. Complacent BPC officials made few friends. A man with periodic fainting fits, they insisted, had been well treated with a 10 per cent pension. After all, explained Colonel Belton, he missed only 2 per cent of his working time. W.F. Nickle, the independent-minded Tory from Kingston, was outraged: 'I have seen some decisions that ought to be reversed and we know of them where great injustice was being done to the men and I think we are getting entirely too scientific in estimating the degree of disability these men are suffering.'[69] Both Jarvis and Knight argued that pensions of officers and men should be equalized; indeed, Knight confessed that his members had instructed him to do so. Members of Parliament who had been officers were invited, without visible result, to show their support for the principle. Maj. D.L. Redman, a former law partner of Lougheed and Bennett who had been elected in Calgary with GWVA support, remained discreetly silent.[70] More effective with the politicians was the suggestion that ordinary soldiers felt discriminated against in a system run by officers. 'I always take it that there is a kind of fraternal feeling amongst officers,' Jarvis explained. 'Officers are sitting on the board, and if another officer comes in he is always treated with courtesy and very very nice. A man comes in and he is treated as a different subject altogether.'[71]

The veterans cited a specific case to prove their point. Arthur Tooke had joined the 4th Battalion in 1914; at Ploegsteert, German shells had buried him, and when he emerged he had a fair case of 'shell-shock.' Back in England, Tooke rose to the rank of sergeant-major, but successive nervous breakdowns led to his discharge. A former accountant with a family of three, his military pension was only $2.66 a week. Only a good-hearted employer in an Ingersoll foundry kept the Tookes from starvation.[72] Yet the same pension commissioners gave Tooke's former commanding officer a total disability pension of $2,160 a year for himself and two teen-aged children. Moreover, since he was also one of those pension commissioners, Col. R.H. Labatt already earned $5,000 a year. Harry Stevens, a Tory MP from Vancouver with a sensitive nose for scandal, poured out his wrath in a letter to Rowell; Labatt, he alleged, could have secured his pension only through misrepresentation or influence. Stevens's letter leaked to the press, caused a modest public outcry.[73] A grievance circulating among angry veterans was now a public issue.

The Board of Pension Commisioners had been caught unawares. In January, Ross and Todd had left for England, leaving the ailing Labatt and their officials to cope. They returned triumphant, having brought Sir Montagu Allan's separate operation under their control and cutting dependant pensions for Canadians in England to the meagre British scale.[74] If J.K.L. Ross had any business for the Special Committee, it was to share his outrage at the Civil Service Commission. How could he run a businesslike operation if he had to hire the farmers and brakemen the commission sent him as clerks or if he had to follow Ottawa's summer hours of 9:00 to 4:00?[75] Instead, the committee wanted to know why Ross did not give full time to his duties. Precisely who wielded the rubber signature stamp on pension decisions? Bewildering technical issues of 'attributability' and 'functional cases' were soon set aside when the Labatt affair gave politicians, veterans, and the public something they could all understand.[76] John Todd improvised the defence. With Kenneth Archibald, the board's solicitor, he picked out points to surrender and ground to defend. The American experience was cited as an argument against appeals from the board and against decentralization. Regional boards in the United States, Todd warned, had vied with each other in generosity.[77] Perhaps it was reasonable, he conceded, that any man who got as far as France or Flanders should be deemed to have no prior disabilities.

Labatt was finished. 'He is a very sick man who has given excellent service,' Todd noted with uncharacteristic charity, but the government had done little to defend him.[78] Only Sidney Mewburn, the new minister of militia, had risen in Parliament to denounce Stevens's letter and defend an old friend. A misplaced sense of duty had brought the ailing veteran to Ottawa, and he had paid the price of humiliation.[79] Within a year, he was dead. 'I feel sure,' Ross wrote to Rowell, 'that if Colonel Labatt had lost two legs or two arms or showed some outward and visible sign of a large disability that [sic] no question would have been raised.'[80]

The issues had certainly been raised. Labatt had been an extreme example of an excellent principle. In the 'market for unskilled labour,' his heart condition was totally disabling. But Parliament had agreed in 1916 that a pension must not be affected by earnings. Stevens had not protested the rule then.[81] Had Labatt or anyone else been specifically favoured? How could it be proved? Another powerful claimant, Sen. George Bradbury, also a CEF colonel, had been outraged by his 50 per cent pension for angina; he demanded and obtained a report from a different medical board which recommended 80 per cent. Colonel Belton left no doubt as to which opinion the board would accept. Bradbury was, incidentally, only the fourth claimant who had managed to get a second opinion.[82]

When the Special Committee reported on 20 May, its recommendations were more pettifogging than radical. The commissioners were lectured on their duties. At least one of them must sign each pension award. Local medical boards could again offer their assessment of disability; if central examiners disagreed, the should confer. Archibald's hope that MPs would recommend the full pension rates for the militia and for British and Allied reservists was dashed. 'In view of the obligations Canada has undertaken,' Rowell announced, 'we were discharging our duty by providing pensions on the scale at which they are established for our own soldiers.'[83] Of course there would be no pension equalization. The principle of a contractual obligation was proof against any new-found egalitarianism.

The veterans had remarkably little to show for their efforts. They had humiliated the Pension Board; they had not reformed it. They had not even won higher pension rates; conscription had relieved the government of the need to make military service – or its painful consequences – more tolerable. Todd resigned in February 1919, fed up with his wartime work and utterly rejecting the cabinet order that he spend his time scribbling his name on thousands of pension awards. 'I think they are glad to be rid of me,' he wrote to his mother; it was time for 'a general with a wooden leg and lots of medal ribbons.'[84] Ross followed in 1919. A return to the racetrack, where his horse had won the Triple Crown and a million dollars in the 1918 season, now seemed infinitely more congenial than battles with the Civil Service Commission. As for the veterans, political victories had little substance.

Veterans, Aliens, and Politics

Amid the preoccupations of conscription, economic and regional strain, and the frightening see-saw battles on the Western Front that began on 21 March, it was easy to overlook the special committee on pensions. Even the Labatt affair was a one-day wonder. Knight retired on 20 May, having waited out the committee hearings and citing 'ill health and extreme nervous condition.' His successor, Robert Stewart, took over a growing organization. Another newcomer was David Loughnan, an Ulster-born veteran of British Columbia's 16th Battalion. Loughnan had escaped death during the destruction of his unit at Second Ypres by crawling half a mile with his intestines protruding from a gaping wound. Survival after such a wound was rare. When Loughnan appeared at the British Columbia veterans' second convention, a contemporary recalled: 'He was practically a stranger, his pale, pain-worn face bore the impress of many weary months of hospital treatment.' Loughnan's focused energy made him the unanimous choice for provincial president.[85] By November his reputation made him editor of the GWVA's new national organ, *The Veteran*. The first issue, published in December 1917, promised to exercise 'the right of independent judgement and criticism of public men and affairs. It will fearlessly and strenuously attack and expose all proven abuses and injustices in our national administration and public life and will lend its independent support to all sane and enlightened policies of reform and progress.'[86] Loughnan meant it. By June 1918 he had secured a separate corporate existence for his periodical, though its symbolic share capital of twenty-five thousand dollars was wholly pledged by the GWVA. By October *The Veteran* boasted a circulation of 95,000.

By the end of 1917, the GWVA claimed to have grown from 15,000 to 25,000 members; the association's membership was concentrated mainly in major cities, but branches mushroomed in smaller cities and towns and even in the United States. From his new perspective, Loughnan warned that branches were in 'a perilous condition' because they had chosen officers 'noted neither for their intelligence nor good sense.'[87] He accepted re-election as president of the British Columbia command with a speech demanding that aliens be forced to pledge allegiance to the Crown or be deported. Delegates cheered his resolution that the Patriotic Fund, already boycotted by the B.C. labour movement, be replaced by taxation. At Brantford, a hundred Ontario delegates thundered applause as their president, the Reverend Charles Jeakins, demanded free hospital care for dependants, interest-free home-building loans, and special asylums for mentally ill comrades. In Saskatchewan, the GWVA convention boasted of a ten-thousand-dollar provincial grant, insisted that English should be the sole language of instruction in provincial schools, and paused to express its appreciation of nurses for their devoted war service. The convention recommended that the government set 'a reasonable maximum price on all household commodities.'[88]

A war-weary Canada was looking for hope and fresh ideas by 1918. The collapse of traditional party loyalties in 1917, Quebec's alienation over the conscription issue, and seething rural discontent seemed to promise a very different post-war Canada. Labour scarcity meant that any veteran who felt fit to work could find a job, possibly at a higher income than he might have expected; but civilians had done far better. When peace came, what would happen to government clerks or timekeepers in munition factories? Almost every Canadian who served overseas, and many who did not, had felt a new nationalism as the CEF established its identity and pride. It was a mood that obviously excluded those who stood aside from the national crusade.

Canada's labour revolutionaries, remembering the 'workers and soldiers' councils' that reputedly had overthrown the Russian tsar, were initially eager to embrace the veterans' movement. Their overtures were rejected. Ex-soldiers and radicals might hold common opinions on profiteering and immigration, but the war was another matter. Labour radicals identified the war effort as the last decadent phase of capitalism; veterans were resentful at being categorized as dupes, and their loyalty remained with those who continued the struggle. In the West, pre-war radicals had been outflanked by those espousing a new militancy. The fate of Albert Goodwin, vice-president of the British Columbia Federation of Labour, shot while escaping arrest under the Military Service Act, prompted labour radicals to call a general strike. In retaliation, veterans and soldiers smashed their way into the Vancouver Labour Temple, wrecked the premises, and forced the secretary of the Labour Council, Victor Midgley, to kneel and kiss a Union Jack.[89]

Even in the West, GWVA spokesmen tried to distinguish between their sympathy for organized labour and their hostility to revolutionaries and enemy aliens. Both radicals and business did their best to blur the distinction. In the East, where moderates generally dominated labour councils, it was easier for veterans and unions to make common cause. When the GWVA held its second convention in Toronto at the end of July, delegates found Sgt William Varley vigorously campaigning as a 'Soldier-Labour' candidate in the provincial by-election. Prominent returned soldiers and Hamilton's aged Labour MPP, Alan Studholme, shared Varley's platform and denounced both his Tory opponent, Canon H.J. Cody, and the treatment meted out to veterans and their families.[90]

For the GWVA's delegates, politics was a time bomb waiting to go off. Their large numbers (and discreet encouragement from municipal politi-

cians and editors) made Toronto veterans eager to turn the GWVA into a
political movement. To add to their influence, the Toronto branches had
bullied Stewart into allowing them seventeen delegates instead of the eight
their numbers warranted. Proximity and extra representation gave Ontario
94 delegates for 7,563 members, compared with 84 for the 11,573 members
from the rest of the country. This would have mattered less if the Ontarians
had not been bent on pushing the GWVA in a new direction. Wrangling
began on the first day, 29 July, when Jeakins, the Ontario president, moved
to end the 'aristocracy of the trenches' and open voting membership to
anyone who had served in the CEF. Loughnan and the westerners joined
battle. 'You know that the men in your locals, the men who make the most
trouble,' Loughnan declared, 'are those who went the least of the way to
France.' After a day and a half of angry debate and defeat, Winnipeg's ten
delegates withdrew. For different reasons, so did Ottawa's six. The Ottawa
group resented efforts to dragoon them into the Ontario organization; the
Winnipeggers denounced the unfair representation for Toronto. A message
from both dissident delegations was pushed under Purney's hotel door: 'We
are firmly of the conviction that the attitude adopted from time to time by
the Toronto and Ontario delegates of jeering and howling at outside delegates with whom they do not agree is not conducive to harmony or good
results. With the predominance of voting power from Ontario and having in
view a resolution submitted to your convention that this association enter
actively into the political arena, we feel that we cannot assume just responsibility for any action of this convention.'[91]

Peacemakers, headed by Ottawa's Captain Macpherson and Montreal's
acting mayor, Lt-Col. J.J. Creelman, managed to restore harmony over the
weekend. 'We must kill this political business,' announced a Calgary delegate, and a somewhat shaken convention agreed. Purney firmly ruled out
any discussion of politics and was upheld by all but two delegates. He
turned aside efforts to have him announce an election meeting for Varley,
the soldier-candidate. Would it be all right, then, to sit on Archdeacon
Cody's platform? 'I suppose it might be done,' Purney coyly suggested, 'in
the case of personal friendship,'[92]

When the one storm had passed, the convention resumed the more congenial business of exploring pension reform and denouncing aliens. Captain
Power, the new Liberal MP, won applause by urging that the militia staff
might be 'thanked for their services' and replaced by returned men. Aliens
of allied countries, another veteran demanded, should be denied licences for
poolrooms, shoeshine parlours, and ice cream stores so that returned
soldiers could have them. In celebration of the national mood, Canon
Somerville from Peterborough proposed that 'O Canada should take prece-

dence over God Save the King.' Delegates unanimously agreed but, after some embarrassment, deferred singing; they did not know the words. Saskatchewan's Grant MacNeil got unanimous backing for the abolition of every enemy-language publication. 'We in Saskatchewan,' he explained, 'realize that we must look at the problem unprejudiced, for we must assimilate the aliens.'[93]

How they might be assimilated soon became painfully apparent. That evening, 2 August, the midsummer heat filled Toronto's business thoroughfares with civilians, soldiers, returned men, and convalescents from the big hospitals. Rumours that Greek waiters had attacked a disabled veteran at the White City Café on Yonge Street provided a spark of excitement. As spectators cheered, a crowd of veterans and invalided soldiers smashed their way into the restaurant and demolished it. A handful of policemen saved the Colonial and Childs' Restaurant, but ten more restaurants and shops were wrecked and looted when police failed to intervene. Some of the crowd commandeered cars and raced westward, destroying another Greek restaurant a few miles away.[94]

The next day, Mayor Tommy Church immediately denied any municipal liability. Police officials explained that, despite prior arrangements, the military authorities had failed to control soldiers. Restaurant owners, who had been threatened and forced to salute the flag by the crowd, reported losses of $24,300, and retained lawyers. On the next night, crowds gathered again. This time, Toronto policemen were ready and angry. The official offer of a hundred soldiers equipped with rifles, bayonets, and ammunition was curtly dismissed. Armed with batons, the police cleared Yonge Street, managing in the process to bludgeon a drunk and angry legless veteran named Mason Button and an angry but more sober Lt-Col. A.T. Hunter. Hunter, a lawyer and GWVA leader, had intervened in the scuffle.[95]

Inevitably, the GWVA found itself blamed for the Greek-restaurant riots. There was no evidence that delegates had inspired the attack or, apart from Hunter, even formed part of the mob, but the days of anti-alien rhetoric had given a signal. Editors exercised their righteous reflexes: 'Housebreaking and looting,' thundered Hector Charlesworth in *Saturday Night*, 'are no more defensible when committed by returned soldiers and their friends, than when perpetrated single-handed by the ordinary burglar.'[96] Toronto's *Daily Star* directed its indignation at the easiest available target: 'There is evidently need for leadership of returned soldiers, and the Great War Veterans' Association ought to take up this matter and set its face sternly against such outrages.'[97] Indeed, Purney and his executive had hurriedly drafted a resolution for the convention's final day, deploring the actions of 'some returned soldiers.' 'It is just such actions as these that hamper the work of the GWVA and bring our cause into disgrace throughout Canada in the public mind.' Loughnan, in *The Veteran* neatly managed to blame just about everyone: 'Without attempting to justify the conduct of the rioters in Toronto, we would draw the attention of the Canadian people to the fact that many returned men do sincerely feel that the Government and people of Canada have failed to implement the gracious promises of special treatment and consideration made to them ere they sailed overseas. Neglect to control profiteering, to work out a sane land settlement and land policy, and to regulate the alien problem, have all combined as irritants upon men whose nerves have not been improved by their trials in the trenches.'[98]

This seems a laboured explanation for the old-fashioned pleasure of smashing other people's property, but such are the burdens of respectability. Suspended between the government and the growing, anonymous mass of returned soldiers, the GWVA's leadership had become another official element in the business of re-establishment.

Amid internal conflict and schism, the GWVA was changing. There was less talk at the Toronto convention of 're-establishment' and more of 'reconstruction.' The distinction, in the language of the time, separated plans for the disabled from those for the able-bodied. The GWVA had begun as an organization of maimed and ailing veterans of war; the challenge before the association and its leaders was to represent all veterans. Even in the summer of 1918 few dared hope that the war would soon be over, but the defeat of the German spring offensives made an Allied victory seem inevitable. The CEF would be coming home, and the GWVA awkwardly prepared itself for a very different kind of repatriation.

5 The 'Department of Demobilization'

Civilian or Military?

By 1917 the Military Hospitals Commission was pleased with itself. 'I failed to see how a better system than this could have been enunciated,' Lougheed had declared in 1915, and nothing had changed his mind.[1] Even veterans seemed more content: 'We really think that the powers now are really trying to do for the returned soldier all they possibly can do,' the GWVA's Norman Knight had admitted in 1917.[2] There were imperfections. Lougheed had never much liked having to consult his commission and, after a particularly frustrating meeting in September 1916, members were not summoned again.[3] The provincial commissions also varied, from Alberta, where Howard Stutchbury was both efficient and compassionate, to Quebec, whose commission refused any responsibility beyond finding work, a task it delegated to a committee of employers.[4]

The MHC had been born out of the desperate improvisation of a country and government utterly inexperienced in war. In 1916 the prime minister had devoted time and energy to curbing the resulting inefficiency, much of it the responsibility of his defence minister, Sir Sam Hughes. By November Hughes himself was gone, so provoked by loss of control of the CEF overseas that he had forced Borden to fire him.[5] Hughes's successor, Sir Edward Kemp, was a rich Toronto industrialist and a veteran Tory with a pompous manner and tough, orderly mind. With the Militia Department under control, Kemp set out to restore its old authority.[6]

In 1915 Hughes had gladly sacrificed the care of army convalescents to an ad hoc agency. Medical matters did not interest him and the Canadian Army Medical Corps (CAMC) needed the help. In 1914, the corps had had only twenty permanent-force doctors and six hundred militia medical officers. The cream of the CAMC went overseas, leaving the obscure and uninfluential Major Potter in charge.[7] The MHC had relieved his burden, and the medical consequences seemed unimportant. The CEF's sick and wounded would complete their active treatment in England; convalescence could be supervised by volunteer nurses and local physicians. But such assumptions were soon obsolete. As we have seen, the MHC had to cope with tuberculosis, amputations, and, at the end of 1916, the sudden arrival of hundreds and then thousands of active cases.

The MHC had never been strong medically. The medical superintendent, Col. A.T. Thompson, was better known as a Yukon businessman and a Tory MP than as a physician.[8] The hospitals were staffed largely by militia medical officers who preferred to keep their civilian practices and help out part-time. If CAMC officers were not available, local politicians recommended appropriate civilian doctors.[9] By 1917 Canada faced a shortage of medical manpower. In 1914 eight thousand doctors had been too many for the available paying patients, but the CEF overseas absorbed about fifteen hundred, and four hundred more had volunteered to serve with the British or the French.[10] The doctor shortage had helped precipitate the turbulent Bruce inquiry into the CAMC overseas, and a comparable investigation of medical matters in Canada by Colonel Marlow, the eminent Toronto surgeon and gynaecologist who served part-time in command of the medical services of Military District No. 2.

A round-faced, earnest man of thirty-nine, Marlow had been a founding member of the CAMC in 1900. He was immensely proud of his corps, but loyalty to his female patients kept him from active service.[11] Marlow's report, issued in October 1916, had none of Bruce's sensationalism; it recognized the problems of inexperience and rapid growth, exposed the limitations of cramped, decrepit buildings inherited from the pre-war permanent force, and offered practical solutions to the problem of detecting defective recruits. Yet the core of Marlow's report, as one might have expected, was that the Military Hospitals Commission was an error overdue for correction. In principle and in practice it was wrong to put soldiers under civilian control. The MHC Command only aggravated the problem by putting junior combatant officers in charge of doctors and nurses. If details were needed, Marlow recalled the folly of using tiny convalescent homes, the scandal of the Minnewaska sanatorium, and the failure to anticipate the need for active treatment facilities.[12]

Like Bruce's report, Marlow's submission remained secret, circulating chiefly in the form of sensational rumours. Marlow's frustration grew. He remembered the crisis in late 1916 when Perley had tried to transfer thousands of cases to Canada, and Marlow easily persuaded himself that this was the evidence that would demolish the MHC. The price was his resignation. Canadians would be outraged that 'thousands of disabled Canadian soldiers who are unfit for futher service at the front but who have sufficiently recovered from their wounds to permit of their return to Canada, are being retained in Britain.' 'Patronage first, economy second and efficiency third,' trumpeted the headlines as Marlow explained his departure.[13]

For Kemp, Marlow's explosion was infuriating. He had worked discreetly on Lougheed, profiting from the senator's chronic indifference to the affairs of the MHC. On 28 February 1917, after securing Col. John Fotheringham, a prominent Toronto doctor serving in France, as a new director of medical services (invalids), Kemp reported that his department could resume the MHC's medical responsibilities. A board of consultants drawn from leaders of the medical profession would guarantee the highest standards.[14] Marlow had undermined everything, and Lougheed was furious. The 1917 parliamentary committee on returned soldiers could not avoid probing the charges. The transfer to the CAMC, which Marlow had wanted even more than his minister, was stalled. To his friend, the Toronto publisher John Ross Robertson, a weary Kemp complained, 'At least half my problems are due to men putting personal aggrandisement ahead of personal service.'[15]

The parliamentary committee gave Marlow a platform, but it did not necessarily give him an audience. Members of parliament were confused by the difference between active and other hospital beds, and they were slow to see any crime in the MHC's sending its serious cases to civilian hospitals.[16] The committee's travels took it to Montreal. At the Khaki League Homes, a tough-minded medical officer reported no trouble in asserting his authority, but the Grey Nuns Hospital was very different. The army officer in command, a former gunner, was a harsh disciplinarian who had built a 'clink' for unruly patients. His five part-time medical officers gave their civilian patients first priority and agreed that three hundred patients needed no doctor on duty at night.[17] The MPs were not impressed.

At Toronto, on 21 March, Marlow had a second and less happy session with the committee. Among the members was R.B. Bennett, Lougheed's law partner, a political and courtroom heavyweight with a habit of hectoring witnesses. Marlow was an easy victim. Why had he blamed the MHC when the CAMC had dreamed up the convalescent-home idea? Why had he condemned the MHC for sending invalids to live at home when he also claimed credit for devising the out-patient system? Why had he tried to embarrass the MHC over Minnewaska and the bed shortage when he plainly did not know all the facts? Ultimately, Bennett over-reached himself, accusing the CAMC officer of wanting Colonel Thompson's job. 'I never stooped to such a thing in my life,' shouted an outraged Marlow. As journalists scribbled, Ames moved to expunge the exchange while Marlow insisted that it remain on the record as evidence of his bad treatment.[18]

Fotheringham, now a major-general, was the Militia Department's key witness. The MPs found him a trifle pompous. Handing soldiers over to civilian doctors was 'an experiment of a most pronounced kind.' 'Frankly,' Ames replied, 'we are not very deeply impressed with the medical excellence of the Army Medical Corps as it has been displayed to us individually.'[19] Niggling interference by MHC officials was a more tangible concern: 'It is difficult,' Fotheringham said, 'for the lay mind to appreciate the annoyance of the professional mind caused by interference ... with purely professional matters.'[20] The point lost some of its weight when the general confessed that what was intolerable from the MHC would be wholly acceptable from CAMC officers. The military preoccupation with hospital discipline led one MP to wonder why citizens would be so hard to manage after time in the army. Had they become less disciplined? Fotheringham, an ardent militarist, found the questioning embarrassing.[21]

Five months of testimony led the special committee to make a host of recommendations, ranging from insurance for the disabled to a ban on 'indiscriminate and unauthorized appeals for funds.' On one issue the members were utterly divided: should there be military or civilian control of disabled soldiers? Ames, Bennett, and four Liberals insisted that such men were being prepared for civil life and the MHC was the proper authority to oversee that preparation; three Tories, F.B. McCurdy, W.S. Middlebro, and Donald Sutherland, argued that 'continuity of care' was the prime objective and only the CAMC could provide it. The majority wanted a new department 'under a Minister of the Crown' to take charge of the disabled; the minority called for a 'National Bureau' to co-ordinate measures for returned soldiers. Having reached a deadlock, both sides declared themselves 'reluctantly compelled' to offer no recommendations.[22]

Sir Edward Kemp was furious. The committee had not only delayed a decision, it had dared to dream up solutions that went beyond its mandate. Creating new departments was a matter for the whole government, he reminded Borden, 'and such a scheme should not be thrust upon it from outside in the manner which is proposed.'[23] By now the weary prime minister was fully enmeshed in the conscription dispute. General Fotheringham was left to cool his heels and complain about his salary.[24] For its part, the MHC was entirely satisfied with the special committee report. Witnesses who complained of 'militaristic' methods and negligent doctors confirmed the suspicions of army surgeons. The GWVA had endorsed 'civilianization' and a 'Department of Demobilization' to be 'conducted along strictly nonpartisan and business lines.'[25] With only slight adjustment, the commission could see its image in that mirror.

The MHC's satisfaction had some basis. During 1917, Samuel Armstrong's management ended the commission's amateurism. By the end of the year the commission boasted 115 institutions, 21 of them built that year. Seventy-one were run by the commission; others, ranging from the Khaki League Homes to the Ninette Sanatorium in Manitoba, were managed by provincial governments or private organizations. Sixteen hospital cars delivered patients across Canada. A publicity branch, recommended by the BPC's Major Todd, announced that the MHC institutions covered sixty-five acres of floor space and were served by 2,800 employees.[26] There would be more. The orthopaedic hospital and limb factory had already outgrown its new premises at Davisville. In 1918 it would move to a seven-acre site on Christie Street in Toronto that had been purchased from the National Cash Register Company.

Publicity was helpful in converting Canadians to the MHC's radical philosophy of self-help for the disabled; it was also a weapon of bureaucratic survival. The commission reminded anyone who mattered of British and American praise for its methods and philosophy.[27] That melted no hearts in the Militia Department. While cabinet ministers wrestled with conscription, railway bankruptcy, and the formation of a coalition Union government, Fotheringham and other CAMC staff did what they could to muster support. In Toronto, Marlow's successor won over local doctors by proposing a large military hospital close to the city core. The MHC preference for locating convalescents at Guelph and Whitby forced Toronto specialists, patriots though they were, to journey deep into the country to care for soldiers. At least the CAMC understood that non-paying patients should suit their physicians' convenience.[28]

On 5 October 1917, the day before Borden formed his new Union government, Lougheed summoned Fotheringham and the acting adjutant-general, Maj. Gen. Sydney Mewburn, to settle matters. The commission, he announced, would henceforth take over all medical matters affecting returned soldiers. CAMC doctors and nursing sisters who wished to continue with the MHC would, of course, be welcome.[29] Sir Edward Kemp would have none of it. Guided by Fotheringham, he replied that the MHC, 'conceived, no doubt, in good faith,' had usurped its responsibility.[30] The prime minister, now facing an autumn election campaign, hesitated again.

Within a week of receiving Lougheed's ultimatum, Mewburn had joined him as a cabinet colleague and minister of militia. As a novice minister, eager to end a silly dispute, Mewburn met Lougheed in Borden's office. Agreement seemed easy: the MHC would provide all facilities; a medical staff officer under the MHC command would be responsible for all medical personnel and civilian doctors would serve as temporary officers.[31] When Mewburn and Lougheed returned to their respective offices, they were soon made aware of their folly. The MHC officials insisted that they would be left with responsibility but no control; the CAMC would not tolerate subordination to the Hospitals Commission. At Vittoria Street, Lougheed reluctantly summoned his commission for the first time in fifteen months. Eleven members heard Mewburn issue his own ultimatum: the medical corps must manage everything but vocational training. MHC members responded with a fighting resolution: to abandon its role 'would cast an unmerited slur on its operations in the past, to which the Commission should not consent.'[32] Having created a three-member executive and having agreed to hold quarterly meetings henceforth, members adjourned in the mood of pleasurable defiance. But theirs was not the final word. On 1 December Fotheringham answered Lougheed's earlier ultimatum by withdrawing his medical officers from the discharge depot at Quebec and warning that CAMC officers would no longer run the MHC's medical boards. It was a shrewd blow; the commission's whole sorting process depended on the discharge depot and medical boards, and it had few doctors of its own.

As the implications sank in, word arrived of the terrible man-made explosion at Halifax on 6 December. As the force from the blast that destroyed the *Mont Blanc* roared across the harbour and slammed into the seaport city, fifteen hundred people died, five thousand more were badly hurt, and scores were blinded. At the MHC's Pier 2 the blast flattened walls, shattered glass, and ripped out plumbing. Pier 2 was empty at the time but, since Halifax was the only winter port with berthing facilities and railway connections adequate to receive hospital ships, repairs were urgently needed. Beyond Citadel Hill, the MHC's new Camp Hill Hospital was spared devastation, but 1,200 civil and military casualties jammed into wards designed for 280.[33] Later, the commisson's tireless publicists would report that well-trained dietitians and modern equipment allowed the commission to provide five thousand meals a day. In the crisis the MHC had justified itself.[34] It was eager to do more. Professor Sexton set his vocational trainees to tasks ranging from driving relief vehicles to repairing footwear for the homeless. Later, exasperated by such local suppliers as Hantsport's C.S. Chesley, the Halifax Relief Commission sought help for its amputees. By then, caution prevailed. 'So far,' warned the superintendent of the limb factory, 'it has been an unchangeable rule with the branch that it will not encroach upon the civilian trade.'[35]

Soldiers' Civil Re-establishment

By January 1918 the dispute between the CAMC and the commission had lasted twelve weary months. If the MHC had won the propaganda battle,

Fotheringham's control of medical personnel was now turning the tide. The sudden appearance of articles in rival Toronto newspapers, plainly inspired by the opposite sides, was a warning that unless the quarrel was resolved it would soon become a public scandal. [36] Mewburn proposed compromises; Lougheed rejected them all. [37] MHC devised ingenious theoretical arguments for civilian methods, but the real problem was that the Alberta senator was loath to abdicate his sole wartime function without a fight. [38] R.D. Gill, a latecomer to the MHC, suggested to Borden that he make Lougheed minister of militia and allow Mewburn to go to London as overseas minister in charge of the CEF in France and England. [39]

That was not possible, but it suggested a solution. In 1917 the Special Committee had split between military control and a 'Department of Demobilization.' Why not both? A year before, Scammell had argued hard for such a department, and the GWVA also had asked for one. The British precedent of a Ministry of Pensions would reassure worriers. Lougheed could become a full-fledged minister, and there would be places for the MHC staff. [40] At the Militia Department, Mewburn's successor as adjutant-general, Brig.-Gen. E.C. Ashton, a former Brantford doctor, had already recognized the basis for a solution. The CAMC argued for 'continuity of treatment,' but it lost interest once a man was discharged. In all the furore over military hospitals, no one had come to grips with the continuing medical problem of tuberculars, epileptics, the insane, and the incurable. If the CAMC absorbed such cases, the outcome, Ashton warned, would be 'confusion, the crowding of local and provincial charitable institutions, the congestion of existing hospitals, the retention in the military service of large numbers who should obviously be discharged, the cry for continual expansion of hospital accommodation without bringing us one step nearer the final solution of the problem.' [41]

Even when the answer was obvious, it took three more weeks of tiresome negotiations to have it settled. If any commission survived, Fotheringham insisted, it must not have 'military hospital' in its title. Lougheed stated that no hospital would be handed over without his personal agreement. Mewburn, aware of his colleague's tricky habits, argued for a deadline. Lougheed announced full agreement on 14 February though he took a further week to sign. On 21 February three orders in council created a Department of Soldiers' Civil Re-establishment, transferred most MHC hospitals to the army, and transformed the civilian organization into an Invalided Soldiers' Commission charged with managing vocational training, the provision of artificial limbs, and a range of modest chores performed under CAMC supervision. [42] On 1 March Scammell notified members of the old commission that their arguments had failed and the army medical corps had won. [43]

In the ensuing weeks, a total of 12,359 beds (one-quarter of them still under construction) were transferred to the CAMC, while 5,575 beds, most of them in sanatoria, were retained for post-discharge cases. There were inevitable strains. From Toronto, Gertrude Vankoughnet, the honourary superintendent of soldiers' comforts, complained that four automobiles supplied for the benefit of patients had been taken by army officers.[44] With ill-concealed relish, Samuel Armstrong referred her to the military authorities. Colonel Sharples, whose MHC command had been absorbed by the CEF in December, reassured a nervous subordinate that 'things will carry on pretty much the same as they are now.'[45] He was right. As with many a great battle, the aftermath of the CAMC-MHC struggle was anti-climactic. The CAMC gained less than it hoped and the MHC, in its new guise, could do its best work better. Working under civilian scrutiny gained the CAMC little glory or public esteem. 'In Canada,' wrote Sir Andrew Macphail, the official medical historian, 'the work was done with little hope of recognition, in an atmosphere of comment, criticism and suspicion. The grumbler, the malingerer, and the neurotic never failed to find an audience equally neurotic, and ready to lend an ear to murmurings and complaint.'[46] Scammell, in contrast, saw growth and exciting opportunities in the new department: 'as employment will loom larger in connection with our work, it is probable that in the end we shall have a bigger organization than we have even at the present time.'[47]

Macphail may have been right about collective neuroses. Years of promised but elusive victories had led only to the German offensives of the spring of 1918. When the tide turned, in August 1918, the price of spearheading the triumphant Allied advance was the heaviest Canadian casualty toll of the war. The mingling of collective hope and individual sorrow coincided with the arrival of the dreaded 'Spanish flu,' a mass epidemic that spread panic, death, and suffering across Canada. That the old and ailing should die was understandable; that the young and fit also fell victim was not. The toll in military hospitals could only be due, in the public mind, to the familiar villain, military incompetence and neglect. The Toronto base hospital – in the old General Hospital – admitted 2,100 influenza cases; 270 developed pneumonia and 90 died. These statistics were not unusual before antibiotics were available, but Mayor Tommy Church treated them as a public scandal, and a grand jury delivered a scorching denunciation of poor treatment, bad nursing, and inadequate accommodation. 'It was rather a brutal thing,' remarked the CAMC's local historian, 'for, as the people of the District were more or less hysterical, they were made to suffer severely and unnecessarily with the thought of their relatives dying for lack of care.'[48]

In bureaucratic terms, the influenza scandal was a blow to the victors in the CAMC-MHC fight. The army doctors had won fifty-one extra hospitals, but they were a wasting asset. 'The C.A.M.C. is a very different organization today from what it will be when the war ceases,' Lt-Col. Mackenzie Forbes had warned in 1917.[49] The flow of patients would stop; the best doctors would be desperate to revive their civilian practices and few of the remainder would find a place in the post-war Militia Department. The DSCR, as the new department was soon known, had at least a limited future. It inherited the jobs the MHC had done best – retraining, job placement, and long-term medical care. MHC officials moved easily into the new structure; Armstrong became deputy minister, Ernest Scammell became assistant deputy minister, and Segsworth continued as vocational director. Thomas Kidner, never at ease with Segsworth's brusque, businesslike approach, was loaned to the U.S. government's Federal Board for Vocational Training and soon joined the National Tuberculosis Association. To manage the department's remaining hospitals, Armstrong chose Lt-Col. Frederick McKelvey Bell, an Ottawa doctor who had been senior medical officer at Halifax during and after the explosion. No one could challenge his experience or proficiency. The department's eleven regional 'units' were based on Canada's military districts.[50]

An anomaly in the new structure was the MHC's direct successor, the Invalided Soldiers' Commission. Ostensibly created to manage the remaining MHC functions in military hospitals, it was soon indistinguishable from Lougheed's department. F.B. McCurdy, a young Halifax financier elected in 1911, was assigned to Lougheed as a parliamentary assistant after long, thankless experience in trying to help Hughes and Kemp at the Militia Department. As a senator Lougheed certainly needed help in the House of Commons, but McCurdy was not made welcome. He was appointed unpaid president of the Invalided Soldiers' Commission, and was given neither members nor responsibilities. McCurdy loyally soldiered on through the spring and summer of 1918, only to resign in the fall.[51] Armstrong, equally fed up, seized a chance to take a management position in Chicago. His successor, Lt-Col. Frank Healey, a thirty-year militia veteran, gave the DSCR headquarters a brief and illusory appearance of being run by veterans.[52]

Restoring the Disabled – Theory

The Military Hospitals Commission had functioned nicely without its political hierarchy; so would the new department. After his position was secure, Lougheed showed little interest in veterans' problems. Once philosophy and policy were clear, perhaps he was not needed.

It was certainly now evident, as it had not been before, that returned men came to the DSCR only after discharge and, for the most part, when medicine and surgery could do no more for them. The remaining hospitals were for men forever unfit for military service or for veterans who had relapsed after earlier release. Those veterans too severely disabled to return to former jobs could be retrained; the majority were sent on to provincial returned soldiers' commissions for help in finding work.

Having been almost overlooked in the shuffle of activities and institutions, the MHC's artificial-limb factory was acquired by Lougheed. The acquisition was a mixed blessing. Maj. R.W. Coulthard, the new head of the branch, insisted that Canadian artificial limbs were the best in the world. His clients, faced with the painful process of fitting and adaptation and deluged with seductive claims from a ruthlessly competitive private prosthetics industry, were not easily pleased. Artificial legs were awkward but adequate; there was no comparable substitute, however, for an arm or a hand. Many veterans concluded that an empty sleeve or a simple hook was preferable to complicated collections of pulleys, gears, and breakable parts.[53] Official propaganda put the onus on the amputee: 'The fact is the usefulness or otherwise of any artificial arm depends far more on the brains and character of the man who had it than on the perfection of the arm itself.'[54] This was, to put it mildly, an exaggeration.

Amputees were a minority, albeit a conspicuous one, among the categories of disability for which the MHC and now the DSCR evolved policies. At the end of 1918 one-quarter of the DSCR's 3,491 patients were tubercular; they benefited from a virtual doubling of facilities during the war, almost all of it at public expense.[55] So-called incurables – largely paraplegics – were far fewer than expected, and Euclid Hall, with its massive pipe-organ and space for forty patients, proved sufficient. Other institutions would be needed in the post-war transitional period, but in an age when medical and hospital treatment was sold for profit in a free market, elaborate safeguards would be needed to ensure that medical benefits, like pensions, would be dispensed only to the deserving. In wartime, it was still possible to give the benefit of the doubt.[56]

The one MHC function the CAMC never claimed was vocational training. In 1917 Segsworth had separated serious retraining from hospitals, but he was happy to continue with 'ward occupations' and 'curative workshops.' The University of Toronto's new Hart House, a gift of the Massey family, became a showplace for rehabilitation. Dozens of ingenious machines, devised by the university's mechanical engineering professors, helped rebuild muscles. The blinded Donald McDougall trained fellow veterans as masseurs. It was in Hart House that young women learned to be 'ward aides' to supervise the production of handicrafts by bedridden convalescents.[57] By the end of 1918 Sir Arthur Pearson's famous St Dunstan's

Hostel was replicated by Toronto's Pearson Hall, where blind veterans could learn both a trade and greater self-sufficiency. [58]

At Segsworth's insistence, the DSCR was as rigid as the old MHC in enforcing the 'disability line' as the criterion for retraining. However disabled, a veteran had no claim on a new career if he could possibly return to his old occupation. Even those who were eligible would be firmly guided into training that took full advantage of previous skills or experience. Economy was a motive; so was the continuing fear that prolonged training would entice the 'work-shy' and aggravate 'institutionalization.' How tough the criteria were was evident from the Vocational Branch's report at the end of 1918: of 43,362 veterans interviewed by Disabled Soldiers' Training Boards (DSTBs), only 9,223 were recommended for training. Segsworth's office approved a mere 8,004 courses. [59]

Former students – a small minority of the CEF ranks – posed a special problem. Even though the DSCR had the right to do more, Segsworth had no intention of using public money to allow veterans more than a short, career-oriented course. Harold Innis, a disabled gunner, sought help in pursuing his post-graduate work in economics at the University of Chicago. It was denied. A young soldier who merely wanted to complete high school fared no better. 'This lad,' said Segsworth, 'would not be training for a definite purpose at the Kingston Collegiate Institution.' [60] A happier exception was Sydney Lambert, an amputee, who was grudgingly supported in his training at Knox College as a Presbyterian clergyman.

Normally, training was limited to six or eight months, wherever possible on the job. Supervision, Segsworth maintained, would prevent exploitation, and a firm would have an incentive to retain a successful trainee. When courses had to be offered in technical and vocational schools, Segsworth needed no persuasion by the GWVA to insist that fellow veterans, not professional teachers, made the best instructors. He also believed that the school-day should conform to the hours of a normal workplace. Veterans were not children, and they were being 'taught how rather than why, therefore the instruction does not entail so much mental effort.' [61] Finding facilities was sometimes hard. In Manitoba the DSCR ran its own schools. The University of New Bruswick's patriotic offer of facilities turned out, on inspection, to be a dank gymnasium basement which a DSCR official pronounced unfit for a root cellar. 'Most of these start out with a blare of trumpets,' noted Norman Parkinson, Segsworth's assistant, 'and end up with very little.' [62] The DSCR acted on its own and rented an exhibition building in Saint John.

Ontario, big, rich, and better endowed with training facilities than any province, continued to pose the biggest problems. Alone among the provincial agencies, Ontario's Soldiers' Aid Commission had insisted on running vocational training, at Ottawa's expense. In Segsworth's opinion, the results were unsatisfactory. The man appointed by the Ontario commission as vocational officer, W.W. Nichol, was the product of a system that had 'completely dwarfed his imagination and initiative.' Instead of fitting courses to the men, Ontario officials shoved them into any available program. As a result, men were demoralized and employers resentful. [63] Finally, Segsworth had created a parallel organization, headed by his old friend Herbert Haultain and modelled on the University of Toronto and its engineering faculty.

The Ontario government, and particularly W.D. McPherson, chairman of the Soldiers' Aid Commission, was not pleased. Provincial control of university funds gave the government a lever, which it pulled. By late 1918, Sir Robert Falconer, the university's respected president, was caught between his provincial paymasters and the DSCR. Lougheed politely reminded him of the damage his institution might suffer if it refused help at a time when 'practically every other University in Canada is contributing its share.' [64] More to the point, the department dealt directly with McPherson. The result was a compromise: the DSCR would choose the courses and Ontario would provide the training. Segsworth's insistence that instructors 'should not have had any long experience in ordinary teaching methods' vanished from the final draft, but it survived in the spirit of the agreement. [65]

By the time of the Armistice the machinery for retraining and re-establishing the small army of disabled Canadian soldiers was in place. Industrial surveys, with their detailed job descriptions, had identified hundreds of occupations for the disabled, from sign-painters and movie projectionists to tractor mechanics. [66] Vocational officers had been trained in the importance of placement and follow-up. Helen Reid's pioneering work for the Patriotic Fund in Montreal had become a full-fledged DSCR social service department helping veterans and their families adjust to disability. Financial and industrial magnates, from Sir Edmund Walker of the Bank of Commerce to Lord Shaughnessy of the CPR, lectured employers on their duty to the disabled. Walker was sure that many a machine shop could use a one-legged or one-armed man with 'hardly any loss of efficiency.' [67]

As the DSCR often reminded Canadians, nine-tenths of the disabled would suffer from 'unseen diseases.' The most troubled (and troubling) would be those who suffered mental breakdowns. 'One hates to say it,' Dr C.K Clarke admitted to the 1916 pensions committee, 'but our country is so far behind in the care of the insane that we should be almost ashamed of ourselves.' [68] Canadians suppressed their shame by maintaining that the insane were victims of their own or inherited vice. Alcohol and syphilis, the MHC's Colonel Thompson had assured the 1917 committee, 'are the two great factors in insanity that is not altogether of an hereditary type, and even if you trace the hereditary insanity back far enough you would probably find its inception was due to either of the two influences mentioned.'[69] Such scientific reassurance was needed to counter a wartime feeling that soldiers should not share the fate of civilian lunatics. Surely it was the terrible strain of war, not liquor or venereal disease, that had driven heroes mad? Military authorities were also reluctant to admit that numbers of feeble-minded and insane volunteers had easily slipped into the CEF, though few had seen action.[70]

A society that regarded mental illness with horror and treated its victims with inhumanity had good reason to be concerned if war rendered sons insane. A primitive psychiatric profession properly rejected the popular diagnosis of 'shell-shock,' preferring the portentous letters NYD-N (or Not Yet Diagnosed – Nervous). By 1917 the term 'shell-shock' had even been banned from army medicine. Other terms – 'neurasthenia,' 'functional disability,' 'battle neuroses' – emerged from the professional need to reduce the inexplicable to categories. Were such disorders real or due to cowardly malingering? If real, could they be cured? If feigned, how was it that normal men were so deeply transformed by war?[71]

There were questions to which authorities in Canada could give no special answer. The MHC's sole expert was Capt. C.B. Farrar, American-born and trained, who had come to Canada in the summer of 1916 to take charge of a special camp for shell-shocked veterans in the Rideau Lakes. While the MHC sent insane soldiers to provincial asylums, public outrage had forced it to use the former Ontario mental hospital at Cobourg as a centre for shell-shock treatment. Therapy varied from whirlpool baths and electro-shock – the notorious wire brush – to sports. A former bank accountant allegedly had been cured by golf. Pickering College, as a classification centre for more conventionally mentally ill soldiers, helped sort out cases amenable to easy cure; others were returned to the provincial authorities.[72]

Treatment of the insane remained a storm-centre for the DSCR. Veterans protested, through the GWVA, the consignment of their comrades to the notorious public asylums. Some medical officers, caught up in the mental-hygiene movement, insisted that the army itself must protect society from 'mental defectives' and epileptics. Advising Sir Edward Kemp on the dimensions of the military-medical problem in Canada, Lt-Col. John McComb and Maj. John Russell warned that 'individuals of constitutionally inferior type will form a class of tramps, ne'er do-wells and criminals that history shows has always followed a war. If at large and allowed to procreate, they will beget their kind.'[73]

As one of its last acts, the MHC summoned provincial premiers or their representatives to Ottawa on 15 January 1918 to tackle the problem of absorbing fifty to sixty insane soldiers each month. It was not easy. Pre-war population growth and a wartime freeze on capital spending left many provinces with mental hospitals run-down and acutely overcrowded even by harsh contemporary standards. There was no more blithe talk of absorbing a patriotic burden. Lougheed offered $250 per patient per year and, after an afternoon of haggling, settled for $275 a year for subsistence, $75 for capital costs, and nothing at all for the new buildings needed for insane veterans. [74] As a sop to critics and as self-protection, the DSCR arranged for a cross-country tour of asylums by Captain Farrar and Dr C.K. Clarke, the controversial reformer who was the medical director of the Canadian National Committee for Mental Hygiene. The committee was also commissioned to devise a course for special social workers to provide after-care for discharged psychiatric cases. [75] The war had changed attitudes toward at least some of the insane, and the DSCR had to be careful.

Like the paraplegics at Euclid Hall, and the sad, resentful men in the sanatoria, the insane were among the 'incurables.' The marvel, insisted the DSCR, was how few of them there were after a war that had drawn 600,000 Canadians into uniform and left one-tenth of them dead. Scammell had insisted in 1915 that almost every returned man could be made self-sufficient; the DSCR believed that it could make that claim come true. Far from neglecting the problem of re-establishment, Canada was ready with a clear philosophy, articulated policies, and a range of institutions, from the Board of Pension Commissioners to the Great War Veterans' Association, to offer the disabled a mixture of sympathy, opportunity, and challenge.

When the Fit Return

There was, of course, one vast lacuna in planning for returned men: the able-bodied. Every agency, from the DSCR to the Great War Veterans, had been shaped by the disabled and their problems. With the Armistice hundreds of thousands of fully fit soldiers would return. What would be waiting for them?

In the early years of the century Canada had easily absorbed hundreds of thousands of immigrants in a season; now, returning soldiers would have enormous added assets in their family and friends. But in 1914 Canada had been deep in depression, with a hundred thousand men looking for work. [76] Recruiting and the new munitions industry had eliminated the manpower surplus. The provinces had cheerfully accepted the wartime responsibility of finding jobs for returning soldiers, but the post-war period might prove more difficult to deal with. At the MHC's regular meeting on 6 and 7

September 1916, commission members had focused on the problem. At Lougheed's inspiration they had urged 'a comprehensive Land Settlement Policy of an attractive character.' The inspiration for 'a National Highway' was less obvious but even more popular. With the dawning of the automobile age such a project would be 'a most practical memorial to Canada's part in the great War.'[77] No public work could absorb as many ex-soldiers at so small an outlay until the post-war economy could employ them. Scammell was satisfied. 'The machinery is so constituted,' he assured his South African counterpart, 'that I do not anticipate any very great difficulties at the time of demobilization.'[78]

Others were not so sanguine. The Borden government stubbornly refused any proposal that might make it the employer of last resort for veterans. When the National Service Board applied its data-gathering resources to determining the post-war expectations of CEF members overseas, it found that close to one-half expected to return to skilled urban jobs. Not only would such men have to be accommodated, warned the board's C.W. Peterson, but there would also be 'a problem of some magnitude to be solved in finding employment for an army of women now replacing men overseas.'[79] The board, created as an expedient to promote enlistment, had by now assumed responsibility for the labour-market implications of demobilization. A flutter of letters to employer associations, labour unions, and other organizations solicited advice. When, unions were asked, was the the best season to release men? Should soldiers be discharged by length of service or because they had jobs waiting? The best minds in Canada were 'needed to assist us in outlining plans that will provide machinery to deal reasonably effectively, at least, with the first shock of demobilization, having regard to economy as well as efficiency.'[80]

The NSB's involvement in demobilization planning owed much to the British example. Begun in 1916, British reconstruction planning had evolved by 1917 into a full-fledged ministry. The possibility that Germany might continue the war on an economic front, plus the marvellous potential revealed by wartime mobilization, excited planners. Visionary schemes for a New Britain, combined with the necessity of not disturbing old business and industrial arrangements, contributed to a wildly complex demobilization scheme. Soldiers identified as 'demobilizers' and 'pivotal men' would be the first out of uniform to help restore the industrial wheels to their peacetime tracks. Others would follow as the economy adjusted. No one noticed that the survivors of 1914 and 1915 would be the last to be released.[81]

Canadians were observers of the British planning. An avuncular Whitehall enquiry about whether 'self-governing dominions' had ensured that enlistments would not expire with the war and whether problems might arise if troops were kept for post-war duties provoked a starchy Canadian reply: 'The Government has the power, under terms of enlistment, to require six months' service after the war, but considers that this power should not be exercised except for Canadian military purposes.'[82] Planning for those or other purposes had a low priority in war-time Ottawa. Newton Rowell, the chief Liberal recruit in the new Union government, was the chairman of a cabinet committee on reconstruction whose members found their time devoured by routine and short-term crises.

Among the few federal politicians who addressed reconstruction was Sen. J.S. McLennan, the Cape Breton industrialist who had been among the MHC's hardest-working members. One reward was a 1918 visit to the second inter-Allied conference on the war-disabled in London. McLennan returned convinced that the DSCR would have to worry about the able-bodied as well as the disabled.[83] No one in Canada or Britain, he discovered, had addressed the problem of 'rusty skills.' Many CEF members thought of themselves as skilled workers, but wartime conditions had changed the standard of precision in industry from the 'footruler to the micrometer.' Without retraining, veterans would lose their jobs and become bitter and potentially dangerous drifters. The benefits of training, McLennan believed, would pay off over two generations.[84] Such messages were not welcome. The 1917 special committee dismissed the possibility of a post-war employment crisis with vaporous optimism: 'A new country like Canada, with vast unexplored natural resources, which we all believe will be developed after the termination of this Great War, contains countless opportunities for ambitious men to win their way.'[85] From the opposition benches, Sir Wilfrid Laurier denounced state intervention. A million Civil War veterans had been absorbed without difficulty: 'I would rather trust the manhood of the man, if he comes back sound in limb and body, than depend ... upon the existence of a paternal government.'[86]

The Union government had only a little less faith than Laurier in laissez-faire. Under the aegis of Rowell's reconstruction committee, a few proposals took shape: a $25 million 'Housing Fund' to be loaned to the provinces at 5 per cent, a trade mission to London to obtain post-war business. The Employment Offices Co-ordination Act, proclaimed on 24 May 1918, allowed Ottawa to pay half the cost of provincial employment bureaus. Both the wartime shortage and a possible post-war glut encouraged efforts to create a truly national labour market.[87] An earlier innovation was even more important for the CEF. On 18 April 1917 the Militia Department had belatedly introduced post-discharge pay. After regulations refined the system, soldiers who had served at least six months, part of it overseas, could claim three months' pay. Later orders extended the pay to the navy, denied it briefly to volunteers from the United States, and refused it altogether to former civil servants and members of the permanent force; since their jobs were guaranteed, they had no need of a financial cushion. [88] For the able-bodied, further examples of paternalism would be shunned. The sovereign cure for military discipline and dependence remained a brisk immersion in civilian life.

There was one exception to Ottawa's determination to let fit veterans seek their own survival. It was unprecedented and therefore unthinkable that a war could end without some effort being made to settle soldiers on the land. Tradition, mythology, and concern about rural depopulation overruled memories of the waste and failure of 'military bounty.' From the moment Senator Lougheed assumed the chairmanship of the Commission on Natural Resources in October 1915 (in tandem with the presidency of the MHC) a soldier-settlement plan was inevitable.

From the ancien régime until 1908, countless Canadian acres had been transferred to disbanded soldiers with remarkably consistent results. Either the resulting farms were lamentably poor or the location tickets disappeared into the hands of speculators. In either case the victims were blamed. A scornful Robert Gourlay reported from the military settlement at Perth: 'Soldiers in general choose their trade only to indulge in idleness and give rein to a roving disposition.' [89] Certainly military life fostered gregarious automata, not the inner-directed workaholics demanded by frontier conditions; but few old soldiers had the more basic requisites: capital, experience, arable land, and a little luck. [90]

Canadians had cursed the British custom of military bounty, but their own young dominion was just as extravagant: in 1870 and again in 1885 vast tracts of land in the Northwest were given to militiamen sent west to save Confederation; as usual, speculators were the main beneficiaries. In 1908, the Volunteer Bounty Act made available 2.3 million acres in Alberta and Saskatchewan to 7,340 male and female veterans of the South African War: only 657 of them even tried to become settlers. One melancholy consequence was that there was no longer remotely enough cultivable public land available for any future military bounty. [91]

That would not kill a tradition. With the certainty accorded unwritten law, soldiers and the public simply assumed that veterans would be offered farms. Ontario arranged to ship interned aliens to Kapuskasing to clear clay-belt land for soldier settlements. Other provinces explored schemes to locate returned men on abandoned farms or in Crown timber limits. The Natural Resources Commission seemed a fitting vehicle for developing a national settlement plan, and Lougheed's choice for its secretary, W.J. Black, the former principal of the Manitoba Agricultural College, was the logical man to work out the details.[92] Scammell's 1915 report had also reflected Lougheed's concerns. The war, he had warned, created problems as well as potential for repopulating the land: 'One difficulty to be faced will be that men from the country districts will be inclined to congregate in the larger centres.' On the other hand, 'large numbers of men who previously followed an indoor occupation, both those who are able-bodied and those who are partially disabled, will after their long open air life in the trenches, decide to find employment on the land.'[93] Whatever the basis of this intuition, Scammell proposed a system of loans, training, and land grants – but only for those who actually took up homesteads.

The MHC treated agriculture as a major component of rehabilitation and as an important form of retraining. The war-blind were encouraged to believe that they could make a living rearing poultry. Convalescent homes proudly displayed produce grown by patients. MHC propaganda claimed that a man with a wooden leg and sufficient fortitude would suffer no real handicap as a working farmer. The mythical and one-legged 'Private Pat' proclaimed: 'The country life's the life for me, with a cow and a hen and a honey-bee – and a few other things.'[94] Realists admitted that farming was heavy labour, but a DSCR handbook asserted that 'continuous hard work is not weakening but strengthening.'[95]

Soldier settlement was not exclusively a Canadian concern; the British also faced the demobilization of a huge army. Precedents from the Napoleonic and South African wars suggested that ex-soldiers might lead a mass emigration. Imperial-minded Britains wanted that vast movement kept within the empire. In 1916 the novelist, publicist, and imperialist Sir Rider Haggard circled the globe on behalf of the Royal Colonial Institute to promote British agricultural settlement. Lougheed sent Scammell to meet him in Vancouver and to escort him through a wearing series of speeches and banquets to Ottawa.[96]

On 11 July, as Haggard harangued sweaty but enthusiastic members of the Canadian Club in Regina, Lougheed unveiled the report of his Natural Resources Commission. Faithful to the concerns of the clamorous mayors who had inspired the commission, Lougheed and his colleagues agreed that 'there is [a] greater probability of settlers establishing new homes being able to make comfortable and satisfactory livings if engaged on the land than if employed in towns and cities.' Accordingly, the commission urged a settlement scheme designed for the inexperienced and the gregarious. Soldiers' colonies would be based on township-size blocks, with schools, churches, shops, and a recreation ground, and a central farm to train would-be settlers. A farming background was not required. Each township would be managed by a man of 'business ability' supported by 'working foremen.'

Settlers who accepted such a regime could look forward to a 160-acre farm and a loan of up to fifteen hundred dollars. [97]

Sir James found his colleagues utterly unenthusiastic. He had to prod the prime minister to have the report forwarded to the departments most affected. When Sir Rider Haggard arrived, the British visitor was politely received by several ministers and then reminded that six of Canada's nine provinces controlled their own public land and that Ottawa's own prairie land had largely been given away. Experts in the departments of Agriculture and the Interior politely noted that no vacant townships fit for farming were close enough to railway lines. Whatever the CPR might claim, group colonies had a persistent record of failure, and no prairie settler could survive on only 160 acres. [98]

There were exceptions. Howard Ferguson, Ontario's ebullient minister of lands and forests, concluded that the wretched internees at Kapuskasing had made enough progress in clearing land, and proceeded with his clay-belt colony. Five northern Ontario townships were reserved for the purpose and settlers were promised a hundred acres (one-tenth of them pre-cleared), five hundred dollars in loans for stock and equipment, and the prospect of a sawmill and a common pool of heavy farm machinery. A farming school at Monteith would prepare them for the adventure. [99] Ontario's example spurred Ottawa. So did internal cabinet politics and the external goal of an interprovincial conference on land settlement, scheduled to be held on 10-12 January in Ottawa. A cabinet committee composed of Sir Thomas White, W.J. Roche, the minister of the interior, and Martin Burrell, the minister of agriculture, and Arthur Meighen set to work on draft legislation. Lougheed was conspicuously absent.

By the time the Soldier Settlement Bill appeared in May 1917, veterans had contributed their views to the special parliamentary committee. At least some returned men were unenthusiastic about the program. If farming was so necessary, one Vancouver Island veteran observed, let 'slackers do it.' [100] Returned men had suffered enough. The GWVA, in contrast, demanded 320 acres for each man who had served overseas, a loan of $2,000 and access to all the arable land still held by the railways or available on Indian reserves. [101] As presented by W.J. Roche, the government's bill came close to the GWVA's expectations. A three-member Soldier Settlement Board could distribute an extra 160 acres of Crown land in addition to the 160 acres any homesteader could claim. The board could also loan up to $1,500 for stock, equipment, buildings, improvements, or more land, repayable at 5 per cent in twenty years. All undisposed-of government land within fifteen miles of a railway would be reserved for returned men. Roche boasted that the government was doing 'something for the able-bodied returned soldier.' [102]

It was not doing very much. Roche's maps and charts showed six million acres of available land on the prairies, most of it in Alberta and most of it, he had to confess, covered with forest, dense scrub, or swamp. [103] Veterans, said a Liberal backbencher, were being offered a gold brick. [104] In fact, they were being offered a harsh and exacting business opportunity temporarily sweetened by huge and unprecedented wartime farm prices. Not only would soldier-settlers have to be physically fit for their ordeal, they would have to demonstrate prior farming experience. J.G. Turriff, a liberal MP and a veteran Saskatchewan homesteader, warned that 'not one in fifty soldiers from Canada or from other countries who have not been accustomed to living on farms can possibly make good under this proposal.' [105]

Turriff's caution was ignored. The GWVA was first ecstatic over the plan and then indignant when the government, preoccupied by conscription, railway finance, and its own survival, promptly forgot all about soldier settlement. In October, when Borden formed the Union government, Roche retired to the Civil Service Commission and Arthur Meighen inherited his portfolio. Then, during the last three months of 1917, an election had to be fought. Only in January 1918, when it was almost too late to plan serious settlement for the year, did the government finally name the membership of the Soldier Settlement Board. It was undistinguished: Maj. E.J. Ashton was a CEF veteran, but he was better known as a Regina furniture dealer and undertaker; Charles Roland, a Winnipeg civic booster, had been secretary of the unpopular Winnipeg Patriotic Fund; the acting chairman, Samuel Maber, at least had had experience in the Dominion Lands Branch. *The Veteran*, reflecting the GWVA's disappointment, noted that of those who were named, two were 'delightfully and completely innocent of ... qualifications.' [106]

Whatever might be said of his colleagues, Maber knew his job. The land made available in Roche's legislation, culled by generations of homesteaders, would be hopeless for settlement. [107] On 3 April 1918, Meighen responded to Maber's pleas by reserving all dominion lands within fifteen miles of railway lines. Gradually, forest reserves, grading leases, school lands, Doukhobor grants, Indian reserves and Hudson's Bay Company allotments were made available for soldier-settlers. [108] The pressure to expand soldier settlement came from the GWVA. Few of the association's wartime members had homesteading ambitions, but the tradition of military bounty was too powerful to be questioned. As for the land shortage, the GWVA had an easy solution: expropriate homesteads held by speculators, corporations, and such 'enemy aliens' as Mennonites and Doukhobors. The GWVA was also enthusiastic about schemes for co-operative colonies and group settlements. At its 1918 convention, the GWVA complained that the 1917 Soldier Settlement Act was 'merely tinkering with a vast question.'[109] The veterans were right. Roche had considered the idea of purchasing land and reselling it to veterans. He had held back; the whole point of soldiers' bounty was that it would cost the government nothing. Moreover, from a business standpoint, both the investment and the risks of return would be staggering. It soon became evident that without land purchase, soldier settlement would be a trivial scheme. The venturesome Arthur Meighen might take the plunge.[110]

Neither Meighen nor the government would breach the principle that soldier settlement was a commercial undertaking. As was usual in Canada, the state acted because no private corporation was large or bold enough for the venture; the Soldier Settlement Board was simply a colonization company on a grand scale. The able-bodied and their friends might believe that they were heirs to the long tradition of military bounty, but time and brutal experience would show them the truth.

The government's promise of full re-establishment for its soldiers took many phantasmagorical shapes in the minds of potential beneficiaries, but its essence was brutally simple: returned men would have the renewed privilege of fending for themselves in a business-like, profit-driven society. Far from being an exception, soldier settlement would be part of the rule.

6 The Year of
the Bonus

Demobilization Planning

Whatever the eventual fate of veterans in Canada, they would first have to
be brought home. Despite prodding, the Militia Department showed little
interest in the problem of demobilization until 1918. Perley and the Overseas Ministry exhibited more initiative. In the spring of 1917 Sir Montagu
Allan and a committee of surplus officers began working spasmodically on
details. A small step was taken when twenty-two thousand Canadian wives
and children were persuaded to go home during 1917 and 1918; but twice as
many dependants remained overseas.[1] Gradually, a few principles evolved
for the post-Armistice period. Canadians at the front would sail from
France; troops would select one of twenty-two 'Dispersal Areas' scattered
across Canada to take their discharge; the order of return would depend on
length of service, with priority being given to married men. As Ames of the
Patriotic Fund kept insisting, husbands cost more than bachelors to
maintain.[2]

Another committee of more senior officers, meeting in London in June
1918, changed the plan. The complicated British scheme of 'pivotal men'
finally had its influence. Economic factors, not military considerations,
must guide Canada too. When the war ended, the entire CEF would have to
be reorganized on an occupational basis. To discourage jockeying for an
early return, information about pre-war skills would have to be collected
before the fighting ended. It was now out of the question to give priority to
soldiers who had seen the most fighting. 'There is only one Canadian Army
overseas,' the committee declared. 'The principle which underlies the control of this Force is that all Officers, N.C.O.'s and men must serve in France
unless the Government ... determined that a man's service in England is of
more value than if he served in France.'[3] Since the National Service Board's

1917 survey was out of date, the DSCR devised a new questionnaire, based on twenty-three occupational groups, and in October 1918 350,000 cards were printed.[4] For its part, the Militia Department began planning to reverse the increasingly efficient system it had devised for funnelling Canadian conscripts to the front. A 'Clearing Services Command,' responsible for the loading of ships and trains and the provision of conducting staffs, could surely adapt to moving soldiers home.[5]

For much of 1918, that seemed a remote prospect. The dreaded German spring offensives cracked the British and French armies and virtually eliminated a Portuguese army corps. The imperial war cabinet agreed that the war would last until 1920; all that would be possible until the Americans arrived in strength would be a few limited offensives. One of them required the Australian and the Canadian army corps to drive the Germans back from a vital rail junction at Amiens. On 8 August the two corps plunged forward, with powerful air and tank support, and almost cracked the German line. Before the offensive could bog down, the Canadian commander, Sir Arthur Currie, insisted on stopping and trying elsewhere. Through the rest of August and into September and October, the Canadians attacked continually, suffering their heaviest casualties of the war but, in the brutal calculus of combat, winning victories. The Australians, bled white but forced to rely on volunteers, came close to mutiny. Conscripts – 'MSA men' – filled the ranks of the Canadian Corps and kept it fighting. To the south, American divisions spearheaded assaults on a German army that was as exhausted as its major adversaries. By mid-October the worst year of the war for the Allies had become the year of victory.

In Canada, 1918 was the year in which the hardships of war finally came home. Food and fuel shortages were aggravated by labour shortages and failing crops. Politicians and publicists tried to lighten the war-weary mood with visions of post-war reform. The concept of 'reconstruction' was seized for a dozen rival causes. 'We cannot go back to old conditions, if we would,' cried Newton Rowell, 'and we ought not to, even if we could.'[6] Even Lord Shaughnessy of the CPR called for better relations between labour and employers.[7] In 1918 the crusaders for prohibition and women's suffrage had their dreams fulfilled. In practice, such reforms meant little to people fed up with regimentation, inflation, appeals to sacrifice, and the eternal gap between promise and fulfilment. Even when victory suddenly seemed close at hand, the prospect of peace coincided with the demoralizing scourge of Spanish influenza. The Armistice itself came to Canada as an anti-climax. On 9 November a rumour had sent people cheering into the streets; the war really ended two days later.

In much of Canada, 11 November was a cold, grey day. Borden was on the ocean, summoned to help formulate the empire's policy for the post-war world. Newton Rowell presided over the national thanksgiving service on the steps of the burned-out Parliament Building.[8] Then, with the acting prime minister, Sir Thomas White, in the chair, the cabinet met to contemplate the new problems of peace. In theory all the mechanisms for a return to normality were ready; in practice they had been deferred, forgotten, or set aside. At the DSCR, Colonel Healey had plainly been the wrong choice for deputy minister. The minister of labour, responsible for employment bureaus, had long since resigned. At the Department of the Interior, Meighen had finally recognized that soldier settlement simply had to be recast.[9] On 15 November White formally established a cabinet committee to cope with 'The absorption into civil life and occupation of discharged soldiers' and 'industrial labour conditions which may arise from industrial dislocation and readjustment.' J.A. Calder, the minister of immigration and colonization and a highly competent Liberal from Saskatchewan, took charge. The members included Lougheed, Rowell, Meighen, Thomas Crerar from Agriculture, and Sen. Gideon Robertson, the ponderous Tory trade unionist who had become minister of labour.[10]

Calder's committee became the heart of a congeries of advisory councils, co-ordinating committees, field secretaries, and publicity agents. Municipalities, women, trade unions, and the GWVA were invited to participate. A committee from the Union of Canadian Municipalities promised to co-ordinate local welcoming committees. The women's committee, under Mrs J.T. Robson of Winnipeg, struggled to avoid competition and rivalry among a host of women's organizations. A GWVA advisory council, composed of W.D. Tait, a McGill professor of psychology, R.B. Maxwell from Winnipeg, an ex-sergeant, and David Loughnan from Vancouver, reflected a judicious spread of ranks and regions. Only organized labour, preoccupied by its own post-war turmoil, failed to take its appointed place as an advisory body.[11]

The key figure in the Repatriation Committee was Herbert J. Daly, 'a brisk, bustling Ottawa businessman who believes that system is three-quarters of success.' A vigorous example of the new business élite, Daly had risen to the top in the National Cash Register Company in thirteen years. At thirty-six he was the president of James Ogilvy & Co., Murray Kay, and, as many depositors would soon realize to their cost, of the Home Bank. As a Catholic, Daly was a useful reminder that Presbyterians did not necessarily monopolize fiscal acumen in Canada. As an equally devout believer in business, Daly could be counted on to respect and support a return to laissez-faire.[12]

Under Daly and his assistant, Lt-Col. Vincent Massey, the Repatriation

Committee was a clearing-house for information and a rich source of advertising. 'Very quickly,' its first report warned, 'will the world realize how much easier it was to make war than to make peace.'[13] Canadians, it insisted, would have to be patient: 'It can hardly be expected that the natural processes of industry, guided only by the somewhat wayward compass of public demand, will secure the immediate reabsorption of the thousands of men and women whom the war caught up out of their former trades and scattered into new and temporary occupations. But Canadian industry is extremely adaptable, and with careful planning on the part of Governmental agencies and sympathetic co-operation from all classes of the public, it is hoped that the extent of unemployment and the length of the period of dislocation will be reduced to a minimum.'[14]

Unemployment would certainly be a problem. Within weeks of the Armistice Sir Joseph Flavelle had dismissed a quarter-million employees of the Imperial Munitions Board in a season when jobs were chronically scarce.[15] The crisis finally spurred the Department of Labour to establish the long-promised unemployment offices. By the end of December, half of the sixty-four labour exchanges were open and information clearing offices in Winnipeg, Halifax, and Ottawa made a faltering start in clearing nationwide labour market information.[16] The DSCR responded by creating an Information and Service Branch, headed by Maj. L.L. Anthes, the chairman of the Toronto branch of the Canadian Manufacturers' Association; Anthes was assisted by T.A. Stevenson, a Toronto union leader. The new branch would station representatives at each government employment office to protect the interests of returned men. Other officials would be assigned wherever demobilized soldiers might seek information about pensions, soldier settlement, or the War Service Gratuities that now replaced post-discharge pay. Two officers of the branch were sent to England, and others were dispatched to travel on troop-ships, lecturing and distributing pamphlets. As with Daly's committee, Anthes's branch would be more involved with propaganda and exhortation than with substantial aid.[17]

In practical terms, the most difficult problem in repatriation planning was simply getting Canadians home. The war had ended in the most inconvenient way. The German army was beaten but intact. An armistice, by definition, was not permanent; hurried Allied demobilization might bring the Germans back. The Canadian Corps, whose 3rd Division reached Mons on 11 November 1918, was expected to provide two divisions for the Allied occupation of the Rhineland. Meanwhile, soldiers and dependants who could be repatriated faced the Atlantic at its midwinter worst in troop-ships stripped of every comfort. Only Canada's winter ports would be available, and, to the planners' surprise, the real limiting factor of repatriation was not shipping but the worn-out, undercapitalized railways. No more than twenty thousand passengers a month could leave from Halifax, or ten thousand from Saint John. [18]

Given the constraints, in what order would the men go home? Within two months a series of bloodless mutinies had persuaded the British to abandon their system of 'pivotal men' and 'demobilizers' in favour of demobilization based on length of service. [19] In Canada, employers, unions, and even veterans persisted in demanding that economic factors take precedence. Speaking for its sixteen thousand members, the GWVA's executive insisted on 'the vital necessity of the most careful and unhurried demobilization in order that every reasonable provision and assurance of training and employment be given to the returned soldiers.' Dumping hundreds of thousands of ex-soldiers on the Canadian labour market in mid-winter guaranteed hardship; W.P. Purney asserted that 'a further enforced absence of a few months would be fully compensated for in returning to Canada when conditions would be more favourable.' [20]

For his part, the corps commander had very different priorities. Sir Arthur Currie soon abandoned his dream of displaying 'the most wonderful fighting machine in the world's history' in a grand review on the Plains of Abraham, but he did insist that the infantry battalions and artillery batteries of the Canadian Corps must return intact to the towns and cities that had bade them farewell. [21] A 'first over, first back' policy would rob the CEF of cooks, clerks, and others who had served in safe occupations. The troops, Currie claimed, shared his feelings: 'I have yet to hear a single instance in which the men do not express not only a preference but an intense desire to return to Canada by units.' [22] The general had a more powerful argument than sentiment: discipline. Throughout the war, civilians and even some soldiers had worried about the impact of wartime savagery on a soldier's character. Reorganizing the corps for demobilization, putting men under strange officers, would weaken the bonds of discipline when they should be strongest. Currie offered his own passionate warning: 'Discipline has been the foundation of our strength, and the source of our power. It has been the principal factor in the winning of our battles and is worth preserving for the national life. For God's sake do not play with it, for you are playing with fire.' [23]

Pressed hard by the absent prime minister, alarmed by Currie's warnings, and assured that Australia had adopted a similar policy, Ottawa accepted a compromise: major units in the corps – 100,000 men – would return under their own officers, with some shuffling of personnel to allow them to be disbanded in a single dispersal area. The rest of the CEF would be formed in drafts based on locality and length of service. Married men would have priority; special occupations would not. One victory was not enough for Currie; he insisted that Canadians in France and Belgium must pass through England for a farewell to friends and relatives. The War Office, with many problems of its own, grudgingly added 125,000 Canadians to its cross-channel shipping load.[24]

Shipping Problems

During November and early December, the Canadian Corps moved to its post-Armistice position. The 1st and 2nd Divisions crossed the Rhine at Cologne and Bonn on 13 December and settled down with varying degrees of resignation to await relief. The rest of the corps stayed in Belgium. Officers organized sports and courses. The Khaki University, an adult education program launched by the Canadian YMCA in 1917, donated textbooks and assistance. At Ripon in Yorkshire, the Khaki University offered matriculation and university courses, and three hundred Canadians with partially completed degrees attended British universities.[25]

Educational pursuits were an inadequate distraction for men bent on going home. Arrangements for repatriation rushed ahead. Once Currie's views had been absorbed, two big camps in Surrey, Bramshott and Witley, were assigned to corps units. Soldiers' families would be sent from the former convalescent depot in Buxton, near London, while other 'concentration camps' served miscellaneous drafts. Since one of the more certain means of preventing the 'pension evil' was detailed documentation and careful medical examinations on discharge, soldiers would pass through a bureaucratic maze before enjoying a two-week embarkation leave and a short wait for a ship.[26]

Theory struggled with reality. Demobilization took place in a world turned upside down by war and revolution. Influenza had invaded Britian as well as Canada; by March 1919 half the population had been affected. The virus coincided with the coldest winter in memory. Miners, dockers, seamen, and even the police marked the return of peace by striking for higher pay.[27] Canadians reflected the turbulent mood. Post-armistice riots at Witley, Bramshott, and Kinmel were attempts to pay off old scores. A brief mutiny at Nivelles in Belgium on 17 December showed that even Currie's corps was not immune.[28] Negligent officers and sagging discipline explained riots and mutinies; they were also factors in the miserable voyage of the troop-ship *Northland*. When soldiers landed at Halifax on Christmas night, waiting journalists found plenty to report. A difficult crossing, two cold, unappetizing meals a day, decks reserved for officers and civilians, filthy sanitary conditions, and a cold, hungry Christmas day in quarantine added up to a scandal. The government moved fast. A royal commissioner, Mr Justice Frank Hodgins, reported within a month. His report excoriated the crew, soldiers, and conducting staff on the *Northland* and ensured that later drafts would come home in greater comfort.[29]

Politicians in Ottawa could feel righteous, but the *Northland* affair made repatriation more difficult. Canada now insisted on shipping standards even Americans did not expect. A sadder case was the *Scandinavian*, a dependant ship that sailed on 28 December. Of 1,175 passengers, 282 were children, 174 of them under twelve. As the steamer headed into the worst weather of the winter, conditions in the overcrowded third-class quarters were nightmarish: seasick mothers, wailing children, blocked latrines. A YMCA worker and two nursing sisters did their utmost; the ship's medical officer, a CAMC major, allegedly stayed drunk. Four first-class passengers gave up their cabins to sick mothers; the captain thought it unreasonable to ask for more volunteers. By the time the *Scandinavian* docked in Saint John, two soldiers and two mothers had died, leaving four children orphaned.[30]

Even though officials maintained that unhappy passengers of the *Scandinavian* could take their grievances to the steamship company, that the medical officer had been sober, and that the hospital sergeant had not fondled women's breasts, changes did ensue. The government undertook, retroactive to 11 November, to reimburse dependants for a third-class passage and rail fare to a Canadian destination and to transfer responsibility for dependants from the Militia Department to the Department of Immigration and Colonization.[31] Better food, medical care, and recreation, to say nothing of better weather, made later voyages easier if never pleasant. J. Obed Smith, the dominion immigration commissioner in London, wasted no sympathy on his hapless charges: 'Just so long as the ocean gets rough in bad weather and people suffer from mal de mer and many travel third class who never travelled that way before, these complaints will continue.'[32]

The kind of patient forbearance Smith expected was scarce among Canadians in England in the winter of 1919. 'One cannot blame the soldiers for kicking and complaining,' said the overseas minister, Sir Edward Kemp.[33] He was doing so himself: 'You are living in paradise in Canada as compared with this place.'[34] The CEF had become an army of homesick civilians, cold, restless, fed up, and constrained only by fear of losing their place in the demobilization queue. The compromise over Currie's demands meant that thousands of men from miscellaneous drafts waited at Kinmel, a vast, dreary camp on the rain-sodden hills of North Wales. Their exasperation mounted with news that the 3rd Division, full of MSA conscripts, was already embarking at nearby Liverpool, and reached its peak when a large draft learned that its ship had been cancelled because it had failed the standards set by the *Northland* enquiry. The result was a two-day riot on 4 and 5 March 1919 that cost five Canadian lives before it ran out of steam.[35]

The men gambled that the rioting would bring ships, and they were right. While the London *Times* matched the gutter press in spreading fantasies of rape and murder by drink-crazed Canadians, most of the rioters left for home.[36] The British authorities even made available one of their few 'monster ships.' the huge liner *Olympic*.[37] In April, when strikes and a prolonged Easter holiday again delayed sailings, there were more disturbances in Canadian camps. In May there was a further rampage at Witley; in June, a riot at Epsom ended in the death of a British police sergeant. When the king expressed his deep displeasure at the event, Canadian officials had a chance to present their own grievances against His Majesty's government and subjects.[38] Once again, the British found more ships. By the end of the summer, repatriation was virtually over.

Not all of the Canadian soldiers chose to return. Concerned by the potential loss of population in Canada and the likelihood that CEF members would fail to succeed in England and would clamour belatedly for repatriation, Kemp made it as hard as possible for a soldier to be discharged in Britain. In the end, 15,182 CEF members signed away their right to a free passage to Canada, joining another 7,136 who had been discharged during the war. They were outnumbered by 24,753 'imperials,' who chose Canada. In all, 267,813 Canadian soldiers and 37,748 dependants crossed the Atlantic in the year after the Armistice. Only a handful of convicts in British prisons remained as sad vestiges of the enterprise that began at Plymouth on 13 October 1914.[39]

Soldier to Civilian

Canadians waited nervously for their returning heroes. Underneath the hope and excitement were fears that army life and warfare had brutalized sons and husbands. Had young men been perverted by a sinful Europe? Had they been contaminated by the strange Bolshevik notions that had seemingly undermined German resistance?

The Repatriation Committee shared the anxiety. 'The Socialists are having too much to say in the Veterans' Association,' complained Herbert Daly. There should be a 'Soldier's Trouble Bureau' with staff to meet returning soldiers and encourage 'a proper line of talk.'[40] Returned men needed money in their pockets. Years of pressure had raised the soldiers' clothing allowance to thirty-five dollars, but that was little enough when a respectable suit cost forty-five dollars. On 18 December 1918 the government finally announced a War Service Gratuity: three or more years overseas entitled a soldier to six months' pay at a minimum rate of seventy dollars a month for a single man; a married private would have one hundred dollars. A year's service in Canada earned the minimum gratuity, seventy dollars. Another grievance, the cost of bringing dependants home from England, was satisfied in January.[41]

Though Ottawa had contributed to the shipping delays in England, it wanted no hold-ups on its own side of the Atlantic. Ottawa was no more eager than Whitehall to welcome the *Olympic* and other 'monster ships'; their loads of five thousand passengers easily swamped facilities at Halifax. The militia's clearing services and the railway companies insisted on smaller liners that could be emptied in a couple of hours. A devastated and overcrowded Halifax simply had no place to shelter held-over homesick troops. Until the spring break-up, Halifax and Saint John were the only Canadian ports available, though a few ships destined for the Pacific trade carried men to Vancouver via the Panama Canal. The harbour facilities of Portland, Maine, were made available for hospital ships. In principle, Saint John was reserved for 'dependant ships,' and shiploads of unaccompanied men were to land at Halifax. In practice, no such distinction was possible. Troops disembarked in their 'dispersal drafts.' At the gangplank, officers checked landing cards and issued five-dollar bills as 'train money.' As one train was loaded another was shunted into place in the vast Pier 2. Halifax's North Station, left roofless by the 1917 explosion, served as a marshalling yard. Officers soon boasted that they could load and dispatch a thousand men an hour.[42]

On shipboard the men carried no arms, but rifles and bayonets were reissued to Canadian Corps units to guarantee the brave show hometown crowds expected. As the CEF battalions and batteries paraded from the railway station to the armouries, the bonds of discipline fell away. Sometimes ranks dissolved in the throngs of relatives, friends, and well-wishers, leaving civic dignitaries with their speeches unread. The command 'Dismiss!' was the last order most men ever intended to hear from the army.[43] Soldiers of Winnipeg's 27th Battalion were asked if they would mind staying in uniform until the city's general strike was over. They would mind very much indeed and the unit was disbanded like the others.[44]

After a night at home, men from CEF units and the miscellaneous draft shared their final experience of military administration at local dispersal stations. Soldiers handed in equipment (little notice was taken of missing items) and moved down rows of tables as they were issued with back pay, a service badge, a discharge certificate, the first instalment of their War Service Gratuity, the clothing allowance, and, if they needed it, a transportation warrant. The larger the depot, the faster the process; Toronto's dispersal station boasted that it had speeded up discharges from two to eight per minute by June.[45] Once released, the new civilian met railway officials, cashed his cheques at an improvised bank, and ran the gauntlet of benevolent societies eager to dispense coffee and advice. The chaplains' services distributed a booklet of welcome from assorted Christian and Jewish religious leaders. A detachable front page could be filled in and returned so that pastors would be advised of lost sheep returning. The DSCR's Information and Service Branch was on hand to provide details of pensions, soldier settlement, and employment offices, and, as Scammell recalled, as a 'tranquilizing influence.'[46]

Soldiers with dependants were discharged at the port of arrival, often as their families were being interviewed by immigration officials. However chilly the welcome awaiting war brides from their new families and communities, they were an immediate focus of concern for voluntary groups. The YWCA and the IODE organized canteens at ports and railway stations. The Red Cross provided a trained nurse for each trainload of dependants; the Rotary Clubs organized cars and drivers; the Boy Scouts carried luggage. Officials from the Canadian Patriotic Fund issued advice and occasional small sums of money to hapless or improvident families who had failed to realize that they must buy their own food for the interminable journey across Canada. For the frugal, the Clearing Depot at Quebec sold food packages for $1.50: a couple of tins of meat, jars of jam and peanut butter, and a packet of soda biscuits would keep two people for two days.[47]

On the whole, procedures in Canada were smooth and efficient. Winter storms delayed trains. Bootleggers and 'runners' at Quebec defied the prohibition law and sold bad whisky to thirsty soldiers. There were complaints that at least one trainload of soldiers arrived 'fighting drunk.'[48] The painstaking efforts to welcome CEF members did not always extend to those Canadians who had served as British army reservists or in the Royal Air Force or to the thousands who had spent the war in British munitions factories.[49] By good management as well as luck, 827 special trains brought soldiers and their families home without accident. Without significant difficulty or delay, a third of a million soldiers had become civilians. Some, still under treatment for venereal disease or with unfinished dental work, would be treated by army doctors or dentists, and many more would file claims for back pay, gratuities, or lost personal possessions. Otherwise, veterans were no longer the responsibility of the Department of Militia and Defence.[50]

A host of federal, provincial, and municipal agencies took over. Five federal departments shared responsibility for the returned men; the Civil

Service Commission would administer the new program of 'veterans' preference.' Each of the provinces boasted of its determination to help ex-soldiers. Alberta and Saskatchewan promised free education for the children of dead soldiers; Manitoba voted to extend soldiers' property tax relief until its veterans were re-established; New Brunswick devised a scheme to settle disabled soldiers on small holdings; British Columbia promised twenty-two thousand acres in the interior to its veterans.[51] Towns and cities urged wartime agencies to continue their good works. Toronto's Repatriation League invited citizens to volunteer their services, one for each of the city's returned soldiers.[52] 'Mother Molson' announced that her Khaki Club would stay open to help ex-soldiers feel at home with old comrades, and the YMCA's Red Triangle Huts followed suit.

Finding work proved to be less of a problem than anyone had expected. Shipping delays had kept many men in England until spring. Most found their own jobs while others, to the dismay of the righteous, gave themselves a holiday on their War Service Gratuity. This was probably just as well, since it was easier to open employment offices than to make them useful. Joint federal-provincial jurisdiction over the offices did not help, nor did the lack of qualified staff. Anthes reported that 'the Provincial Governments have not been judicious for the most part of their selection of representatives.'[53] Anthe's own branch was not perfect. A flying visit to Vancouver revealed that his staff were so busy pursuing their own get-rich-quick schemes that they were neglecting their proper clients. In Manitoba, veterans had to wait for Ottawa to resolve a bitter jurisdictional dispute between the province's Liberal minister of labour and the eminent Tories of the Returned Soldiers' Manitoba Commission. Job-finding for ex-soldiers, insisted the commission, was its responsibility; the province angrily disagreed.[54]

Such problems made little difference to the employment situation. Jobs were available in 1919. The Information and Service Bureau reported 130,000 applications and placed 111,001 workers, one-quarter of them in manufacturing and one-sixth in civil service jobs.[55] 'It is a matter of common knowledge that there was no glut of the labour market in Canada during demobilization,' said Francis Carman. 'The reasons for this fortunate state of affairs are in part to be found in the world-wide demand for Canadian products; but in part also in the measures taken by the government with a view to preventing the flooding of the labour market.'[56] Since governments not infrequently fail, their triumphs should be recorded.

As a gesture of good will, Ottawa permitted returned men to claim a year's free medical care – without pay and only so far as the facilities of the DSCR's hospitals and treatment centres permitted. The gesture was not wholly altruistic; generosity might avert many a borderline 'moral claim' and, noted an official publicist, 'where that is the case it is one of the teachings of history that it is exceedingly difficult to resist a demand for pension.'[57] Heroes they might be, but already a grateful nation was bracing for the onset of symptoms of veteran greed and the pension evil. Walking a second mile might avert a longer journey later. Indeed, it did not take long for Canadians to become suspicious of the men restored to them. Out of a population of 8.5 million, more than half a million had been marked by an experience their fathers and grandfathers had never known, one that could not have been beneficial. Knowledgeable experts advised against coddling ex-soldiers. Col. Alexander Primrose, the first post-war president of Toronto's Academy of Medicine, warned colleagues about his former comrades: 'They have become accustomed to having everything done for them, they lose all ambition and have no desire to help themselves.'[58] Brig.-Gen. J.A. Gunn, the founder of Toronto's Repatriation League, warned that ex-soldiers had suffered a dangerous psychological transformation: 'As I have said his training had been to think of nothing but killing the Boche. Every other thought has as far as possible been excluded from his mind. His whole habit of thought has been changed from what it was in civil life. He has not had to worry about any of the responsibilities which form part of civil life. To a very great extent, he has been relieved from instituting things and above all that self-interest which is essential to success in civil life has been suppressed.'[59]

Gunn and Primrose were a long way from the ranks of the CEF. Veterans were anything but a homogeneous group. In age they ranged far beyond the official span of eighteen to forty-five; in service there was little in common between the 'Old Originals' of 1914 and the young conscripts who joined famous battalions only after the fighting was over. Returned men perceived a deep distinction between themselves and those who had stayed in Canada. Front-line soldiers despised men who had found themselves 'bomb-proof' jobs behind the lines. The emphasis on equality in veterans' organizations underlined how deeply the privileges of officer status had annoyed other ranks in the CEF. Yet some generalizations are possible. The 1919 DSCR survey of soldiers overseas found that 83.9 per cent claimed no more than a public-school education; a mere 1.5 per cent had attended university.[60] By common observation, veterans returned with a predilection for short hair, regular showers, and clean clothes, to say nothing of the minor vices of swearing, drinking, and gambling (and the fungus of athlete's foot).[61] Soldiers had shared in the profoundly modernizing experience of submission to a vast, highly regulated bureaucracy. Many survivors would not reminisce about experiences they preferred to forget; others, not always the most heroic, were 'line-shooters,' full of tales. To escape the memory of Flanders' cold, many fled as far as British Columbia and even California. [62]

Everywhere, restlessness was the common characteristic of the returned soldier. It was as much a part of war as a wooden leg, claimed the journalist and veteran George Pearson. 'It is that terrible restlessness which posseses us like an evil spirit; the indefinite expression of a vague discontent, the restlessness of dying men, little children and old soldiers.' [63] Colonel Bell, the DSCR's medical director, explained that soldiers had been used to rapid changes of environment: 'It cannot be expected that he will settle down to the humdrum existence of civil life, or that his initiative may be invariably relied upon without judicious encouragement.' [64] Soldiers had lived in a passionate present, spending their pay as though there were no tomorrow because, quite literally, a future was a prize beyond their means. Even far behind the lines, soldiers knew that the holocaust of the trenches lay between them and a normal life. Unexpectedly, on 11 November, their future was restored. As lottery winners discover, the grand prize can be a disequilibrating blessing.

Employers were the first victims. Restlessness undermined Scammell's assumption that most men would go back to their old jobs. Even patriotic employers who offered promotion and wage increases to veterans, were spurned. Bryce Stewart of the Employment Service complained that returned men tried for any kind of job, qualified or not: 'It is a mental attitude that unfits him.' [65] Pierre van Paassen, a Dutch-born theology student who had joined the CEF, recalled his own post-war mood. 'There had been a thunderstorm and the atmosphere had failed to clear. It was the same petty, monotonous, joyless, suffocating world of three years before, only now I was more intensely aware of it.' [66] The DSCR urged tolerance on the part of employers and patience on the part of soldiers, but few paid much heed. Late-returning veterans found that job-hunting was easier if they left their service buttons at home. 'Mother Molson' complained of ex-soldiers 'unwilling to help themselves': 'The present conditions invite gatherings in low surroundings, which are nothing but breeding places for Bolshevists and Revolutionists. A walk through certain districts of Montreal will reveal that a surprisingly large number of returned men live anything but right and honourable lives.' [67]

A British veteran recalled 1919 as 'the year of disillusionment.' [68] Returned Canadians contrasted the frigid reality of Canada with the homeland idealized from afar. Civilians harped on the misery of meatless Fridays or fuelless Mondays, but soldiers, who had seen a drab Britain or a ravaged France, found a people who had done very well out of the war. Only soldiers and their families, made threadbare by a tight-fisted Patriotic

Fund, seemed to have missed out on affluence. Wartime inflation had halved the value of the dollar, but most Canadians had adjusted and in many cases improved their income. The soldier's pay, $1.10 a day, was unaltered from 1914.[69] To veterans, the automobile was a symbol of luxuriant wealth: motor vehicle registrations had soared from 69,598 in 1914 to 341,316 in 1919. Most of these were private cars, often worth more than an 'Old Original' had earned for his entire war service.

History keeps little record of those who did fit in. Most CEF veterans found their way to old or new jobs and quietly resumed their lives. Soldiers who left records or diaries of wartime service rarely had much to say of their post-war experiences. A professional photographer in a small Ontario city reopened his studio and resumed business. An army mechanic started a trucking business with war surplus vehicles. If they chose, civil servants, teachers, and other public employees could easily return to their former work. Compared with the veterans of a later war, few CEF members had acquired marketable skills. Flyers were an exception, though supply exceeded demand. Most men tried to fit in. One soldier found temporary work as a carpenter at the University of Toronto. Thirty-five years later, when he was forced to retire, he was denied the pension the university paid its 'permanent employees.' Would he have fared better if he had never enlisted? It was a question most veterans sooner or later asked themselves.[70]

The question was not hypothetical. Businesses abandoned during the war could not be rebuilt. Professionals found that clients had deserted them for stay-at-home rivals. Battlefield surgery and morning sick-parades were irrelevant to middle-aged physicians compelled to rebuild a practice or to young doctors such as Frederick Banting, hurriedly qualified in wartime courses, who had no practice at all. John Todd had predicted that 'the fact that former sailors, soldiers and their families are protected against risks of death, accident and ill health will inevitably lead towards the extension of social, health and life insurance to all citizens.'[71] The inevitable would take a long time. Briefly, medical associations contemplated state-run medicine for the poor – if only to provide work for former medical officers. The interest soon faded. Veterans themselves might have had reservations after their foretaste of 'state medicine' in the army.[72]

The war had brought domestic tragedy and marriage breakdown to many families. Canada's stringent divorce laws encouraged bigamy and desertion and caused a great deal of misery. It was easier to blame the war for husbands who abandoned faithful wives or for wives who had turned to prostitution or other men.[73] Crime, drug addiction, and alcoholism were all part of the heritage of military service. So too was the seeming radicalism of the veterans' organizations, which railed against profiteers or demanded public ownership or intervention in housing, education, and health services. Less apparent but more profound was the conservatism of the returned men. Their sacrifice had earned them a stake in their country. Veterans, in Howard Palmer's phrase, saw themselves as 'guardians of national orthodoxy.'[74] In their resolutions, veterans espoused a racially exclusive citizenship in which Asiatics were even more unwelcome than Germans. Returned men never challenged suffrage for women, but they bitterly resented the most obvious by-product of that reform, prohibition. Temperance forces could always find a soldier-spokesman, but veterans formed the core and essence of the Moderation Leagues that struggled to reverse the ban on liquor.[75] Veterans were equally firm in demanding that working women give way to men, unless widowhood or poverty made a job an economic necessity.

Many returned men consciously obliterated memories of their service, shunning veterans' organizations and Armistice Day ceremonies, and claimed neither pensions nor benefits. To post-war policy makers, they set an example more should have imitated. Col. Clarence Starr, returning early in 1919, urged waiting reporters to forget about the war: 'The sooner we in Canada get away from military titles and everything connected with the war, the better it will be for the country and the average citizen.'[76] This advice was easily given by a prominent orthopaedic surgeon; for his humbler comrades, it was hard to take. Disillusioned by the country they had defended, former soldiers lived off their gratuities, clung together, and kept hoping for some of the pleasures they had expected peace to bring. 'We had grown so accustomed to being treated as mere automatons,' Van Paassen recalled, '... that we all seemed to be waiting for the next word of command.'[77]

Organization and a Bonus

If returned soldiers wanted to stick together, they had a choice of organizations to join. Size, status, and an Ottawa headquarters gave the Great War Veterans an enormous advantage over the Winnipeg-based Army and Navy Veterans. On 10 October 1918 some of the Torontonians who had failed to drag the GWVA into active politics officially launched the Grand Army of Canada, an organization pledged to open membership, independence, and a network of co-operative stores and factories to help veterans re-establish themselves.[78] The special problems of British veterans and their families led to the almost simultaneous formation at Winnipeg of the Imperial Veterans in Canada.[79] Officialdom preferred to deal with a single organization, even if it was the demanding and ambitious GWVA. The Great War Veterans took credit for the War Service Gratuity, the enlarged clothing allowance, and free transportation for dependants, and it wanted still more benefits. If some dependants had had their fares paid, what about the rest? Widows should have the gratuities their late husbands might have received; so should men who had served with British or Allied forces. [80]

When R.M. Stewart resigned in January 1919, the GWVA executive found a more dynamic successor. Grant MacNeil, twenty-six, was the son of a Presbyterian minister and the former press agent and manager of Regina's only vaudeville theatre. Wounded as a machine-gunner in 1916, he had come home to work as an MHC instructor at Moose Jaw. He helped build the GWVA in Saskatchewan and emerged, in 1918, as its full-time provincial secretary. Harris Turner, the blind veteran who represented Saskatoon in the legislature, detected in MacNeil 'an impulsive enthusiasm' that sometimes led him to extremes, but he also noted that 'when MacNeil speaks, the province listens.' [81]

MacNeil inherited a growing organization and powerful influence. In February alone the GWVA could boast of forcing the pension commissioners to decentralize their decisions and of persuading Arthur Meighen to expand the limits of soldier settlement. In the West, military commanders were warned that on no account must they risk tangling with the veterans' organization. At Winnipeg, the army provost marshal, Colonel Godson-Godson, announced that disorderly veterans in uniform would no longer be arrested by military police; instead, their names would be handed over to the GWVA. [82]

No one could pretend that veterans or the GWVA in 1919 were firm guardians of social order or public peace. Disabled veterans had led anti-alien riots in 1917 and 1918, and the returned men of 1919 would be just as violent. New GWVA branches were as enthusiastic as old ones in their support for policies of repression, confiscation, and deportation. Grant MacNeil himself had earned his spurs leading the GWVA's nativist crusade in Saskatchewan. Under David Loughnan *The Veteran* was an organ of Anglo-conformity. 'In justice to the returned man,' he wrote, 'it must be admitted he has always argued there are two sides to the much discussed enemy alien question – our side and theirs. Our side stretches from Halifax to Victoria, theirs lies on the other side of the Atlantic ocean.' [83]

Words were not enough for restless and resentful men. Winnipeg socialists, denied the use of theatres because of threats made by veterans, braved the cold of Market Square on Sunday, 26 January. A mob of returned men and sympathizers drove them away, wrecked the Socialist Party of Canada headquarters, and smashed nearby restaurants on the pretext that they were owned by 'enemy aliens.' Next day, a rowdy crowd of ex-soldiers marched to the Swift's packing plant in Elmwood, vowing to chase out the aliens and put 'white men' in. Winnipeg's Mayor Charles Gray and Brig.-Gen. H.D.B. Ketchen, the district officer commanding, persuaded the men to disperse by promising that their demands would be met. Through the day, mobs wrecked more restaurants, visited more factories, and beat the few luckless foreigners they encountered. Police followed at a discreet distance, arrested a few youths for looting, and comforted victims with the genial assurance that they could always sue their assailants. [84] Far from deploring lawlessness, the Winnipeg *Telegram* sneered at the 'cowardly and furtive behaviour of the alien'; the respected *Free Press* supported the veterans' demand for alien registration as a preliminary to mass deportation. [85] The Manitoba government obliged.

That spring, veterans rioted in Hamilton, Toronto, Vancouver, and Calgary. 'The men who fought for democracy,' declared Arthur Hazelden of the Calgary GWVA, 'are not going to go hungry while aliens and slackers get all the jobs.' [86] At the time, hunger and unemployment were simply not factors; restlessness and nativism were. Even enemy status was not necessary; China had sided with the Allies, but that did not keep rioting veterans in Halifax and Lindsay from demolishing Chinese businesses. When the government asked the GWVA to control its members, MacNeil replied with a curt lecture: 'Certain groups of aliens have been exceedingly arrogant in their attitudes, thus arousing the passions of men trained to deal relentlessly with the prototype at the point of a bayonet.' [87] As president, Purney appealed for patience and self-discipline. World conditions, he explained, had created insuperable difficulties in getting rid of foreigners, and the aliens were exploiting the country's difficulties. [88]

Nativism, of course, was by no means a veterans' monopoly. In a year of ferment, returned men shared their civilian neighbours' concerns. Those who came home to rural townships often echoed the farmers' rejection of traditional party politics. Trade unionists, fresh from the ranks of the CEF, participated fully in the hottest year for strikes in Canada's history. Where veterans and probably most other rank-and-file union members parted company with their leaders was over the new post-war alliance between radicals and 'foreigners.' The One Big Union, conceived at Calgary in March and born in Winnipeg in June, offended GWVA branches because its organizing appeal was so conspicuously directed at foreign-born workers in the mines of Alberta and the forests of northwestern Ontario. The Winnipeg General Strike, in contrast, though led by many OBU enthusiasts, won the backing of most returned soldiers because foreigners were conspicuously absent from the strike committee. [89]

In the midst of the 1919 turmoil, GWVA leaders tried hard to be statesmen; they attempted to mould veterans into a progressively conservative constituency above the claims of class or party. Political guidance was issued with careful impartiality. 'Embers from the intermittent fires of rampant socialism,' warned *The Veteran*, 'are being zealously fanned to white-hot heat by revolutionary "labour leaders," ' but the real culprit was the blind optimism of government and the laissez-faire beliefs of employers. 'The millionaires may be in control now,' Loughnan wrote, 'but they are playing with fire and courting revolution for there is a limit to human endurance.'[90] During the Winnipeg strike MacNeil was sent to the city to keep the GWVA neutral. He found returned men serving the Citizens' Committee as special constables and the Strike Committee as demonstrators and marchers. On Bloody Saturday, 21 June 1919, members of the Royal North-West Mounted Police, many of them fresh from overseas, charged a crowd thick with veterans and their families. Among the strike leaders arrested was Roger Bray, a butcher and a Methodist lay preacher who had enlisted in 1916.[91]

On one issue veterans were neither neutral nor independent. Almost by accident, Calgary veterans had given Canada's returned men a cause of their own. On a bitterly cold 23 February ex-soldiers had crowded into the Allen Theatre for the regular Sunday forum. George Waistell, a former sergeant and British merchant skipper, had an idea. While other citizens had prospered, soldiers had been left with their meagre $1.10 a day. Politicians had promised them full re-establishment; that promise could easily be redeemed at $2,000 per man for those who had served at the front, $1,500 for those who had gone to England and $1,000 for those who had served in Canada. An Alberta Liberal MLA at once endorsed the idea; a cash grant would prevent paternalistic meddling on the part of the state. Soldiers could use the money to take up whatever vocation they chose. A sole veteran protested that the scheme did not seem very sensible to him, but he was disregarded. The Calgary Resolution was born.[92]

Since meetings filled time, veterans met often and the Waistell proposal was an obvious topic of discussion. A gratuity of two thousand dollars per man seemed little enough in a rich country that would have paid far more if the war had lasted into 1920. As soldiers gradually realized that there would be no 'military bounty,' that the War Service Gratuity was all they would ever have, support for the Calgary Resolution grew. It was soon echoed in the West by town councils, women's institutes, and chambers of commerce. Who could refuse the boys what they wanted when 'someone else' would pay? Bob Edwards of the Calgary *Eye-Opener* described the bonus as 'one grand solution for virtually all the troubles due to unrest, unemployment, discontent and Bolshevism.'[93]

In Ottawa, the bonus demand created dismay. A quick calculation suggested that it was a billion-dollar threat to national solvency, already menaced by a two-billion-dollar national debt. GWVA officials, torn between their sense of responsibility and the realization that the bonus was the chief attraction for new members, tried to avoid the issue. Finally, *The Veteran* fought back, insisting that returned men would not 'so cheapen themselves as to give a quit-claim ... for a paltry $2,000.'[94] It was too late. Brig.-Gen. W.A. Griesbach, elected in 1917 by the soldier vote, was booed by Edmonton veterans when he condemned the bonus.[95] The Army and Navy Veterans officially scolded the GWVA for favouring its own greedy members at the expense of widows and orphans, but the ANV's powerful Winnipeg branch recorded its support for a handsome cash gratuity.[96]

MacNeil's western trip convinced him that the bonus movement would not dry up.[97] The general strike in Winnipeg allowed the GWVA to postpone its third national convention from June to July and to organize opposition. With the membership soaring to an estimated quarter-million, the bonus issue might be all that newer members needed to overthrow the GWVA's pre-Armistice leadership. On 30 June, as the convention opened in a Vancouver high school, Willard Purney set out to outflank the bonus-seekers. The delegates, he declared, were soldier-citizens whose chief concern must be widows, orphans, and disabled comrades. A host of resolutions, ranging from the shortcomings of soldier settlement to a demand for a Canadian air force 'with the workers sharing in the management,' was designed to keep the delegates busy.[98] Albertans were determined to keep the gratuity issue alive. 'If the soldier is repatriated and given the opportunity to be contented by being helped to his feet,' said Calgary's Walter S. Woods, 'then Bolshevism will disappear, disloyalty will disappear.'[99] For two rancorous, weary days, GWVA leaders laboured in back rooms to bring forth a resolution that bore little resemblance to the Waistell scheme. Bonus payments were 'the most satisfactory and effective means of re-establishing the soldiers,' the convention agreed; the compromise was buried deep in the wording: 'the granting of such a bonus upon an equitable basis [should] be limited only by the country's ability to pay,' a question, along with other details, that was to be 'agreed and decided upon by a joint parliamentary and G.W.V.A. committee.'[100]

The GWVA leaders felt pleased with themselves. They had blunted the force of the bonus drive and provided what they saw as a basis for reasonable compromise. There had, of course, been much criticism of Lougheed, DSCR officials, and soldier settlement, but this was delegate froth. Surely the Borden government would respond.[101] The Liberals certainly did: in an interval between ballots at their national leadership convention, Lt-Col.

J.L. Ralston and Henri Béland moved a motion echoing word-for-word the GWVA proposal.[102] Then they chose the plump and unmilitary William Lyon Mackenzie King as their new leader. In the government, General Mewburn urged sympathy. Lt-Col. J.W. Margeson, Labatt's successor on the Pension Board, submitted his own bonus scheme, based on a dollar for each day's service. 'If [the veteran] does not make good afterwards,' Margeson argued, 'it is not the fault of the government.'[103]

The government was not budging. 'In my judgment,' insisted Lougheed, 'we should not go beyond the formal assistance given.' Meighen agreed. Sir George Foster, the acting prime minister, dismissed the bonus demand as greedy and absurd. 'The result would be that in a great many instances the beneficiary would, if left to himself, be no better off in a few months after the benefaction, and the same old discontent would cry again and again for relief.'[104] On 27 August Borden gave his answer: Canada had done all she could for her soldiers. The War Service Gratuity had cost $130 million; soldier settlement would cost as much or more; pensions would be an annual burden of $35–40 million; and there was a frightening national debt to service. 'This country,' Borden concluded, 'is face to face with a serious financial situation which will call for rigid economy and careful retrenchment.'[105]

The GWVA leaders were nonplussed. What they thought was a reasonable proposal had been rejected without even a face-saving gesture. Pressures, barely contained at Vancouver and growing during the summer, might now burst. MacNeil tried again. Surely the prime minister could at least appoint a royal commission. An ailing, exhausted Borden refused. There would be 'no larger or further gratuity.' There would be no royal commission. The government had all the facts it needed.[106] Two days later, Foster noted in his diary, 'The G.W.V.'s have broken loose.'[107]

'Flynnism' and Parliament

Across the country many veterans had persuaded themselves that the Calgary Resolution was just, reasonable, and, once Germany paid its war reparations, well within the country's means. Nowhere was support stronger than in Toronto. No city had been harder hit by the shutdown of the munitions industry; no city had more returned soldiers; and few had politicians more eager to seek veterans' votes. On Sunday, 7 September, returned men thronged to Queen's Park to denounce Borden, the *Globe* (which had opposed the bonus), and their own timorous leaders. 'Let us put a peaceful demand,' shouted J. Harry Flynn, 'and if it is not answered, I say let us take it by force.'[108]

Flynn was a smooth-faced demagogue who had crossed from the United States in 1917 and joined the medical corps. He had been slightly wounded in France, and had come home a sergeant. He was hired by the DSCR as a commercial teacher.[109] By Sunday night he was also president of the Returned Soldiers' Gratuity League. In a series of packed meetings, Flynn raged at editors, politicians, and GWVA leaders. When Bill Turley, the disabled ex-boxer who was GWVA secretary for Ontario, tried to answer Flynn on his own platform, veterans howled him down and tried to beat him. Flynn charged that Turley and other officials were on the government payroll; the GWVA answered by suing Flynn for slander. By the end of September, Flynn's organization had blossomed into the United Veterans' League. Most of the GWVA's Toronto branches had either defected or elected leaders pledged to support the unadulterated version of the Calgary Resolution.[110]

Flynn had powerful backing. Mayor Tommy Church was as eager as ever to forge the kind of alliance with veterans that had kept the Republican party in power in the United States after the Civil War. Flynn's scurrility and his billion-dollar bonus inhibited neither the mayor nor a sympathetic Toronto *Telegram*.[111] In Ottawa the government felt the pressure, not only from Toronto but from Hamilton, Winnipeg, Montreal, and anywhere else veterans could hold a rally and draft a telegram. There would be a small concession. Parliament had to meet anyway to debate the peace treaty and the costly Grand Trunk Railway settlement; another special committee on veterans could be arranged. The chairman would be J.A. Calder, chairman of the Repatriation Committee and, a critic claimed, 'the smoothest chap north of the boundary.'[112] A preponderance of ex-soldier members of Parliament on the committee and ample opportunity for MacNeil to question witnesses and elucidate the veterans' viewpoint left a somewhat misleading impression of government open-mindedness.

From 19 September to 31 October Calder's committee met in the intervals of parliamentary business and explored all the problems of re-establishment, from widows' pensions to unemployment. Scores of groups and individuals, from the Soldiers' Wives League to university presidents, made their appearance. Only Harry Flynn cracked the mask of tolerance. Earlier, he had boasted to Toronto audiences of forcing Borden from his sick-bed. The night before giving his testimony, he told cheering Ottawa veterans that the politicians were on notice for their jobs. On 1 October the politicians had their turn. Led by Calder and urged on by MacNeil, committee members probed Flynn's American origins, his modest war record, his teaching career, even his Catholicism. It was a serious tactical error; returned soldiers were enraged by the personal abuse of a fellow veteran.

Few noted Flynn's surprisingly feeble defence of the bonus. He had dismissed the injustice of giving the same $2,000 to both an 'Old Original' and a conscripted latecomer as an attempt to split veterans. Flynn's proposal to finance a billion-dollar gratuity by taxes on Sunday movies and by lotteries had passed unnoticed. [113]

A week later the GWVA had its turn to speak. The bonus idea had travelled a long way from Calgary. Now the GWVA proposed that aid be given only to the veteran who could 'demonstrate that State assistance in re-establishment is a real necessity for the welfare and future security of himself and his dependants.' A complex bureaucracy, jointly run by the government and the GWVA, would determine need and issue credits ranging from $1,000 to $2,500 to be spent on debt reduction, tuition fees, buying a home, even on Victory Bonds. Surely Parliament would not refuse a veteran in need? What veteran, an MP rejoined, would *not* be in need? George Waistell was at least ingenious: 'I maintain, from the huge amount of opposition that we have received, that there are going to be many thousands of gentlemen who are so well established that they will not make the claim for this re-establishment aid.' [114] More to the point, he and other GWVA spokesmen maintained that they were 'sitting on a safety valve.' 'If by any incomplete or insufficient measure which this Parliament may adopt, you unceremoniously throw us off that safety valve, our control is gone.' [115]

This brought to mind Currie's misgivings of a year before; but this time big money was involved. The government was obdurate. 'Either or both,' declared Sir Thomas White of the Flynn and the GWVA proposals, 'the thing is impossible.' [116] Would a soldier who spent the war in England be satisfied with $225 while a comrade who went to France with a forestry company got $1,125? [117] By dint of incorporating every past or projected expenditure on pensions and re-establishment, Calder calculated that Canada already had committed half a billion dollars to its veterans. That was enough. Some injustices would be resolved: those who had gone from Canada to the imperial forces would have the same gratuity as the CEF; dependants who returned before the Armistice could claim their passage money; a sum of $25 million in a Winter Emergency Appropriation fund would help tide veterans over the coming harsh season. Otherwise, if MPs wanted to do more, there is only one course, and that is that some other Administration must carry on.' [118]

After that, only a handful of Toronto-based Tory MPs still backed the bonus: Horatio Hocken, past-master of the Orange Lodge, the maverick Billy MacLean from York South, and, above all, Col. J.A. Currie, a former journalist whose command of a CEF battalion had ended abruptly in 1915. Colonel Currie was an embarrassing ally. By the end of a long parliamentary evening on 6 November he had antagonized the House, quarrelled with a fellow Tory, slapped another member in the face, and been hit on the head with a stick.[119] That night the bonus died, and the GWVA might well have died with it. The association's claims to special influence were obviously hollow. Purney and MacNeil took what credit they could for concessions to imperial veterans, but channelling winter relief through the detested Patriotic Fund was pure humiliation. Tait, Loughnan, and Maxwell resigned at once from the Repatriation Committee. Angry branch members poured invective on the government, the opposition, and their own leaders. Surely it was time to get into politics? Leaders pleaded for caution. 'The Great War Veterans' Association, like the sword of Damocles, hangs heavy over many a political head just now,' wrote Loughnan. 'Why let it fall and dent the edge on a few bone-heads when so much use may be found for it in the future?'[120]

Behind their barrage of bombast, GWVA leaders assessed the heavy price of the bonus campaign. Veterans who had flocked into the association now flocked out, some to more radical organizations such as the Grand Army of Canada or Flynn's United Veterans, most to find their own answer to re-establishment. When barely one-fifth of the Winter Emergency Appropriation was spent, the GWVA asserted that delay and mismanagement had forced veterans to turn to private charities; the government, more plausibly maintained that the GWVA had over-blown the problem.[121] Never again would politicians accept the association as the sole and authoritative voice of returned men. The bonus campaign had undermined the GWVA's painfully acquired prestige; what remained were the two worst characteristics any pressure group could have – greed and weakness.

Yet the bonus issue would not die. Months after the Calgary Resolution, the new American Legion had devised its own demand for 'adjusted compensation' to make up for miserable wartime pay. The American proposal was adopted by Walter Woods, a Soldier Settlement Board employee and now the president of the Calgary GWVA. On 8 March 1920, Calgary's People's Forum heard Woods's argument for a dollar per day's service for men who had served in France – less for those who had served in Canada, England, or Siberia – and voted unanimous support. As the GWVA prepared for its fourth convention at Montreal on 24 March, a new enthusiasm for a bonus scheme broke out in the west.[122]

This time, GWVA resistance was weaker. On doctors' orders, Purney abandoned the presidency on the eve of the meeting. Other officers retired. Woods and the Albertans found allies in Quebec and Ontario delegates. Capt. Léonce Plante, recalling wartime complaints that French Canadians were 'too noisy,' boasted that their uproar on behalf of the bonus would be welcome now. Delegates chose R.B. Maxwell as their first rank-and-file president and declared that they would adjourn to Ottawa until the government caved in. White's successor as finance minister, Sir Henry Drayton, had claimed that Canada would look like a squeezed orange if the bonus was conceded. A Kingston delegate brought cheers when he declared that the country, indeed, might look like an orange, 'perhaps with the financial pips taken out of it and the juice equally distributed throughout the orange, and that's what we want in Canada.'[123]

There were contradictory voices, too. Colonel Ralston had moved the bonus resolution at the Liberal convention in August 1919, but at Montreal he warned that business condemned any idea of handing money to able-bodied veterans who did not need it. 'Chubby' Power, his fellow Liberal, agreed. Grant MacNeil, stung by reflections on his lobbying zeal, warned the convention that it was hopeless to pressure a government that had 'definitely declared itself as being against an indiscriminate cash bonus.' A majority – 112 to 57 – voted to continue the fight.[124] Dutifully, on 30 March, Bob Maxwell and a GWVA delegation met with Sir George Foster, the acting prime minister. The outcome was predictable. 'The Government,' Foster announced, 'is not and never has been of the opinion that the best way to reconstitute, re-adjust and re-establish the returned soldier is by placing in his hand a sum of money over which there should be no government supervision, and without any reference to the peculiar and differing circumstances of each returned soldier.'[125] Privately, Foster noted his disdain for the new state of the GWVA: 'The Resolutions were crude, the management has gone into extremist and weak hands.' The leadership had passed to 'Ne'er do wells' and 'English rads and roustabouts.'[126] When other veterans' organizations followed the GWVA to Ottawa a few days later, Flynn was barred for using 'insulting language,' but the outcome was the same.[127]

Government firmness and rapid absorption of most veterans in the labour force defeated both Calgary resolutions. It remained for the GWVA to bury the bonus or be buried by it. Both Maxwell and MacNeil decided to find other interests and issues for their shrinking membership. The new president focused on seeking unity among the quarrelsome veterans' organizations, while MacNeil struggled to make the GWVA the defender of pensioners and other claimants. When the bonus issue surfaced again at the GWVA's fifth convention in Port Arthur in 1921, MacNeil gave delegates a blunt and final message: 'Let us be honest about this. There is not a party, as a party, in the Dominion of Canada ... that can say they will come out for a cash gratuity. You throw yourself directly into opposition to the financial interest and the Manufacturers' Association.'[128]

The Grand Army of United Veterans, formed in 1921 from a merger of the Flynn organization and the Grand Army of Canada, remained more sanguine. Since Liberal candidates had received handbooks repeating their party's 1919 bonus commitment, the GAUV put its faith in Mackenzie King in return for a written pledge to form a committee 'with the widest power to consider all matters relevant to these proposals.' King had words of assurance for the GAUV: 'I should not hesitate to endorse the principles underlying all the several resolutions.'[129] After the Liberals' narrow victory, it fell to Sir Arthur Currie to explain to Harry McLeod, the GAUV's troubled secretary, that King's mushy prose signified precisely nothing.[130]

In common with farmers and labour, veterans lost their battles in 1919. Profiteers would remain unplucked. The 'enemy alien' remained to undermine the 'Anglo-conformist' image of Canada. Above all, the claim to equality of sacrifice with those who had stayed home was rejected. Canadian veterans remained a political factor; they could never claim, as did the American Legion, that they were invincible. In the United States 'adjusted compensation' had triumphed by 1924 over presidential vetoes, if only in the form of a promissory note.[131] Canadian veterans had no such triumph. There would be no Canadian GAR for Tommy Church to manipulate. The GWVA had to accept defeat and try again.

7 Re-establishment and Settlement

Restoring the Disabled – Practice

By defeating the veterans' bonus, Parliament kept the government's re-establishment blueprint intact. The able-bodied would be purged of the irresponsibility of army life by a stiff dose of self-sufficiency. Even the slight concession of relief from the War Emergency Appropriation was designed to help provinces and municipalities rather than the returned men. If anyone believed that soldier settlement was a new 'military bounty,' it was not for lack of explanation. As for the disabled, the route to independence was only slightly more circuitous; they would be treated, trained, and even pensioned only in ways that would emphasize that a veteran's life was again his own to make or mar.[1]

How many veterans were disabled? By the end of 1919, 8,012 were still in hospital; by the end of 1920, 69,202 men and women had qualified for disability pensions. Others, ostensibly cured, would for the rest of their lives find in their wartime service the source of debility, pain, sickness, and personal failure. While a number of departments had dealt with aspects of demobilization, the Department of Soldiers' Civil Re-establishment emerged as the focus for disabled returned soldiers. A department that preached self-sufficiency evolved into the cradle of Canada's welfare state.

The wartime medical demarcation between the department and the army soon lost its meaning. The CAMC met the hospital ships at Portland, but its hospitals no longer distinguished between long-term and short-term cases. The DSCR acquired the better military hospitals. In London, where the CAMC had erected the five-hundred-bed Westminster Hospital south of the city, the DSCR located a centre for its mental and neuro-psychiatric patients. In Calgary, a random collection of downtown buildings was christened the Colonel Belcher Hospital. By early 1920, Toronto's Christie Street Hospital had become the DSCR's largest and best-known institution.[2]

In addition to its inheritance of sick, wounded, tubercular, and insane patients, the department provided medical care to ex-soldiers who suffered recurrences of illnesses or injuries incurred in wartime. A year's free treatment was available to all veterans 'where space permitted'; the program was extended to the DSCR's trainees.[3] At the peak of demand, during the week of 20 September 1919, such 'non-attributable' cases represented 1,005 of the DSCR's total patient load of 13,775. Most were out-patients; the peak for in-patients, in February 1920, was 7,618.[4] By the end of 1920, the department was already busy closing institutions and 'demobilizing' staff.

Meanwhile, the DSCR's medical responsibilities ran a broad gamut, from war-wounded to syphilitics to persons addicted to morphia and other pain-killers.[5] Tuberculosis, the earliest medical problem of the MHC, remained with the DSCR to the end. The 99 'incurables' were fewer than anyone had expected in 1915; other problems went beyond measuring.[6] The neuroses the public insisted on calling 'shell-shock' would not soon vanish. Neither would other 'problem cases'; men who seemed unable to function for themselves, whatever contribution, large or small, they may have made to the war effort. Even in 1919 the psychological consequences of war were an iceberg of submerged misery and frustration.

Amputees, in contrast, were visible sufferers from war. Out of the 126,594 wounded in the CEF, the survivors in 1922 included 1,013 who had lost an arm, seven who had lost both arms, 2,490 who had lost a leg (most often the left) and 95 who were legless. Three men were each left with one arm, and one tough survivor, Private Curly Christian, had lost all four limbs.[7] Amputees lived with awkwardness, phantom pain, and the cords, belts, straps, and pulleys that tore clothes and chafed skin without ever quite fulfilling the inventors' promise of 'a perfect prosthesis.' Two single amputees, Marshall MacDougall and William Hinks, set off from Calgary to Ottawa as part of the post-war cross-country walking craze. They stopped at the Lakehead when their stumps broke down. One-armed men did their best with inadequate gadgets and wore gloves to spare a squeamish public. Through the Soldiers' Comfort Branch of the DSCR, the tireless Mrs Vankoughnet supplied 'invalid tricycles' to those who needed them.[8]

The DSCR limb factory struggled with suspicious clients and scornful private competitors. Colonel Starr, progenitor of the factory, was unrepentant about the lack of choice: amputees did not 'know what's best.'[9] The manager, Maj. J.A. Coulthard, had a better idea. In 1919 he dispatched his most pertinacious critic, Arthur Hazelden of the Calgary GWVA, with Mrs Hazelden, on an all-expenses-paid trip to England, France, and Belgium. Hazelden dutifully inspected factories and hospitals and returned, Coulthard reported, 'well satisfied' on all but a few details. Another prominent amputee, W.S. Dobbs, was hired to give two-week courses on using the

'Canadian convertible arm' and as a consultant on amputee problems. As many amputees as possible were trained and employed at the Toronto factory.[10] Other disabled veterans also benefited: 1,000 men were supplied with glass eyes; 20,000 orthopedic boots were issed to ex-soldiers with foot injuries; and 16 men with horrible facial scars were given masks and spectacles.[11]

By 1920 the DSCR had taken over dental treatment from the CAMC, providing the extractions, fillings, and vulcanite dentures that helped make 38,000 returned men 'dentally fit.'[12] Dentists helped with the agonizing work of restoring the disfigured. Free dental treatments for tuberculosis sufferers also produced some unexpected cures. TB remained a major problem, and tubercular patients occupied 2,248 of the DSCR's 7,374 beds at the end of 1919. By 1921, the MHC and the DSCR had treated 8,571 tuberculosis patients, but almost 1,000 were already dead.[13] A Board of Tuberculosis Consultants, convened by the DSCR in April 1920, agreed that the incidence of the disease for veterans seemed to be double that for civilians, though the experts believed poison gas was a minor causative factor. Few of the sufferers had been exposed to gas. Perhaps the truth was that soldiers were tested for TB; civilians were not. More significant was the board's advice to rely on civilian institutions for the treatment of TB. Civilians adapted better to the niggling discipline of sanatorium routine and set an example for ex-soldiers.[14] By 1925 the DSCR operated only one sanatorium outside Calgary; thirteen civilian sanatoria housed ex-soldiers.

Civilian institutions were more controversial for mentally disturbed veterans.[15] The public's double standard for civil and military cases offended psychiatric reformers. The 1919 tour by Captain Farrar and Dr Clarke of the National Committee on Mental Hygiene was Col. McKelvey Bell's scheme to reassure critics and put a little discreet pressure on provincial authorities. Clarke's reports were unsensational, if unflattering. In western asylums the two men found understaffing, overcrowding, and such vestiges of barbarism as crib beds. They criticized Alberta's policy of sending ex-soldiers to the new facility at Ponoka merely because it was new. Civilians should not suffer because soldiers, however briefly, were in official favour.[16] In Ontario the two doctors ran into the DSCR's nemesis, W.D. Macpherson. Only official provincial inspectors, insisted Macpherson's deputy, were allowed to visit provincial hospitals. In Quebec, Farrar inspected alone. The Protestant hospital at Verdun, he found, was too crowded to take more military patients. At the huge Beauport asylum outside Quebec, he found fifteen hundred men and women jammed into dark, narrow wards under the supervision of a single young physician. Treatment, Farrar wryly noted, was the 'expectant method.'[17]

Action in Quebec was precipitated by Canon Frederick Scott, the CEF's most famous chaplain. As an Anglican, Scott was outraged that Protestants might be confined in a Catholic hospital.[18] His threat to publicize his concern forced the DSCR to reserve four hundred beds at the new Montreal veterans' hospital, Ste-Anne de Bellevue, for 'neuro-psychiatric' patients. By 1920 the $2 million Westminster Hospital was also ready. Clarke toured the institution, approved the staff, facilities, and the fact that most patients admitted themselves, and concluded that 'the educational effect ... will bring about the reforms asked for much more quickly than any other method.' The DSCR could congratulate itself on its generally progressive influence on the treatment of some of Canada's saddest cases.[19]

At the end of 1923, the DSCR reported 1,097 'mental' and 447 'nervous' cases in its care.[20] War neuroses, however labelled, were only reluctantly linked with insanity. Colin Russell, who had headed the CAMC special hospital for neuro-psychiatric cases, Farrar, and many of their colleagues insisted that cure was for such patients a matter of will power. Hospitalization, like pensions, only encouraged men to escape work as they had escaped danger. Former army doctors, their credentials strengthened by experience under fire, tended to confirm the doctrine.[21] A flat and final pension payment of five hundred dollars was deliberately punitive – a 'moral prosthesis' for a weak will.[22]

The whole DSCR treatment policy had a consistent goal: to reduce disability as much as medically possible. Retraining and pensions took over after doctors had done their best. Three years of wartime experience in retraining had put Canada ahead of her allies. A visit to Britain in the summer of 1919 persuaded Segsworth and T.A. Stevenson, Anthes's deputy, that the British program was 'wide and ambitious ... very little of which was carried out.'[23] With ten times Canada's casualty toll, the British had only a few more men than the dominion under training and in only thirty different trades. As for the Americans, DSCR observers merely confirmed journalistic exposés of mismanagement and corruption in the U.S. Vocational Training Board.

Retraining in Canada, Segsworth boasted, was comprehensive, realistic, and economical. The cost, $19.46 per student-month, compared favourably with the $32.16 a month charged by respected U.S. land-grant colleges. The MHC's original 39 occupations had been expanded by industrial surveys to encompass 380 trades, from adding-machine mechanic to x-ray operator.[24] Trainees could be found in 66 schools, colleges, and universities and in 2,965 industrial establishments. Where no vocational institutions existed or where provincial authorities refused to help, the DSCR had improvised 53 schools and training centres, usually staffed by returned men. The program was varied and widely dispersed. The University of Toronto taught courses ranging from massage to motor mechanics; Knox College offered theology courses to one disabled veteran; and the nearby Central Technical School instructed students in movie-projection, showcard writing, and a dozen other skills. McGill University contributed its heating plant as a school for stationary engineers. A tailor in Charlottetown supervised two apprentices, while a Dr Watson in Montreal tutored three would-be dental mechanics. Massey-Harris, Acadia Sugar, the Russell Motor Car Company, the railway workshops, and a host of other industries, large and small, did their patriotic duty. [25]

Even *The Veteran* emphasized that retraining must not become 'a well-paid medium for the encouragement of loafers.' [26] More than five thousand applicants were rejected because they could go back to their former occupations. A disabled school teacher from Alberta was told that he did not really need an extra year in teachers' college to return to the classroom. [27] As Harold Innis had discovered, the DSCR gave little encouragement to university students. The British example of helping former undergraduates resume their studies cut no ice in Canada. [28] Even when aid was granted in special cases, it was only for a few months' duration; and elaborate efforts were made to ensure that necessary textbooks were loaned, not given, and then only to students who could not afford their own. [29] Anything more, insisted Segsworth, would be 'class legislation.' The sole breach in the 'disability line' benefited minors – soldiers who had lied about their age and enlisted below the age of eighteen. 'These boys were immature at the time their decision was made,' Segsworth explained, 'and it is questionable whether the Government is not in a large measure responsible for any disadvantages accrued to them.' Politicians and officials agreed that it would be a tragedy if such youthful patriots were condemned to the ranks of unskilled labour for the rest of their lives. [30]

In December 1919, 27,602 men were in training, a sixty-fold increase in a year. [31] By the end of 1922, as the program neared its end, the DSCR reported that 52,034 veterans, including 11,384 minors, had begun courses, 42,605 had completed them, and 3,666 had been dismissed for persistent absenteeism, misbehaviour, or 'lack of interest.' Others had left voluntarily, half of them to take jobs. Segsworth had insisted on courses of no more than six to eight months; the final average was 7.7 months, but 24,018 trainees had been permitted extensions and 5,500 had switched from unsuitable programs. [32] More than half the trainees took courses related to industry or trades; almost one-third overcame 'Private Pat's' inspired aversion to 'paper-scratching'; and 15 per cent chose branches of agriculture.

Segsworth and the DSCR had developed an impressive theory, but how successful was the practice? The rush of students, the inexperienced instructors, and the inadequate equipment created difficulties. In 1920 veterans from Kingston complained that vacancies, not aptitude, determined their choice of courses. The DSCR itself broke the rule that pensions must not affect income by allowing pensions to be suspended when training pay and allowances were provided.[33] In January 1919 instructors and students at the DSCR's improvised Winnipeg schools went on strike over low pay and lack of equipment. Lougheed bluntly warned a civic delegation that he would close every school before he surrendered to such mob action. Segsworth's assistant, Capt. Norman Parkinson, was sent to reopen the schools with a pledge that equipment would follow.[34] The strike had other results. The meagre training allowances authorized in 1917 were raised on 1 March 1919 and again in 1920. One unintended result was that trainees with families soon complained that potential employers rarely offered them as much in wages as their training pay.[35]

The GWVA's early enthusiasm for DSCR training methods soon cooled. Writing in *The Veteran*, Loughnan claimed that 'the greatest curse and cause of unrest in Canada is found in the partially trained man.' That was what the DSCR was producing, and it would lead to 'a waste of valuable time, money and energy, trouble with the unions, and an increase of partially trained men who eventually drift into the discontented ranks of manual labour.'[36] Segsworth knew the argument: the DSCR's courses were designed to build on old skills, restore self-confidence and direct men to jobs that paid a full wage within a few months. No one started from scratch. What about men with few skills, little education, and no aptitude? Of the trainees, 83.9 per cent had no more than a public-school education.[37] A residue of veterans was too old, too sick, or too emotionally disturbed to find real work. Even many trainees, an investigation concluded in 1923, had merely put in time.

Retraining policy for one group of veterans was rarely criticized. Blindness or defective eyesight afflicted 2,252 CEF members; 154 were totally blind.[38] By 1919, Pearson Hall was operating in Toronto as a replica of Sir Arthur Pearson's St Dunstan's Hostel, with additional responsibility for teaching trades. Some programs were based on dubious lore; the myth that blindness 'improved' other senses led to a misguided but short-lived enthusiasm for teaching piano-tuning. Massage was more promising until after 1920, when DSCR hospitals began to close. The blind turned to poultry-rearing, stenography – Pearson had insisted that the blind should type – or such traditional blind trades as broom-making or boot repair.[39] The new philosophy of self-help for the blind, reflected in the young Canadian National Institute for the Blind, supplanted the more traditional blind charities. Capt. E.A. Baker made a natural transition from the DSCR's Blind

Section to the CNIB.[40] The outstanding could not be the norm; blindness was often only one disability among many. One blind veteran had also lost an arm, broken his jaw, and suffered skull damage. Another never quite recovered when a fixed knee had sent him tumbling down the stairs of a London Underground station. Full pension, attendance allowance, and free transportation ('if infrequent') never compensated men with few inner resources and little education or skill. Even the special benefits were available to a minority: most blind veterans, like the other disabled, could attribute only a fraction of their affliction to 'actual service.'[41]

Re-establishing the Disabled

Even more imaginative than the commitment to retraining the war-disabled was Segsworth's system of employment surveys, job placement, follow-up, and social service for men and their families. Mere exhortation would not easily overcome a Canadian tradition of hiding the handicapped or leaving them to charity. Segsworth's travelling salesmen helped find jobs for the disabled in twelve hundred different industries. A detailed description, for example, determined that a man with fair upper-body strength and no respiratory problems could do the work of a prairie elevator manager. Early in 1919, a Handicap Section was added to the Information and Service Branch to help the disabled overcome employment obstacles. Vocational supervisors eased friction for trainees learning on the job. Patriotic employers and valiant veterans would do the rest. Even the quadruple amputee, Pte Curly Christian, suitably equipped with limbs and an invalid tricycle, found work as a billiard-marker.[42]

Segsworth claimed a uniquely efficient statistical follow-up for his work. When the Handicap Section was disbanded at the end of 1923, it had recorded 94,038 applications and found 58,058 jobs.[43] More than 90 per cent of trainees found work, claimed the DSCR's Vocational Branch, and 60 per cent found work in areas for which they had been trained. Veterans who learned on the job fared best, but half of those trained in the DSCR's own schools were able to apply their new skills.[44] The government took one-fifth of the trainees. GWVA pressure and a directive from the special parliamentary committee on pensions and re-establishment, created in 1920, led the Civil Service Commission to order dismissal for female federal employees whose husbands could afford to support them.[45] The fragile young merit principle was bent to put veterans who met the minimum qualifications for a job at the head of the list. Any qualified disabled ex-soldier took precedence over the able-bodied.[46]

The veterans' preference was only a partial blessing. By 1921 William

Foran of the Civil Service Commission could announce that 95 per cent of post-war appointments had been reserved for returned men or women. Veterans held 8,000 permanent and 29,000 temporary positions.[47] Rural postmasterships, normally a patronage plum, were held for the disabled, a great benefit to men who could no longer earn their living in farm work.[48] Provinces and municipalities that did not follow the federal example faced the wrath of the GWVA and its sympathizers. Civil servants were still ill-paid, however, and they no longer enjoyed job security. Wartime expansion was temporary, and the cuts fell on the tens of thousands of veterans who had sought re-establishment in a bureaucratic niche. The DSCR was only an extreme case: it employed 9,035 men and women in March 1920; by 1925 that number had shrunk to 2,190. A special and highly publicized training program for disabled veterans led to only 66 jobs, most of which were positions as elevator operators, cleaners, and weights-and-measures inspectors.[49]

Parliament tackled the successive problems veterans faced in the labour market. By the end of 1919 it had approved five-hundred-dollar interest-free loans to disabled men who needed capital to buy equipment or tools or to finance courses the DSCR could not provide. By 1922, 1,630 loans for tools and 31 for further education had been approved, though one-fifth of them had already led to repossession.[50] Another problem was workmen's compensation for the disabled. A one-eyed veteran who lost his remaining eye on the new job would claim a full blind pension; compensation boards also suspected that amputations, chest ailments, and other disabilities would add to their claims. Accordingly, they raised premiums for such employees. Only in December 1921 did Ottawa announce that it would pay the extra compensation cost for veterans pensioned at 20 per cent or more. By the end of July 1924, after an experimental period of three years, the total cost had proved to be $50,571, most of which was spent in Ontario and Alberta. Other provinces, with feeble compensation systems, had made scarcely any claims.[51]

A more general problem for returned soldiers, with special application to the disabled, was insurance. John Todd had foreseen the difficulty as early as 1917: 'A disabled man,' he had reminded the parliamentary special committee, 'cannot get accident insurance nor can he always get life insurance on the same terms as can a healthy man.'[52] Even able-bodied veterans needed help; many had cancelled pre-war policies because a war exemption made them useless or because the premiums were too costly for a soldier's pay. In France, the government and private companies had jointly financed a special insurance fund, and in 1919 the GWVA had pressed for a similar Canadian solution. The government was unresponsive: 'Having ... incurred the liabilities that we have and made the provisions that have been made.' grumbled Sir George Foster, 'it is asking a good deal to arrange, in addition to all these a system of Government-supported insurance.'[53]

After further veterans' urging and a firm reminder that insurance was part of a tradition of thrift and self-help, that was precisely what the 1920 special parliamentary committee proposed. Under the scheme developed by the dominion superintendent of insurance, G.D. Finlayson, and by Thomas Bradshaw, who had managed Toronto's wartime soldiers' insurance, the government would provide a simple term life policy available in five-hundred-dollar increments up to five thousand dollars with no medical examination. Only immediate dependants could be named as beneficiaries; rates would be based on age alone; premiums might be deducted from pensions, though policies would certainly not be reserved for the disabled. If survivors qualified for a pension, their premiums would be returned with interest.[54]

Returned soldiers' insurance, or RSI, met little opposition. The venerable Liberal, Sen. L.G. Power, raged against the proposal: 'There seems to me to be a disposition to leave our ordinary common sense behind when we come to deal with men who went to the front.' But even he was mollified on learning that the able-bodied would share the risks.[55] In the House of Commons, his unrelated namesake, Maj. C.G. 'Chubby' Power, complained that even conscripts could apply.[56] The few who argued that private insurance companies should be involved were assured that only the state could carry such a risky and unprofitable scheme. Veterans had their own misgivings – and little spare cash. In the first of two years when sales were open, only 2,400 policies were sold. More vigorous promotion and the extension of the scheme to a third year left the government with 33,850 policies worth $82,815,000 by the end of 1923. Despite warnings about deathbed applications, early premiums kept pace with early claims and a first-year death rate of 22.87 per thousand fell to 8.21 per thousand in the second year.[57] Perhaps there was fraud, admitted Sen. Sam Sharpe, 'but what is there that we go up against today in which there is not some fraud?'[58] The existence of returned soldiers' insurance was also an answer to veterans and dependants who claimed pensions for post-war misfortunes. It was part of the restoration to self-sufficiency.

Re-establishment would never be perfect. The temporary relief problem of the winter of 1919–20 recurred with greater severity in 1920–1, and DSCR units faced renewed appeals for help. This time the department drew the line at pensioners and former trainees; it also distributed vouchers, not cash. Even tight-fisted management could not keep the cost below $51,500. The need for relief programs continued through the decade.[59] The DSCR also faced a growing residue of seemingly unemployable 'problem cases.' Few employers could offer the light work, frequent rest periods, and clean conditions needed for convalescent tubercular cases, and it was not easy to overcome 'phthisiophobia' among fellow workers. 'Thirty-niners,' men who had enlisted when they were over-age, often returned too worn out to compete in the labour market, but few had qualified for pensions. 'They are crocks,' explained Grant MacNeil; 'they cannot receive vocational training, you cannot place them in employment, and they are constituting, I think, the major part of our problem cases.'[60] They were almost rivalled by 'nervous and mental cases' not serious enough to be hospitalized but plainly unable to support themselves. 'In only a few cases,' Scammell reported, 'has it been found that military service has been a determining factor in producing the conditions described, and then only as a slight aggravation.'[61] That was enough. Families or municipalities that otherwise would have had to absorb the burden demanded that Ottawa meet its responsibilities to all ex-soldiers.

As usual, Scammell had foreseen the problem in 1915. His solution had been 'Soldiers' Homes' similar to those in the United States. Reflection had persuaded both veterans and the MHC that such institutions were undesirable. 'Homes' carried the stigma of the poor-house, and soldiers had had enough of regimentation. Even proposals for village colonies for tuberculars and epileptics were discarded.[62] Working in all weathers and in dusty conditions would amount to a death sentence for most lung cases, and, as one witness confessed, there was no such thing as light work on a farm.[63] The DSCR's Board of Tuberculosis Consultants urged (with unhappy phrasing) 'sub-standard' workshops for their charges. From September 1919 the DSCR was reluctantly drawn into the provision of sheltered workshops.[64] Wherever possible, management was delegated to the 'capable businessmen' of the Red Cross Society, but in Ontario the DSCR itself had to manage its 'Vetcraft' shops. By the end of 1924 ten such workshops existed across Canada, employing 347 'problem cases' to turn out toys, simple furniture, and their best-known product, imitation poppies.[65]

The DSCR's role was not limited to Canada. Thousands of Canadian veterans remained in Britain; many more returned to the United States after wartime service with the CEF and thousands of Canadian ex-servicemen joined the post-war migration to California. Meanwhile, more than fifty thousand 'Imperials' returned to Canada.[66] Ernest Scammell spent much of the summer of 1918 in London, negotiating reciprocal arrangements with a harried and disorganized British Ministry of Pensions. The agreement was surprisingly generous. British pensioners in Canada could choose imperial or Canadian rates – at British expense. Veterans in either country would have access to treatment, training, and emergency help.[67] Arrangements in England that took months to conclude required only a single meeting in Washington on 18 October 1919. Once again the neighbouring countries agreed to reciprocal access to veterans' hospitals and treatment centres, with each country paying its own bills.[68] By the end of 1920 a DSCR Foreign Relations Section had signed comparable agreements with Belgium, France, Australia, and Italy. Out of 63,000 Canadian pensioners more than 12,000 lived abroad in 1923, scattered from Australia to the Isle of Skye. A DSCR office in London was responsible for 6,894 pensioners in the British Isles, while 4,297 CEF pensioners in the United States had to look to Ottawa.[69]

For several years after its creation in 1918, the DSCR publicized its achievements and regularly congratulated Canadians on their generosity to disabled veterans. No ally or enemy paid higher pensions or provided more lavishly for men under treatment or training.[70] An American journalist, Stanley Frost, agreed. Concluding a 1923 magazine series excoriating the U.S. Veterans' Bureau, he depicted Canada as the country 'Where Veterans Fell among Friends.' American officials had excused waste and corruption with the claim that in a democracy 'all Government work must of necessity be done very poorly.' Canada was a democracy, Frost reminded readers, and her work shone: 'Her men have had the best of medical care where ours have not; her rehabilitated soldiers step back into civil life without friction and with success; there is no delay, almost no bungling, no flurry at all.' Almost all 'complainers' were 'foreign born.'[71]

Frost's data and references suggest that he took his evidence from DSCR officials rather than from first-hand observation, but the department could point to other favourable reports. G.M. Wilson of the Grand Trunk Railway shops reported that disabled veterans had mastered skills in six months. The Toronto *Telegram* found local employers happy with DSCR trainees. At Consolidated Optical, R.F. Reid had trained seventeen workers and he wanted more.[72] *Maclean's Magazine* published glowing success stories: Madeline Jaffray, a nursing sister who had lost a foot when her hospital was bombed, was now a TB nurse; Jimmy Harrison, a farm boy with a missing leg, now prospered as a typewriter salesman. Donald J. McDougall, the blind masseur, had won a scholarship to Oxford, and Maj. Ralph Webb, another leg amputee, was mayor of Winnipeg.[73]

The achievements were public, but the strains were hidden. The strike at the Winnipeg vocational school, another at the limb factory when Coulthard took over, and a host of other minor disputes reflected the problems of improvisation.[74] In June 1919 Col. McKelvey Bell suddenly quit over an effort by Segsworth to secure his own vocational medical advisers. General Fotheringham joyously predicted the collapse of the DSCR;

Lougheed sneered that Bell merely wanted more money. Bell's successor soon escaped to a vacancy on the Pension Board, and the third director of medical services, W.C. Arnold, was a young Saskatchewan doctor who was too junior to assert any professional pretensions. Segsworth left soon after.[75]

By 1919 the GWVA had become a persistent critic of the department and its senior officials. Lougheed's arrogance in the Winnipeg strike rankled for months. His latest deputy minister, F.G. Robinson, had spent the war with the British Cheese Commission until Armstrong hired him as his assistant in the MHC. Surely, Loughnan argued, there were qualified ex-servicemen for such posts.[76] The GWVA executive claimed that the deputy minister lacked 'that qualification of sympathetic understanding of returned men and their needs which can only exist in those who have themselves seen active service.'[77] In 1920, when Robinson resigned, he was succeeded by the man who had defeated the Winnipeg DSCR strike, Norman Parkinson, an artillery veteran.

Veterans were not inherently opposed to government. Soldiers overseas had developed little love for such private agencies as the Red Cross or the YMCA, and their wives had resented the CPF's affluent 'lady volunteers.'[78] MacNeil and the GWVA opposed government efforts to shuffle responsibilities to charities. Surely, veterans regularly insisted, the government should bury destitute veterans instead of subsidizing the Montreal-based Last Post Fund.[79] In 1921, MacNeil irritated some MPs by arguing that the DSCR, with all its faults, was more efficient than a private agency: 'You usually have to wait sometime for a decision from the governing body who are men engaged in other activities, and who find it impossible to specialize on the particular problems under discussion.'[80]

The problem was that members of Parliament, the government, and even some senior DSCR officials wanted to believe that re-establishment was over, that traditional institutions could now take over, and that most of the specialized agencies created for returning men could be demobilized. The 1920-1 depression made cost-cutting seem all the more urgent. Yet to veterans that same depression underlined the failure of re-establishment and the permanence of the veteran problem. On 15 April 1921, the GWVA secretary addressed the fourth post-war parliamentary committee on re-establishment: 'The circumstances of a large class of men [are] worse than when they were demobilized. Their resources are exhausted, they are discouraged in many ways, they are facing increased living costs, and their outlook is uncertain.' These were not the casual labourers normally victimized by the business cycle: 'We found ... that many men formerly regarded ... as in comfortable circumstances, were absolutely, at certain stages last winter, without a crust of bread in the house. They had not regained their footing at all in civilian life.'[81]

Alarmism is the stock-in-trade of all pressure groups, but no one argued with MacNeil. His claims were echoed by W.F. Nickle, now the honorary secretary of a fast-dwindling Patriotic Fund.[82] The newly formed Amputations Association claimed that one-quarter of its members were out of work. One-fifth of able-bodied veterans had lost their jobs in the new depression, MacNeil declared, and no one could even estimate the extent of the plight of the disabled.[83] The GWVA and other veterans' organizations demanded drastic remedies: five years of free medical care, unemployment insurance, and a housing scheme to create jobs and give urban veterans some of the benefits rural comrades obtained from soldier settlement. The government should adjust its spending to the seasons to minimize winter layoffs and summer overtime.[84] The veterans got cold comfort. The DSCR's Norman Parkinson solemnly opposed each of MacNeil's proposals. Free medical care would cost too much. Business loans to veterans might work in New Zealand, but Canada's northern climate was harsher and veterans could never compete as shopkeepers with Jews, Italians, or Chinese.[85] The MPs agreed. Distress was a normal part of the aftermath of war. The national debt was too high for fresh commitments. Unemployment – or insurance against its consequences – was no longer a federal concern. Returned men must share the plight of their fellow citizens.[86] Some veterans protested; a few hundred of them trudged from Toronto to Ottawa in May of 1922, only to be sent home by train.[87]

In Germany, employers were compelled to accept a 3 per cent quota of disabled veterans, and they devised work and machinery to make their obligation profitable.[88] But Canadians were in no mood to learn from a former enemy. Even Britain's system of genteel persuasion – a 'King's Honour Roll' – for those who hired maimed veterans was more than Canadians would accept. The war was over, and so was re-establishment.

Soldier Settlement

There was no irony intended in MacNeil's suggestion that soldier settlement was a bounty that entitled others to compensation. Much of the western heat behind the Calgary Resolution had been generated by the apparent favour shown to the minority of soldiers who had qualified for free land and cheap loans. For their part, cabinet ministers scarcely understood the confusion; soldier settlement was never more than a business proposition, albeit an excellent one with wheat at $2.02 a bushel in 1918.[89]

Admittedly, the 1917 scheme had begun badly. Delays in implementation, a limited land base, and applicants who were usually disabled, guaranteed short-term trouble. Of two thousand soldiers drawn into the scheme by early 1919, ninety had already given up.[90] No one noticed. From editors to humble citizens, no re-establishment policy was as popular as soldier settlement. The DSCR found tens of thousands of CEF members eager for a farming life. 'If the members of the government are so incompetent that they cannot grapple successfully with this problem,' Saskatchewan's Harris Turner scolded, 'they should call the garbage waggon and have themselves removed to the nuisance ground.'[91]

Except on the prairies, where Arthur Meighen's new department controlled land and resources, the provinces would have to be involved. New Brunswick, Nova Scotia, and Quebec had cautious loan schemes; Ontario and British Columbia had conceived their own more ambitious colonization plans. British Columbia's farmer-premier, 'Honest John' Oliver, had even insisted on a post-war interprovincial conference to ensure that settlement, immigration, and agriculture would be on Canada's peacetime agenda. When the premiers and their key ministers met in Ottawa on 19 November, Meighen was in England and the radical new federal version of soldier settlement was unveiled by J.A. Calder. To bring millions of acres of wild land and abandoned farms into cultivation would demand huge outlays and an end to federal-provincial bickering. Helping soldiers buy farms and pre-empting vacant homesteads would spread settlement to all nine provinces.[92] The premiers applauded, reflected on the costs, and agreed, subject to a strict interpretation of the British North America Act, that Ottawa could look after settling returned soldiers. By the time Meighen returned, Calder had won carte blanche for him to proceed.

The ambitious Manitoban had big ideas: soldier settlement could make him a latter-day Clifford Sifton, peopling the west not with foreigners but with patriotic native sons and selected fellow-Britons. First Meighen had to find land. Roche's critics had been right; public land was inadequate and culled. More land could be squeezed from Indians, Doukhobors, and railway companies, but the only real solution was to lend soldiers the money to buy their own farms. That would extend soldier settlement to the nine provinces and would please veterans and local farmers alike.[93]

On 11 December 1918 Meighen described his plans to Borden. Would-be settlers who wanted to buy a farm would have to pay 10 per cent down and borrow the balance, up to $5,000, from the Soldier Settlement Board. Loans would be paid back over twenty years at 5 per cent interest, half a point lower than the cost to the government of current borrowing. Settlers could borrow an extra $2,000 to cover stock and equipment, repayable over four years, and $1,000 for improvements – normally a house or shack for the family, a shed for livestock, and minimal fencing. From first to last the SSB would protect the government's investment. Applicants would be checked for experience and aptitude as well as for overseas service. Many would have to take training or gain experience with an established farmer. The SSB would make its own valuation of a farm before it paid over the purchase price, and supervisors would watch over both the settlers and the government's equity.[94]

By 11 February 1919 Meighen had cabinet approval. A slight reduction was made to the maximum loan: no more than $4,500 could be advanced for each farm and no settler could borrow more than $7,500. Soldiers on free dominion land could borrow up to $3,000; a veteran with his own farm could borrow $2,000 to clear a mortgage and $3,000 for stock, equipment, and improvements.[95] Parliament, which dealt with the new legislation in late June, presented no obstacle. The Liberal opposition grumbled about too much spending, and two veteran homesteaders in the Senate, J.G. Turriff and Robert Watson, solemnly warned that no homesteader should assume such a weight of debt.[96] They were properly abused by fellow westerners for lack of faith in their own region. Meighen himself set aside the business arguments for his scheme to plead for soldier settlement as a bulwark against the sedition and disorder he had glimpsed in the Winnipeg General Strike:

We believe that we cannot better fortify the country against the waves of unrest and discontent that now assail us, as all the rest of the world, than by making the greatest possible proportion of the soldiers of our country settlers upon our land. Of course, every class of citizen is necessary to constitute the national life, but the class of citizen that counts the most in the determination of the stability of a country against such forces as I mentioned a moment ago is undoubtedly the basic class – the agricultural class. That class is the mainstay of the nation. So the purpose of this bill is a national one primarily. Its purpose is to strengthen the fibre of this country by building into the basic industrial structure ... the best blood and bones of our nation.[97]

Meighen had not waited for Parliament to launch the Soldier Settlement Board on its enormous task. Hundreds of competent farmers would be needed to serve on local qualifying boards. The SSB required experts in appraising the fair market value of working farms. A vast localized bureaucracy must be created to process applications, arrange loans, supervise settlers, purchase and distribute thousands of horses, cattle, sheep, swine, poultry, and farm machinery, and make allowances for all the vagaries of soil, climate, and human nature. Between March 1919 and June 1920 the

SSB staff grew from a couple of hundred to 1,594 employees. Most were returned soldiers; not all could possibly be wise, competent, or even honest. [98]

Only CEF members who had served overseas and those originally domiciled in Canada who had seen action with imperial or Allied forces were entitled to the full benefits of the act. Ex-soldiers from British and dominion forces – neatly excluding veterans from India and non-white colonies – were also eligible if they provided a 20 per cent down payment and served at least a year's apprenticeship on a Canadian farm. [99] Soldiers' widows could qualify if they had sons strong enough to cope with the rigours of pioneering. Nursing sisters, though technically eligible, were urged to look elsewhere for re-establishment. 'They cannot qualify,' Meighen explained, 'for the rough and strenuous duties of settlers.' A 1920 amendment formally excluded them. [100]

There was no lack of applicants. Almost a quarter of the 262,000 soldiers who returned in 1918–19 filed applications. Whole battalions filled out forms. Soldier settlement was promoted both as a lavish benefit for returning heroes and as a strictly commercial undertaking. Of course, it could be both. Veterans with sufficient knowledge of farming to consider making it their future would certainly be aware of the level of agricultural prices. With good returns, paying back the SSB would be easy. Pamphlets, newspapers, and even *The Veteran* proclaimed the achievements of men 'making good' on the land. [101]

Demand soon overwhelmed the improvised SSB machinery. In all of March, only 400 applications were received. From May to July there were 400 a week; by August 600 would-be farmers were submitting forms every week. Serious applicants were interviewed by a qualification committee of agricultural specialists and successful farmers. The screening criteria, based on service, reference, physical fitness, and farming experience, eliminated women and most disabled veterans. Those without experience were referred to local agricultural colleges or urged to sign on as hired hands with recommended farmers. [102] In April the SSB was allowed to offer its trainees and apprentices a small allowance. Meagre by DSCR standards, it was a foretaste of the poverty that awaited many of these would-be-farmers. [103] About three-quarters of the applicants interviewed in 1919 and less than two-thirds of those interviewed in 1920 were granted certificates of qualification. [104]

Once his application was approved, a settler had to find a farm. If the man must be fit to farm, insisted the SSB chairman W.J. Black, so must the land. Politicians and promoters claimed that veterans were ideally suited to assault the northern tree belt or the rugged interior valleys of British Columbia; Black had no such illusions. the Kapuskasing colony, finally shut down by Ontario's Farmer-Labour government in 1920, was testimony to his wisdom. [105] Until Black took over, the SSB had described land in Saskatchewan's Porcupine Forest Reserve as 'of the finest quality and within close proximity to rail transportation.' It was neither. British Columbia tried hard to unload Merville, Camp Lister, and other hopeless ventures of its Land Settlement Board on the SSB, [106] but the board did its best to avoid them. In its first report it firmly spelled out its policy: 'The board does not contemplate the settlement of soldiers as pioneers in remote locations or under isolated conditions, removed from markets, in virgin forest areas or on lands not suitable without reclamation or other development. Lands not cultivable as above explained afford neither attractiveness for the average settler nor the possibility of immediate returns necessary to the settler's subsistence, nor reasonable security for money advances, all of which are essential to make the settlement plan a success.' [107]

About one soldier-settler in six obtained a free grant of 160 acres of dominion land plus the standard 160-acre homestead; one in twelve borrowed money to remove encumbrances; the vast majority borrowed to buy land from private owners. [108] The would-be settler had to find suitable property, negotiate a price, and present the proposal to the nearest SSB office. Board appraisers then made their valuation of the farm. So did a local loans committee composed of farmers and real estate agents. By standing firm, the SSB might persuade the owner to drop the price. But, as the SSB itself confessed, it could not always outsmart local agents or save every gullible veteran. Thomas Caldwell, a farmer elected in 1919 as an Independent from New Brunswick, had served seven months on a loan committee. 'We had a number of these men coming in with absolutely ridiculous propositions to buy a farm equipped with a nice house and all conveniences, which would not produce anything, and we have had them come back two or three times.' [109] Not all loan committees were as tough-minded or as honest. Soldiers whose proposals were rejected could always try again.

Once the board accepted the price, the settler paid his 10 per cent (some settlers were exempted from this requirement 'under very special conditions') and the SSB paid the balance and legal costs and commissions. The new farmer could then use his extra credit to buy stock and equipment and make necessary 'improvements,' with a couple of years' grace before any payment was due. Quantity purchases of machinery, harness, hardware, and lumber allowed the board to pass on discounts as high as 20 per cent. [110]

Meighen originally had sought the power to expropriate suitable settlement land anywhere in Canada. The 1919 act only allowed the board to force owners of large tracts of unimproved land to put the land on the market or face compulsory sale. The Hudson's Bay Company parted with

100,000 acres of its western holdings, and the Pope Ranch, near Eastview, Alberta, contributed 18,000 acres. The act also allowed Meighen to reorganize the mixture of individual and communal holdings on the Doukhobor grant near Kamsack, Saskatchewan. The communal land was consolidated and purchased for ten dollars an acre though, as Meighen boasted, the real value was closer to forty or fifty dollars. 'I may say that the plan of dealing with the Doukhobor reserve ... met with the satisfaction not only of the community, but of the other people of the district, including the returned soldiers' organization.'[111] The GWVA's only objection was that similar treatment had not been meted out to Mennonites, Hutterites, and other 'undesirable aliens.'[112]

Indian veterans were eligible, under the amended Indian Act, for a special version of soldier settlement. Reserve land was exempt from Meighen's special powers, but bands in Alberta, Saskatchewan, and British Columbia were persuaded to part with seventy-eight thousand acres at prices ranging from nine dollars an acre on the prairies to eighty dollars an acre on a small British Columbia reserve.[113] Frank Stacey, a Liberal Unionist MP from British Columbia, would have preferred to expropriate native land: 'In doing justice to the Indian let us not do an injustice to the white man or the country.'[114] To its credit, the GWVA opposed any threat to Indian reserves, and Meighen insisted that valid surrenders must be negotiated.

The minister and the board knew what they wanted. The colony schemes that had intrigued Lougheed and Roche were unacceptable. One loan committee, Black reported, had let soldiers borrow jointly, but the entire loan had to be salvaged when individuals refused to meet their share. 'It early became apparent,' the SSB explained in 1921, 'that the settler must succeed under this scheme the same as any farmer succeeds in the ordinary farming community ... New and experimental projects for overcoming the ordinary burdens of farming or short-cutting on the road to success have not been indulged by the Board to any extent.'[115] Waiver of the down payment, a persistent GWVA demand, led to regular failure. Maj. John Barnett, Black's successor, reported in 1921 that the last of seventeen loans to Ontario settlers exempted from making a down payment was being salvaged. Such men felt little stake in their venture, and they had not learned 'thriftiness in the preservation of their money.' MPs were impressed.[116]

The SSB displayed a cautious common sense, appropriate to the trustee of over one hundred million dollars in public investment. Poultry-rearing and market-gardening, regularly urged as opportunities for the disabled, struck the board as a trap for the unwary. A single error in judgment or an accident could cost a settler his entire crop or flock. Small holdings, another popular panacea, demanded more skill, energy, and luck than a whole farm, not less.[117] The board was a fervent promoter of mixed farming at a time when specialization was in style. A variety of crops and animals preserved fertility, reduced waste, spread labour through the year, and avoided debt: 'With cows, pigs, poultry, and a good vegetable garden much of the foodstuffs that contribute to a healthy livelihood are obtained from the farm.'[118] Such old-fashioned wisdom was conveyed by the SSB's field supervisors. Two or three calls a year – or more frequently, if a settler was floundering – protected the government's investment and distributed counsel where needed. Settlers were encouraged to be patient, hardworking, and realistic. Such fads as the gasoline tractor were discouraged; a team of good horses was all a settler needed to work 160 acres.[119] A Home Service Branch helped settlers' families, especially English war brides, make the harsh transition to homesteading. Short courses subsidized by the Red Cross brought women together to learn unfamiliar skills and to find reassurance in shared experiences. Men, however, did the visiting; women homemakers, Barnett explained, would be too expensive.[120]

Between them, Black and Meighen created a system that drew on a generation of settlement experience. Local committees provided knowledge and experience. Qualified settlers, reasonable valuations, and systematic supervision surely guaranteed that public money was not only safe but certain to yield a rich return. Writing in 1921, the Manitoba author Agnes Laut described soldier settlement as 'one of the biggest pieces of constructive legislation ever enacted in Ottawa.'[121] By any statistical test, the spread of settlement was impressive. At the end of 1919, the board had provided $51.6 million in credit to 17,218 returned soldiers. On the prairies, soldier-settlers had opened 144,000 acres for settlement. Every province shared in the program. By the end of 1920, when the tide began to slow, the SSB claimed 19,890 settlers, 3,056 of them in the eastern provinces, 13,874 on the prairies, and the balance in British Columbia. On 31 March 1921, when the SSB published its first report, 25,433 settlers had been placed on the land, 19,771 of them on privately purchased farms. More than $80 million had been approved in loans, and $77 million had gone toward first mortgages on land and livestock and equipment; the average loan per settler was $4,035. Soldier-settlers had produced 2.6 million bushels of wheat, 6.5 million bushels of oats, and produce valued at $13.9 million.[122]

By then Meighen had become prime minister and leader of a restored Conservative government. Appropriately, he chose the organizer of soldier settlement, W.J. Black, to become a full-time national organizer for the Tories. The SSB would be safe under Maj. John Barnett, a New Brunswick-born lawyer, an adopted Albertan, and a CEF veteran.[123] Barnett could manage success. The sickly failure of 1918 had become what the *Canadian*

Annual Review called 'the largest real estate and loan business in Canada, if not in the British Empire.' [124] In 1919 the GWVA had had plenty to say about soldier settlement, but its sixteen resolutions added up to a demand for still more land and even more credit. The success of the program created demands not only for a bonus but for alternative loan schemes. [125] David Loughnan of *The Veteran* asserted that urban soldiers were entitled to five-thousand-dollar housing loans. Col. Cy Peck insisted that only a fisherman's version of the SSB could keep whites from being driven from the Pacific Coast by the Japanese. [126] Members of Parliament dismissed such schemes as mere versions of the notorious bonus, and concluded that 'a grant to any class or classes, no matter how worthy or pressing their needs might be,' would merely open the door to all. [127] Land colonization was somehow different, in part because of tradition and in part because of an ideology of the soil. It was sound national policy, the SSB stated in its first report, 'to add to the agricultural citizenhood of Canada as great a number as possible of the best of its manhood, those who had seen active service.' [128] Despite the early rush, the board was disappointed that twice as many settlers had not been placed on the land.

The Testing of Success

No one could have expected perfection from the Soldier Settlement Board. However sensible its policies and regulations, their implementation depended on the wisdom of its boards and committees and the honesty and good judgment of hastily recruited officials. Frank Stacey, who was sent to British Columbia to revive a languishing SSB operation there, reported that local realtors 'seemed to possess the spirit of the age to such an extent that they deemed it was up to them to get all they could' even if it meant 'doing' soldiers. [129] In 1920 the Manitoba GWVA launched its own investigation of the Winnipeg SSB office. Evidence that a ring of land agents was operating from the St Regis Hotel and fleecing soldier-settlers brought Maj. John Barnett to the scene. Local officials were fired, a few dealers prosecuted, and other dealers transferred their operations to the United States. Meighen offered revaluation to the affected settlers and formally thanked the GWVA, though he did not refund their legal costs, which amounted to $1,265.28. [130]

SSB boards and committees were moved by sentiment, pressure, and the liberating sense that they were handling public funds. Agnes Laut found that 'pull' from Ottawa or advice from a friendly MP sometimes concealed an applicant's lack of character or experience. When SSB officials tried to prevent a man from buying sandy or swampy land, 'up goes a kick from the relatives, from the returned man, from the returned man's local soldier association.' When the board scaled down prices, it faced charges of bias or corruption. 'There is no man feels so aggrieved as the crook caught in the act and failing to put it through.'[131] Apart from the St Regis ring, corruption was less a problem than inexperience, a fondness for making rules, and hiring errors inevitable in an organization that had grown so fast. C.W. Marshall, who had been fired as a field supervisor, avenged himself by publishing a long list of charges against colleagues and superiors. Black could answer most of the charges, but he also had to explain that Marshall had failed every test of farming knowledge and that he had been hired as a favour to Bob Maxwell of the GWVA.[132] By 1920, the SSB had rid itself of many incompetents; but its meagre salaries made it hard to find good replacements. Appraising land or livestock, as Black explained in 1920, was a scarce skill, but the SSB could offer valuators only $1,800 to $2,400 a year, while the National Trust's Edmonton office offered $2,400 as a starting salary.[133]

The SSB also suffered the unpopularity of any agency that has to say no. Qualification was a major issue. For example, at age forty-five, with twenty-five years of farming experience, was James Robinson young enough to fight but too old to farm? Black was unrepentant. Robinson's farming had been done in Scotland and Northern Ireland, the SSB explained; it would be no favour to him or his large family to load him with debts he would never have the time or the strength to pay off.[134] 'It is no kindness to a returned soldier to put him on a farm when the thing is hopeless from the start.'[135] Decisions about land were equally controversial. Grant MacNeil felt that Alberta's famous Matador Ranch was ideal for soldier settlement. On the contrary, replied Black; most of the Matador was thirty to thirty-five miles from any railway, and it was impossible to find water without drilling deeper than any settler could afford.[136]

Board officials could harden their hearts because the inevitable cycle of failure and salvage had already begun. By November 1920, when the first collections were due, a thousand settlers had given up. The benefit of the doubt had benefited no one. Agnes Laut described 'intelligent duds' whose brilliant theories did not compensate for laziness, and a 'horse nut' whose family was in rags because he spent his money on breeding stock. One man, who planted hay on excellent wheat land, boasted that he did not intend to slave away the only life he had.[137] Such cases were predictable. Their land could be sold for as much as the SSB had invested and often for more. For the board, as for Canada, a brilliant long-term future was the ultimate safeguard against loss. In 1920 parliamentarians concluded a searching review of the SSB with the judgment that its operations 'appear to have been beneficial.'[138]

Yet in retrospect the 1920s were not good years in which to invest in Canadian agriculture. The war had effaced the salutary lessons of the 1913–14 depression and drought. After the bumper harvest of 1915, prairie wheat yields fell as steadily as prices rose. The 1919 spring wheat crop was among the worst in memory – 9.5 bushels to the acre – at unquestionably the highest price – $2.36 a bushel. [139] This was the counterpoint to the grim warnings from Turriff and Watson in 1919 and to predictions by the Alberta Liberal-Unionist, Dr Michael Clark, that 'we are launching a huge scheme ... which is foredoomed to failure, and we are committing almost a crime against the men whom we send farming.' [140]

Ottawa knew that gloomy forebodings, plus denunciations of the tariff, were as much part of the ritual rhetoric of prairie politicians as a florid faith in their region's ultimate prospects. The SSB knew there would be good years and bad. The 1920 crop year was a fair test. A hard winter, a hot dry summer, and a plague of grasshoppers did not prevent a better wheat crop than had been produced in 1919, but prices, thanks to a restored Winnipeg Grain Exchange, took a mid-harvest tumble. By all the most recent standards, even $1.60 a bushel was no disaster. At the end of the year, 9,802 of the 12,233 settlers with payments due had met their obligations in whole or in part and 390 had paid off their loans completely. [141] In 1921, a very mild winter and an 'extraordinary and prolonged drought,' as the *Canada Year Book* noted, caused crop failures even on Cape Breton Island. On the prairies, disaster was averted by rain in late June; but when the rain returned during the September harvest, delivery was delayed, grades dropped, and so did prices – to eighty cents a bushel for wheat. That was higher than the sixty-six cents of 1913, but in the interval inflation had halved the value of the Canadian dollar. [142]

The 1921 crop year began a prolonged agricultural depression. By 1924, the economist C.R. Fay would observe that if a Canadian farmer had paid himself wages at the going rate for an unskilled city labourer, he would have put himself out of business. [143] Instead of paying themselves, most farmers had to pay banks and mortgage companies for loans contracted in more buoyant conditions. Soldier-settlers had arrived too late for wartime profits, but they had paid wartime prices for land and stock, and their debts must be paid off as farm incomes plummeted. From 1918, when the SSB began operations, to 31 March 1920, 1,270 settlers were 'salvaged'; by March 1923, 2,115 more had walked away from their investment. [144] The general disaster blunted public awareness of the special plight of veterans struggling to clear land in the Peace River country or the Porcupine Reserve and of the men on Nicoaman Island in the Fraser River, who were flooded out three years running while Ottawa and Victoria quarrelled over who should build dikes. [145]

Belatedly, veterans' organizations began to realize that soldier settlement had not been a bonus. In December 1921 the GWVA's Alberta command demanded an extension on repayments and a revaluation of all land and equipment purchased through the SSB. [146] 'I am informed that millions of dollars set aside for land settlement purposes has [sic] been absolutely wasted,' wrote Sir Arthur Currie. [147] That was an exaggeration in 1922, but the impression mattered more than the facts. 'Viewing it from every possible angle,' warned *The Veteran*, 'the failure of soldier settlement would be a national calamity.' [148]

Meighen, defeated as much by the 1921 depression as by wartime unpopularity, could no longer intervene. The new Liberal government, elected on 6 December 1921, was too dependent on votes from skittish rural Progressives to ignore the problem. The temptation to denounce a predecessor's follies had to be muffled in the non-partisanship appropriate to veterans' concerns and so vast a national enterprise. Major Barnett, summoned to a meeting of the latest special committee on 21 April 1922, admitted that the SSB repayment plan was too heavy: 'My own opinion is that the original act was wrong ... when it said a man could pay for his stock and equipment in four annual instalments, because even in 1919 that was impossible.' [149] A prairie Progressive, Alfred Speakman, agreed that it was wrong for settler's four heaviest annual payments – for stock and equipment, as well as for land – to come at the start of his career. The answer was to consolidate the two loans, make them repayable over twenty-five years, not twenty, and, in recognition of earlier high prices, forgive interest payments until 1923. When Meighen mocked the folly of collecting loans on stock that would be long since dead and equipment that would be utterly worn out, Speakman, as co-chairman of the committee, reminded him: 'Our object was not to frame a law that would read well or sound well or that was even particularly consistent; our object was to bring about conditions of re-payment on the land which would enable these men to succeed on a return to normal agricultural prosperity.' [150]

The GWVA and even Speakman would have preferred a revaluation of all SSB properties, but both attitudes and evidence were against them. In 1923 Barnett could boast that the profit on 1,306 parcels of salvaged land more than covered the SSB's losses on salvaged stock and equipment – though obviously there was painfully little to show for the settler's down payment or his labour. [151] Revaluation also challenged the optimism inherent in the residents of 'Next Year Country.' It was difficult to accept that the prices and values of the wartime years were gone. Making Ottawa wait a little longer for its money seemed infinitely preferable. Soldier-settlers, claimed the Saskatchewan GWVA yearbook, 'finished the 1922 season in splendid shape.' Next year's crops would be better, and the debt handicap had been eased by a total of $10.2 million.[152]

For soldier-settlers, as for disabled veterans, the post-war depression revealed the shaky foundations of plans and policies that had seemed completely logical and realistic. In both cases a modest initial investment had promised prosperous self-sufficiency for veterans and a generous dividend to the nation. In both cases, Canadians could congratulate themselves on programs that exceeded, in efficiency and promise, anything that their allies could boast. Then, because of a predictable and short-lived economic depression, both re-establishment and soldier settlement had apparently come unstuck.

In fact, 1923 would be no better. By the end of that year the SSB reported 30,604 soldier-settlers with loans totalling $103,150,098, but almost one-fifth of them had already abandoned the struggle. The SSB was transferred to the Department of Immigration and Colonization in order to implement the '3,000 British Family Scheme,' the latest device of the back-to-the-land movement. Operating as the Land Settlement Board, the SSB could now give its latest clients a choice of more than three thousand abandoned and unsaleable soldier-settlement farms.[153]

Agriculture was not the only industry to go sour in post-war Canada. Although it had been delayed by post-war demand and the furious readjustment to peacetime markets, the pre-war depression returned with a vengeance in the autumn of 1920. By the summer of 1921, even the Department of Labour estimated that two hundred thousand Canadians were unemployed.[154] Many of them were returned soldiers whose gratuities were spent and whose fragile hold on re-establishment was easily broken. Unemployment relief, doled out by the DSCR only to the disabled, was collected that year by one in five pensioners. Those who imagined that their war service would somehow give them a claim to work and wages felt bitterly deceived.[155]

In 1915 Ernest Scammell, acutely conscious of the pre-war depression, had envisaged the need for special provision for returning soldiers; a year later, the Military Hospitals Commission had urged, as a transitional measure, such massive public works as the building of a national highway.[156] Such ideas were forgotten during the wartime prosperity, and they were overshadowed by post-war fiscal anxieties. Unemployment was a provincial problem for which no prudent federal government could possibly assume responsibility. Besieged by municipal officials made nervous by unemployed veterans, Arthur Meighen had offered half a million dollars to help with direct relief in 1921 on the ingenious argument that the depression was the tail-piece of a wartime crisis. There must be no precedent for a general federal assumption of those 'charitable and eleemosynary' functions the constitution had providentially reserved for the provinces. As for the veterans, re-establishment was over.[157]

What Meighen and his colleagues forgot was that re-establishment, particularly for the disabled, was not an end in itself. As John Todd had foreseen in 1915, successful re-establishment was the only certain antidote to the 'pension evil.' Only if veterans were able to move from dependency to self-sufficiency would endless pressures to enhance the pension system be curbed. Only if veterans came to see themselves as taxpayers would they and their friends resist ingenious appeals to broaden the basis of pensioning. The depression of 1921 effectively undid all that Scammell, Todd, and Segsworth had hoped to achieve just as certainly as it undermined soldier settlement.

The trouble was not temporary and could not easily be repaired.

8 The Ralston Commission

Pension Principles and Law

'One of the greatest advantages enjoyed by a new country,' John Todd had written in 1915, 'is that when it is confronted by an unaccustomed situation it is usually possible for it, by a consideration of the history of other nations placed in similar circumstances, at least to avoid the mistakes of others.'[1] Todd and his colleagues had had several cautionary models: the American 'pension evil,' the British 'military mendicancy,' even the Canadian 'soldier's bounty.' Todd had not only devised principles; he remained, even after he left the Pension Board, an active advocate. Readers of the *North American Review* were reminded in 1919 that 'to serve good pension law we must fortify and guide our desire to deal fairly with fighting men by understanding what should be done for them and the manner and cost of doing it.'[2]

Whatever his minor defeats, Todd believed that he had given Canada a 'good pension law.' Separating the analysis of disability from the ultimate pension decision eliminated sentimentality. Most Canadians, bewildered by the complexity of pension administration, would be content only to know that Canada's pension rates were the highest in the world. By September 1920 a totally disabled private collected the same pension as a lieutenant: $900 a year. Even when the U.S. Congress raised its rate to $1,200, the BPC could point out that a totally disabled Canadian with a wife and two children received $1,380, while the Americans made no extra provision for families. The British equivalent for a private was $728; the Australians, once the leaders in pension payments, could afford only $696 a year.[3]

Prudently, the board rarely mentioned that barely 5 per cent of Canadian pensioners collected the full rate; 80 per cent received under 50 per cent of the maximum, and most received 20 per cent or less. The Americans also added disability percentages, so that a U.S. counterpart of Curly Christian got more than twice the total disability rate. The BPC deducted one disability before assessing the next: for example, a missing leg was calculated at 40 per cent; its mate would be 40 per cent of the remaining 60 per cent. A bilateral amputee might qualify for only a 64 per cent pension.[4] Since the man still had two good arms, the board left him plenty of incentive to test his earning capacity. Nor were pensions permanent. Veterans lived in anxious expectation of the next examination. Time, experience, and new prostheses might make even a permanent injury less disabling.

The board, as it reminded critics, was a trustee for the public as well as for soldiers. Veterans insisted that pension commissioners and their staff should be returned soldiers, but such men were not always sympathetic. Former medical officers were less tolerant of battlefield neuroses than civilian practitioners. The army encouraged its doctors to suspect 'scrim-shanking' and 'malingering' among the sick. Officers considered soldiers who argued for their rights 'barrack-room lawyers.'[5] Such attitudes were not easily shed. Moreover, the magnitude of disability claims and the resulting fiscal burden alarmed those of a conservative disposition. From 1 April 1918 to 31 March 1920, the total pension burden soared from $7.27 million to $25.18 million. Disability pensions grew from 15,335 to 69,203. By the end of 1920, 177,035 men, women, and children were being supported in whole or in part by pension cheques.[6]

Politicians were no help. MPs had cheered Lt-Col. Cy Peck, the Victoria Cross winner, when he declared: 'This great and chivalrous country does not care and never will object, though the expenditure involved for these purposes reaches ten, twenty or even two hundred million dollars.'[7] Sir Henry Drayton, freed of the burdens of the Finance Department, could be equally expansive in 1922: 'This whole pension scheme has nothing to do with strict rules of law. It is an endeavour to do the right thing, and to do it to the fullest extent.'[8]

In fact, pension legislation defied this blithe spirit and became increasingly intricate, technical, and bewildering. Experts boasted of the anomalies they discovered; veterans were merely mystified. For fifteen years the Pension Act became a primary focus for veterans' organizations, an almost annual ordeal for Parliament, and, after service of the public debt, by far the largest single burden on the national finances. Veterans' pensions drew the federal government into areas of social policy, administrative law, medical expertise, and political values in which there were few precedents.[9]

Parliament used its first post-war session in 1919 to turn the wartime pension regulations into law. The special committee, headed by Newton Rowell, could draw on three years experience with the 1916 order in council.

Basic drafting seems to have been left to the BPC's solicitor, Kenneth Archibald. Making his debut as GWVA secretary, Grant MacNeil argued for pension equalization, the rights of Imperial veterans, and the need to appeal BPC rulings, but his main concern had been pension rates, unchanged since 1917. Rowell's committee had recommended adding a temporary 20 per cent bonus, removable when prices came down.[10]

Neither the committee nor Parliament delved deeply into the intricacies of the pension bill. By the time the special committee reported, it was late June. The burning of Parliament in 1916 had relegated members to hot, stuffy quarters among the dinosaurs in the Victoria Museum. Attendance was small and attention wandered. Only on the third day of debate, late in the committee stage, was there a spurt of excitement when an MP finally noted that pensions might be paid to 'unmarried wives.' Was the phrase a Yankeeism? demanded a backbencher. 'It is not a Yankeeism,' responded the venerable Rodolphe Lemieux; 'it is paganism.' Two days later, flourishing a copy of a Toronto magazine that proposed easy divorce as a solution to the post-war lack of single men, Lemieux was afire with moral virtue. 'It is time to say Halt,' he roared. 'Do not listen to every passing whim and every passion of the moment.'[11] Government members rose to the challenge. Fresh from their experience with the Patriotic Fund, Sir Herbert Ames and W.F. Nickle recalled how the war had lifted the veil on all manner of family relationships. Rowell reminded Lemieux that he had belonged to the 1916 committee that originally endorsed pensions for 'unmarried wives.' Col. Robert Mackie, an Ottawa Valley lumberman, scolded self-righteous MPs for their hypocrisy: 'it has been the duty of men from Christ down to the present time to throw the stone at woman.'[12] A motion to remove the offending words and replace them with 'a woman awarded a pension under subsection 3 or section 32 of this Act' passed on division.[13] In the Senate, Raoul Dandurand teased the dignified Lougheed: 'Does this payment to the concubine of the soldier do any violence to my hon. friend's sense of propriety?' Evidently, it did not.[14]

The core of the new act was section 11: 'The Commission shall award pensions to or in respect of members who have died ... when the disability or death in respect of which the application for pension is made was attributable to or was incurred or aggravated during military service.' The entitlement was far broader than Todd himself had recommended in 1918. A soldier on leave who lost his leg in a bus accident would have as valid a claim as a soldier who suffered the same injury from a German shell. Rowell admitted that the act was really 'an insurance system.'[15] As with an insurance policy, there were provisos: death or injury on 'occupational leave' – usually for harvesting – were excluded. Soldiers serving after the official 'Declaration of Peace' (still two years away in 1919) could be pensioned only if death or disability was 'the direct result of military service.' No pension could result from 'improper conduct,' which was defined as 'wilful disobedience of orders, self-inflicted wounding and vicious or criminal conduct.'[16] Venereal disease was considered to be self-inflicted; continence or prophylaxis would prevent it. Few politicians wished to argue the point, but drunkenness was another matter. An impassioned plea from Colonel Peck for 'full-blooded fellows who would get into scrapes by giving rein to their inclinations' persuaded MPs to remove a reference to inebriation. Boys would be boys.[17]

With the conspicuous exception of the insurance principle, Todd's pension policies survived intact. Pension commissioners would remain immune from appeal and would be insulated from politics by ten-year terms. Pensions would be based on disability, not on service or past income: 'The occupation or income or condition of life of a person previous to his becoming a member of the forces shall not in any way affect the amount of pension award.'[18] The loss of an arm was deemed an identical disability for a bricklayer or a barrister. No pension was permanent; the board would review the cases of disabled beneficiaries regularly. Men who failed to appear would lose their pensions, and they could be penalized if they refused operations or treatments that might reduce the degree of disability.[19]

Todd's understandable preference for principle over murky pragmatism had one limitation: reality is more imaginative than theory. The Pension Act presumed that men were fit on enlistment, yet the evidence was clear that thousands of unfit recruits had slipped into the CEF. Accordingly, BPC examiners rapidly became ingenious at assessing pre-enlistment disability, even without records. The board also distinguished between soldiers who had reached 'an actual theatre of war' from those who had not. The former, Rowell explained, had obviously passed so many medical exams that they must have been fit; others could be pensioned only for whatever 'aggravation' military service had caused to their previous disability.[20] Strict enforcement of the policy accounted for the thousands of cases of veterans with tiny pensions who were too sick or disabled to support themselves. The public, unaware of this subtlety of pension policy, assumed official neglect. Doctors who stretched a point for hapless veterans were furious when BPC examiners scorned their opinions.[21]

Hard cases made headlines. Had Gunner Kennedy, who drowned near London, Ontario, after a sweaty route march, really known that swimming was prohibited? No sign had been posted, yet 'misconduct' ruled him out of a pension. Private Lockwood, paraded in January 1916 for inspection by

Sir Sam Hughes, went home to die of pneumonia. His wife got no pension because the board discovered that Lockwood had had a pre-enlistment case of rheumatic fever. Soldiers trapped in a YMCA dugout without their respirators had no recourse for injuries from poison gas; they had disobeyed orders. So had a man who had deliberately exposed himself to a German sniper; his widow would suffer for his self-inflicted wound.[22] So would many more, including dependants of men shot for cowardice.

Dependants' pensions created many problems. The board accepted the legal burdens that a man would have exercised himself. A widow's pension was an absolute right, Rowell stated in 1919, 'because it was the duty of the husband to support her, and the State, recognizing that fact, grants the pension regardless of her financial position.'[23] Parents were another matter. Surely a son had a duty to his widowed mother, or even to both parents if they were destitute. In Quebec, provincial law enforced that obligation; other provinces relied on custom. The Pension Act could do no more. Mothers, fathers, even helpless sisters and brothers would receive pension benefits as a dutiful son and brother would have wished, but only after their means were carefully scrutinized. Widows of two pre-war brigadier-generals found that their meagre five-hundred-dollar government pensions were large enough to bar them from receiving mothers' pensions of behalf of sons killed in the war. Helping them would be 'class legislation.'[24] C.G. 'Chubby' Power launched a popular, if unavailing, crusade by demanding automatic pensions for widowed mothers who had lost sons in the war. The cause became more popular because of the obtrusive BPC surveillance to ensure that its means tests had not been subverted. One sympathetic MP complained that there was 'nothing more nauseating to the widowed mother of a fallen soldier than to have these inspectors coming around to see whether the small amount of pension on which they can barely live is being augmented in any way.'[25] Calling them 'visitors' did not make the BPC investigators more popular.

The board was parent and guardian to orphans and provider to widows' families. Pensions now ended at age sixteen for sons and at age seventeen for daughters unless a child, 'through mental or physical infirmity,' had to be supported to the age of twenty-one. The act also allowed support to age twenty-one for students 'making satisfactory progress in a course of instruction approved by the Commission.'[26] The BPC chairman would later explain that approval was rarely given except for technical courses that helped a youngster earn a living; academic education usually led to 'inferior clerical positions.'[27] Widows were spared a means test, but their claims were not necessarily easy to establish. Some wives found themselves 'unmarried' because the war had exposed a bigamous relationship in England. In a choice of wives, the BPC usually preferred the latest; but Mary Knight lost her pension when the board discovered that an earlier husband, who had deserted her in 1903, was still alive.[28] A soldier who came home insanely persuaded that he was married to Lady Astor left his real wife and three children penniless when he bolted from the escort taking him to an asylum. A deserter's dependants had no claim. CQMS W.J. Ball had been posted as a deserter months after he vanished in France in 1919. The GWVA dutifully campaigned for a pension for his wife and sons, since the man must be dead. But at the end of 1921 Ball showed up in Saint John with an elaborate tale of robbery, amnesia, and a hitch with the brutal Spanish Foreign Legion.[29]

Parliament, the Pension Board, and most Canadians agreed that marriage was a lifelong contract. Women who remarried lost their pensions, but a lump-sum payment for one year provided them with a dowry. Board investigators pursued faint and anonymous hints of immorality with the ardour of a jealous spouse. Any widow suspected of cohabitation, prostitution, or even so minor as sin a bootlegging lost her pension without notice or appeal.[30] Pensions were intended to keep a widow at home. When Brig.-Gen. H.H. McLean, a Liberal-Unionist MP from Saint John, suggested that such women could earn a living, a shocked CPF official demanded: 'Why should the widow of a man who laid down his life for his country be expected to work?' An embarrassed McLean compounded his offence by mumbling that, after all, private's wives came from the servant class. The resulting uproar from veterans and parliamentarians terminated McLean's political career.[31] Widows, of course, worked when they could, as women did in growing numbers in post-war Canada.

One category of widow was strictly denied a pension: the woman who married after the appearance of her future husband's disability was considered to be the author of her own misfortune. Grant MacNeil and T.W. Caldwell, a New Brunswick Progressive, urged such cases in the face of invariable reminders of the 'pension widows,' the conniving American harpies who still lived on the avails of deathbed marriages.[32] 'Every woman would want to get married if she thought she was going to be maintained,' warned a major's widow in 1919.[33] MacNeil's examples included a widow whose husband had been healthy enough after their marriage to earn a Military Cross and another whose mate had been accepted for the post-war permanent force. His arguments were in vain.[34]

'Tightening Up'

Pension commissioners always insisted that they were the mere instruments of Parliament. The enormous rush of claims in 1919 and a complete change of personnel kept the board from straying into innovation in at least the first post-war year. Col. John Thompson, appointed in December 1918, became chairman six months later. The eldest son of Canada's first Catholic prime minister, Thompson had raised a CEF battalion in Ottawa and earned the DSO in France. He was a bachelor, a shrewd lawyer, an austere conservative, and a rigid guardian of the public treasury. His colleagues were lesser men. Stanley Coristine, secretary to the board from its inception, replaced Todd until August 1920, when the DSCR's second director of medical services, Dr E.G. Davis, took over. The third member, Lt-Col. J.W. Margeson, a former paymaster, politician and a GWVA stalwart, used the board as a stepping-stone to a Nova Scotia judgeship at the end of 1921.[35]

Thompson rapidly became as dominant in the BPC as Todd had once been. When the usual parliamentary committee met in 1920, he arrived with what he described as 'one or two changes where we have thought it was rather working a hardship on the individuals concerned.'[36] Thompson then rushed away, leaving Margeson and E.G. Ahern, the board's new secretary, to explain such details as an added thousand dollars for each commissioner and the commutation of all pensions of 10 per cent or less. The GWVA had certainly pressed for the arrangement, and the amounts, $700 and $300, were well below actuarial expectation.[37] Seemingly innocuous was a revised section 11, which promised pensions for death or disability 'attributable' to military service.' Removing six words, Ahern explained, merely brought the Canadian act 'into line with the general law of other countries.' It would affect only the permanent force. Margeson echoed the assurances. Nothing would interfere with the rights of the men of the CEF: 'I can assure you that when the final Act comes to be drawn up it will be carefully seen to that there is none in this war will have any rights taken away from him as far as aggravation is concerned.'[38]

Suitably reassured, the committee and veterans' representatives turned to other matters. Continuing inflation persuaded the committee to raise the 1919 bonus to 50 per cent, though only for pensioners living in Canada. It would be unfair, claimed Hume Cronyn, the committee chairman, to give CEF pensioners living in the United States more than their American counterparts. On the other hand, widowed mothers would henceforth be deemed to be getting ten dollars a month from any unmarried sons. According to Cronyn, the public demanded it: Canadians were shocked when a widow with 'three or four strapping sons' claimed a full pension.[39]

In fact, Margeson's reassurances about section 11 were disingenuous. The board had decided to tighten up. The deepening economic depression was argument enough for restraint. Like Todd, Thompson rejected the 'insurance principle' as a basis for war pensions, and he had used his legal ingenuity to eliminate it. To confirm the matter, in 1921 section 11 was again amended: only 'military service *as such*' would henceforth make a disability pensionable.[40] The change was not retroactive; no pensions were cancelled. Instead, Colonel Thompson had blocked future claims. When, in the course of illness, injury, or old age, veterans rediscovered wartime disabilities, the 'due to service' principle would frustrate their efforts to link present pain and past injuries. Thompson had cleverly foreseen a flood of 'missing link' pension claims, and he had moved deftly to plug the dyke. Parliamentarians hardly noticed. With an election due, it was more important to increase pension rates than to get tangled up in legal technicalities. The board, declared E.W. Nesbitt, was 'very generous.' In the bipartisan spirit of veterans' affairs, no one cared to argue.[41]

The election campaign that ended on 6 December 1921 was the longest in Canadian history. Considering the veterans' role in 1917 and the anathema the GWVA had pronounced on the Unionists in 1920, veterans had remarkably little to say in the contest. J.V. Conroy, secretary of the Toronto GWVA, claimed that veterans had most to gain from Arthur Meighen's election. Ed O'Flynn, the new president of the Ontario command of the GWVA, assured Mackenzie King that the veterans were all against Meighen. O'Flynn was, King recorded, 'a good Liberal and pleasant young fellow.'[42] In fact, veterans probably split in all directions and no party claimed – though all politely solicited – their support.[43] Few ex-soldiers stood as candidates, and most of the officers elected as Unionists in 1917 were either called to the Senate or were buried in Meighen's debacle.

Grant MacNeil had his hopes for the campaign. By 1921 he had created an efficient 'Adjustment Bureau.' An entire floor of Ottawa's Citizen Building was crammed with desks and filing cabinets; GWVA advisers tried to guide soldiers, widows, and orphans through the mysteries of government bureaucracy. Members and non-members, great and small, benefited. *The Veteran* reported that a prominent western colonel, having exhausted official channels and political influence, had turned to the GWVA bureau. An adviser looked over his case, noted the points that officialdom expected to be covered, and won the claim. The colonel promptly took out a membership.[44] The Adjustment Bureau, however, devoured money, and the GWVA by now was in a financial crisis. In the wake of the bonus defeat, membership had slumped. Saddled with the cost of grandiose buildings, the local branches postponed or forgot their per capita dues to the dominion command. To MacNeil, the Adjustment Bureau embodied the GWVA commitment to the disabled and dependent; without it, the association was no better than the Army and Navy Veterans or the bonus-hunting GAUV. Yet without money and members the commitment would collapse.[45]

Inspiration came from the United States. President Warren Harding's Veterans' Bureau had launched a 'Clean-Up Campaign' aimed at settling every last claim from the war. The GWVA would push Canada to follow suit with a 'Clean Sweep.' Any veteran could use the GWVA to argue on his behalf for pay, pensions, gratuity, or medical treatment. If the local branch or provincial command failed, the Adjustment Bureau would take over. 'If you have a claim,' posters urged, 'present it now.'[46] The election campaign helped make ministers and officials unusually obliging. Departments assigned staff to settle veterans' problems. The Militia Department announced that it was holding $350,000 worth of undelivered cheques. Claims poured through GWVA branches. Bill Turley, the Ontario secretary, had so many applications that he bundled them into parcels and shipped them to Ottawa by express.[47]

When the election produced a parliament of minorities, all parties needed friends. To manage both the DSCR and the young Department of Health, King turned a little reluctantly to Henri Séverin Béland, a country doctor who had represented Beauce County since 1902. Captured by the Germans in 1914 when he was visiting his wife's home in Belgium, Béland had spent much of the war in prison. In a prisoner exchange in 1917, after his wife's death, he came home a martyr. In 1919 Liberals had used him to second their veterans' bonus resolution. The new minister was an affable light-weight. 'The truth is, these two departments are far too much for Béland,' King noted in his diary. 'I doubt if he will make a good administrator.' Still, a veteran Quebecker had been rewarded and ex-soldiers appeared pleased.[48]

As James Struthers has argued, the shape of the new Parliament had enormous consequences for the kind of government the GWVA and unre-established veterans needed. Whatever his personal reputation as a reformer, Mackenzie King had committed his party by 1921 to reassuring business by cutting taxes and farmers by cutting tariffs. The Progressives, whose support he needed, made it clear through their leader, T.A. Crerar, that 'rigid economy' was among their strict conditions. Laurier's old finance minister, W.S. Fielding, summoned back to the same portfolio, could promise a 'great slashing' in public expenditure. Colonel Thompson might espouse the wrong politics, but he would have allies in his efforts to resist pension extravagance.[49]

Veterans' organizations met the new government with high hopes and clear demands. The Ottawa GWVA branch had called for a royal commission to probe re-establishment grievances. When MacNeil and Bob Maxwell, the GWVA president, met King and Béland, they settled for the promise of a new parliamentary committee. As chairman the Liberals picked Herbert Marler, a former CEF major and Montreal lawyer, elected in 1921. With brisk efficiency, Marler split his members into subcommittees and pressed them for early reports. MPs agreed to extend the 1920 bonus, to give RSI applicants a further year, and to repatriate CEF veterans who had failed to find work in England. So high was the level of satisfaction, Marler concluded, that an appeals tribunal for pension claimants would have nothing to do. The government would agree to the formation of a medical advisory board; three Ottawa doctors would hear appeals from veterans denied pensions or treatment on purely medical grounds.[50]

MacNeil found Marler's committee frustrating and its chairman unfriendly. Splitting the committee certainly speeded its work, but it prevented MacNeil from attending every session. In his absence, veterans' cocerns lacked effective advocacy. Marler himself was fulsome in his praise for the Pension Board. He frustrated an attempt by a Tory backbencher to restore the 'insurance principle' to section 11 and insisted that he had heard no feasible ideas for getting unemployed veterans back to work. MacNeil, who had provided a good number of such ideas, could rightly feel insulted.[51] But he had a much more serious concern than Marler. Only in 1922 had the GWVA absorbed the impact of the amendment of section 11. The 'Clean Sweep' helped. BPC decisions had never been explained, even to claimants, but the flood of cases began to show a pattern. Widows whose pensioner-husbands had died of their disabilities found their own pension claims rejected. Men whose wartime injuries or diseases suddenly flared into a fresh disability learned that there was now a 'missing link' in their claim. Dying veterans who sought returned soldiers' insurance now had their applications rejected. Someone was tightening up the rules, but with what authority?[52]

Late in May 1922 someone slipped MacNeil a copy of a BPC minute dated 29 September 1921. Henceforth, the board had ruled, once a pre-enlistment disability had improved to its former state, any pension for aggravation would be cancelled. MacNeil realized that this ignored the blanket protection that section 25(3) gave men who had served in 'an actual theatre of war.' Here was evidence of a board conspiracy to subvert the law. On 12 June, as Marler struggled to wind up his committee and bask in his achievements, he faced an irate MacNeil armed with his proof that the Pension Board had defied Parliament. BPC officials, hurriedly summoned, failed to reassure the GWVA official. Colonel Thompson, who met him late on 12 June, did not even try. The board, Thompson maintained, followed the Pension Act to the letter. The insurance principle had been dead since 1920. What about all the assurances from officials and MPs? MacNeil asked. Thompson was blunt: he didn't give a damn; he enforced the law as Parliament wrote it.[53]

MacNeil was now worried as well as angry. If Thompson was right, thousands of veterans and widows had lost any hope of a pension. Marler was no help: by arranging the meeting, he felt he had done his duty. He now had a report to finish. MacNeil summoned his executive. The young secretary's fury seeped into the draft telegram that circled the table at the hurriedly convened meeting. Even cooler heads agreed that there would never be a better time for the GWVA to strike. On the afternoon of 15 June news services tapped out the fiery telegram MacNeil had dispatched to Marler's committee: 'Following recent disclosures surrounding Parliamentary inquiry, we openly charge Pensions Board with contemptible and cold-blooded conspiracy to deprive ex-service men of rights previously granted by Parliament. There has been deliberate concealment, secret regulations, pensions and insurance in direct violation intention of Parliament and deliberate attempts to disguise facts before present Parliamentary Committee. This is culmination unsympathetic policy of increasing severity during recent months.'[54]

The GWVA telegram and seven accompanying charges created instant editorial uproar. Marler had to act. His special committee hurriedly met and, with a certain resentment, recommended that a royal commission investigate the allegations. The House concurred. The Senate sent its own special message by savaging most of the Pension Act amendments the Liberal government had just pushed through the lower house. Pensions for widows who had married disabled soldiers, a belated triumph for Caldwell, were firmly rejected. 'We know very well,' Fred Pardee reminded his fellow senators, 'that there were many marriages contracted during the war simply for the purpose of obtaining the returned soldier's gratuity.' In such matters, Lougheed added, 'we had better make haste slowly.'[55] If the Pension Board chose to resist original sin and extravagance, the Senate would be its bipartisan ally.

Except for the expense, King's government had nothing to lose from investigating the veterans' charges, since neither the board nor the Pension Act were its creations. For MacNeil and the GWVA, the stakes were much higher. In 1918 Harris Turner had warned of MacNeil's 'impulsive enthusiasm.' Now that enthusiasm had burst. For MacNeil, as for many a person who has spoken in hot conviction, reflection proved chilling. Reginald Bowler, the able, one-armed lawyer who headed the Winnipeg GWVA, was summoned to act as MacNeil's counsel. He knew that Colonel Thompson's interpretation of the Pension Act was probably right in law. Words like 'conspiracy,' 'concealment,' and 'defiance of Parliament' made fine invective, but where was the proof?

Everything depended on who formed the royal commission. The DSCR's new deputy minister grasped the point. Early on 22 June Norman Parkinson ordered Scammell to draft an order in council appointing two venerable Liberal judges, Renwick Riddell and Charles Archer, and Col. J. Fenton Argue, president of the College of Physicians and Surgeons. They would surely save the BPC from MacNeil's demagoguery.[56] The Liberal cabinet preferred to make its own choices. The chairman would be Lt-Col. J.L. Ralston, Halifax lawyer, leading Rotarian, defeated Liberal MLA, and renowned ex-commanding officer of Nova Scotia's 85th Highlanders. Col. Walter McKeown was an associate professor of medicine at the University of Toronto; Lt-Col. Arthur Dubuc, the engineer in charge of government canals in Quebec, had served with the French-speaking 22nd Battalion of the CEF. Moreover, to the dismay of both DSCR officials and the Pension Board, the mandate of the new commission was extremely broad: the commissioners would explore the full impact of retraining, pensions, and soldier settlement. Canada's entire experience of soldiers' civil re-establishment would be on trial.[57]

At the end of July 1922, Ralston met with his new colleagues at the Château Laurier in Ottawa, appointed staff, and set to work. On 28 August the hearings opened. From the outset, Bowler made no effort to prove the literal truth of the GWVA charges; nor did Ralston allow the issues to be settled on narrow grounds. Instead, the GWVA counsel forced board officials and unit medical directors to reveal the confusing instructions, one-sided reports, and arbitrary rulings that had fuelled the veterans' grievances. Colonel Belton, displaced as the BPC's chief medical adviser by Dr W.C. Arnold and exiled to Toronto as a mere pension examiner, obviously relished the opportunity to contradict Colonel Thompson's interpretation of the 1920 amendments. Margeson, summoned from the Nova Scotia bench, insisted, on the contrary, that CEF veterans had lost the 'insurance principle' in 1920. Reminded of his earlier assurances to the parliamentary committee, Judge Margeson conceded, a little weakly, that it was 'a hard act to interpret.'[58]

However frail in fact and in law the GWVA charges might be, Ralston and his colleagues were plainly dismayed by the attitude of the Pensions Board. As a medical professional, McKeown was shocked by the easy confidence with which pension advisers rendered verdicts. 'If that is your attitude,' he remarked after Maj. W.A. Burgess, the BPC's leading medical advisor, had justified a seemingly arbitrary judgment, 'all I can say is that you are not competent to handle these cases.'[59] McKeown apologized the next day; but his opinion remained unchanged. Dubuc's sense of justice was aroused by the board's perception that it had no obligation to help claimants prove their case. For that matter, Colonel Thompson made it clear that he did not think himself obliged even to explain pension act amendments to politicians. 'I just interpret the Act,' he stated. 'I do not pay attention to what any member of the Pension Committee may have thought about any proposed amendment or about any section or about any legislation. I take the statute as I find it.'[60] Of course, Thompson had to admit that the Pension Act was very much as he and the board had drafted it.

In October the commission looked at a couple of hundred actual pension cases. For the first time the board had to justify its decisions publicly. Private Newman, wounded in the hand and pelvis, had been pensioned only for his hand because an official forgot to mention his hip injury. When he protested the board had ruled that the injury must have been slight if it had been overlooked. Alexander Smith, discharged in August 1917 with a fractured tibia, sclerosis, rheumatism, a corneal ulcer, a suppurating ear, and injured left arm, and a 40 per cent pension, spent the remaining two years of his life in a DSCR hospital. His death, from pneumonia, was labeled 'non-attributable.' Charles Garbutt, who could barely walk, was recommended for a 15 per cent pension but got nothing. In truth, argued Bowler, 'they hated to admit that a man with flat feet, an old man, was entitled to pension as a result of aggravation on service, but on the other hand there never was a clearer case presented for a pension.'[61]

Board officials insisted that such decisions were matters of judgment. Where was the illegal conspiracy? Days of testimony revealed that the BPC, eager to cut back on the 'insurance principle,' had acted only on rumour when it dated the 'Declaration of Peace' January 1920. Without admitting the error, the board had devised the 1920 Pension Act amendment partly to cover its tracks. As a result, CEF veterans and dependants had lost their rights a full year and a half before the actual Declaration of Peace in September 1921. Given responsibility for Returned Soldiers' Insurance – largely because most of the insured used their pension cheques to pay their premiums – Colonel Thompson had been horrified by the loophole that allowed deathbed applications. After vain attempts to get politicians to amend the law, he plugged the hole himself in December 1921, after death claims suddenly soared from $50,000 to $90,000 in one month. By holding up applications until the 'deathbed cases' died, Thompson had devised a crude medical screening not permitted by the 1920 RSI act. The new Liberal finance minister, William Fielding, had belatedly approved this course.[62]

These were minor bendings of the law, which public opinion might well uphold. Indeed, in his summation, the board's counsel, Dr Gordon Henderson, insisted that 'tightening up' had been an administrative reflection of a political mood. Self-preservation was the first law of nature, 'and those who were at home were prepared to make promises to those who enlisted ...

They were prepared to go a long way to assist the returned soldier. But human nature is human nature, and when the war was over, and we were safe, we commenced to regret many of our extravagant promises.'[63]

This was not the view of the royal commission. When Ralston tabled his first report in February 1923, he acknowledged that the GWVA had 'failed to sustain the charges of conspiracy, plot and deliberation ... by the Pensions Board in dealing with the rights of ex-service men.'[64] That was all the comfort Colonel Thompson and his officials could find from the report. Ralston found that the board had failed to make its policies known, had ignored the will of Parliament, and had reached its conclusions in needless secrecy. Even though MacNeil's specific charges were unfounded, he had acted 'after a cumulation of circumstances which might well have produced the conviction that a system of clandestinely whittling away rights had been inaugurated.'[65] No one could question the BPC's integrity: 'It could have courted popularity and lightened its load by taking a less determined and zealous attitude,' but it had neglected its whole duty: 'A ground for strong criticism, by the Commission, is that the Pensions Board gave undue prominence to the idea that its duty was ... that of a Trustee of Public Funds. This function was, after all, secondary to the duty of the Pensions Board as a Trustee of the rights and benefits which Canada intended for ex-service men and their dependents.'[66]

Veterans Aggrieved

Months before its first report appeared, the royal commission had anticipated its assessment of MacNeil by dispatching him at public expense to prepare veterans across Canada for the second phase of the inquiry. As secretary of the Dominion Veterans Alliance, a loose federation of the major associations formed in 1921, MacNeil was the logical man for the job of preparing deputations and co-ordinating briefs, but Ralston would hardly have chosen an agent whose credibility he planned to demolish. By the standards of the time, the Royal Commission on Pensions, as it had been officially styled, was determined to canvass opinion widely. But Ralston had no intention of wasting his time with repetitive briefs or personal grievances. Posters and advertisements in English and French heralded the hearings. In some localities publicity was issued in Yiddish, Chinese, and Japanese. To involve more veterans, 150,000 questionnaires were distributed through the Post Office (only 3,442 replies were received).[67]

Beginning at Camp Hill hospital in Halifax on 24 January 1923, the commission headed west to Saint John and Montreal, crossed the continent to Vancouver, and returned via Calgary, Regina, Winnipeg, and Toronto. In thirty-eight days the commissioners heard 160 witnesses, collected 5,800 pages of testimony, and visited seven hospitals, six sanatoria, an orphanage, an insane asylum, and several sheltered workshops. Almost everwhere MacNeil had managed to persuade local veterans to agree on six-member deputations representing regional problems and the specialized concerns of amputees, soldier-settlers, tuberculosis sufferers, and the blind. At Vancouver and again at Winnipeg and Toronto the GAUV stubbornly insisted on taking up time with bonus demands. MacNeil wearily conceded that they were entitled to raise the issue. Ralston ran each session as a conference, collecting and even debating views with an informality that pleased veterans but sometimes exasperated the accompanying government officials. 'Anyone who followed the proceedings throughout,' he reported, 'would readily agree that despite an occasional explosive utterance by an individual or small group, the average returned soldier once properly informed, is instinctively fair and reasonable.'[68]

Ostensibly, the commission had the full support of the DSCR; in practice, officials knew that they were on trial and resented it. Dr A.E. Lunden, the unit medical director at Montreal, gleefully reported to Scammell that MacNeil had been obliged to wait for forty-five minutes for a sufficient 'agglomeration of the Comrades.'[69] The GWVA 'speech-fest,' Scammell responded, would soon be over. The conduct of a DSCR official who helped Peterborough veterans organize their grievances was judged 'most undesirable.' At Victoria, a veterans' representative who asked to see DSCR files was shown the door. Ralston was assured that the incident was a pure misunderstanding. At Toronto, medical officers preferred not to have the commission hold its meeting at the Christie Street hospital; it might cause too much excitement among the patients.'[70]

Since contented veterans had little to tell the commission, the dissatisfied predominated. Amputees spoke of the harshness of the BPC's disability tables and the cost of replacing clothing worn out by the straps, belts, and pulleys of their prostheses. Toronto veterans found a spokesman in Maj. Bert Wemp, a diminutive air ace and a future mayor, who insisted that half a million dollars had been wasted in relief. What destitute disabled veterans needed was work, he said, not charity. At Montreal, tubercular soldiers spoke of their grim alternatives – relapse on a meagre pension or demoralization in the atmosphere of a sanatorium. Venereal disease sufferers with gallant war records complained of being denied any pension even though their afflictions predated their enlistment. At Halifax, Regina, and Toronto witnesses bitterly reported how war widows had been harassed by Pension Board investigators acting on anonymous allegations of immorality. Mrs Lesten of Winnipeg, an elderly war widow, had taken in a disabled friend of her late husband as a boarder. Malicious gossip altered the board; a 'lady visitor' concluded that misconduct could not be proven, though Mrs Lesten was 'ill-advised.' On that ground she was stripped of both pension and reputation. Mrs Bland of Toronto, similarly accused, even had support from the DSCR, but to no avail.[71]

Everywhere the BPC was the main target. From Vancouver Scammell reported that the DSCR would emerge with credit. 'The further this enquiry goes,' he advised Parkinson, 'the more apparent it is that we have an efficient organization which is working satisfactorily.'[72] The board, in contrast, appeared remote, arbitrary, and increasingly unfair. In each community veterans pleaded for the right to appeal the board's rulings, preferably to local tribunals whose members could judge a man's disabilities with their own eyes. With pressure on the royal commission to show its usefulness and the equally inevitable difficulty of sorting through the enormous complexity of re-establishment issues, Ralston and his colleagues drafted an interim report as a kind of political down payment. Since a parliamentary committee was not appointed in 1923, Ralston and his colleagues provided that year's only input to veterans' legislation.

The report on the GWVA charges had urged reinstatement of the 1919 version of section 11, recognition of the 'missing link' cases, and restoration of any application forfeited by the BPC's illegal attempt at imposing a medical test on RSI claimants. The royal commission's second set of proposals, tabled in April 1923, dealt with a number of urgent issues. The commission recommended that the DSCR's handicap employment sections be shifted to the provinces. There should be no further extension of applications for Returned Soldiers' Insurance. Three years of the deathbed loophole were enough.[73]

Far more radical was the commission's insistence that the Pensions Board must allow appeals, as was done in Britain and the United States. The lack of appeals had troubled Ralston more than any other feature of the pension system: 'To those familiar with judicial systems it will seem somewhat striking that the Pension Act ... vests in a body, consisting of three Commissioners at Ottawa, the sole, original and final jurisdiction to determine the right of applicants for pension for the whole of Canada. There is no appeal, control or effective review by any outside body, and the Pension Board is not subject nor amenable to any ministerial or departmental instruction.'[74]

Ralston's proposed system resembled the U.S. appeal process – three-member district review boards in each of the nine DSCR units, and a federal appeal board with final jurisdiction; remoteness has been one of the BPC's worst problems and the veterans' most common grievance. Like the royal commission itself, each board would have as members a doctor, a lawyer, and a layman, any two of whom were to be returned soldiers. Veterans should have a year to make their appeal, but the only ground would be the issue of attributability. Board rulings on pension rates, misconduct, or other matters of judgment would not be subject to appeal. By themselves few veterans could hope to prepare an effective case for appeal, but it hardly seemed appropriate to channel all appeals through the GWVA's Adjustment Bureau. Other veterans' organizations would not stand for it. The solution, hinted at by Ralston during the cross-country tour, was a system of 'Official Soldiers' Advisers' who would prepare and present claims at no expense to the veterans. Those who wished to have their own legal counsel would have to pay the fees. [75]

Any appeal system would be controversial. At the very heart of J.L. Todd's original 1916 plan for pension administration was the concept of an all-powerful board. Marler's committee in 1922 had complacently rejected any real need for appeals: 'If such a Board was provided it appears manifest ... that the great majority of decisions made by the D.S.C.R. and/or the B.P.C. but appealed from, would be confirmed.' [76] Ralston and his colleagues had come to a harsher conclusion, but the board's status as Canada's bulwark against pension profligacy would be upheld by powerful political defenders and Thompson's legal ingenuity. The Medical Advisory Board, finally established in December, six months after an authorizing order in council, found that the Pension Board employed every artifice of law and delay to resist any critical finding. The chairman, Dr J.L. Biggar, complained that the BPC's medical advisers were out of touch by comparison with 'medical men in the active practice of their profession,' but he had no hope of matching Thompson's legal expertise. As for the Pension Board, it had nothing to say to Ralston or to veterans. The GWVA demanded that the board declare its intentions, and even sent a two-man 'patrol' to take back the response; the demand was met by silence. [77]

Like any government, the King cabinet was moved more by politics than law or justice. It was convenient to remember that for seven years veteran's matters had been non-partisan. The royal commission had proposed; Parliament would decide, with a minimum of guidance. In the 1923 session of the House of Commons, MPs narrowly supported a second attempt, backed by Caldwell and labour's J.S. Woodsworth, to get pensions for the luckless widows who had married too late. They also turned down an eloquent bid by a British Columbia member, Leon Ladner, to restore the 'insurance principle' for any man who had served anywhere in the CEF. Marler warned that doing so would give a veteran a pension for any disease contracted any time. The Ralston proposal, which was limited to men who had seen overseas service, went far enough. [78] The appeal procedure proposed by Ralston passed almost without debate, apart from a brief populist appeal from a Yukon Conservative, Capt. George Black, that ex-staff officers be kept off any of the boards. 'I have never seen on active service a staff officer, or a brass hat or an officer wearing a full collar on his military coat, that was human.'[79] Black was politely ignored.

The Senate was in a different mood. Senators had created their own special committee in 1923 and met late into the evening from 20 to 30 June to consider Pension Act amendments. DSCR and BPC witnesses spoke at length. Thompson assured the senators that the BPC would not alter its ways; Parkinson insisted that appeals must be administered by the DSCR. When the committee finally allowed MacNeil to speak, the tone was set by a few angry senators who were furious at being bombarded by telegrams from GWVA branches. When the senators demanded to know if the GWVA charges had been withdrawn, Raoul Dandurand intervened: 'Soldiers of the CEF never withdraw,' claimed the Senate leader with courtly irrelevance. In 1920 senators had been annoyed when their elderly Halifax colleague, L.G. Power, had reminded them that 'gentlemen here can afford to be independent in a way that the members of the other House cannot.' Now, with the Liberals in power, a predominantly Tory chamber stirred itself to vigilance. Soldiers should certainly be properly treated, Sen. F.L. Béique, the committee chairman, agreed, but it was also necessary that 'the expenditure be curtailed if it was possible to curtail it.' Accordingly, the committee tore up most of the House of Commons proposals. The hapless 'pension widows' were stricken from the bill; so were other categories of beneficiaries inserted by vote-seeking MPs. The modified 'insurance principle,' was again deleted. Instead of the nine review boards and a federal tribunal, which would have cost an estimated half-million dollars a year, the senators grudgingly consented to a single Federal Appeal Board, with five to seven members, that would travel the country. The new board would consider only evidence already presented to the BPC; new facts (or opinions) were not its concern. As a final reminder of where the senators' hearts lay, Béique congratulated Pension Board witnesses for sticking strictly to the facts. MacNeil, he regretted to report, had been the only witness to offer 'opinions.'[80]

On 26 June the senators enjoyed themselves praising the board, denouncing the Ralston commission, and serving the cause of fiscal integrity. It was all very well, General Griesbach said, for the Ralston commission to talk of rights and justice, 'but what good is it to arrive at a conclusion as to justice and right when we have exceeded the financial ability of the country?'[81] Griesbach and H.W. Laird, an ex-colonel from Saskatchewan, did argue for the 'insurance principle.' That issue was settled when a somewhat flustered Senator Dandurand confessed that the government had advised him only that morning that he must insist on keeping the new section 11 unaltered. An angry Lougheed declared that he would never have worked past midnight on the special committee if he had known that his work would be wasted.[82] On the insurance principle alone the senators capitulated.

The senators had not wholly wasted their time. If section 11 was given back most of its 1919 meaning – growing in the process from eight lines to fifty-two – the Senate had put a stop to local appeal tribunals, held the line on women who married the disabled, wiped out four other categories of potential pensioners, and rendered the new Federal Appeal Board largely nugatory by restricting the evidence available to it. As a compromise, the Senate allowed a joint meeting of pension commissioners and members of the new Federal Appeal Board to consider pensions for 'meritorious cases' not covered by any other section of the act. Since almost any conceivable 'meritorious case,' including venereal-disease sufferers, was mentioned elsewhere, the clause was meaningless. Perhaps that was the Senate's intention.[83]

Appraising Re-establishment

From July until May, the Ralston commission worked with little interruption, accumulating mounds of paper and intermittently acquiring new tasks such as determining how to distribute wartime canteen profits among the men who had contributed to them. Like most commissions, it then went into a long subterranean phase as members tried to catch up with reading, reflection, and their own lives. By the same token, veterans, editorial writers, and politicians began to clamour for action. As the 1924 session slipped past, Ralston reluctantly extracted part of his final report and submitted it in May.[84]

The *Second Interim Report* was a dense collection of recommendations on the Pension Act and the Soldier Settlement Act which, on the whole, suggested that a year's interval had cooled some of the sympathy generated during the 1922 and 1923 hearings. Certainly there were flashes of indignation and a continued refusal to hide behind conventional morality. It was eminently unfair, the commission argued, that a man who enlisted with tuberculosis should be eligible for a pension while a man who joined with venereal disease was not. 'The country availed itself of the services of both of them and put them to all duties and dangers of fit men. They both may have given flawless service and this service probably had a more serious effect on the health of the "immoral" man than on that of the other, but the State rids itself of its responsibility to him and his dependents because of his ancient indiscretion.'[85]

On other issues the report showed a harder edge. The GWVA had argued that it was wrong to stop a man's pension because he had been sent to prison (no such deduction was made in the United States), but the commission was unconvinced. In the issue of 'pension widows' the commission could recognize a minefield. The cases presented, some of them already familiar, were often heart-rending. Surely there could be no fraud if pensions were limited to widows who had married within a year of a pensioner's discharge. That was all: 'The Commission is strongly of opinion that in the amendment suggested it has gone at least as far as can possibly be justified on any sound ground, and that no further general extension in respect of these cases should be entertained.'[86] As for widows who lost their pensions on remarriage and then lost their second husbands, the commission could play with the British anomaly that an officer's widow in such a predicament regained her pension while a widow of a lower-ranking soldier did not. Clearly, the state profited from remarriage, but hasty marriages should not be encouraged. The answer was a cautious compromise: if she was widowed again within five years and left destitute, the woman's pension might be restored, with the lump-sum 'dowry' deducted.[87]

These and dozens of other recommendations – many of them rejecting such popular veterans' demands as a reversal of commutation and the linking of pensions to former incomes – led to the hurried formation of yet another special House of Commons committee under Jean Dénis, a Liberal from Joliette. Committee sessions dragged on through June and July of 1924 as the familiar parade of witnesses reported pensioner poverty, pleaded that the 1920 bonus be made permanent, and repeated the claims of widows, 'venereals' and tuberculars. Despite pensioners' high hopes, the new Federal Appeal Board had made little difference. Colonel Belton, the chairman, C.B. Reilly, the lawyer chosen as vice-chairman, and Maj. C.B. Topp, the secretary, solemnly explained that the narrow grounds for appeal, exclusion of fresh evidence, and the BPC's consistent rejection of each unfavourable finding had stalled the process.[88] When Colonel Thompson appeared, he cheerfully announced that there had been no meritorious cases, since every one of them was covered by some other section of the act, notably section 12, which dealt with misconduct. Yes, he agreed, syphilis did imply immorality.[89] Veterans and even MPs began to wonder whether an appeal procedure would make much difference so long as the board itself was so inflexible. Maj. M.A. Macpherson, the president of the Regina GWVA and a future eminence in the Conservative party, wanted Thompson removed: 'We feel that however honest and upright he may be, he is not serving the country or serving us.'[90]

The sessions of Dénis's committee, however hurried, left little time in the 1924 session for either house to consider Pension Act amendments. It was only 16 July that the House of Commons approved a bill incorporating virtually all that Ralston had recommended, from pensions for pre-enlistment venereal cases and dependent widowed mothers to an extension of the 1920 bonus for another three years.[91] On 18 July Mackenzie King had already summoned the governor-general to prorogue Parliament when an embarrassed Senator Dandurand introduced the bill to the upper House. His apologies and Lougheed's anger simply invited the senators to rebel. 'A wink is as good as a nod to a blind horse,' declared General Griesbach as he and his fellow senators set out to tear the bill apart.[92] In fact, the former general soon found himself defending the cause of the 'pension widows' while his colleagues, full of righteous claims that the lower House had abdicated responsibility, slashed merrily away. Dandurand offered no protest. It was perhaps wise, he confessed, to go slowly in extending benefits. The American experience was a warning.[93] In the end, the Senate allowed nothing beyond an extension of the pension bonus. Impatient MPs weighed the prospect of defying the Senate attempt to blackmail against the imminence of prorogation. They opted for the summer vacation. After Mackenzie King promised angry members that he would introduce Senate reform at the next session, Parliament broke up.[94]

By then the Ralston commission had completed its fourth and final report. The report dealt with a miscellany of concerns, from employing handicapped veterans to the problems of Canadian and imperial ex-servicemen in the United States. It was the DSCR's turn to suffer criticism when the commission condemned its restrictions on granting treatment; nowhere in the world were treatment and pension decisions made with so little co-ordination.[95] Yet in the end the report's harshest comments were reserved for the BPC. Taking up the theme that had recurred in meetings across the country, the commission pleaded for openness in board procedures. Obviously, BPC officials did not welcome invidious comparisons and plea-shopping, but these were hardly abhorrent to any lawyer. 'There need be no more mystery about Pension and Treatment decisions than about a case at law where the view of each individual judge is known.'[96] The commissioners could hardly deny the need to enforce the law, but at least half the allegations raised against pensioned widows were untrue or spiteful. 'All, however are investigated with a thoroughness which is undaunted ... Enquiries are frequently made as to whether any man lives in the house, how many beds there are, and where placed. Young children, even those of the widow herself, have been questioned on these and other suggestive subjects.'[97] Plainly, the experience of Mrs Bland, Mrs Lesten, and their wronged sisters had deeply shocked the commissioners.

Much of the commission's final report was devoted to 'special disabilities,' the blind, amputees, the insane, the tuberculous, or elderly survivors of the war. The commission had special praise for the persuasive skills of the Tuberculous Veterans' Association, but it turned down the TVA's pleas for sheltered workshops and an extra one-third on any pension to meet the special costs of food and shelter. That would be 'rank discrimination.'[98] On the 'neurasthenics,' deprived by law of a pension for their own good, Ralston felt that five years had been long enough for the experiment. Some, perhaps many, had 'made good'; the rest were by now entitled to a pension. Prematurely aged and helpless veterans posed an insoluble problem. Old age was not a disability, and the commission showed little enthusiasm for a Canadian version of the Chelsea Hospital or American-style 'soldiers' homes.' The answer, of course, was a general old age pension, but how that could help the prematurely aged the commission could not say.[99] Instead, the report endorsed sheltered workshops, but only under Red Cross or other private management. Despite criticism of the Last Post Fund by the GWVA, the commission also recommended a grant of $10,000 a year to the fund. Destitute veterans should be spared paupers' graves, and a patriotic charity would be wiser and cheaper than any government-run funerals. Dependants should not be included in the benefit.[100]

There were many veterans' problems the commission would not or could not solve. It had no sympathy with men who had chosen to be discharged in England and who now sought repatriation. Nor could Canada be expected to open offices to serve veterans in the United States. 'It goes without saying that Canadians living in foreign countries cannot be expected to have the same intimate relations with, or service from the institutions of their own country as those residing in Canada.'[101] Almost everywhere, soldier-settlers had brought their grievances to the commission: denial of qualification certificates, refusal of a second chance on better land, the rejection of small holdings, and (with growing fervor) the complaint that lands were overvalued.[102] The commission was unmoved. The Soldier Settlement Board had a two-way contractual agreement with its clients. If the SSB was sometimes stern, it was within its rights. Like the board, the commissioners blamed individuals, not circumstances, for failure. Three-quarters of settlers were 'holding their own'; among the exceptions, 'personal factors and failings have contributed to the lack of progress.'[103] On revaluation the commission argued that a few bad years could not justify a policy that could cost millions. As for small holdings, they were 'nothing less than the State investing in a separate open-air Vetcraft Shop for each individual applicant.'[104]

Faced with choices, Ralston and his colleagues retreated instinctively to a cautious faith in law. On pensions, for example, applicants were entitled to know their rights. Officials owed veterans 'correct and clear statements as to the principles on which pensions were granted ... the lines along which evidence is required and where possible ... any available staff in assisting the soldier in procuring and putting into shape this information.'[105] Openness did not mean paternalism. The GWVA's request that the government survey unemployed disabled veterans and reopen training programs got no encouragement. The men had had their chance. That the disabled veterans could 'depend on pay and allowances for a substantial period of his transition from military to civil life was in very many cases almost as genuine a benefit as the instruction actually received.'[106] Germany and France might compel employers to hire the disabled: Canada need not. Voluntarism was not exhausted. In Toronto a 'Committee of Rehabilitation' had found jobs for disabled veterans with help from a federally funded wage supplement. Once combined wages and pension reached 32.5 cents an hour, the supplement ceased. This was a worthy model for all.[107] What if voluntarism failed? The commission reluctantly acknowledged an ultimate federal responsibility: 'The State is not obsolved from liability until employment opportunity in proportion to that enjoyed by the normal man for his 100 per cent capability is provided for whatever substantial remnant of working capacity the pensioner may have.'[108] How that could be made to happen Ralston and his colleagues left to a conjectural future.

Humane, conscientious, and conservative men had explored the Canadian experience of civil re-establishment. Ralston and his colleagues had not sought to upset fundamental policies. For all their limitations, most of Todd's principles still looked better than the alternatives. The royal commission brought little innovative ingenuity to its task, but it would not have been welcome in any case. Veterans, officials, and the public had no taste for revolutions. What they gained from Ralston was a cautious infusion of equity, common sense, and a hint, albeit faint, of a future in which all citizens, not merely veterans, might share entitlement, not charity.

9 Veterans' Unity

Veterans of the World, Unite

'The gravest danger that besets the veterans of the great war,' warned *The Veteran* in 1919, 'is lack of unity.' Instead of the comradeship and co-operation of 'over yonder,' the GWVA's organ found 'the returned men of Canada already split up into a number of organizations, each professing similar aims and objects, each endeavouring to advance the interests of the ex-service man and his dependents, and each alternately deriding and cutting the other's throat.'[1] If veterans had lost the bonus fight in 1919, if the Pension Board was obdurate in 1920, if governments had abandoned returned men to the depression of 1921, disunity was an obvious explanation. In turn, failure bred massive defections. By the winter of 1921 the GWVA and its rivals were in visible decline.

The experience was worldwide. Almost everywhere, huge citizen armies had shared the experiences of demobilization. Problems and the policies that had been developed to meet them were widely compared. Canada boasted the world's highest pension rates, but Australian veterans shared in the home-purchase plan Canadians were denied. Britain's infant welfare state supplied unemployment insurance – soon derisively rechristened 'the dole.' The American Legion had launched its bonus campaign as the GWVA was abandoning the struggle.[2]

What was sadly unique among Canadian veterans was their disunity. By 1918 Australia's Returned Soldiers' and Sailors' Imperial League had absorbed or eliminated its rivals.[3] After 1920 the American Legion had no serious rival. As the effective voice of 4.7 million U.S. veterans, the Legion became the heir to the GAR as Washington's most irresistible lobbying group. On 15 July 1921 the Legion's bonus scheme passed the U.S. Senate; by 1924 'adjusted compensation' had overridden persistent presidential vetoes and had become law.[4] So had much else that American veterans wanted. By 1931 Legion pressure had eliminated the last vestige of attributability from U.S. disability pensions.[5] Even when Legion membership declined in the mid-1920s, the organization faced no rival more serious than the Veterans of Foreign Wars, an older, more conservative group that limited its membership to those who had served overseas.[6]

For Canadian veterans, the British experience was at least as influential as the American. During the war years, four rival ex-service organizations had emerged, ranging from the conservative Comrades of the Great War to the National Union of Ex-Servicemen, better known as NUX, which was committed to the class war. The largest group was the National Federation of Discharged and Demobilized Sailors and Soldiers – radical, egalitarian, and closed to officers unless they had come up through the ranks.[7] Bitter rivalry complicated an otherwise pleasant 'problem': sharing about seven million pounds in wartime canteen profits. The War Office finally turned the problem over to Lord Byng of Vimy. With the common touch that had helped him when he commanded the Canadian corps, Byng managed to inveigle all but NUX into sharing the management of what the press promptly titled 'Byng's Millions.'[8] The next step depended on Sir Douglas Haig. Little known and little loved by his huge, long-suffering army, Haig had won sudden popularity by refusing to accept a title until Britain's government bestowed a gratuity and improved pensions on his men. As Earl Haig he used his new prestige for a purpose. First, he persuaded almost a dozen officers' self-help organizations to merge in a single Officers' Association. Next, he turned down the presidency of the Comrades of the Great War. Neutrality was an asset when he agreed to address the much larger National Federation. As Haig's biographer suggests, a bad speaker can sometimes make a most persuasive argument. Haig's message was simple: unity. Prior preparation and a shared financial desperation had already persuaded most of the other associations to seek merger. Access to the Canteen Fund was a powerful magnet. By June 1921, the basis for a British Legion was established. Only the troublesome NUX remained outside, and it faded into insignificance.[9]

Practical arguments for veteran solidarity were interwoven with sentiment. Surely the comradeship of the trenches could contribute to keep the world at peace. The bonds of empire, forged in war, must unite all Britons everywhere. In February 1921 the merger of four South African veterans' associations brought Haig and delegates from Britain and the white empire to Cape Town to launch a British Empire Service League. Since the GWVA could not find money for the fare and the Canadian government would not find it for them, Bob Maxwell somehow managed to pay his own way to appear as a spokesman for Canada's veterans. He returned, via the Red Sea and his native Armagh, with a brave new vision of a veterans' movement pledged to British values, imperial unity, and controlled immigration.[10] Idealists and even some of their hard-headed critics would eventually go farther and endorse the Fédération inter-alliée des anciens combattants (FIDAC), which grouped French and Allied veterans and, after long and passionate debate, their former German enemies.[11]

As returned men elsewhere came together, Canadian veterans seemed to be falling apart. Since 1917 the GWVA had almost annually spawned a bitter rival. The Army and Navy Veterans had remained aloof from the association in 1917 because its members who had served in earlier wars had been made unwelcome. The GWVA blamed the machinations of 'certain Toronto politicians' for the creation in October 1918 of the Grand Army of Canada, with its commitment to co-operatives and political action. Machinations were even more in evidence a year later when Toronto's Mayor Tommy Church and Col. J.A. Currie had encouraged the formation of Harry Flynn's United Veterans' League.[12] In 1920, Flynn's organization and the Grand Army found enough common ground to merge as the Grand Army of United Veterans. A shared commitment to the bonus and the concentration of members in the Toronto-Hamilton area made the marriage easier. The group's executive, claimed a scornful GWVA official, could meet 'for the price of car fare.'[13] In fact, GAUV membership grew as disillusionment with the GWVA's half-hearted bonus compaign increased. In late 1920, as part of military monitoring of ex-service organizations, Sir Willoughby Gwatkin, the chief of the general staff, reported of the GAUV that 'at Winnipeg it is rather extreme in its views, whereas in Victoria it is well thought of, or was when I was last there; whereas in Vancouver some of the worst elements are associated with it.'[14]

The GAUV mustered most of the stormy petrels among the returned men – no small contingent when so many veterans felt bitter and disillusioned. The Army and Navy Veterans, in contrast, tended to patriotic conservatism. In his final speech at the ANV's 1920 convention in Victoria, Major W.J. Tupper boasted that his organization had helped save the nation during the Winnipeg General Strike a year before: 'If it had not been for the stand that the Veterans took on that occasion, there is little doubt that Canada might have been in a very serious condition to-day, and that Constitutional Government might have been a thing of the past.' If governments had not done all they might, 'no organization obtains everything we wish.'[15] In a convention studded with majors, captains, and stalwart ex-imperials, Tupper's successor, Maj. M.J. Crehan of Vancouver, firmly repelled bonus-seekers with a resolution that re-establishment should be no more generous than the nation could afford. [16] The GWVA condemned the Last Post Fund; the ANV loyally endorsed such good works. The ANV certainly reflected a proper concern for pensions, unemployment, and soldier settlement, but its members were older, more settled, and more satisfied than those of rival organizations.

Within their limits, the GWVA, the GAUV and the ANV were national organizations that claimed to serve all veterans. The Imperial Veterans in Canada represented imperial reservists across the country, as well as others whose pensions and benefits derived from the British government. Theirs was a complex and specialized concern which the purely Canadian organizations had, perhaps inevitably, tended to sidetrack. Ottawa's generosity in supplementing imperial pensions did not eliminate the difficulties of dealing with a combination of British and Canadian regulations and the officials who enforced them. "The boys have no appeal,' complained H.B. Willing, the IVC's secretary, in 1920. 'They have great faith in Chelsea and they want the idea of Chelsea carried out here.' It was not easy to do. [17]

Whatever its origins or purpose, each of the national associations had to measure itself against the Great War Veterans. Despite the losses from the failure of both Calgary resolutions, the GWVA remained far and away the largest Canadian ex-service organization. In February 1920 the association had 761 branches stretching from Dawson City to London, England. [18] MacNeil reported to Ernest Scammell in midsummer that the total had risen to 857 branches, with an estimated 200,000 members. [19] The branches controlled property worth millions of dollars, from the tiny portable hall of the Fairbanks branch in suburban Toronto to Edmonton's Memorial Hall, complete with a lounge, a billiard-room, a 3,000-seat auditorium, and a dormitory to house transient or homeless comrades. [20] Under David Loughnan's editorship, *The Veteran* delivered a monthly package of news, fiction, and advertising to 70,000 paying subscribers. The GWVA's adjustment service was unique among veterans' organizations. When the GWVA met, journalists referred to it tritely but not inaccurately as 'the Soldiers' Parliament.' [21]

It all cost money. To finance the dominion command, its Ottawa headquarters, the GWVA depended on a per capita levy of sixty cents a year from members and the revenue from selling lapel badges. The arrangement relied on a flow of new members eager to decorate their buttonholes and on the willingness of branch treasurers to place the needs of a distant national headquarters ahead of local priorities. Beyond assigning a convention delegate for each one hundred paid-up members, the dominion command had no way of enforcing per capita payments. If, as MacNeil claimed, the GWVA had had 200,000 members, the 1920 income from the per capita levy would have been $120,000. In fact, in the nineteen months between the 1920 and 1921 conventions, the branches remitted only $39,454.[22] The GWVA and its branches were losing members faster than they could find them. An 'open-door' policy of accepting men who had not gone overseas produced the bitterest debate of the 1920 convention, but it was implemented because Ontario and prairie delegates needed members to share the cost of their splendid new facilities.[23] Even a Japanese-Canadian branch was eventually accepted, in spite of the GWVA's persistent racial prejudice.[24] Whatever the precise membership figures, the trend was unmistakable: before the 1920 convention, per capita levies averaged $3,048 a month; before the 1921 convention, the average dropped to $2,076, and between the fifth and the sixth convention a mere $794 a month reached Ottawa.[25]

David Loughnan's solution was to transform the GWVA into a kind of fraternal organization, complete with rituals, regalia, and secret oaths, that had attracted generations of North American males. When he retired at the end of 1921, Loughnan promoted his 'Fourandex,' a secret society for 'good fellowship and solidarity' within the GWVA, but MacNeil's priorities prevailed.[26] The GWVA remained a service organization, but it was a costly and difficult role. The British and American examples, a growing financial crisis, and an awareness that the veterans' critics profited from internal divisions all suggested the need for merger. If 1919 had been the year of the bonus, 1921 became the year of amalgamation.

The Year of Amalgamation

The virtue of unity was obvious to a movement that revelled in the rhetoric of comradeship, sacrifice, and solidarity. At the same time, the army had focused soldiers' loyalty on the battalion, the company, or even the section of a dozen men. Allegiances made merger unwelcome. At Victoria in 1920 the ANV's chaplain, Canon Hinchcliffe, patiently secured a cautious resolution on amalgamation; when an enthusiastic delegate suggested that the association should even, if need be, sacrifice its name, he was answered by cries of 'No, no!'[27]

If the ANV was reluctant, the GAUV was eager for solidarity. Having united the two youngest splinter groups in the veterans' movement, the Grand Army of United Veterans fervently endorsed amalgamation. At Winnipeg, from 3 to 5 May 1921, delegates to the GAUV's first convention announced that amalgamation was their first order of business and, by extension, that it must become the top priority for the association's rivals. A convention committee suggested that the government should designate the third Friday in September as Amalgamation Day. While citizens celebrated both the living and the fallen among their defenders, veterans would presumably unite.[28] Politicians would have to heed an organization of 100,000 men. How else could veterans achieve a GAUV program whose objectives ranged from five years' free medical care to interest-free loans? In a dig at the GWVA, Maj. W.J. Morrison, the GAUV's founding president, declared that 'such organizations as were not in favour of political action must see by now how fruitless their efforts have been.'[29]

The GWVA was not inclined to bow to an organization that allegedly mustered only nineteen delegates for its first convention or that chose Harry Flynn as its first vice-president.[30] A month after addressing a noisy Winnipeg rally of fifteen hundred veterans, however, Flynn and his constant travelling companion, Herbert Capewell, were 'asked to retire' from the GAUV on the obscure ground of 'housecleaning in the organization.'[31] Scandal was only partly avoided when Flynn hurriedly departed for Boston. Flynn's departure improved the GAUV's reputation and removed a large personal barrier to collaboration among veterans' associations.[32] Gordon McNichol, a decorated hero, soon replaced Morrison, and Flynn's successor as vice-president, Sgt Walter Rayfield, had won the Victoria Cross. Among returned men, these were better credentials than most of the GWVA's leaders had acquired as 'Old Originals.' With about as much precision as MacNeil, the GAUV's secretary, Fred Marsh, claimed that his organization had seventy thousand members in Canada, twenty thousand more in the United States, and as fine a record of service as any veterans' association in Canada. Unquestionably the GAUV was influential in two of the regions where returned men had concentrated, Toronto-Hamilton and Vancouver-Victoria.[33]

For rank-and-file members of all groups, unity had a simple, straightforward appeal. Had internal conflict not interfered with the campaign for "full re-establishment" and pitched returned men into the miseries of 1921? Worse was to come. Pensioners knew that the 50 per cent bonus had only been temporarily allowed in 1920. As the economic depression deepened and public revenue fell, only a united voice from veterans could save the pension bonus.[34] Unity always made most sense at the local level. By 1921 a number of GWVA and GAUV branches in Toronto had amalgamated. In Winnipeg, GWVA leaders pre-empted the unity cause by proposing an alliance with their major local rival, the Army and Navy Veterans. Leading figures in the two organization, including J.R. Bowler for the GWVA and Maj. Fawcett Taylor of the ANV, chose a name – the British Empire Veterans' Association – and after due reflection agreed to convene a meeting just before the GWVA's 1921 convention in Port Arthur.[35]

As for the GAUV, it chose Toronto as the city in which to launch its unity campaign. On 11 June 1921, under lowering skies, a thousand veterans assembled in Queen's Park to hear spokesmen for the GWVA and the ANV, as well as the GAUV, proclaim their devotion to the common cause. Resistance was easily blamed on selfish national officials who were only anxious about their jobs. On 22 June most of the leading figures from the rally met privately with Rayfield and Marsh. 'The small men will say that it is a ruse on the part of the G.A.U.V. to get control from the G.W.V.A.,' Marsh warned a reporter, 'but the person who takes that attitude is not fit to be an official any longer.' [36] Indeed, that suspicion was so strong that the two GAUV leaders withdrew. What remained was indeed a new organization; a Canadian Legion of War Veterans with the sole goal of complete amalgamation of veterans' groups. If, as the organizers claimed, 95 per cent of veterans wanted unity, they could join the new Legion and thus bypass their officials. [37]

Although the first response of the GWVA was anger, a more creative policy obviously was needed. [38] A welcoming banquet held on 25 June 1921 for Bob Maxwell, safe home from his Cape Town journey, was an opportunity to unveil ideas. The new British Empire Service League might be the catalyst that would allow seven million imperial veterans to speak with one voice. In October Marshal Ferdinand Foch, the former Allied generalissimo, would be visiting North America, and there was every likelihood, Maxwell claimed, that Sir Douglas Haig would join him to meet old comrades in Canada. By postponing its Port Arthur convention from July to October, the GWVA would put itself at the centre of Haig's unifying influence and emerge once again as the single agency representing Canada's veterans. [39]

While convention delegates hurriedly changed their plans, GWVA executive members and officials gathered at Port Arthur to discuss Maxwell's amalgamation plans. What kind of an organization did Canadian veterans need? It must have a national charter and an effective organ, and it must be active in all nine provinces and have its headquarters in Ottawa. It needed a non-partisan, non-political constitution and policies that embraced a concern for the disabled and dependent, an intelligent interest in world affairs, and an 'unswerving loyalty to Canada and the Empire.' On each count, by no coincidence, the GWVA qualified. [40] But MacNeil, for one, understood that more was needed. The Winnipeg experience suggested that the ANV might accept some form of federation. The Imperial Veterans approved of unity but they themselves would do no more than affiliate. Visits and contacts made in the summer of 1921 warned the GWVA secretary that the forthcoming convention would be stormy unless he could report progress, particularly since it soon became apparent that Foch was not coming to Port Arthur and Haig had never even planned to cross the Atlantic. [41]

On the whole, senior officers from the CEF had chosen to leave veterans' organizations to their own devices. Recalling the GWVA, Col. Frederick F. Clarke later admitted: 'I felt it was not place for an officer, and like a great many, like so many thousands of officers and men in the expeditional [*sic*] force, I dropped out of the organization.'[42] The former Canadian Corps commander had never belonged. Maxwell's enthusiasm for Foch and Haig had put Sir Arthur Currie's nose out of joint. Haig had told the former Canadian commander of his invitation to visit Port Arthur. Why had the Canadians not turned to their old chief? As Currie explained to a friend, 'The fact of the matter is that I have never been invited to this convention, which would seem to indicate that I am not wanted.'[43]

On that same day MacNeil had written to Currie, belatedly reporting on the problems of amalgamation and presenting a characteristically elaborate scheme from David Loughnan for a Canadian BESL. The letter and an invitation to Port Arthur, delivered by an embarrassed Maxwell, came too late to appease the former corps commander. 'I do not intend to commit myself in any way,' Currie replied, 'until I have given the question further thought and study.'[44] J.H. Craig, the provisional secretary for the Canadian Legion, also made an attempt to enlist the CEF's most distinguished general.[45] Currie demurred; the prominence in Legion ranks of his egregious namesake, Col. John Currie, 'did not engender any degree of enthusiasm on my part.'[46] Some of Currie's comrades were not as fussy; by October 1921 Captain Craig had gained the support of two members of Parliament, five generals, and assorted colonels as part of the bid to put officers back in command of the veterans' movement.

The new Legion may have boasted officers, but the GWVA still had the troops. It also had a strategist in Grant MacNeil. The Winnipeggers had set the stage for a pre-convention meeting; the GWVA secretary-treasurer set the terms. Each nationally chartered veterans' organization was welcome to send delegates to an amalgamation conference scheduled for the weekend before the GWVA convention. That meant the ANV, the GAUV, and the IVC, but if the Legion wanted to come it also was welcome. So were the Naval Veterans of Toronto, the Comrades of the Great War from Vancouver, the Old Originals, and the Veterans of France.[47] In the year of unity, new organizations had proliferated. Among them were the amputees. Local associations of amputees, having contended with the DSCR's Orthopaedic and Surgical Branch, met in Toronto from 29 September to 1 October to form a national organization. Between civic receptions and banquets, the 'Fragments from France' formulated resolutions on pensions, employment, and wear and tear on clothing, and proclaimed themselves the Amputations Association of Canada. Capt. the Reverend Sydney Lambert, who had lost his legs while serving as a private in the 50th Battalion, became president.[48]

The amputees could afford to send no more than greetings to Port Arthur, but the ANV, the GAUV and the IVC each sent two-member delegations to a day-long session that concluded with an agreement to meet again in Winnipeg in the new year. Even so modest a gesture was opportune. When the GWVA convention opened on the following day, Monday, 17 October, delegates from British Columbia forced civic and political dignitaries to delay their welcoming speeches while they tried to make amalgamation the first order of business. If that was not done, warned Capt. Ian Mackenzie, the GWVA would die in British Columbia.[49] When Maxwell finally regained control of the meeting, the Sunday session was his most powerful debating point: who could deny the executive's efforts to win unity? Representatives from the GWVA's rivals and from the American Legion presented fraternal greetings and, by convention vote, joined in the debate on veterans' unity.[50] In an ebullient mood, delegates voted to allocate three thousand dollars for Maxwell's trip to Cape Town, re-elected him as a salaried president, and left the executive with a mandate to negotiate federation. Anything more, said Dr W.D. Sharpe, the president of the Ontario command, would go too far.[51]

The structural potential of a federation was illustrated by tubercular veterans. Since 1918 branches of the Invalided Tuberculous Soldiers' Welfare League could be found in most DSCR sanatoria, but the league was an organization in name alone until October 1921, when a few delegates met in Winnipeg. Unlike the amputees, they were barely noticed; TB sufferers were commonly stigmatized as clannish and quarrelsome as well as infectious. They also were poor. The formation of the new Tuberculous Veterans' Association (TVA) was made possible only after GWVA delegates agreed to provide a salary and office support for its national secretary, E.S. Keeling. In return, the adjustment bureau would have a new specialist on a complex problem and the GWVA would have a new ally.[52]

The alliance with the TVA proved opportune. On 6 February 1922, a month later, the promised amalgamation conference opened in the Manitoba legislature. MacNeil was present; so were pairs of delegates from the ANV, the GAUV, the IVC, the new TVA, and, despite the lack of a charter or members, two representatives of the Canadian Legion. Maj. Fawcett Taylor, past president of the ANV, future Manitoba Conservative leader, and host for the occasion, took the chair.[53] That office was no sinecure; in the closed room, bygones were not bygones. Men who had abused each other publicly and privately were not comrades. The split was clear: total amalgamation or, at best, federation. Speaking on behalf of the Legion, Lt-Col. A.M. Hunter had plenty to say. From Toronto to Winnipeg, attempts at federation had failed. Associations were shrinking. Everywhere, he claimed, veterans were 'groping in the dark and accomplishing nothing, depending on outside contributions to keep these moribund organizations alive and on their feet.'[54]

MacNeil was unmoved. After two days of wearying rhetoric, he had had enough. Amalgamation, he declared, was a catchword that ignored what ex-soldiers really wanted. 'What they want is amelioration of the conditions under which they are suffering and they want unity as a means to accomplish that end, and the tragic phase of this conference is we have been focussing on the means and entirely overlooking the end.'[55] That was rhetoric too, but it led to the result MacNeil had chosen and tried out in advance. By 9 February his weary opponents concluded that they had spent too much time to go home empty-handed and that the only acceptable solution, as MacNeil had anticipated, would be a 'Dominion Veterans' Alliance' run by a virtual continuation of the conference, with Fawcett Taylor as chairman and Walter Rayfield of the GAUV as vice-chairman. MacNeil would be secretary and chairman of the legislative committee – the only function of the new organization he had ever recognized as important.[56] Certainly, if it pleased the GAUV, and the Legion, the DVA might 'educate' veterans to accept amalgamation, but then again it might not. That was not MacNeil's concern, and without him nothing much seemed likely to happen.

What did matter was that the DVA allowed veterans to speak with a united voice to a new and untrusted Liberal government. In April 1922 MacNeil summoned members to a three-day session of the new legislative committee. A long list of DVA proposals, ranging from pension reform to Asiatic exclusion, descended on Herbert Marler's special committee with an authority veterans' resolutions had not possessed for years.[57] If MacNeil was not on hand to help the GAUV president, Gordon McNichol, defend the bonus, Marler's system of splitting up the committee gave MacNeil a useful alibi.[58] Under MacNeil's guidance the entire alliance found itself committed to unemployment insurance, state control of resource development, and expansion of the Employment Service. It was not entirely clear that the majors, colonels, and generals of the Legion or the ANV would have concurred, but surely that was the price of unity.

The alliance had nothing to do with the GWVA's 'Clean Sweep' campaign or with its sequel in June 1922 – MacNeil's sensational charges against the Board of Pension Commissioners. Repeatedly and explicitly, the GWVA secretary excluded the DVA from the risky course he had adopted. Once the Ralston Commission had dealt with the charges, however, MacNeil resumed the mantle of DVA secretary for the second phase of the inquiry. The alliance performed a real function in preparing and programming sessions that involved every veterans' organization, local and national, as well as the unorganized. It was the GAUV, the noisy proponent of amalgamation, that regularly broke with the united front by demanding time to reiterate well-worn arguments for the bonus. Both MacNeil and the royal commission showed a prudent forbearance. By the summer of 1923 the Dominion Veterans' Alliance had demonstrated its value. It had also ignored the deadline, set fifteen months before, for proceeding to amalgamation. Within its limits, federation had sufficed; it was evident from *The Veteran* that MacNeil and other GWVA leaders had no plans to go beyond those limits.[59]

The Canteen Fund

The common problems of most veterans' organizations – money and members – persisted. Rival associations guarded their true strength from each other (and posterity) with precautions more appropriate for military or commercial secrets, but even MacNeil's inflated estimates of GWVA strength fell to 180,000 by 1921 and 170,000 in 1922. Thanks to the service bureau, the GWVA was spending as much in a couple of months as the Army and Navy Veterans budgeted for an entire year.[60] Yet without its legislative and adjustment work, MacNeil believed, the GWVA would betray the veterans and dependants it was pledged to serve.

In Britain the Canteen Fund had been the catalyst in uniting veterans' associations. Since Canadians had contributed to the profits of the Navy and Army Canteen Board, CEF veterans were entitled to their share of the British fund, to say nothing of profits from film shows and surpluses accumulated by the miscellaneous Canadian regimental accounts. From a distance Canadian officials and veterans had monitored the savage wrangling in Britain. Meanwhile, like impoverished but expectant heirs to a large estate, veterans made grand plans to spend the money. What better topic could old comrades discuss as they gathered in clubs and branches to enjoy their small oases in a prohibition-dry Canada?[61]

From all sources, Canada's share of the Canteen Fund amounted to about $2 million.[62] The 1921 Special Committee had agreed with the GWVA that the funds must be kept for returned men and their dependants, but it also recommended that the government consult all three of the major national veterans' organizations for advice on how to use the money.[63] MacNeil needed no urging. What organization did more for all veterans and their dependants than the GWVA? 'This service,' MacNeil claimed in a letter to the acting prime minister, C.J. Doherty, 'is being continued on an extended scale, and is promoted to the benefit of all ex-service men irregardless [*sic*] of membership affiliation.' He hinted at an even more ambitious role for the future: 'It is the intention of the Association, if assistance may be obtained, to conduct more intensive organization in preparation for any serious unemployment that may recur. Organized co-operation, in all industrial communities, of all interests will undoubtedly do much to eliminate the necessity for unemployment relief on the part of the Federal Government.'[64]

MacNeil's letter was opportune and almost certainly prearranged with the minister. In an election year the government would conciliate a former critic, relieve itself of an unwanted and unconstitutional responsibility for unemployment relief, and confound its critics by pointing to an unanimous report of a parliamentary committee. Within a week the Canteen Fund's trustees were ordered to hand over $50,000 to the GWVA. In return, the association would publicize re-establishment through *The Veteran*, replace the DSCR's recently disbanded Information and Service Branch, organize against unemployment, and in general 'expand its scope and usefulness.'[65] It took the rival associations until September to make their own bids for money, but the government promptly obliged with $20,000 for the GAUV, $12,500 for the ANV, and smaller grants for a total of twenty-one different organizations – even $3,000 for the barely existent Canadian Legion and $100 for the troublesome radicals of the Soldiers' and Sailors' Labour Party. Having watched its rivals, large and small, reach the trough, the GWVA had only to ask to receive a further $80,000, this time (like its rivals) 'for the purpose of relieving unemployment.'[66]

In all, $180,000 of the Canteen Fund was expended in subsidies to veterans' organizations in 1921. Both the plans justifying the subsidies and the subsequent accounting were sketchy. The GAUV said that it wanted a grant mainly for office expenses.[67] The Army and Navy Veterans simply distributed its money to branches in amounts ranging from $100 to Fort Francis to $1,500 for Winnipeg.[68] The GWVA had a single bank account, and the $130,000 from the Canteen Fund was deposited along with the dominion command's meagre regular revenue, leaving the branches to wonder and complain when news of the government's largesse finally leaked out.[69] Norman Parkinson, after vain efforts to exercise his responsibilities as trustee for the Canteen Fund, pleaded that the pressure of other duties forced him to resign.[70] The truth was that neither the government nor the associations were in a mood for rigorous accounting. Only the GWVA seems to have worked out an auditing method with DSCR officials; four years later the ANV and the GAUV could report only from memory.[71]

It was also clear that the proceeds from the Canteen Fund gave the veterans' organizations a second wind. When Lord Byng, the new governor-general, reached Ottawa in the summer of 1921, he was ready to repeat his British experience of unifying veterans. 'Spoke of his plan with returned men, a democratic self-governing organization; he had ear-marked part of the money before leaving England,' an approving Mackenzie King recorded in his diary.[72] But with money of their own to spend, the GWVA and its rivals had other priorities. The GWVA's special executive meeting at Port Arthur in July 1921, which cost $5,316, was billed as an 'unemployment conference.' Over $46,000 was channelled to *The Veteran* in the name of 'publicity and propaganda.'[73] MacNeil's 'Clean Sweep' was one of the few tangible outcomes of the Canteen Fund bonanza. At the Winnipeg amalgamation conference, MacNeil could boast that far from being impoverished, his organization had a $60,000 surplus.[74]

In the eyes of rank-and-file veterans, subsidizing officials was not a suitable way to dispose of canteen profits. *The Veteran* filled its columns with suggestions for schemes ranging from scholarships to a fund to help ailing veterans escape to the California climate. Tom Lapp, Loughnan's successor as editor, wanted the money invested in a 'non-competitive industrial enterprise' that would provide both jobs and dividends.[75] The 1921 ANV convention expressed a fondness for building soldiers' homes. True to the special parliamentary committee recommendation, the DSCR convened a Canteen Funds Disposal Committee on 3 November. The GWVA insisted that only a referendum among veterans could settle the issue of how best to allocate the funds. The government printed 550,000 ballots and distributed them to veterans in Canada, the United States, and Britain. Only 22,594 were returned. The ballots contained five printed choices. A plurality – 5,764 voters – favoured spending the money on sheltered workshops. The next largest group – 3,750 voters – simply wanted the money 'distributed.'[76]

The meagre response forced the new Liberal government to keep looking for an answer. The coincidental creation of the Ralston commission provided a place to refer the problem. In their final report Ralston and his colleagues announced that the fund stood at $2,142,245, admitted that the commissioners had discovered no consensus among veterans, and recommended that the money be split among the provinces and used as a loan and grant fund for indigent veterans. An ingenious formula, based on provincial percentages of enlistments, discharges, and pensions, determined the shares; unpaid local committees made up largely of ex-servicemen would administer the program. The American Red Cross and the British United Services Fund would each receive $50,000 to care for expatriate Canadian veterans in distress. As a sop to the associations, the commission recommended that $100,000 be used to maintain an adjustment bureau independent of the DSCR.[77] The Ralston recommendations, essentially unaltered, passed the House of Commons without opposition at the end of the 1924 session, only to fall foul of the Senate's end-of-session stubbornness. As it had with most of the Pension Act amendments, the Senate simply announced that it had been left too little time for close study. 'I cannot for the life of me see any reason for rejecting the ... bill,' protested Béland. 'It is not our money; it is the soldiers' money, the distribution of which was recommended by the royal commission.' [78] That, of course, was the Senate's reason: the wisdom of the Ralston commission on the subject of canteen funds was no more dependable than it was on pension matters.

By mid-1922 the previous year's windfall had vanished, and it was clear that the Canteen Fund, now a storm-centre of controversy, could provide nothing more. The GWVA once again needed money. A special 'Keeping Faith' appeal netted only $2,236. Exploiting the new idea of 'Poppy Day' looked more promising. In 1921 paper poppies, produced by French and Belgian orphans from the war zone and sold for their benefit, invaded the United States and Canada. GWVA branches turned over a total of $60,780 to the French consul. [79] Here was a product that the DSCR's Vetcraft shops could manufacture and that the GWVA's dominion command was ideally situated to market. MacNeil seized the chance. The alternative, said *The Veteran*, was to leave the field to commercial 'vandals of sentiment.' [80] For Armistice Day 1922 the Vetcraft shops delivered $23,487 worth of large and small poppies, wreaths, and sprays. The GWVA headquarters sold them to provincial commands for $34,716, deducted $5,222 in expenses, and recorded a modest profit of $6,007. Provincial commands and branches added their own mark-ups, and John McCrae's fellow Canadians paid about a nickel each for a symbol of sacrifice that had cost the GWVA 1.3 cents. [81] The scheme was not a big success, however. Members of the DVA were suspicious that MacNeil was making far more from his partnership with Vetcraft than he admitted. Poppy Day made the GWVA a little money and many more enemies. [82]

The Liberal government was sympathetic to the GWVA's plight. It paid J.R. Bowler $4,575 for his work as GWVA counsel before the Ralston commission; MacNeil was given his travelling costs for preparing the way for the commission in 1923; and an extra $5,411 compensated the GWVA for the cost of preparing cases. In August 1923, with a Canteen Fund settlement pending, the cabinet authorized a $5,000 'loan' to the GWVA for its adjustment work until the new soldier advisers took over. [83] The money was promptly covered in supplementary estimates. This was helpful, but it was far from enough. By the summer of 1923 the GWVA faced a financial crisis.

The symptoms were acute when the GWVA, having skipped its 1922 convention on the pretext of preoccupation with the hearings of the Ralston commission, finally met in Vancouver in July 1923. A deluge of internal propaganda reminded members of how much the GWVA had accomplished:

200,000 claims adjusted, 400 permanent buildings acquired, $2 million spent on relief; surely it was an investment worth protecting.[84] For the first time the problem of overdue per capita levies was tackled by proposing the establishment of a national membership card. Maxwell had quit at the end of 1922, citing 'personal economic reasons.' His successor, Dr W.H. Sharpe, was a hearty but aging surgeon from Brampton, Ontario, who had served in Serbia with a Royal Navy hospital and ended the war as a CAMC major. He would at least work for nothing. Even more responsibility would now fall on MacNeil; delegates voted that he should become 'Assistant to the Dominion President' to liberate the GWVA's ablest official for legislative and, even more, organizational work.[85]

This was no real financial solution. MacNeil and the new executive faced a galloping deficit and no hope of rescue. *The Veteran* had been published weekly since 1921, but increasingly it was filled with trashy advertising for dubious oil properties and shifty-looking investment opportunities. On 1 September 1923 the magazine was closed down. The Tuberculous Veterans' Association was abruptly told that it would have to make other arrangements for its national secretary. The resulting shock, and a hurriedly organized 'Carry On' campaign, managed to shake $9,637 from branches and benefactors. On 3 November, when the DVA met at the GWVA offices in Ottawa for its third session, MacNeil took advantage of the prevailing good will and a vote of thanks for his role in the Ralston inquiry to urge other organizations to share the GWVA's burden of service. Needless to say, they hedged and evaded; as MacNeil later recalled, 'The understanding then became applicable that the GWVA would undertake these responsibilities, and finance the bureau as well as could possibly be done.' On the same date, a smaller and less ambitious version of *The Veteran* resumed publication, promising more news from branches and no more questionable advertising. In return for a monthly contribution, the TVA regained a share of the adjustment bureau's services, and the GWVA struggled on.[86]

Through most of 1923, MacNeil had pursued another financial source. Since 1915 the Disablement Fund had become a vague, half-forgotten mystery, suspended in some unaccountable limbo. Surely it was intended to support work that assisted every veteran and dependant. Sir Arthur Currie might be persuaded to influence its chief contributor, James Carruthers. Carruthers had already withdrawn $35,000 of his money to benefit the CNIB, and the GWVA's unique Legislative and Adjustment Service might seem an equally worthy cause. The prime minister and Dr Béland, MacNeil reported to Currie, were both sympathetic.[87]

So was Currie, and, he discovered, so was Carruthers. The Montreal grain magnate was frankly disappointed that his money had done so little conspicious good. Yet neither man was eager for the money to benefit the GWVA. 'I ... am firmly convinced,' Currie told MacNeil, 'that the Prime Minister should create a small independent unpaid committee who would be responsible for organizing what you call the "adjustment service" in order that the staff of that service should feel independent of Government control.'[88] In a letter to Mackenzie King, Currie was more explicit. If it was proper to fund such a service from the public treasury, it was also important to give it independence. He would even offer to serve on the committee that he recommended be established, but both Carruthers and he agreed that 'we have to be careful that the money placed in our hands would not be used for the purpose of keeping the headquarters of the G.W.V.A. going.'[89] Béland was not persuaded.[90] Small, independent-minded committees were not something a politician could be expected to relish, and certainly Béland had no complaints about the GWVA. If there was a Disablement Fund – and after a year and a half in the department, Béland obviously knew nothing about it – why not use it? It was the Disablement Fund, at Béland's firm insistence, that provided the GWVA with $5,000 in 1923, an amount recouped later from a supplementary vote.[91] It was a practice that might become habitual. With unconscious irony, MacNeil gratefully acknowledged Sir Arthur Currie's influence in the transaction. The general was suitably chagrined.[92]

MacNeil, Currie, Béland, and almost everyone else had overlooked the Disablement Fund's trustee and devoted guardian. Since 1915, Ernest Scammell had protected, husbanded, and restored the fund, guarding it from provincial Returned Soldiers' Commissions in 1918 and from assorted predators since. Despite Carruthers's substantial withdrawal, a refund of the Yukon's $6,600 contribution, and a long list of loans and tiny grants to distressed soldiers, Scammell had retained $117,000 of the original $128,000. Carruthers, for one, was entirely satisfied when he received Scammell's overdue explanation: the fund's innumerable loans, grants, and other good works were indeed best done by stealth. Next, Scammell had to deal with MacNeil and his own minister.[93]

By the time of the Ralston commission hearings, Scammell's distaste for the GWVA secretary-treasurer was evident. Nor, as he confessed later, did Scammell see any particular necessity for the adjustment work.[94] It was, after all, a reflection on the perfection of machinery he had helped devise. Nor did Scammell wish his fund to be devoured piecemeal by the likes of Grant MacNeil and the GWVA. Still, the Disablement Fund would be repaid when the Canteen Fund bill passed, and Scammell dutifully agreed to a further fifteen-thousand-dollar loan, with five thousand dollars to be paid by instalments beginning in June 1924. The unexpected failure of the Canteen Bill gave Scammell qualms. What if the minister or the cabinet never paid back the money? It was certain that the GWVA never would. Béland, fussing over preparations for an imminent European trip, proved amenable to Scammell's request for an approving order in council. Perhaps, the civil servant suggested, it might be as well to direct the loan to the entire Dominion Veterans' Alliance; that would answer the rival organizations when they came clamouring for a share. Béland agreed, the cabinet barely noticed, and the minister could depart in peace.[95]

Scammell was no fool. He knew that MacNeil was desperate for the money. He knew that the DVA remained the paper organization it had been in February 1922: it had no adjustment service. But once the alliance received the money, MacNeil would see little of it again. MacNeil knew that. When he collected the next cheque on 2 October 1924, he immediately assumed that a mistake had been made; the cheque was payable to the alliance. Scammell never showed MacNeil the order in council. Instead, with obvious guile, he suggested that MacNeil, as an official of the DVA, must have the authority to endorse such cheques. Their purpose – supporting the adjustment service – was not in doubt. As an outsider to the veterans' organizations, Scammell sweetly confessed, he could not know their rules. MacNeil needed no prodding; the financial urgency was too great. Having consulted Dr Sharpe, his president, MacNeil endorsed both the first five-thousand-dollar cheque and another on 7 January 1925. With a deft shove from Ernest Scammell, MacNeil had put himself in his enemies' hands.[96]

The dénouement came in 5 March 1925, when an unsuspecting Béland introduced a new Canteen Bill. How much Arthur Meighen and the opposition knew in advance is not clear. The Conservatives certainly smelled an issue. Plainly, the Senate's actions had not had the expected consequences: the GWVA's adjustment bureau had survived. Where had the money been found? What was the Disablement Fund? Where was the trust agreement? Why had the DVA been paid ten thousand dollars? What had happened to the money? Was it true that no one but MacNeil had ever seen it? Béland could not say. Perhaps there was no trust agreement. Scammell was in Montreal, Béland confessed, and had no time to explain. What about Carruthers? 'No man,' Meighen stated, 'is giving $100,000 without saying what it is for'[97] It was, the Montreal *Star* judged, 'an exceedingly futile rumpus,' with MPs hair-splitting on the Trusts Act while the GWVA and the DSCR pursued their vendetta. The Canteen Bill would pass the Commons, the *Star* predicted: 'Its reception in the Senate is altogether an uncertain quantity.'[98]

The *Star*'s reporter was right. As early as February General Griesbach had begun to organize an attack on the payment from the Disablement Fund, presumably as a personal contribution to a pre-election assault on the Liberal government. It is not clear when he discovered that MacNeil and the

GWVA provided an even more vulnerable and attractive target. Nor is it clear when the DVA's other members learned about MacNeil's appropriation of cheques ostensibly intended for their organization. Major Taylor, still chairman of the DVA as well as Conservative provincial leader in Manitoba, insisted that he learned the truth only from the House of Commons debate on 5 March (though it is hard to believe that Arthur Meighen never consulted his fellow Tory from Portage la Prairie). Whatever he knew in advance, Fawcett Taylor's response was dignified and restrained. In his report to all the DVA's constituent associations on 17 April he summarized the facts, observed that the alliance had made no progress towards amalgamation, and loyally asserted that he meant no reflection on the GWVA or its work. 'I have not the slightest doubt,' he said, 'that the money received from the Disablement Fund was properly expended for the maintenance of the G.W.V.A. service bureau, and that no one benefited personally by it to the extent of one cent.' That of course, was not the point: 'I felt rather humiliated and embarrassed when I ascertained that certain of these cheques had been made to the Dominion Veterans' Alliance, and don't purpose [sic] that such a thing shall occur in the future.'[99] The DVA was dead.

As the *Star* had predicted, the Senate was waiting for the Canteen Bill when it cleared the House of Commons on 5 May. Senator Griesbach had peppered the order paper with questions on both the Disablement Fund and the earlier payments from the Canteen Fund; on 12 May, when the Canteen Fund bill emerged, he was ready to demand that a special committee look into pensions and both of the supplementary funds. 'I venture to assert that ex-service men in the country will not approve of the manner in which the sum of money accounted for has been spent,' he told his fellow senators. 'There are items here which I greatly question.' Veterans deserved answers.[100] Griesbach's colleagues happily obliged. A venerable Ottawa Liberal, Senator Napoléon Belcourt, could be counted on to protect the government from harm. Liberals were no longer Griesbach's quarry. For five years MacNeil had plagued senators and their friends; now he would have his comeuppance. Both the GWVA's secretary-treasurer and the association's financial records were curtly summoned. When the records proved immobile, DSCR auditors descended on the GWVA's Sparks Street offices.

As the rival organizations lined up to respond to Griesbach's damning questions, MacNeil and the GWVA stood alone. This time, there was no Bowler to assist. Grudgingly granted counsel at his own expense, MacNeil turned to Capt. J.T. Shaw, an Independent from Calgary. As an MP Shaw could not charge a fee; and, in the circumstances, he was not likely to be very successful in appeasing vengeful senators.[101] What auditors might have found in the records of the ANV, the GAUV, or the Canadian Legion was irrelevant; those organizations were not in the dock. MacNeil's $4,500 salary, the payment to Maxwell, the salaries and travel expenditures, the thousands of dollars spent on 'publicity and propaganda' made a rich commentary on an organization that had absorbed $130,000 to combat unemployment but had not spent a penny on the unemployed. Day after day vengeful rivals had their chance to attack the GWVA's leading official. Even the Poppy Day monopoly joined the Senate's list after W.S. Dobbs of the Amputations Association claimed that the GWVA had attempted to copyright the poppy symbol. Officials of Winnipeg's Poppy Day Committee offered evidence that the GWVA's dominion and Manitoba commands had acted as profiteers.[102] In Col. F.F. Clarke, the CNR's chief surveyor and the grand commander of the Canadian Legion, senators finally found a veterans' leader to their taste. The hapless Shaw failed utterly to get Clarke to admit that MacNeil had been anything more than hard-working. 'It has always been my point,' Clarke said, 'that, as long as we had paid officials, we would have men who were energetic in keeping their jobs.'[103] Hugh McLeod, Marsh's successor as secretary of the GAUV, insisted that his organization had performed as much adjustment service as the GWVA. The proper thing, McLeod suggested, would have been for the DVA treasurer to summon a meeting, 'say that they had had a pretty nice wind-fall, and it would be nice to get together again and split the odd bottle.' Griesbach promptly terminated that line of questioning.[104]

During the two weeks of hearings Belcourt had insisted that MacNeil faced no charges and needed no counsel. The senators' report, published on 18 June 1925, belied those assurances: Canteen Fund money had been squandered and salaries and honoraria for the GWVA's headquarters officers; not a penny had reached unemployed servicemen and their families. The GWVA had shamelessly commercialized the poppy and had sought to turn the symbol of sacrifice into a private monopoly. As for MacNeil, he had deliberately subverted the intent of a minister and an assistant deputy minister and had 'committed a breach of trust ... as an official of the Dominion Veterans' Alliance.' The indictment was complete.[105]

The Canadian Legion

Barely a week after the report was published, the GWVA's seventh convention gathered in Ottawa. The first order of business was a unanimous and noisy vote of confidence in the embattled leaders. Delegates crowded around Sharpe and MacNeil to offer their support.[106] But the GWVA secretary-treasurer had no illusions; he was finished. The federated version of veterans' unity had dissolved with the DVA. The bitterness of veteran politics and the financial plight of his own organization had been ruthlessly exposed. Even the TVA, the GWVA's loyal satellite, had been torn into bitter factions. E.S.B. Hind, still furious at the GWVA's financial 'betrayal' of 1923, had used the Senate committee to pour out his venom on MacNeil only to be deposed by the TVA's president, Capt. T.M. Downing. In sanatoria across Canada, Hind and Downing factions battled. [107]

At the British Empire Service League's London meeting in 1923, Haig had proposed that the next biennial gathering should be held in Ottawa as an occasion to heal Canada's fractured veterans' movement. In May 1925 W.D. Lighthall, the GWVA's venerable progenitor, offered MacNeil some cautious advice. Electing 'the untruthful and self-seeking' Maxwell in 1920 had been a dreadful misfortune. So too, by implication, was the GWVA's subsequent activist course. Now, he urged, 'the G.W.V.A. and all its friends – of whom I count myself one – should distinctly adopt as their next object, a general gradual conciliation, especially of the officer element.' [108] The Haig receptions might be the opportunity for further reconciliation. But Sir Arthur Currie, for one, would not help. 'No, Dr. Lighthall,' he replied. 'Union cannot be accomplished unless the board is swept clean and all sinister, ulterior and personal motives squelched and eliminated.' Haig was warned that the unattached veterans, and officers particularly, because of the past antipathy shown them, would be unlikely to join. As best, Currie suggested, he might 'plant a seed.' [109]

Currie's predilection for a conspiratorial view of the world was not shared by his wartime rival. Lt-Gen. Sir Richard Turner VC had retired to run his family's grocery business in Quebec. He was willing to help the GWVA but solely on the condition that he would serve as its final president. The day after they welcomed Sharpe and MacNeil, delegates of a chastened GWVA unanimously elected Turner and, on a motion by Col. Jimmy McAra of Regina, placed their charter in the hands of Haig's personal representative. [110]

The board was being wiped clean. If Haig's example in 1921 had helped inspire a 'Canadian Legion,' his approach in 1925 induced even more senior officers to supplant the privates and sergeants who had dominated the major organizations. Colonel Clarke of the Canadian Legion summarized the new philosophy when he told the Senate committee' ''Gentlemen, we feel that if a veteran organization is to take hold in Canada and give real service, the officers should be men who can give a little time and money, for the honour that is in the cause.' [111] Senator Griesbach, the former brigadier-general, inherited the presidency of the Army and Navy Veterans from the succession of majors who had managed its affairs. Even the populist and egalitarian GAUV chose Col. R.H. Steacy, the former chief Protestant chaplain overseas, as its new president. [112]

By the time Earl Haig arrived, a new veterans' leadership and a unity movement were taking shape. Twenty thousand people met the British field marshal on the lawn of the Parliament buildings. GWVA delegates had voted to hold their next convention in Halifax, but when adjournment came on 30 June, in the presence of Haig and four thousand spectators, the GWVA was virtually wound up. [113] After the British Empire Service League concluded its proceedings over the Dominion Day weekend – with the usual theme of empire immigration predominating – Haig set off across Canada. In an age that saw celebrities only in the flesh, enthusiastic crowds thronged to meet the famous general and listened dutifully to his lectures on imperial and veterans' unity. In Montreal at the end of July Haig announced that Sir Richard Turner would be his trustee in the cause of veterans' unity. A cheering audience at the Canadian Club clearly agreed that when the veterans came together 'we shall have forged a link in the great chain of ex-soldier organizations which will bind them to one another and to the Empire and to the great principles of which the Empire stands.' At Halifax, Haig appealed to unattached veterans and especially to officers to join the movement: 'Your proud boast during the war was that you never failed to reach the objective that was set for you. I ask you to assist me in bringing about this objective which has for its aim the betterment of the conditions and circumstances of ex-servicemen and all the peoples of the Empire.' [114]

Turner met his new responsibilities. In each province he nominated a provincial trustee, usually a dependable senior officer. The Ontario meeting, held on 19 August, was the first and a model for the others, with Maj.-Gen. J.T. Fotheringham in the chair and Brig.-Gen. J.A. Gunn in charge. Unity was approved unanimously. [115] By November veterans in every province had committed themselves to attending a 'unity' meeting to be held at Winnipeg's Marlborough Hotel on 25 November 1925. Haig's man, Sir Richard Turner, was in the chair. A procession of delegates from the larger organizations declared their commitment – guarded or wholehearted – to unity. The Imperial Veterans seemed newly enthusiastic; but General Griesbach of the ANV was unexpectedly suspicious and resentful. So were delegates from the Amputations Association, who bridled at receiving 'mere sympathy' from fellow veterans and who feared that their special concerns might be overlooked in a larger organization. The groups of 1921 were now outflanked and outnumbered by a flurry of new participants, from the Naval Veterans and the South African Veterans to the Veterans' Civil Service Guild and Lt-Col. J. Keiller McKay's Disabled Veterans' Association. [116] Despite all the months of rhetoric and planning, the outcome was uncertain until Sharpe of the GWVA and Downing of the TVA forced a vote: would the convention proceed to choose a name and a constitution? Reporters, who had been locked out of the meeting, listened at keyholes as an angry Griesbach shouted that amalgamation meant annihilation. But the vote carried, thirty-five to eleven. Committees were formed to develop constitution, policies, and 'ways and means.' A banquet, with Lt-Gen. Sir Percy Lake, a prewar builder of the Canadian militia and a wartime commander of the disastrous Mesopotamia campaign, in the chair, celebrated unity with fresh speeches. The few GAUV delegates celebrated elsewhere. [117]

In three more days of resolutions and debate, interspersed with greetings to and from Currie, Lord Byng, the Prince of Wales, and other symbols of past devotion and future loyalty, a new organization evolved. The constitution, devised in large measure by W.D. Lighthall, opened membership to any veteran who had served in any war of the empire or for at least three months with an Allied force. Women's auxiliaries were permissible, though their by-laws would be subject to branch and provincial approval. Finally, 'no avowed Anarchist, Communist, or other person who advocates the destruction of ordered government in Canada by force shall be permitted to become or remain a member.' [118] Harsh experience persuaded the ways and means committee that there must be a national membership-card system to ensure collection of annual dues of one dollar per member. On the matter of a name there was unexpected unanimity: the organization was to be called the Canadian Legion of the British Empire Service League. General Lake, who had come from Victoria as a delegate of the old Canadian Legion, went home as president of the new one. Turner and Currie would be honorary presidents, and Brig.-Gen. F.S. Meighen, who had been involved in the veterans' movement early on, would be vice-president. Haig had warned that officers would dominate the British Legion unless deliberate efforts were made to include other ranks. The Winnipeg meeting remembered that warning; for the largely symbolic office of chairman, the meeting chose a former machine-gun sergeant, Labour member of the Manitoba legislature, and president of the Winnipeg GWVA, A.E. Moore. He was buffered by Lieutenant-Colonel McKay as vice-chairman and Lt-Col. L.R. LaFlèche as treasurer, and by a phalanx of colonels, majors, and captains on the executive. [119]

On 30 November the Unity Conference adjourned. It remained to be seen if the veterans approved of the decisions that had been taken. Across the country, the smaller conferences that had chosen the Winnipeg delegates provided the framework for creating the new organization's provincial councils. In Saskatchewan, where the GWVA under Col. James McAra had never faced much competition, the provincial council was established on 18 and 19 February 1926. The Manitoba council followed on 18 and 19 March, with Winnipeg's one-legged mayor, Ralph Webb, presiding. On 12 April a committee of the new national executive took over the GWVA's Legislative and Adjustment Service, and a month later Thomas Lapp changed mastheads from *The Veteran* to *The Legionary*. By the end of June all nine Canadian provinces had formed their councils. On 24 January 1927, when the Canadian Legion returned to Winnipeg for its first convention, General Lake could report that there were now twenty-thousand paid-up members and that charters had been signed for three hundred branches. [120]

Unity was still not complete. The Legion could tolerate the absence of the Veterans of France or the departure of the Veterans' Civil Service Guild. It was more painful that the Amputations Association had refused the offer of a special department. The absence of the Army and Navy Veterans, the third largest national organization, hurt most. Certainly, as MacNeil had always known, of all the associations the ANV had the strongest sense of its own identity and the greatest reluctance to see itself as part of a larger veterans' association. The ANV convention at Regina that chose Griesbach as president had debated amalgamation for hours, only to affirm that the identity and assets of the organization would have to be preserved. Far from leading the Army and Navy Veterans into the Legion, Griesbach's role was to help keep them out. General Lake reported to Currie on both the motives and the danger. 'Their present attitude is that they consider they have, after considerable effort, purged themselves of all undesirable elements, that they think by joining the Legion they would risk coming into contact again with those same elements, that they are very well satisfied as they are, and that they do not see any particular reason why they should put themselves out for the general benefit.' [121]

It was a viewpoint Currie could appreciate. Once again Canada's best-known soldier felt himself bypassed, first by Haig and now by Turner. Having named him honorary president, Currie complained, the Legion had not yet even been in touch with him. [122] In his reply Griesbach made no effort to hide his contempt for the new organization. The Army and Navy Veterans, he said, insisted on membership 'based upon military service of value and good behaviour in civil life'; membership in the GWVA was based on mere service. Its leaders had been 'usually men of no particular service in the War, and of poor reputation in civil life.' Moore was one of them, 'a politician in the Soldier Movement – & lives off it.' [123] There would be no reconciliation.

The days of wild exaggeration and growth were over, but by October 1928 the Legion claimed 55,000 paid memberships, 594 branches, and 179 ladies' auxiliaries. Among the senior branches were No. 9 (British Columbia), formed by Japanese-Canadian veterans; No. 93 (British Columbia) composed of former nurses and other women who had seen active service; and No. 34 (Manitoba), which united Polish-Canadians. Vigorous fund-raising in 1928, plus firm negotiations with creditors, protected the new

Legionary from the initial financial misery that had pursued *The Veteran*.[124] By 1930, on the eve of the Great Depression, Legion membership had climbed to 70,000.

Griesbach may have been right; the Legion was the heir of the GWVA. The name was changed for the sake of unity, but the line of succession was unmistakable. Like its predecessor, the Legion set out to become the national movement of veterans, political but non-partisan, committed to serving its members. The Legion's Service Bureau inherited most of the staff and all of the concerns of its predecessor. The generals, Lake, Turner, and even Currie (who served as national president from 1928 to 1929 without being present at either convention), passed on, leaving a different generation of leaders. Lt-Col. Léo LaFlèche, a future deputy minister of national defence, Maj. J.S. Roper, a Halifax lawyer, and Winnipeg's J.R. Bowler would see the Legion through the difficult days of the depression.

Grant MacNeil, who had really created the post-war GWVA, departed without fanfare or protest. He worked his way across Canada by showing slides and war films until he reached Vancouver. There he earned a meagre living as a car salesman. In the depression years MacNeil survived as a penniless beachcomber, living in a borrowed shack. The idealism and activism of the young Co-operative Commonwealth Federation caught his imagination. In 1935 voters in Vancouver North bucked a Liberal trend and sent MacNeil to the House of Commons he had once influenced as much as any outsider in its history.[125]

10 The Department of Pensions and National Health

Dwindling Responsibility

The goal of civil re-establishment had always been to reduce Canada's responsibility for her returned soldiers. From homestead loans to insurance, each program was intended to foster self-sufficiency. Such expectations were not easily fulfilled. The benefits of retraining had been vitiated by the post-war depression. Soldier settlement had partially foundered because of the collapse of farm prices. The austere finality of the Board of Pension Commissioners had been at least cracked by the Ralston commission and an appeal system. The merger movement had saved the main veterans' organization from collapse and had guaranteed that Canada's old soldiers would not fade rapidly from public consciousness.

In July 1920, when the DSCR boasted ten thousand employees and scores of institutions, Ernest Scammell had begun planning its long-term future as a Ministry of Pensions, responsible for every veterans' program from hospital care to soldier settlement.[1] Although his plans were ignored, change came fast. By the summer of 1921 the BPC's field staff and head office had been merged with the DSCR. John Todd, reassured that the commissioners had safeguarded their independence, sent his congratulations.[2] By 1927, years of steady shrinkage had reduced the department to eight hospitals, seven provincial units (the Maritime provinces were all served from Halifax) and fewer than two thousand employees.[3]

There was little protest. DSCR employees might be ex-comrades, but veterans' organizations bore them little good will. Morale sagged as able employees fled an ill-paid and uncertain future. Though only the Department of Finance spent more federal money, the DSCR lacked political prestige.[4] Only the most desperate job-seeker wanted a place in a shrinking organization, and pension payments remained mercifully free of political influence. The department was immune from partisanship, of course. In 1926, after the affable Dr Béland had been shifted to the Senate, his place was taken by Dr James Horace King, the former minister of public works.[5] King, who had been demoted for his lack-lustre performance in delivering votes from his native British Columbia, brought nothing to his new responsibilities but a medical degree. His chief initiative was to launch an investigation into alleged political manipulation by the DSCR staff.[6]

For five months in 1927, Lt-Col. A.T. Hunter, a failed Liberal candidate and former president of the Parkdale GWVA, waded through hearsay and innuendo in pursuit of Tories. Proceedings were in camera and cross-examination was forbidden; after all, Hunter said, DSCR officials had regularly denied that right to veteran-clients.[7] An official who suggested to two amputees that a Tory membership was a small price to pay for a job in a government liquor store compounded his offence in Hunter's eyes by adding, 'You don't have to vote that way.' It was, Hunter fumed, 'the most cynically atrocious political principle ever enunciated by a Canadian public official.'[8] Hunter's report excoriated officials – from Parkinson, the deputy minister, to a luckless dentist who could not account for his supply of medicinal whisky – but it offered no solutions beyond advising the DSCR to burn its voluminous regulations.[9]

The Hunter excursion coincided with a less formal but more searching investigation of the DSCR by Gordon Scott, a partner in the accounting firm of P.S. Ross and a future Quebec provincial treasurer. As his sponsor, the Finance Department, had hoped, Scott concluded that the department was over-sized, over-officered, over-organized, and rent by a destructive rivalry between unit medical directors and administrators. Scott's solution was brutal: local functions should be centralized in Ottawa, the BPC should cut out its routine medical examinations, and, above all, the DSCR and the Department of Health should be merged.[10] The report, with its scheme for realizing $100,000 in savings and its solution to Hunter's revelations, was a bonus no government could ignore. Once it was clear that the DSCR's services would continue, veterans' organizations had no objection to make, and pensioners were delighted to escape their annual medical ordeals.[11] Dr King could preside over the new Department of Pensions and National Health as easily as over his two smaller portfolios. Most DSCR functions were assumed by a pensions division of the new department under an assistant deputy minister, Dr R.J. McKee. Ernest Scammell, now demoted to divisional secretary, kept his job. Other senior colleagues were dispatched to private life with the minister's kindly congratulations on making their jobs obsolete.[12]

The new department fell short of Scammell's 1920 design. Perhaps as its reward for sponsoring the Scott investigation, the Finance Department was given jurisdiction over returned soldiers' insurance. Soldier settlement remained with Immigration and Colonization in the fading hope that it might some day regain its businesslike conception.

But by 1924, even shreds of optimism about veterans on the land were scarce. In that year more soldiers left the land than took up homesteads. Even the SSB's John Barnett conceded that errors had been made, notably in Manitoba where soldiers and politicians had insisted on buying remote bush and swamp land.[13] The GWVA, strongest among prairie veterans, was a forceful national lobby for unhappy settlers, demanding easier repayment of SSB loans and revaluation of land, stock and machinery purchased at inflated wartime prices.[14] It was a demand the Ralston commission had rejected in 1923. So did the SSB. 'You can call it a revaluation or a reduction in capital,' said Barnett in 1924, 'but it is a bonus after all.'[15] That year the Senate backed him up, rejecting soft-hearted proposals from the House of Commons for postponing repayment and revaluing stock. Two years later, veterans' pressure did win revaluation from a minority Liberal government, only to lose again when the Senate kept debating the issue as Parliament moved to its chaotic 1926 dissolution.[16]

By January 1927 a new parliament faced the Canadian Legion. At Winnipeg, a Legion committee on soldier settlement had given the organization an imposing list of demands. True to its cautious style, Legion spokesmen asked only for help with interest costs and a chance for settlers to acquire better land.[17] For its part, the renewed Liberal government insisted that revaluation was now its only policy. The Legion briskly changed its mind and took what credit it could: '[The policy's] chief merit is that it will provide the greatest relief to the most deserving cases.'[18] Revaluation began in the summer of 1927 and was finished by the spring of 1930. Of 10,907 remaining soldier-settlers, 8,103 had their farms reappraised. In all, $7.4 million was written off, much less than the estimated $10 million. A good crop in 1927 and a record harvest in 1928, experts agreed, ensured that soldier settlement would now be a success.[19]

No one had ever expected pensions to shrink dramatically, at least until the 1960s, but surely the Ralston commission recommendations would remove them from political contention without permitting abuses. In fact, the 1923 reforms had made a bad situation worse. By limiting the new Federal Appeal Board's jurisdiction to the crucial but narrow issue of attributability, the Senate left the BPC to assess the actual pension. When their judgment was challenged, Thompson and his colleagues were not inclined to be generous. Even if he won before the FAB, a veteran would often receive only a derisory award. The inevitable rivalry between the two organizations had been aggravated by choosing Colonel Belton, a critic of the BPC, as chairman of the appeal board. Official soldier-advisers, nominated by veterans' organizations, lacked the training, experience, and incentive to prepare cases carefully or to discourage frivolous claims.[20] The FAB, claimed Sir James Lougheed, had 'thrown open the doors very widely and the country had been put to a very large expense by reason of the appeals allowed by the Board.'[21] Meanwhile, Colonel Thompson found his own appeal mechanism by referring the FAB's more dubious decisions to the Department of Justice.

Critics in and out of Parliament persisted in believing that reform could come through amendment of the Pension Act. MPs, deluged by sad cases from their constituencies, were easily persuaded; senators, for the most part, remained obdurate. In 1925 pre-election generosity helped make the 'temporary bonus' of 1920 permanent, but the upper House firmly rejected a Commons attempt to allow pensions for what Sen. Napoléon Belcourt described as 'vicious conduct' – the luckless 'venereals.'[22]

In 1927, after a couple of distracting years, Parliament returned to the issue of pensions when an aggressive, ambitious R.B. Bennett decided to make mincemeat of the feeble Dr King. By refusing to establish the usual select committee and by proposing to wind up the FAB, the minister had insulted the new Legion and ignored the opposition. 'Chubby' Power and a newly elected J.L. Ralston rescued their inept colleague by promising extended pension deadlines and that old appeals could be reopened.[23] Bennett went further, urging a 'presumptive' clause that would have put the onus of proof in attributability cases on the Pension Board. Tories, Progressives, and J.S. Woodsworth's tiny labour group echoed Bennett's demand. When the House of Commons divided in the first partisan split on a veterans' question, Liberal whips had mustered ninety-five votes to Bennett's seventy-eight. It was the kind of defeat a politician could use profitably when next he spoke to veterans or their friends.[24]

A year later, the Liberals were ready with a select committee (under the popular "Chubby" Power) and their own list of reforms. So was the Legion.[25] Generals and colonels, not privates and sergeants, headed the veterans' delegation while MacNeil's expertise was reflected in the one-armed Reginald Bowler, by a competent Service Bureau, and by a muster of 'human documents' that illustrated the range of pension issues. There was Private Ross, his crippled leg deemed 'attributable' by the FAB but assessed as only a 4 per cent disability by the BPC. Private Krezanovsky reported that in France he had been knocked on the head and left unconscious near a railway track before a train tore off his arm. At the time, an army court of inquiry had accepted his story. How could the BPC now insist that the man had been drunk and was unworthy of a pension? The pension visitor who reported Mrs Lesten for taking in a male boarder had cost the elderly widow her pension; she was still awaiting a hearing. Alfred Bryan came home from France with wounds on his face, back, arms, and legs and a medical report stating that a bullet had passed through his skull. All agreed that he was now helpless, but the BPC insisted that his head wound was only the scar of an old mastoid operation. The FAB had no jurisdiction; diagnosis was none of its business. [26]

After more than a decade of repetition, the issues and arguments of a pension debate were familiar. The plight of seven hundred 'pension widows' still divided the chivalrous from the suspicious. Mrs J.A. Wilson of the National Council of Women pleaded for the 'honourable girl' who had fulfilled her engagement to marry a crippled veteran. Surely it was wrong to deny a suffering soldier a chance for happiness and cheap home nursing. [27] Surely too, argued Bowler, there must be merit in a proposal that the House had already supported on four occasions. 'There must also be some merit,' rejoined Dr Peter McGibbon, a Tory ex-medical officer, 'in a rejection made four times by the Senate.' [28]

The Senate remained the key. The House of Commons by now paid so little attention to Pension Act debates that the Speaker had to appeal for order. The Senate, in contrast, formed its own select committee and set to plugging loopholes left by feckless MPs. As usual, the 'pension widows' were easy victims. Senator Griesbach read aloud the bewildering prose forwarded from the lower House: 'No pension shall be paid to the widow of a member of the forces who was married to him after the appearance of the injury or disease which resulted in his death unless in the opinion of the Commission the condition of such member of the forces was at the time of the marriage such that it would be reasonable to anticipate that the injury would not result in death.' Since he could not make sense of the words or find better ones, declared Griesbach, it was better to do nothing. The Senate agreed. Members of Parliament fulminated briefly and then subsided. [29]

The Legion emerged from the 1928 session with just enough gains to claim victory. Amputees had finally won compensation for wear and tear on their clothing. 'Meritorious cases' might get a better deal from a joint FAB-BPC hearing, though members of the two boards almost never agreed. 'Unmarried wives,' who lost their pensions the minute they legitimized their relationships, finally got relief. [30] But the Legion's satisfaction faded fast as it became clear that the basic problems still existed. Having raised hopes by permitting appeals, the Pension Act only trapped veterans or their dependants in procedural intricacy and delay. Of 15,075 appeals lodged with the FAB by the end of 1928, barely one-third had been heard and only 1,341 had been allowed. [31]

Old soldiers were not fading away. A decade after demobilization, disability and dependency were greater than ever. For all the BPC's austere ingenuity, more than ten thousand veterans, one-fifth of the total, had qualified for disability pensions between 1925 and 1929. The total would have been far larger if twenty thousand men had not had their pensions commuted in 1921. Most of them had spent the money, but their pain and inconvenience persisted. The image of the CEF as an army of men in their teens and twenties was misleading; the average age was close to thirty, and many were much older.[32] For them, re-establishment had posed special problems, but even younger men insisted that wartime service had left them prematurely aged, easily exhausted, and 'burnt-out.'[33] There were thousands more whose disabilities were specific and invariably were attributed to military service. If medical science doubted that pneumonia, bronchitis, or tuberculosis could be linked to service a decade earlier, economic desperation could provide the arguments.

Sir Arthur Currie was hardly a typical veteran, but he symbolized the physical cost of war service. The robust commander of 1919 had now become a stooped, white-haired man of fifty-four. Poor health as much as pique had prevented Currie from finding a major role in the Legion. In 1928 he accepted election as grand president, but a year later, as he prepared for his first convention, illness struck again. At Regina, Lt-Col. Léo LaFlèche read the absent Currie's message. Delegates were stunned and then delighted as they heard the harsh, unequivocal assault on the Canadian pension system. Currie declared himself 'not only amazed but ashamed that eleven years after the war it is necessary not only to plead but to fight for justice.' The Pension Act must be overhauled, and 'the regulations of the Pension Board must be redrafted from beginning to end.'[34]

A year before, Currie had emerged with enormously enhanced prestige from a Port Hope libel trial. That prestige was now put at the service of pensioners. Organizations from the IODE to trade unions promptly echoed the demand for action. Mackenzie King assured Currie of his profound sympathy.[35] When Parliament met in 1930 for its pre-election session, veterans rivalled the out-of-work as topics of importance on the political agenda. If the government had few specifics, King explained coyly, it was because veterans themselves would share in policy-making. With 'Chubby' Power again in the chair, a select committee assembled in the splendour of the Railway Committee Room to receive the veterans' leaders. Currie, as Legion president, led a single delegation that included Col. W.C. Wood of the Army and Navy Veterans, Capt. Eddie Baker of the Sir Arthur Pearson Club of Blinded Associations, the Reverend Sydney Lambert of the Amputations Association, and the Reverend John Kelman of the Tubercular

Veterans' Section. Currie, reported *The Legionary*, spoke 'with the vigor and clarity which marked his utterances as the leader of the Canadian Forces on active service, but it was quite evident to those present that he himself bore the marks of the rigors of war which he described as having affected every man who served.'[36]

Currie left LaFlèche, Bowler (now the Legion's national secretary), and the Service Bureau to present the veterans' case. LaFlèche, a cruelly mutilated survivor of the French-speaking 22nd Battalion, was a wise choice. Canadians, he said, wanted no American-style pension 'barbecue.' In a veiled reference to the 'presumptive clause' urged by Bennett in 1927, LaFlèche insisted that it was wrong to put the onus of proof on the BPC: 'There would be a danger of making it possible for everyone who enlisted and served to secure a pension without having to submit a fair and reasonable measure of proof in favour of his claim.'[37] While LaFlèche and his colleagues acknowledged that veterans could be undeserving as well as deserving, MPs and senators (included for the first time in the committee) were at their most obliging. Pensions that had been commuted almost a decade earlier would be restored. Returned soldiers' insurance, closed in 1923, would be reopened for three more years. Even the long struggle of the 'pension widows' finally ended; a woman who had married a pensioner before 1 January 1930 would henceforth have as good a claim to a widow's pension as if she had been married in 1914.[38]

The most drastic changes affected procedure. 'Chubby' Power seems to have supplied the blueprint, but it was seized and embellished by politicians and veterans alike. From now on the Board of Pension Commissioners would merely approve applications that fell within the regulations; every other claimant would be referred to a new pension tribunal whose nine members would travel the country to hear applications. Instead of the untrained and sometimes inept official soldier advisers, a veterans' bureau, with qualified 'veterans' advocates,' would prepare claimants' cases. Because justice demanded adherence to the adversarial process, the BPC would have a chief commission counsel, with a small staff, to present the other side. A pension appeal court composed of three members and headed by a judge would be the final arbiter. Veterans were even assured the benefit of the doubt: 'The body adjudicating on the claim shall be entitled to draw and shall draw ... all reasonable inference in favour of the applicants.'[39] At every point the Legion's demands had been met. Even the Senate merely changed a 'herebefore' into a 'heretofore.'[40]

Pensions were only part of the Legion's triumph. The depression, which for prairie farmers began with the unsold 1928 wheat harvest, brought fresh disaster for soldier-settlers. The Legion's 1929 convention at Regina had appointed a special committee under Reg Bowler to hear witnesses and collect exhibits; the committee concluded that the settlement question would have to be treated 'just as seriously as we ever treated the question of pension.'[41] Of 24,708 settlers, almost half had abandoned their farms by 1929; of 11,912 veterans still struggling to pay off loans, 4,785 were described by the SSB as 'likely to fail' or 'barely holding their own.'[42] As victims of a situation utterly beyond their control, Bowler maintained, soldier-settlers were entitled to relief. Power's select committee agreed. By 28 May 1930 the government had written off $11.3 million in soldier-settler indebtedness.[43]

And there was more. Not even the new Pension Act met the needs of the 'burnt-out cases'; a version of the new means-tested old-age pensions, introduced in 1927, might cope with that particular type of 'aging.' An interdepartmental committee met and agreed that the war had aged veterans by an average of ten years. The 1920 session was invited to authorize a War Veterans' Allowance for impoverished veterans aged sixty or more and for younger veterans who were unemployable for physical and mental reasons. The money – $240 a year for single men and $480 for married men – would bridge the gap to age seventy, when the regular pensions took effect.[44] Only the Tories were opposed to the plan; they grasped the significance of allowing the partisan Dr King to distribute such bounty in an election year. In Bennett's words, it was 'the worst piece of political legislation any parliament has had to consider on the eve of an election.' 'It is useless,' responded Mackenzie King, 'for any one to hope to please the hon. gentlemen opposite.'[45] Still, confident that the veterans' votes had been safely tied up, the Liberals graciously deferred the implementation of the new allowances and the new pension structure until the general election was over.

Tribunals and Appeals

Delighted by the 1930 legislation, Sir Arthur Currie offered Mackenzie King his congratulations: 'It is my opinion that you will hear very little more of this matter for many years to come.'[46] On 28 July the voters did their best to make that prediction come true: King and his government were decisively defeated by Bennett and the Conservatives. The new minister of pensions and national health was Col. Murray MacLaren, a wealthy Saint John doctor. 'Excellent man though he was,' Bennett's secretary recalled, 'I can think of no one in the cabinet who was less influential with R.B.' Bennett made the decisions about veterans, as he did about much else in his government.[47]

Apart from naming three nervous members of the War Veterans' Allowance Committee, the Liberals had left virtually every new appointment vacant. Walter Woods, the former GWVA activist, had been summoned from his job as SSB superintendent at Calgary to set up the program. He respected Bennett and, fortunately for him, the feeling was mutual.[48] Under Woods, War Veterans' Allowances soon evolved as one of the most trouble-free of veterans' programs. Other Liberal appointees were less fortunate. Members of the Federal Appeal Board were unceremoniously dumped.[49] Rather than sort through a throng of Tory job-seekers, Bennett allowed veterans' organizations to choose members of the new Tribunal. The resulting collection of captains and colonels excluded former FAB members and representatives of the rank and file.[50] For the new Pension Appeal Court, Bennett chose an Ottawa lawyer, Col. Livius Sherwood, and the Legion's Colonel LaFlèche. As chairman he chose his friend and political crony, J.D. Hyndman, an Alberta judge.[51] The sole survivor of the old order, Col. C. Beresford Topp, took charge of the new Veterans' Bureau. His opposite number as chief commission counsel was Richard Olmsted, borrowed from the Department of Justice.[52]

It took time to make the system work. Hyndman arrived in Ottawa in mid-January 1931. The disbanded FAB had left a backlog of six thousand cases, and the change of government and the 1930 act inspired thousands more. So did the depression. Since a claim cost nothing, hard-pressed veterans had every reason to try. At best, by Topp's estimate, the tribunal's three panels might process four thousand cases a year. By June 1931, after hearing five cases a day five days a week and travelling constantly, the panels had completed 1,582 cases. About half the cases rejected by the BPC were approved.[53] To lighten his burden, Olmsted referred virtually every favourable decision to the pension appeal court. Unsuccessful claimants did the same.[54] When Hyndman and his colleagues compared the fuzzy, amateurish tribunal judgments with the crisp statements of the BPC, most pension claimants got short shrift. The exceptions depended heavily on 'benefit of the doubt.'[55]

Within a year, any joy over the 1930 Pension Act was fast dissipating. About six thousand 'commuted' pensioners rejoined the pension lists, and so did at least some 'pension widows.' Yet, for thousands of pension claimants, delay and rejection soured the hopes that had been raised so high. The Legion and its rival organizations became easy scapegoats for embittered veterans and targets of rebel leaders who despised the caution of their ex-generals and colonels. Currie's successor, Maj. J.S. Roper, was a Halifax lawyer and a faithful Tory. Caught between his frustrated followers and his party loyalty, Roper appealed personally to the prime minister. He could not fault the legality of what was happening, Roper admitted, but veterans were not lawyers. They had been promised a square deal: 'Are they not going to feel that they have been duped again?' Surely the prime minister could persuade the board not to appeal every case and not to 'avail themselves of all the technicalities of the law to defeat a claim.'[56] Bennett, adrift in his own sea of troubles, had time for only a few procedural amendments at the end of the 1931 session: Olmsted would have more staff, the tribunal would have a fourth panel of three members, and the BPC would take a second look at the thousands of pending cases.[57]

To outsiders, the changes made little difference. Olmsted no longer made automatic appeals, and a little work by the Veterans' Bureau helped the BPC accept a few more claims, but the backlog remained. More than thirteen thousand pension applications had piled up by the end of 1931; it was easy to imagine thousands of sick and disabled men dying in poverty, leaving destitute families to starve while Ottawa bureaucrats fiddled with red tape and enjoyed their secure salaries. The *Canadian Veteran*, one of many short-lived papers that blossomed during the depression, had an obvious explanation: far from failing, the government's pension machinery was working perfectly to deprive returned men of their rights for the sake of a penny-pinching administration.[58] Sir Arthur Currie stated publicly that the Pension Board had put sand in the works.[59] The Legion's Toronto and district command denounced its own national leaders: 'The efforts of our higher command officials seem concentrated on their desire to find sheltered employment in highly-paid Government positions to the utter disregard of veterans generally.' Toronto would send no money to the dominion command.[60]

Driven by their members and their own sense of frustration, officials of the major veterans' organizations had to do something. In January 1932 a new united front, the Associated Veterans of Canada, took shape in Ottawa. Linking the Legion, the ANV, and the Amputees Association, the Sir Arthur Pearson Clubs, and the Toronto-based Canadian Pensioners' Association in a loose 'federation,' the Associated Veterans forged a cautious unanimity on an agreement to attack the 1930 procedures rather than the intricate web of entitlement. The problems were obvious enough. By the summer of 1932, some 3,000 claimants had come before the tribunal, but only 650 had won any kind of pension. Almost one-half of the tribunal's favourable verdicts were reversed on appeal, and claimants had virtually no success with Hyndman and his colleagues. Men who had won their cases in person before the tribunal found it doubly infuriating to lose on legal arguments devised by faceless officials in Ottawa.[61]

The prime minister ignored opposition charges and demands that a select committee explore the apparent scandal. If, as the veterans insisted, the issue was procedural, the proper forum would be a joint committee of veterans and officials headed by a Supreme Court judge. The veterans agreed, but were dismayed when the officials turned out to be Colonel Thompson, Col. Thomas Morrison of the tribunal, Colonel Topp, and other key pension authorities. A rancorous series of hearings and meetings filled the autumn of 1932. The first chairman, Mr Justice Thibaudeau Rinfret, gratefully made way for Louis-Arthur Audette, a retired judge of the Exchequer Court. In the end, Audette's committee produced four separate reports. Only Audette, Thompson, Topp, and Dr Ross Millar of the Department of Pensions and National Health could be persuaded to sign the main report. Their conclusions were obviously inspired by Thompson, who blamed the entire mess on the tribunal and proposed its immediate abolition. A few travelling members added to the Board of Pension Commissioners and continuation of the wise and cautious Pension Appeal Court would eliminate the problems.[62] The new appointees, Thompson privately advised the prime minister, would be responsible for the prudent disbursement of huge sums: 'if proper men are selected ... they will daily save their annual salaries.'[63]

The Legion's representative, Brig.-Gen. Alex Ross, had alarmed his own side by stating that he would serve only in his civil capacity as a Saskatchewan judge. Ross, alone among the committee members, seems to have approached the problem with judicial rigour. The enormous backlog of cases, he discovered, was more a statistical apparition than a reality. The free (if inadequate) service of the Veterans' Bureau and a 'no finality' rule for claimants had encouraged thousands of veterans, many of them pensioners already, to file applications. Most of the cases were held up because there was simply no evidence to advance them. Nor could Ross fault the Pension Appeal Court for overturning decisions in support of which there was often neither evidence nor apparent justification. Yet Ross's main recommendation differed in one crucial detail from the Audette report: there should be a single agency for the first-instance adjudication of pension claims; but if that agency was not the result of a genuine amalgamation of the BPC and the tribunal, there would be trouble. 'To my mind,' he reported, 'the publication of a statement that the Tribunal be abolished, would create a public situation with regard to pension administration such as had not existed since the days of the Ralston Commission.'[64]

Ross's advice was ignored. When Murray MacLaren introduced the newest pension bill on 20 April 1933, the tribunal was indeed abolished in favour of an enlarged BPC, now renamed the Canadian Pension Commission. The Pension Appeal Court and the Veterans' Bureau remained, but a 'reviewing officer' with medical training would replace the major villain of the 1930 act, the chief commission counsel.[65] As Ross had predicted, even Tory backbenchers joined the chorus of protest. Only the announcement of the formation of a select committee headed by a Tory veteran, Col. James Arthurs, calmed the House of Commons. A month of sessions moved the House slowly towards Ross's position: an amalgamation of the board and the tribunal, an extra judge to help the Pension Appeal Court reduce its backlog, and greater independence for the Veterans' Bureau. Ex-service-men, MPs, and even senators were content.[66]

But their satisfaction ended abruptly on 1 October 1933, when the eight members of the new Canadian Pension Commission were announced. Firmly in the chair was Col. John Thompson. Of the tribunal members, only Gen. Sir Richard Turner had survived. The rest were dumped as ruth-lessly as the FAB members had been three years earlier. They had been incompetent, Bennet confided, and 'in some cases hopelessly so.'[67] It was a brutal judgment on men caught in a difficult position. Opposition MPs and veterans' representatives felt betrayed. 'It never entered our heads,' con-fessed *The Legionary*, 'that when the appointments came to be made, the government would consider that the Board of Pension Commissioners and its staff alone contains the personnel necessary for the proper operation of the Act.'[68] A Montreal veterans' group angrily demanded that veterans on relief should replace the pension officials, who had enjoyed 'their very reasonable salaries' long enough. In March 1934, when Legion representa-tives met the government, an angry Ross insisted that it had always been Thompson and his board that had provided 'the disturbing element which has made it impossible for any of these new organizations to function in a satisfactory manner.'[69]

A little belatedly, Bennet got the message. The urgent need for a franchise commissioner as a result of the 1934 Election Act provided a convenient change of scene for the incorruptible Colonel Thompson. Special legislation brought Mr Justice Fawcett Taylor from the Manitoba Court of King's Bench to take his place on the pension commission. A former colonel, presi-dent of the Army and Navy Veterans, and chairman of the ill-fated Domin-ion Veterans' Alliance, Taylor proved as acceptable to the veterans' leaders as to the Tories.[70] For better or worse, a decade of institutional turmoil in pension administration was over. In its essence, the new structure would outlast another great war.

It was about time. The Legion itself and probably most veterans desper-ately wanted to change the subject.

The Depression Crisis

The pension struggle and virtually everything else that happened in Canada after 1928 were affected by the worst economic depression the world could remember. An economy dependent on the export of raw materials was an easy victim of falling demand and rising protectionism. Canada's troubles did not come singly: a procession of environmental disasters marched across the prairies during the 1930s, bringing drought, rust, grasshoppers, and some of the coldest winters and hottest summers since record-keeping begun. At the depth of the depression in 1932, one Canadian worker in four was unemployed and one person in six qualified for municipal relief.

Veterans shared in the misery. Jobs created in the fragile prosperity of the late 1920s were the first to vanish, setting adrift men who had never really found a place in post-war society. War service had robbed ex-servicemen of training, experience, seniority, and energy, the only qualities employers valued in their own struggle to survive. By 1932, the average CEF veteran was forty-four – too young to retire, too old to be a likely prospect for employment when younger and more active men were available. Being a veteran, a government report confessed, was an actual liability: since no employer enjoyed the stigma of firing a war hero, it was wiser not to hire him in the first place. [71]

A government desperate to balance spending with vanishing revenues offered little substantial help. Preference was still given to veterans for civil-service jobs, but it was almost meaningless when economy drives resulted in cutbacks. Federal and provincial relief camps reserved staff and foremen's positions for veterans, but their pay and prospects were hardly better than those of the ordinary campers, who earned twenty cents a day. [72]

The most publicized Canadian pension statistics had always concealed how little money the great majority of the war-disabled really received. Such pensions were, of course, no more than a supplement to the wages that John Todd and Walter Segsworth had always assumed to be the outcome of retraining and placement. A minority of unemployed and destitute pensioners had remained a burden on the DSCR and the Department of Pensions and National Health. While Ottawa drew the line at supporting the able-bodied, somehow pensioners seemed an appropriate federal responsibility. Even in 1928–9, the most prosperous post-war year, $367,231 in relief was distributed to a total of 4,647 pensioners. As the depression deepened, numbers and costs soared. In 1931–2, 12,303 pensioners, almost one-fifth of the total, needed some relief; a year later the total reached 14,368. [73] Hard-pressed municipal relief officials used the federal program as an excuse to wash their hands of destitute pensioners. Even the clothing and medical care grudgingly doled out to 'reliefers' was denied to disabled ex-servicemen and their families.

'Departmental relief' might carry a lesser stigma than municipal relief, but the amounts were tiny and the vouchers were just as embarrassing. The official minimum scale was $15 a month for a single man, $25 for a couple, and \$42.50 for a family of eight, amounts that sound meagre enough until compared with those of some municipalities. Verdun, a Montreal suburb, had a veterans' organization vigorous enough to report on the crisis. Robert and Mary Laycock got by on a \$25-a-month pension and \$5.60 in relief until local pension authorities insisted on withholding \$15 for their rent. After paying his rent, Frank Wrigley, a tubercular pensioner, had only \$21.50 a month left to support a family of five. A visitor found that Wrigley had no food or fuel in his house, too few clothes for his children to send them to school, and no shoes or underwear for himself. After he died, Wrigley's wife and children might get an adequate pension; until then, an official admitted, he was 'up against a stone wall.'[74]

For a few thousand destitute ex-servicemen and women, the War Veterans' Allowance was a meagre salvation. Of the 5,790 veterans who had qualified by 1933, fourteen were former colonels and majors and five were ex-nursing sisters. As many more had been turned away, usually because they were not sufficiently destitute or because those under the age of sixty were not utterly unemployable. Impossible economic circumstances were not justification enough for an allowance.[75]

While veterans demanded special recognition of their problems, it grew easier to find Canadians who believed that returned men had been too generously treated, that pensions had been won by fraud or lavished on the undeserving. The depression bred a sour, selfish mood. In 1932, only fervid protests stopped the Bennett government from issuing a 'blue book' listing the names and addresses of pensioners and the benefits received by each of them. The purpose was all too clear: neighbours would be able to spot and report pension fraud.[76] A year later, the finance minister, Edgar Rhodes, announced that military pensions paid to federal civil servants would be cancelled. Another Legion crusade was needed to derail that proposal.[77]

On the whole, Canadian pensioners were protected from depression-era economies. In Britain, Australia, France, and Germany, disabled veterans suffered severely from pension cuts.[78] American veterans, who had thrived in the 1920s on a bonanza of congressional generosity, were obvious victims of a Democratic economy drive in 1933. Franklin Delano Roosevelt, faced with a crisis in fiscal confidence and persuaded to cut pension spending in half, responded by slashing rates and cancelling thousands of payments completely. When the American Legion weighed into the struggle, its legislative muscle persuaded Congress to rescind much of Roosevelt's Economy Bill. Journalists and New Deal sympathizers portrayed the American veterans' organization as a greedy, militaristic, and power-hungry 'King Legion.'[79]

Whatever might be said of its American counterpart, the Canadian

Legion felt anything but powerful as the depression sapped its membership and finances. Money troubles reduced the organization to the same querulous desperation that had afflicted the GWVA. The tiresome internecine squabbling that a stronger organization might have shrugged off seemed to paralyze the Legion's executive. In 1931 Colonel Wood of the ANV tried to involve the Legion in his own association's richly remunerative but wholly illegal sweepstakes scheme. In return for backing the move for legalization, the Legion would share in the take. After a debate that seemed to drag on for months, righteousness prevailed in the dominion command, but the controversy spread to equally hard-pressed and slightly less scrupulous provincial commands and branches. In 1934 the Legion was still tied up in referenda on the topic. [80]

Meanwhile, the Legion's permanent staff suffered drastic salary cuts. The tuberculous veterans seethed when their parent body welshed on commitments to maintain the TVS representative. *The Legionary* sagged and almost collapsed under the weight of overdue advertising accounts and unpaid printing bills. Tom Lapp departed, and an unpaid editor, Capt. W.W. Murray, kept the shrinking monthly issues appearing. [81] Across the country branch dues fell into arrears and landlords foreclosed on premises. To Scammell's dismay, Major Roper almost succeeded in a bid to grab the Disablement Fund as a substitute for the annual government subsidy of $10,000. Carefully edited testimonials from local unit directors helped save the fund, and the subsidy remained at a modest $9,000. [82] In another desperate bid for funds the Legion granted the use of its name for a new brand of cigarettes. [83]

Hectoring members and branches about the Legion's money problems and denouncing 'shirkers' and 'slackers' who failed to pay their dues was no way to build an organization; nor was the Legion's enthusiasm for 'Empire Free Trade,' however ardently the cause was promoted by Major Roper at the BESL conference in London in 1933. [84] In mid-depression, veterans might wonder why their organization had so little to say about unemployment and economic misery. An aging membership, with more memories than hopes, yearned for the comradeship and nostalgia that had seemed superfluous in the immediate post-war years. Despite the depression, veterans' organizations in Britain, Australia, France, and the United States reached peaks of membership, and the reason for their growth was more often nostalgia than politics. In Canada, a new Canadian Corps Association, committed to a grand reunion of veterans, began to compete for the Legion's failing membership.

Desperate measures were needed. Plans for a Vancouver convention were scrapped; Ottawa would be closer and cheaper for most delegates. Sir

Arthur Currie's death on 30 November 1933 helped bring veterans together. One of his last speeches provided a slogan: 'They Served Till Death, Why Not We?'[85] On 11 March 1934, twelve hundred Legion delegates crowded into the Château Laurier to ponder their collective future. After four years, Roper had had enough. So had Alex Ross, the first vice-president. Somehow the crusty old judge was persuaded to stand as president. In turn, he made it clear that the Legion must change. Pension problems must be settled, but the organization must give its whole attention to the unemployment problem. Ross had summoned Grant MacNeil, who had been out of work for years, to chair a convention committee on the problems of jobless veterans. The report was a solemn listing of issues, from malnutrition, sickness, and despair among the unemployed to the callousness of the comfortable majority. Thanks to MacNeil, the Legion would demand higher relief scales, medical care for destitute pensioners, and, above all, a Legion investigation into the extent of veteran unemployment. Five years into the depression, no one in Canada had any idea of precisely how many people were hunting for jobs.[86]

Ross was delighted, and so were the delegates. The Legion had a new, more relevant cause. Moreover, the new president told his audience, it was no longer good enough to lean on governments. In his brusque, bulldog manner, Ross warned: 'Either we continue to live on subsidies until the people of Canada become nauseated by our importunity, or we branch out boldly into a new and wider sphere where the ex-soldier will solve his own problems.'[87] Ross travelled as far as Australia and California to revive and redirect Legion branches. Local branches took on a new life as they collected lists of unemployed veterans and solicited employment grievances. Was it true that the Montreal Harbour Commission had never hired a returned man? What good was veterans' preference if the Civil Service Commission imposed an age limit on new employees? Had railways discriminated when they laid off veterans who had lost seniority through war service? Ross revelled in editorial approval of his message that veterans wanted jobs, not handouts. Nothing could be more objectionable than taking the Legion into politics, he told a well-heeled Toronto audience, but 'if the ex-servicemen of Canada are ever driven into the political field it will be by reason of our failure to assist those men who are at present unemployed or practically unemployable to secure a livelihood for the remaining years of life.'[88]

It helped that Canada, by 1934, was almost imperceptibly climbing out of the depression. It helped even more that in January 1935 R.B. Bennett communicated his unexpected conversion to activist government to a sceptical nation. On 24 January Ross and other ex-service leaders were summoned to state the veterans' case and to hear promises of action. The government itself would inquire into veterans' unemployment. After a delay occasioned by the prime minister's acutely inopportune illness, the membership was announced: Judge Hyndman would preside, with Col. C.B. Price and W.B. Woods as members, and the knowledgeable Ernest Scammell as secretary. Some veterans fumed at the idea of yet another needless investigation; Ross and his associates were delighted. They recognized the leverage that one of Bennett's few remaining confidants could exercise. Hyndman did not delay. By 16 March he had organized his first session. His committee travelled no farther than Toronto and Montreal, with a side-trip to the notorious Verdun, and his report was completed in late May. [89]

Hyndman obviously had no intention of criticizing his friend the prime minister. A country that spent $1.131 billion on veterans since the war, he insisted, had given proof of its generosity. Veterans had no claim to benefits 'as of right,' and assorted schemes to expand the War Veterans' Allowance would simply open the way to an American-style general service pension. At the same time Hyndman legitimized the Legion's overdue concern for unemployed comrades. With a little statistical juggling – mde necessary by lack of better data – Hyndman and his committee agreed that about 38,000 Canadian veterans with overseas service, and 10,000 to 15,000 'Imperials,' were out of work and in need of help. The trip to Verdun had removed any illusion that municipal relief would suffice. After meeting veterans on relief, Hyndman concluded grimly: 'It was obvious that these men were undernourished to the point where many would be unable to undertake manual labour, even were this available.' [90]

Suggestions for job creation, ranging from bush-clearing and cultivation of small holdings to a Canadian Corps of Commissionaires, had poured into the committee. Hyndman suggested that a short-lived 'Veterans Assistance Commission,' with representation from government, veterans, and chambers of commerce, might implement whatever proposals made practical sense. On departmental relief, Hyndman was more precise: distressed veterans had to be a federal concern. Unemployment was not an ex-serviceman's fault. Ottawa should pay the difference between municipal scales and a 25 per cent pension for single men or a 30 per cent pension for families. To eliminate the 'relief' stigma, the payments should be called 'unemployment assistance' and they should be made in cash. Clothing, medical care, and, for home-owning veterans, mortgage interest and taxes must be part of the package. [91]

Despite the attempt at haste, Hyndman submitted his report only as Parliament wrestled with the last stages of Bennett's 'New Deal' legislation. The House, in a re-election mood, chose not to wrangle over details.

Approval from Ross and the Legion was certification enough. The Veterans' Assistance Commission could wait, but $500,000 was added at once to the estimates of Pensions and National Health to improve the lot of out-of-work veterans. In return, General Ross sternly reminded every Legion branch and command of the need for strict political neutrality.[92] Perhaps Canadians needed no last-minute advice. On 31 October 1935, disaffected voters scattered their support among Social Credit, Reconstruction, and Co-operative Commonwealth Federation candidates. With fewer votes than they had received in 1930, Mackenzie King's Liberals swept to a one-sided victory.

In King's new government, the competent if bibulous 'Chubby' Power finally entered the cabinet as minister of pensions and national health. He was, he reminded *The Legionary*, not merely a friend of veterans but a veteran himself.[93] Ian Mackenzie, another GWVA stalwart with a drinking problem, became the minister of national defence. Their presence reassured veterans who knew that the Liberals had more than their fair share of cost-cutters and 1917-vintage anti-conscriptionists.

The new government inherited the Hyndman report. It had no intention of assuming any broad responsibility for unemployed veterans, but it would accept a Veterans Assistance Commission. In July 1936 the commission took shape, with Col. J.G. Rattray, a former head of the SSB and a past president of the Ottawa branch of the Legion, as chairman, Lt-Col. Hugues de Martigny and the Legion's General Ross as members, and half a million dollars to spend through voluntary local committees.[94] It seemed an ingenious solution to an impossible problem. The local committees ranged from active to inert. Three communities sponsored small holdings for a total of forty-six veterans; three others opened workshops employing fifty men. The Department of Transport was persuaded that jobs as door-to-door radio-licence issuers should be reserved for unemployed ex-servicemen. Another scheme subsidized wages while veterans were trained on the job. Rattray's commission also helped launch the Canadian Corps of Commissionaires by securing a charter and granting fifteen thousand dollars for the first year's operations. The corps, said the government, must be 'entirely independent of the Department of Pensions and National Health.'[95] Perhaps the Rattray commission had little real impact, but it did create an impression of purposeful activity at minimal cost. It also eased some local troubles; the Halifax committee gleefully reported that it had found one ex-service 'agitator' a job with such long hours that he would no longer have the energy to organize his comrades.[96]

Power brought an experience and agility to his ministry that none of his predecessors had demonstrated. Both egalitarians and economizers were pleased when he cancelled the practice of paying ex-officers at their wartime rates during stays in veterans' hospitals. Regular medical examinations for pensioners were abolished. Disabled veterans could grow older in the certainty that their pensions would not grow smaller. A 1936 Pension Act amendment confirmed that any errors in a veteran's favour not corrected within four years would stand.[97] Further amendments in 1936 and 1939 virtually ended restrictions on pensions for women who married disabled veterans. The old warnings about 'pension widows' and 'deathbed marriages' had somehow lost their effect. Not all widows were so lucky, however. The Canadian Soldiers Non-pensioned Widows' Association petitioned in vain. It was absurd, Power told to a fellow Liberal, 'that a widow should expect a pension because her late husband had lost a thumb in the war.' To Canada's sole woman member of Parliament, Agnes Macphail, Power offered a somewhat more principled argument. There should indeed be help for widows; but 'the mere fact of service in the army,' he assured the staunchly pacifist Macphail, 'should not be qualification for entry into a privileged class.'[98]

From their inception, War Veterans' Allowances had beckoned as a solution to the problems of an aging army and a substitute for far-fetched and unprovable disability claims. In 1936 the new government cut the age of eligibility for veterans who could no longer support themselves. By 1939 'economic handicaps' joined physical and mental disability as a basis for claims. In recognition of its permanence, Woods's committee became a board. On the eve of war in 1939, twenty thousand veterans collected the allowances; more than half were 'unemployables' under the age of sixty.[99]

War Veterans' Allowances set ex-servicemen and women apart from their fellow citizens. The allowances suggested that there was something special in the poverty, suffering, and humiliation that time and age had brought to the veterans of the CEF. Was their plight so different from that of other aging Canadians? Power's response to Macphail was an ingenious political evasion; it also affirmed a principle of universality in social programs that a richer Canada would begin to accept during a new decade of war and reconstruction.

A Time of Memories

In 1934 Alex Ross had done more than shift the Legion's political focus from pensions to unemployment. In a single stroke he had also committed the organization to an excursion into nostalgia. The Vimy pilgrimage, already once postponed by the world economic crisis, would proceed. In an age of mean and frightened thoughts, the venture became an act of defiance and a test of the Legion's reviving self-confidence. Critics insisted that the pilgrimage could never happen, that the money would be better spent at home, that Canadian veterans would disgrace themselves and embarrass the country. Instead, the Legion's National Pilgrimage Committee, with the implacable Léo LaFlèche at its head, plodded forward, reviving the military organizational skills painfully acquired a generation before.[100]

By March 1936, six thousand Legion members and their wives were committed, ships were chartered, and trains and hotel rooms were reserved. On 16 July five ocean liners sailed from Montreal, packed with aging servicemen and women, most of whom looked mildly ridiculous in the floppy blue or khaki berets that Canadian veterans had adopted as a uniform. Two Canadian destroyers, HMCS *Saguenay* and HMCS *Champlain*, followed as a respectful escort. By 26 July the six thousand pilgrims had swollen to a throng of ten thousand men and women and a few children. They waited under a broiling sun as French, British, and Canadian politicians and a young Edward VIII finished their orations. Unwitting precursors of another war, flights of modern fighter planes swooped and raced over the soaring twin shafts of the new Vimy Memorial. The veterans could go home again.[101]

To those who had shared the experience, the Vimy pilgrimage would be one of the rare happy epiphanies that give meaning to life; for most Canadians, it was one of those events that slide softly out of history, leaving their trace in souvenir books, faded memorabilia, and yellowed photographs. For all veterans of the First World War, the Vimy pilgrimage marked the time when the second battle ended. Two decades of conflict with officials, politicians, and fellow veterans had forced the creation and reformation of systems to support the disabled and aging survivors of the Great War. The results were not what Scammell, Todd, Segsworth, and others had envisaged, but they would serve the young men and women who would be veterans themselves in another decade.

All history is an unfinished story. Beginnings and endings are a narrative convenience. The veterans of the First World War survive in shrinking numbers. In 1986, 12,404 collected disability pensions, and 10,695 women and children maintained their claims as dependent pensioners. The $80 million collected that year was, at face value, at least twice as much as was paid for pensions in an inter-war year.[102]

Canada has changed almost beyond recognition since those years, and the veterans of the First World War did more than their share to create that transformation. In 1915-17, Scammell, Todd, Segsworth, and Black, armoured with social theory, had built on conjecture. The creators of the Veterans' Charter of 1944 - Ian Mackenzie, Walter S. Woods, Robert

England, Léo LaFlèche, and many more – had lived the consequences of those theories. The million Canadians who came home from the Second World War would have rehabilitation credits to cover the cost of furnishing a new home. There would be a guaranteed return to former jobs, with pension and seniority rights assured. There would be access to education and training, and a month of free tuition and maintenance for each month of active service. There would be grants to veterans to start businesses and to maintain themselves and their families until the enterprises became profitable. The Veterans' Land Act was a conscientious and cool-headed attempt to remedy the defects of the Soldier Settlement Act, from its fixation on homesteading to its unintentionally burdensome debt loads.[103]

Veterans of the Second World War were, on the whole, far more fortunate in their war service than the soldiers of the earlier war. All three of Canada's armed services became vast training schools to develop types of skills the CEF had never contemplated. Even ordinary soldiers could profit from their long years of waiting in England or in North American garrisons. Training and education were available on a scale and at a level of sophistication unimaginable in the earlier war. While Canada mobilized far more men and women than in 1914–18, her ultimate casualty toll was one-third smaller than that of the earlier war, and the country itself emerged unscathed in a devastated world. These were foundations for a prosperity unlike anything Canadians had known before. These were advantages that might have been dissipated without the generous and imaginative policies created by veterans of an earlier war for their comrades-to-be. Under Power's successor, Ian Mackenzie, the Department of Pensions and National Health became the cradle of Canada's post-war welfare state.

Democracies, according to tradition, are forgetful and ungrateful. That proposition is based in part on evidence of the hardships and suffering of a nation's former soldiers. If there is any popular impression of the fate of veterans of Canadian Expeditionary Force, it is that they were treated with a shabby indifference – granted meagre pensions or left to fend for themselves by a country that rapidly turned to the pastimes of the 1920s, making money and having a good time. Fragmentary impressions, contributed by historians who stumbled across the track of veterans' issues, have contributed to the general image: the defeat of the 1919 bonus campaign, the dreary ordeal of soldier settlement, and the plight of destitute pensioners all provided an appropriate backdrop for the contemporary feeling of revulsion against war.

Patient readers of this book may have had those impressions confirmed. Depending on the extent to which experience has eroded their natural capacity for moral outrage, readers may also have a more sophisticated understanding of how and why re-establishment failed both its architects and its intended beneficiaries. But in no one's eyes was that failure necessarily complete. Thanks to Todd and to Colonel Thompson, Canada avoided the 'pension evil.' A militant American Legion and a dutiful Congress allowed the United States' pension burden almost to quadruple between 1919 and 1932, while Canadian pension payments fell by almost one-third. [104] If one-fifth of disabled pensioners needed relief at the depth of the depression, had most of the remainder been sufficiently re-established to escape a common indignity? Soldier settlement might seem an acknowledged disaster, but were the causes inherent in the scheme or in the economics and the ecology of the era? The cruel process that left a mere eight thousand ex-soldiers on the land by 1939 was at least comparable to other Canadian land-settlement ventures in far more favourable circumstances. Homesteading, as the architects of soldier settlement had always maintained, was for the lucky and the strong.

Perhaps the chief discovery of this study is that Canada's policies for returning soldiers were not at all based on accident or neglect. Ernest Scammell, John Todd, Walter Segsworth, and other framers of civil re-establishment were careful and far-sighted planners, alive to the post-war difficulties their clients would experience. They were, of course, men of their time, as convinced of the virtues of economic individualism as they were of scientific expertise. For able-bodied veterans, they believed, a swift transition to civilian self-sufficiency was the best way to remove the vestiges of soldierly dependency. Even for the disabled, the transition must be as swift as possible. What policy-makers did not foresee could fill a volume – and has. They did not anticipate the post-war depression in its delayed but virulent form. Both retraining and the compensatory nature of disability pensions were undermined when disabled veterans, at their most vulnerable, were cast adrift.

Above all, the planners did not anticipate the soldiers themselves. Deliberate government policy made soldiers poor. Whatever their previous standing, a wage of $1.10 a day placed servicemen and their families at the bottom of the income scale. Once pensions were linked to the wages of 'the class of unskilled labour,' disability made the status permanent. This had enormous implications. Canadians had blamed poverty on bad luck or individual failings; for soldiers, it became the result of conscious public policy. When armies were recruited from the slums or from the ranks of landless rural labourers, a soldier's meagre pay produced few social strains. When armies were recruited from across the social spectrum, a soldier's poverty could fuel a social revolution.

One of the revolutions in progress during the First World War was the overthrow of old notions of social entitlement. Canadian society, like its counterparts elsewhere, began by treating soldiers as objects of fashionable charity; veterans gradually mobilized their forces to demand benefits as of right. The transformation was imperfect and incomplete, but the aversion to charity permeated the veterans' movement, from the resentment of Winnipeg's Returned Soldiers' Association in 1916 to the Legion's final rejection of the sweepstakes scheme in 1934. The concept of entitlement fuelled the veterans' long struggle against Colonel Thompson and the Board of Pension Commissioners. At the same time it undermined the 1919 battle for the bonus because, to many veterans, the Calgary Resolution was an illegitimate demand. Never before, however, had the government's clients formulated and presented their own demands; it was a revolution in thinking that posterity would come to take for granted.

The planners for civil re-establishment and their clients established another vital principle of social policy: need is based on family size. In the first month of the war Ottawa acknowledged that a family required more income than an individual by paying separation allowance to married members of the CEF. The Patriotic Fund supplemented that allowance as its contribution to a soldier's peace of mind. The MHC and the DSCR followed suit with allowances paid to veterans in hospital and in training programs; so did the Board of Pension Commissioners when it assessed even the smallest pension. No other employer followed suit. One sad consequence was that the DSCR trainee, receiving the bare minimum to sustain his family as a training allowance, often lost income when he took a job. In 1920 a trainee with a family of five earned $137 a month; few firms would pay that much to a new, semi-skilled employee with a physical handicap. Hundreds of thousands of Canadians understood the concepts of family poverty and family allowances a full generation before 1945.

In a whole range of policies, from pension assessment to the provision of prostheses, Canadians broke new ground during and after the First World War. Without Kidner, Sexton, and Segsworth, and without the veterans who made the effort, Canadians would have been far slower to realize that the disabled could perform serious and demanding work. Without Eddie Baker, Sydney Lambert, and their organizations of blind and maimed veterans, all sightless and amputee Canadians would have faced a longer and more difficult struggle against tradition and prejudice.

In the second battle, as in the first, the combatants knew only of their own struggle and their own suffering. They knew little of the progress of the battle, and only a minority survived long enough to share a sense of victory. Indeed, few of the veterans who joined the second battle had any vision of creating a more generous, humane, and caring society than they had known.   If taxed with such idealism, they would have responded, like soldiers in any war, with little understanding and much profanity. Yet the veterans' second battle, even more truly than their first, ended in a victory that all of us have shared.

Statistical Appendix

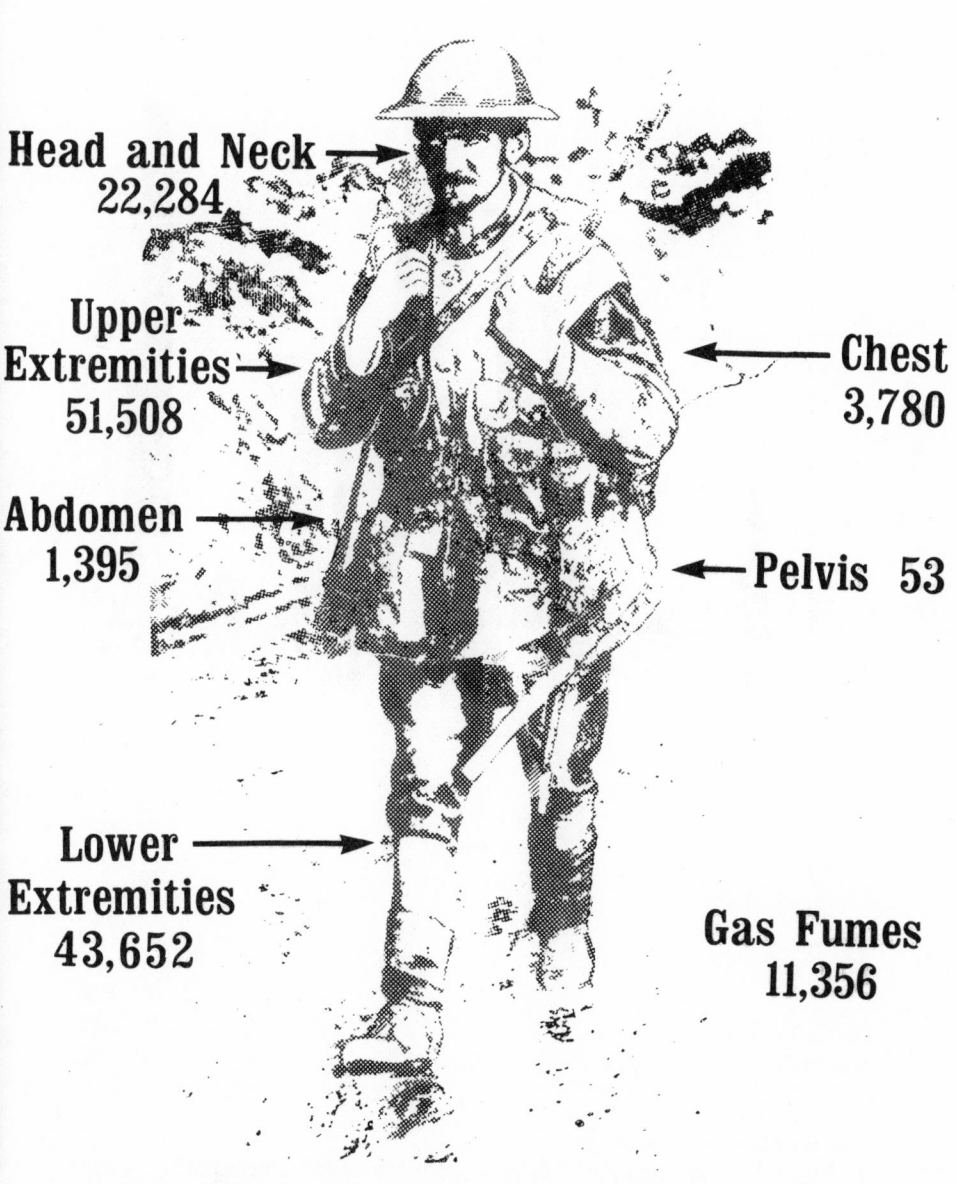

Head and Neck
22,284

Upper Extremities
51,508

Abdomen
1,395

Lower Extremities
43,652

Chest
3,780

Pelvis 53

Gas Fumes
11,356

Canadian Wounds in Action, 1914–18
This illustration is a graphic reminder that it was probably fatal to be wounded in
the trunk. Wounds in the arm or leg had an excellent prognosis, but abdominal
wounds usually were fatal. A surprising number of soldiers with head or neck
injuries reached treatment.

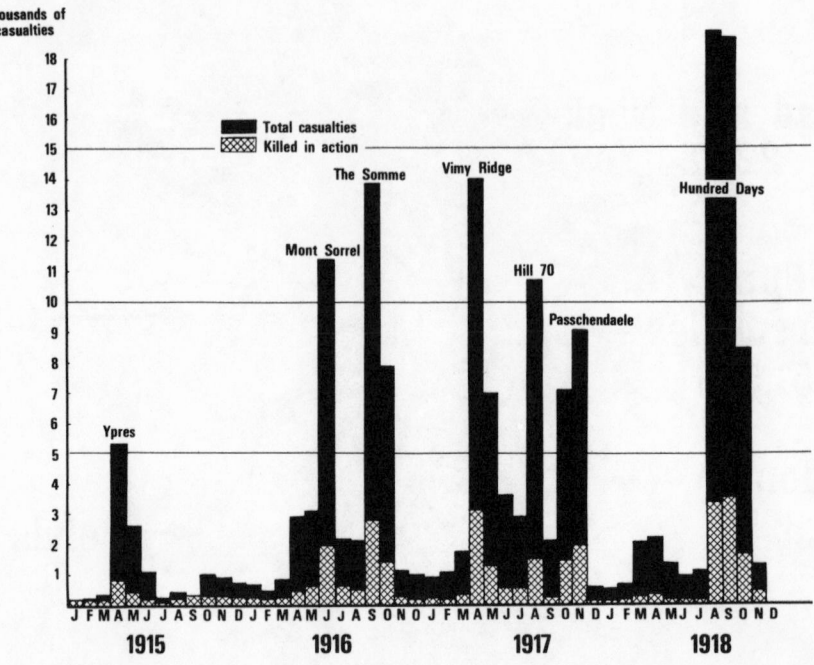

Canadian Corps Casualties, 1915–18

The toll of dead and wounded was continuous from the moment the first Canadians entered action at the end of 1914, but the greatest number of casualties occurred during the major battles. The cost of Vimy Ridge and Hill 70 was borne in a single month; the appalling toll of Passchendaele was spread over October and November 1917. Particularly striking are the enormous losses of August and September 1918, when the Canadian Corps served as the spearhead for the British armies. Source: RG 24, vol. 1883a, f. 27.

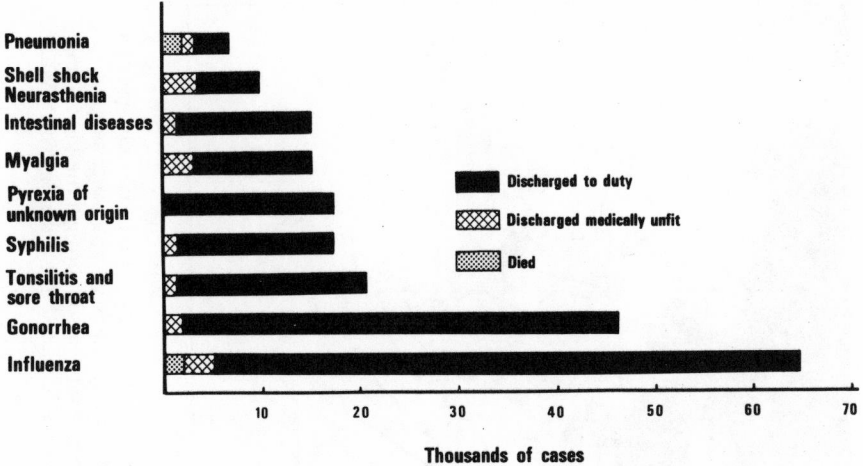

Major Diseases in the Canadian Expeditionary Force, 1914–19
This illustration underlines the killing impact of pneumonia and influenza, diseases no longer treated as serious hazards to healthy young people.
Pyrexia of unknown origin (PUO) was more commonly known as 'Trench Fever' and was due to an organism carried by the fleas that infested almost every serving soldier. The illustration also indicates the seriousness of syphilis and gonorrhea as health problems in the CEF.

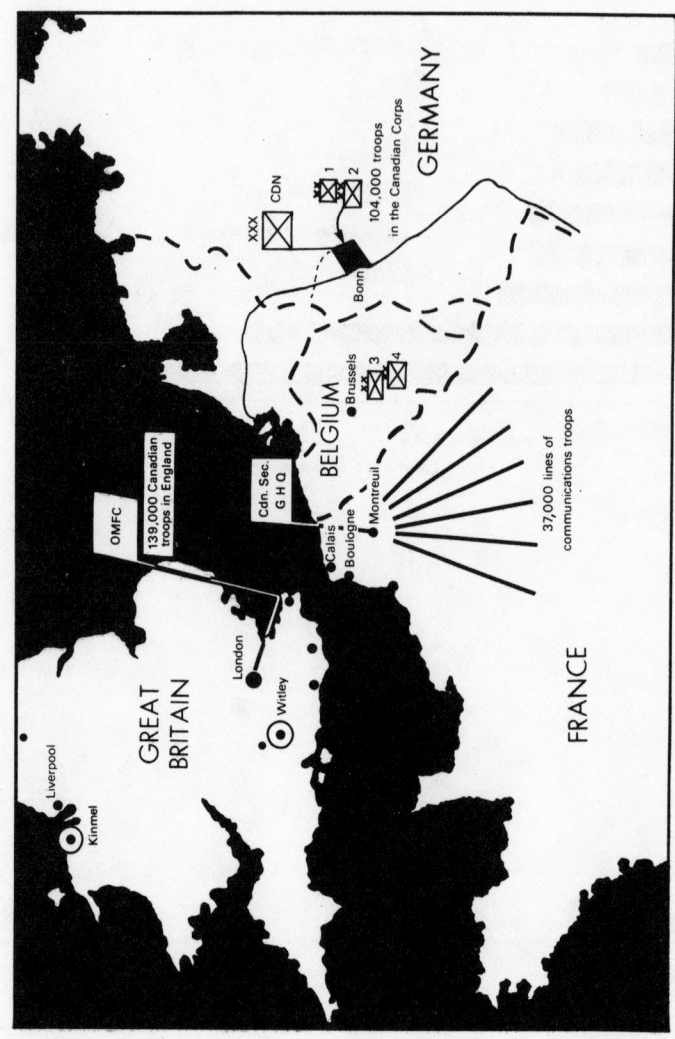

Canadian Demobilization, 1919

Bringing home the Canadian Expeditionary Force involved the repatriation of two divisions from the vicinity of Bonn, two others from Brussels, 37,000 railway, forestry, and other support troops in France, and 139,000 soldiers in England. Corps units passed through the big staging camp at Witley in the south of England; miscellaneous drafts waited at Kinmel in North Wales for ships at the nearby seaport of Liverpool.

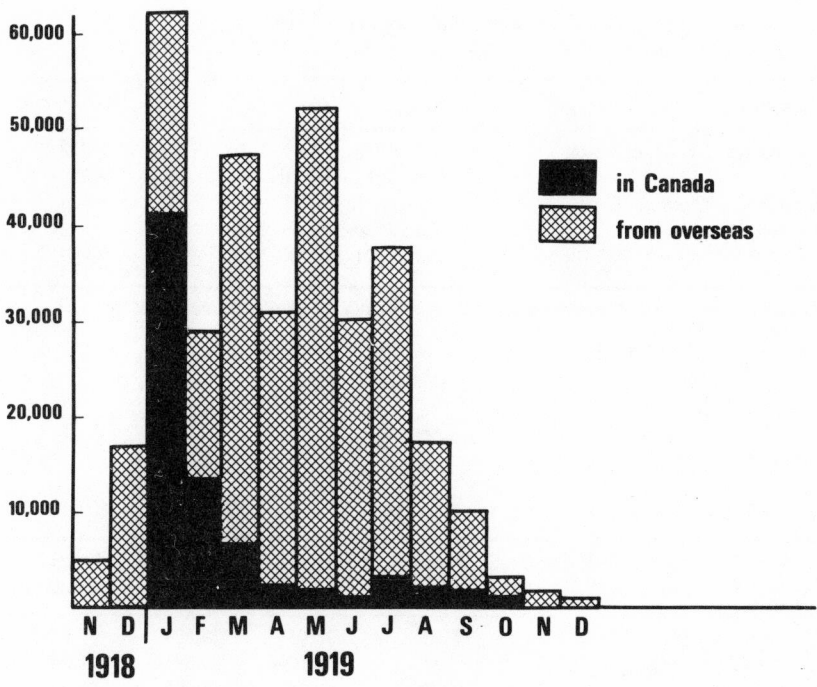

Demobilization of the Canadian Expeditionary Force, 1918-19
Despite plans for orderly demobilization linked to economic need and the capacity of industry to reabsorb soldiers, the diagram shows that the process was rapid
and that it was virtually complete by September 1919 – as soldiers, relatives, and
taxpayers all desired. Source: Duguid Papers, vol. 1, no. 2

Hospital Admissions by the Military Hospitals Commission and
Department of Soldiers' Civil Re-establishment, 1915–21

Organization	Dates	Admissions
Military Hospitals Commission	1 July 1915–31 Dec. 1916	22,742
	1 Jan. 1917–31 Mar. 1918	28,258
Department of Soldiers' Civil	1 April 1918–31 Dec. 1919	36,625
Re-establishment	1 Jan. 1920–31 Dec. 1920	23,592
	1 Jan. 1921–31 Dec. 1921	13,890

SOURCE: *Report of the Department of Soldiers' Civil Re-establishment*, 1921, p. 4

Pensions in Force under the Pension Act, 1918–39

Year	Dependant pensions	Pension value ($000)	Disability pensions	Pension value ($000)	Total pensions	Pension liability
1918	10,488	4,168	15,335	3,105	25,823	7,274
1919	16,733	9,593	42,932	7,470	59,685	17,063
1920	17,823	10,841	69,203	14,335	87,026	25,176
1921	19,209	12,954	51,452	18,231	70,661	31,185
1922	19,606	12,687	45,133	17,991	64,739	30,679
1923	19,794	12,280	43,263	18,142	63,057	30,422
1924	19,971	12,038	43,300	18,787	63,271	30,825
1925	20,015	11,804	44,598	19,816	64,613	31,621
1926	20,005	11,608	46,385	21,457	66,390	33,065
1927	19,999	11,419	48,027	22,811	68,026	34,231
1928	19,975	11,209	50,635	24,374	70,610	35,584
1929	20,002	11,090	54,620	26,095	74,622	37,185
1930	19,644	10,743	56,996	27,059	76,640	37,803
1931	19,676	10,986	66,669	29,226	86,345	40,212
1932	19,308	10,859	75,878	30,999	95,186	41,858
1933	18,745	10,625	77,967	31,125	96,712	41,749
1934	18,236	10,339	77,855	30,453	96,091	40,793
1935	18,241	10,373	78,404	30,406	96,645	40,779
1936	18,175	10,381	79,124	30,473	97,299	40,854
1937	18,186	10,417	79,789	30,365	97,975	40,783
1938	18,105	10,411	79,876	30,270	97,981	40,682
1939	17,896	10,318	80,104	30,094	98,000	40,413

SOURCE: *Canada Year Book*, 1940, p. 1066

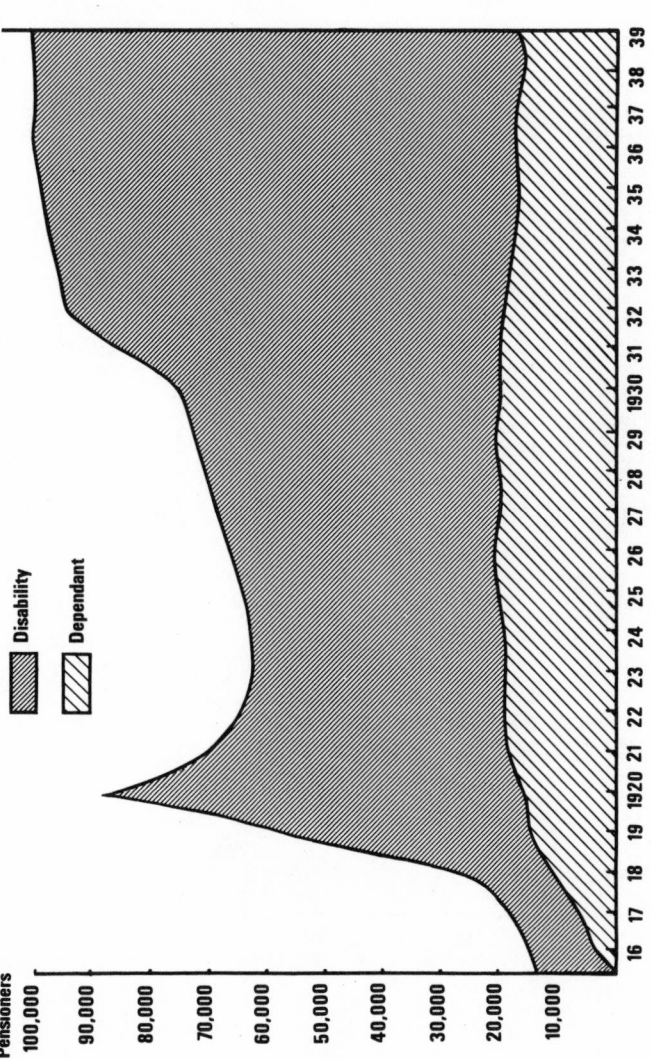

Canadian Disability and Dependant Pensions from the First World War, 1916–39
This diagram indicates the number of pensions in force from 1916 to the eve of the Second World War. It illustrates the dramatic rise in pensions immediately after the war, the sharp decline as small pensions were commuted or cancelled, and the steady subsequent rise in rates, particularly after the 1930 amendments to the Pension Act restored commuted pensioners and a more generous administrative system allowed many claims. Source: Report of Department of Pensions and National Health, 1940

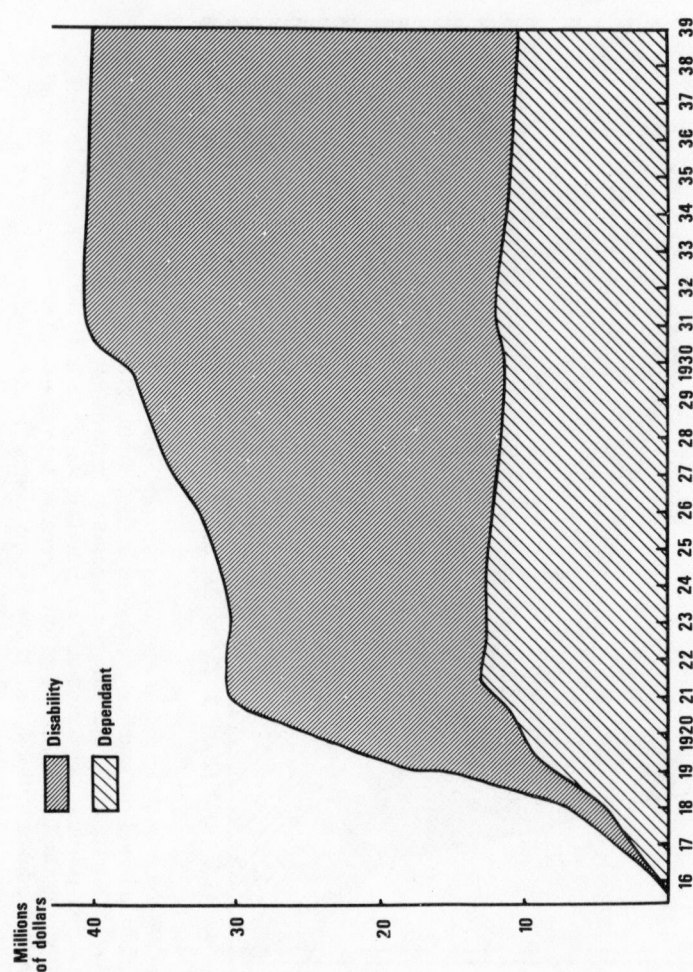

Canadian Disability and Dependant Pension Liability from the First World War, 1916–39
While the 'pension burden,' or liability, rose rapidly from 1916 to 1921 and increased more slowly into the 1930s, the slow decline in the cost of dependant pensions compensated for the rise in disability pensions and the generosity of the post-1930 legislation and appeal arrangements proved to be rather more apparent than real. Source: Report of Department of Pensions and National Health, 1940

Disability Pensions by Classes as of 30 September 1926

Class	Percentage of disability	Number	Percentage of total
1	100	3,337	7.06
2	95	39	0.08
3	90	289	0.61
4	85	164	0.35
5	80	1,094	2.32
6	75	1,258	2.66
7	70	1,241	2.62
8	65	523	1.11
9	60	1,700	3.60
10	55	232	0.49
11	50	3,083	6.53
12	45	610	1.29
13	40	3,496	7.41
14	35	1,247	2.64
15	30	3,777	8.00
16	25	4,079	8.64
17	20	6,878	14.57
18	15	7,233	15.32
19	10	4,898	10.38
20	5	2,031	4.30
TOTAL		47,209	

SOURCE: RG 38, vol. 179, f. 8502
Note that about twenty thousand of the smallest pensions at 5–10 per cent of disability were eligible for commutation from 1920.

Canadian Pensions in 1933
Where pension liability incurred

Country	Disability pensions	Dependant pensions
France	67,825	16,403
England	6,809	1,240
Canada	2,875	947
Other	458	155

Disability pensions by rank

Rank	Number	Amount ($000)
Private	66,314	26,375
Sergeant	7,103	2,730
RSM	303	113
Warrant officer	176	65
Lieutenant	2,215	892
Captain	967	465
Major	375	216
Lieutenant-colonel	120	95
Colonel	13	11
Brigadier general	8	14
Nursing sister	371	144
Matron	2	2

Diseases or injuries

Category	Temporary	Permanent
General	5,803	611
Nervous system	4,021	155
Special senses	3,963	2,330
Circulatory	8,043	742
Respiratory	12,333	363
Gastro-intestinal	2,510	558
Urinary-genital	1,673	143
Amputation	174	2,730
Gunshot wound – joints	2,083	8,893
Gunshot wound – injury	6,177	16,599
General disease	1,561	1,302
Venereal disease	86	114
TOTAL	48,427	34,500

SOURCE: *Canada Year Book*, 1934

The Cost of Veterans' Benefits as a Percentage of Canadian Federal
Budgetary Revenue, 1914–40

Year	Veterans' benefits ($ million)	Budgetary revenue ($ million	Veterans' benefits as a proportion of revenue (%)
1914	0.7	133.0	0.5
1915	0.8	172.1	0.5
1916	2.8	232.7	1.2
1917	8.2	1,609.8	3.1
1918	30.3	312.9	9.7
1919	74.6	349.7	21.3
1920	76.1	436.9	17.4
1921	56.1	395.0	14.2
1922	48.0	409.6	11.7
1923	45.1	407.8	11.1
1924	45.1	352.5	12.8
1925	46.1	383.3	12.0
1926	46.0	401.1	11.5
1927	61.9	430.8	14.4
1928	63.2	461.6	13.7
1929	50.1	453.0	11.1
1930	57.0	357.7	15.9
1931	61.1	334.5	18.3
1932	55.9	311.7	17.9
1933	55.1	324.6	16.9
1934	54.6	361.9	15.1
1935	55.1	372.6	14.8
1936	56.8	454.1	12.5
1937	56.2	516.7	10.8
1938	57.4	502.1	11.4
1939	60.4	562.1	10.7
1940	59.9	872.1	6.9

SOURCE: M.C. Urquhart and K.C. Buckley, *Historical Statistics of Canada*, 1st ed.

Notes

Chapter 1: Veterans

1 *Canadian Annual Review* (cited hereinafter as *CAR*), 1914, Special Supplement, pp. 47–51. On Hughes's role, see Winter, *Sir Sam Hughes*, pp. 44–73; Morton, 'The Cadet Movement,' pp. 64–6.
2 Struthers, *No Fault of Their Own*, pp. 13–14; Brown and Cook, *A Nation Transformed*, p. 199; Thompson, *The Harvests of War*, pp. 47–8
3 See Wilson, *Ontario and the First World War, 1914–1918* (Toronto 1977), pp. xvii–xix, 3; Wade, *The French Canadians*, vol. II, pp. 642–5; Mewburn to Borden, n.d. (May 1918), PAC, R.L. Borden Papers, vol. 243, f. RLB 2687, p. 136056.
4 Estimates of reservists are given in Duguid, *Official History*, vol. 1, pp. 61–2; the figure shown there is 3,232 British reservists. The annual report of the Department of Soldiers' Civil Re-establishment for 1919 estimated the number at 3,500 (p. 75), while Morris, *The Canadian Patriotic Fund*, p. 7, estimated 10,000. Whether in Britain's volunteer regular army or in European conscript armies, soldiers served for a term of years 'with the colours' and for a further term in the reserves, subject to call-up in time of need. Although such men are not counted among the 628,462 Canadians who served in the CEF (nor are most of a further 45,000 Canadians in the British flying services and other components), they formed a considerable part of Canada's post-war pension and disability burden, and they help to complicate the serious problems of statistical computation.
5 Nicholson, *CEF*, pp. 20–1; Montreal *Herald*, 27 July 1914; *CAR*, 1914, pp. 275–8
6 Duguid, *Official History*, vol. 1, app. 86, reports 9,159 born in Canada, 18,495 in the British Isles, 652 in other British possessions, 756 in the United States, 523 in other foreign countries, and 1,032 who gave no information.
7 Nicholson, *CEF*, p. 18
8 Ibid., pp. 20–5; Macphail, *Medical Services*, pp. 21–2, 253–6. On decisions about vaccination and inoculation, see Duguid, *Official History*, vol. 1, pp. 75–6. PC 2830, 9 October 1917, made typhoid inoculation compulsory for all in the CEF.
9 On pay, see Duguid, *Official History*, vol. 1, app. 91, pp. 61–2; PC 2264, 3

September 1914. Following a new British lead, the government approved a separation allowance in PC 2266, 4 September 1914, for those who were not receiving their civilian incomes (later restricted to those receiving federal or provincial civil service salaries). Rates ranged from $20 for a private's wife to $60 for a colonel's lady. Soldiers with families were first permitted and later (under CPF pressure) compelled to make assignments of their own pay to their dependants. See Morris, *Patriotic Fund*, pp. 29–30.

10 On insurance, see Wilson, *Ontario*, p. xxiv, n. 10. Toronto offered its men $1,000 in coverage. Many life insurance companies patriotically cancelled their war risk clauses – for an added premium of $50. No one anticipated the duration or mortality rates of the war.

11 Duguid, *Official History*, vol. 1, p. 59; PC 2102, 11 August 1914

12 On the background, see Morris, *Patriotic Fund*, pp. 8–9, and Stacey, 'The War of 1812 in Canadian History,' in *The Defended Border*, p. 332.

13 Lt-Col. C.F. Winter to Col. Minden Cole, 11 August 1914, Canadian Patriotic Fund Records, McGill University Library

14 Canada, House of Commons, *Debates* (hereinafter cited as CHC *Debates*), 22 August 1914, pp. 87–92; Morris, *Patriotic Fund*, pp. 9–16. On Ames, see *The City below the Hill* (Montreal 1897) and *The Housing of the Working Class* (Montreal 1907). Ames was knighted in 1915 for his role in launching the CPF.

15 Morris, *Patriotic Fund*, pp. 21–6; Wilson, *Ontario*, pp. xxiv, 10–12; *CAR*, 1914, 222–7; 1915, pp. 217–21; 1916, p. 330; 1917, pp. 451–2

16 Morris, *Patriotic Fund*, pp. 32, 42. The fund boasted of its 'Third Responsibility' as a paternal guide to the soldiers' wives and families. 'There were few branches of the Fund,' said Morris, 'that did not, in some measure, endeavour to inculcate into soldiers' dependants the principles of thrift' (at p. 42).

17 Ibid., p. 36

18 CHC *Debates*, 30 June 1919, p. 4277. The Militia Department had immediately approved separation allowance on the same basis, although it eventually felt obliged to form a committee under Maj. J.W. Margeson to sort out problems of bigamy, desertion, and alleged immorality. See *Special Committee, 1918*, pp. 180–5. The British were not quite so broadminded. Under protest from the Archbishop of Canterbury and others, the phrase was officially deleted. See Wooton, *The Politics of Influence*, p. 26.

19 Florence Cole to Herbert Ames, 9 October 1914, 15 January 1915; Canadian Patriotic Fund to Cole, 21 January 1915; Canadian Patriotic Fund Records. See, for a more general account, Morris, *Patriotic Fund*, p. 9.

20 Duguid, *Official History*, appendix 94

21 Ibid., pp. 141–2; see also Lt-Col. Frank Reid to Col. J.W. Carson, 24 March 1915, RG 9, III A 1, ser. 8, vol. 37, f. 8-2-17. 'There is a tremendous lot of detail with this work,' Reid stated – including ordering twelve pairs of handcuffs for the party that returned on the *Missanabie*.

22 George C. McIntosh to J.E. Armstrong, MP, 3 April 1915, Borden Papers, vol 71, f. OC 323 (1)(a), p. 36555

23 Ibid., pp. 36657–8; Mowbray S. Berkley to Gwatkin, 30 August 1915, ibid., p. 36760A.

24 Case of Pte W.A.R. Holmes à Court, ibid., pp. 36631–3

25 Gwatkin to Loring Christie, 1 October 1915, ibid., 36766; also Gwatkin to Christie, 30 August 1915, ibid., 36760A.
26 See Hughes to Borden, 1 May 1915, ibid., p. 36579; PC 959, 1 June 1915; on arrangements in England, chief staff officer to deputy assistant adjutant-general, 21 May 1915, RG 9, III A 1, ser. 8, vol. 37, f. 8-2-17; Carson to Hughes, 15 June 1915, ibid., f. 8-2-8. On arrangements, see Col. J.G. Adami, 'Draft History of the C.A.M.C.: The Military Hospitals Commission,' RG 9, III B 2, vol. 3753.
27 Ibid., pp. 205; Macphail, *Medical Services*, pp. 316–17
28 Borden to Ryerson, 2 June 1915, Borden Papers, vol. 71, f. OC 323 (1)(a), p. 36641a
29 Brown, *Robert Laird Borden*, vol. 2, 1914–37, pp. 37–8
30 PC 1540, 30 June 1915; *CAR*, 1915, p. 263
31 On Lougheed, see PAC, Daly Papers, vol. 2; Gadsby, 'The Government Leader in the Senate,' p. 123.
32 Military Hospitals Commission, minutes of 20 July 1915; RG 38, vol. 225
33 On Scammell, see C.F. Hamilton to William Foran, 6 November 1918, RG 32, C-2, vol. 232, f. 862; ibid., 'Memorandum re Services and Activities of Ernest Henry Scammell,' 7 July 1935. On the Canadian Peace Centenary Association, see Hamilton to R.B. Viets, 17 October 1924, ibid.
34 See Lt-Col. G.S. Maunsell to secretary, Militia Council, 10 July 1915, RG 38, vol. 225, f. 3506, with 49 pages of offers ranging from the use of Hume Blake's summer home to the assistance of J.G. Turriff's daughter Edith, who was described as being 'good at housekeeping.'
35 Scammell to adjutant-general, 29 September 1915, RG 38, vol. 137, f. 7-12
36 Scammell to Lougheed, 19 July 1915, RG 38, vol. 225, f. 8-63
37 Minutes of the inaugural meeting, MHC, 20 July 1915, ibid. See *CAR*, 1915 p. 263.
38 Roland, 'War Amputations in Upper Canada,' pp. 73–84, illustrates the problem for the war of 1812.
39 In the Boer War, the British Army reported 57,684 cases of typhoid and 8,022 deaths out of 380,605 soldiers present. In all, 5,774 British troops were killed. *American Medicine*, XXV, 6 (June 1919) calculated comparable death rates if the American Expeditionary Force had been engaged in earlier wars. Out of a strength of 2,121,396, the AEF would have lost:

	In the Civil War	In the Spanish-American War	Actual losses 1917–19
Typhoid fever	57,133	68,164	213
Dysentery	63,898	6,382	42
Pneumonia	38,962	61,086	41,747

40 On CEF casualties, see Nicholson, *CEF*, p. 548, and Macphail, *Medical Services*, pp. 248ff. See also RG 24, vol. 1867, f. 27.
41 Estimating total disability at the end of the war is surprisingly difficult, since the majority of sick and wounded were considered (and considered themselves) to be fully recovered; only later did they attribute their disability to wartime conditions. By February 1919 113,766 men had returned to Canada; the great majority of them were unfit for further service, yet significant

numbers of men re-enlisted in the CEF during the war and defied the odds by returning to France. By 1919–20, when all had returned and a backlog of pension cases had been handled, Canada had 60,203 disability pensioners. The total fell for a number of years. Age and perhaps the strain of the depression brought an increase. In 1934, at the depth of the depression, Canada had 77,855 disabled pensioners: see RG 38, vol. 195, f. 65-123.

42 Robert England, 'Discharged Soldiers', reviews the tradition of military bounty.

43 On the society, see Craig, 'The Loyal and Patriotic Society.'

44 Roland, 'War Amputations,' pp. 81–2

45 *Regulations and Orders 1883*, paras. 1008–10. Among the cases were those of a sergeant who died of heat-stroke waiting for a train and a private who was granted $17.75 for the costs of attendance and transportation after being stricken with smallpox.

46 Report of the Committee of the Privy Council, 8 July 1885, Canada, *Sessional Papers*, 80e, 1886; *Militia General Orders*, no. 14, 9 July 1885. See *Regulations and Orders, 1887*, paras. 917–38.

47 CHC *Debates*, 3 June 1887, p. 746; 23 June 1887, p. 1268

48 On the Valiquette case, see CHC *Debates*, 28 February 1890, pp. 1268, 1272.

49 Ibid., pp. 1274–9, 1268

50 On the Neely case, see RG 9, II A 1, vol. 185, A 3744; Col. H.G. Grasett to Sir Adolphe Caron, 17 April 1888, PAC Caron Papers, vol. 98, f. 56380 et passim. (Mrs Neely had been backed by Lt-Col. Otter, the Reverend Charles Ingles, and N. Clarke Wallace, MP, all of whom seem to have thought better of their advocacy.)

51 On Mrs French, see RG 9, II A, 1, vol. 185, f. A 3744; on Mrs Ryan, see CHC *Debates*, 28 February 1890, p. 1268. On both, see Canada, *Sessional Papers*, 80d, 1886.

52 On Mulloy, see RG 38, vol. 69, f. 175; RG 7, G-21, vol. 365, f. 2425; and *Special Committee, 1920*, p. 210. Not everyone approved. See Norman McDonald to Borden, 10 August 1904, RG 24, vol. 22, f. 49-5-1; McDonald threatened to shoot someone if Mulloy got any more money!

53 See, for example, A.F. Messervey to Borden, 17 March 1915, Borden Papers, vol. 71 f. OC 323 (1)(a), p. 36548. In 1914, three British major military charities existed to handle problems that otherwise might have fallen to taxpayers. The Royal Patriotic Fund Corporation provided support for the widows of soldiers and sailors; the Sailors' and Soldiers' Families Association supported wives, children, and other dependants left destitute by an absent serviceman, while the Soldiers and Sailors' Help Society, under the distinguished and concerned patronage of Lord Roberts, endeavoured to help disabled veterans become self-supporting. The three major charities were supplemented by a host of county, regimental, and corps associations, private trusts and specialized appeals which, when obliged to register in 1916, numbered over 6,000. See Wooton, *Politics of Influence*, pp. 16–37.

54 James Bryce, *The American Commonwealth*, vol. 1, p. 180

55 Dennis, 'Provision for Crippled Soldiers,' p. 177

56 Dearing, *Veterans in Politics*, expresses only a modest doubt about the Grand Army's alleged influence. A detailed and relatively dispassionate account of American pension legislation may be found in Weber and Schmeckebier, *The Veterans' Administration*. On U.S. veterans, see Mayo,

Soldiers What Next! pp. 18-37; Waller, *The Veteran Comes Back*, pp. 197-9; Wecter, *When Johnny Comes Marching Home*, pp. 211ff; and Ross, *Preparing for Ulysses*, pp. 6-7. On Tanner, see Waller, *The Veteran*, p. 199.

57 CHC *Debates*, 19 February 1875, p. 252. On applicants, see 'Return of Militia of 1812-13,' Canada, *Sessional Papers*, no. 25, 1875.

58 CHC *Debates*, 26 February 1875, p. 392

59 Weber and Schmeckebier, *Veterans' Administration*, p. 33; Waller, *The Veteran*, p. 218.

60 CHC *Debates*, 27 March, 1912, pp. 6252-3. See also ibid., 1908, pp. 3757-9, 3775; and England, 'Disbanded Soldiers,' p. 15.

61 On the Fenian Raid bounty, see RG 9, II A 4, vol. 28, especially *Report of the Board of Inquiry relating to Claims of Applicants for Fenian Raid Volunteer Bounty in ... Nova Scotia, 1914*; see also CHC *Debates*, 28 March 1913, pp. 6677ff.

62 Morton, *The Canadian General*, p. 320

63 *Report of the Auditor General*, 1912-13, p. O-2. (Of $70,020, $17,689 went to pay pensions from the 1885 campaign, $1,821 for pensions from the Fenian Raids, and $40 for pensions from 1837-8.)

64 As J.G. Adami of McGill University warned; see Adami, memorandum, 10 May 1917, Borden Papers, vol. 73, f. OC 327, pp. 38315-29.

65 See Lougheed to Mr Justice Meagher, 24 August 1915, RG 38, vol. 152, f. 8464, suggesting the fund's potential; Willison to A.R. Forde, 4 August 1915, ibid.; on the Machine Gun Movement, see *CAR*, 1915, pp. 207-14. (While there was later talk of returning the contributions, $661,272 seems to have found its way into the government coffers: Sir Sam Hughes, statement reported in the Ottawa *Journal*, 3 February 1916.)

66 Borden's activity and the problem of finding scattered Canadians is evident in Borden Papers, vol. 52, f. OC 237 (2)(B).

67 White to Borden, 9 September 1915, ibid., p. 25220

68 Ottawa *Journal*, 28-29 May 1915; *CAR*, 1915, pp. 265-6

69 F.H. Sexton, 'The Training of Disabled Soldiers for Suitable Occupations,' reprinted in the Halifax *Morning Chronicle*, 27 October 1915. On Sexton, see Hunt, *Nova Scotia's Part in the Great War*, pp. 330-2. On Sexton, see Verma, 'Frederick H. Sexton,' pp. 18-26 and Macleod, 'Technical Education,' pp. 73ff.

70 Departmental Committee on Provision of Employment for Soldiers and Sailors Disabled in the War, *Report*, Cmnd. 7915 (1915). On the report, see Wooton, *Politics of Influence*, pp. 13, 28-30. On charity-mongering, see Wooton, pp. 23ff. The phrase is from Cole, *Labour in Wartime*, p. 95.

71 Scammell, *Provision of Employment*, p. 5; Scammell to Rowley, 19 September 1915, RG 38, vol. 198, f. 6091

72 Scammell, *Provision of Employment*, p. 5

73 Ibid., p. 5

74 Ibid., p. 10

75 For the state of vocational training in Canada, see Royal Commission on Industrial Training and Technical Education, and Sexton 'Education for Industry,' pp. 68ff.

76 Scammell, *Provision of Employment*, p. 9

77 On Carruthers and the Disablement Fund, see Scammell to Beland, 7 March 1925, citing Carruthers to Lougheed, 31 July 1915 and 26 August 1915,

RG 38, vol. 153, f. 6954 et seq.; and Scammell's testimony, *Special Committee, 1917*, p. 971. On contributions, see RG 38, vol. 152, f. 8454.
78 PC 2412, 14 October 1915. See Borden Papers, vol. 71, f. OC 323 (1)(a), p. 36769; Scammell testimony, *Special Committee, 1917*, pp. 231–2, and *Report of MHC*, May 1917, Canada, *Sessional Papers*, 158, 1917, pp. 15–16
79 Minutes of the Interprovincial Conference, 18–19 October 1915, RG 38, vol. 225, f. 8-62

Chapter 2: 'A Motherly Touch'

1 On provincial committees, see *Proceedings, Special Committee, 1917*, pp. 544–8, 647–651, RG 38, vol. 225, f. 7289; *Canadian Annual Review*, 1915, p. 263.
2 Ottawa *Free Press*, 7 October 1915
3 On facilities, see *Report of MHC*, pp. 17–32; *Special Committee, 1917*, 233–8.
4 Ibid., p. 238
5 Minutes of Military Hospitals Commission, 10 November 1915, RG 38, vol. 225, f. 8-62
6 On procedure, see *Report of MHC, 1917*, p. 52; Maj.-Gen. J.L. Hughes, report, 24 November 1915, RG 38, vol. 137, f. 7-12; *Special Committee, 1917*, pp. xviii–xix; on civilian clothing, see ibid., pp. 963–5.
7 The proportions remained fairly constant. By March 1917, of 12,843 returnees examined by medical boards, 2,891 had been ruled to have no claim, 828 had been sent to await a pension decision and 9,124 had been recommended for further treatment. A further 864 had been returned for non-medical reasons (*Report of MHC, 1917*, p. 58).
8 On the depot and discipline, see minutes of MHC, 18 October 1915, RG 38, vol. 225, f. 8-62.
9 Minutes of MHC, 10 November 1915, ibid.
10 On consequences, see *Special Committee, 1917*, p. 231, and Borden to Hughes, 27 November 1915, Borden Papers, vol. 52, f. OC 237 (2)(a), p. 25344; Lt-Col. A.D. McRae to Hughes, 6 November 1915, ibid., pp. 25331–3. (The authorities in England were delighted with their economy and efficiency in loading so many into a single ship!)
11 Scammell to Borden, 30 November 1915, ibid., pp. 2538–9; Scammell to C.W. Rowley, 13 December 1915, RG 38, vol. 198, f. 6091.
12 *Special Committee, 1917*, p. 232
13 Ibid., p. 238
14 For Lt-Col. Walker's testimony, see ibid., pp. 503–5; minutes of MHC, 13 June 1916, RG 38, vol. 226, f. 8610.
15 On Rowley's activities and views, see RG 38, vol. 198, f. 6091.
16 Scammell to Rowley, 1 February 1916, ibid.
17 Rowley to Scammell, 7 February and 25 February 1916, ibid.
18 Rowley to Scammell, n.d., ibid., noted that Mackenzie was 'a man who never writes letters and only answers telegrams occasionally.' See also Rowley to Scammell, 16 June 1916, ibid., and report of the secretary, 29 April 1916, RG 38, vol. 225, f. 3506.
19 F.W. Peters to Scammell, 16 April 1916, Borden Papers, vol. 53, f. OC 238 (2)(a), p. 25652; Mrs W.J. Thomas to trustees of the Canadian Club,

4 April 1916, ibid., pp. 25388–91; Maj. J. Reynolds Tite to DOC, Military District No. 13, 30 September 1915, ibid., vol. 52, f. OC 237 (3)(a), p. 25230; minutes of MHC, 13 March 1916, RG 38, vol. 225, f. 8-62

20 Scammell to Rowley, 5 April 1916, RG 38, vol. 198, f. 6091

21 On Montreal facilities, see *Special Committee, 1917*, pp. 417–18.

22 Pellatt to Lougheed, 23 October 1915, RG 38, vol. 162, f. 1430, part 1; Riddell to Scammell, 3 November 1915, ibid. (Toronto members continued to meet as a 'board' and continued to raise both Riddell's salary and that of his assistant, Miss Whitton, until that of the former far exceeded Scammell's.)

23 George to Scammell, 4 November 1915, ibid.; see also George to Scammell, 22 October 1915, ibid.

24 Minutes of MHC, 10 December 1915, RG 38, vol. 225, f. 8-62.

25 Scammell to Borden, 30 November 1915, Borden Papers, vol. 52, f. OC 237 (3)(b), p. 25359; and 'History of the CAMC, Military District No. 2,' RG 9, III B 2, vol. 3752. See also Toronto *Telegram*, 15 December 1915.

26 Macphail, *Medical Services*, p. 316

27 On pay, see Riddell to Scammell, 22 December 1915 et passim, RG 38, vol. 162, f. 1430, part 2; Toronto *Telegram*, 23 December 1915; Scammell to Riddell, 27 December 1915 (cf *supra*), reflected annoyance that Riddell and Harris had left the impression that they had secured pre-Christmas payment of the aggrieved soldiers.

28 On reinstatement, see PC 508, 24 February 1916; minutes of Toronto Committee, RG 38, vol. 162, f. 1430, part 1.

29 Howard Stutchbury to Scammell, 11 May 1916, RG 38, vol. 127, f. 7-12, part 1; Scammell to AAG-1, 11 March 1916, ibid.

30 *Special Committee, 1917*, Table III, p. 962

31 Ibid. One explanation for the small numbers was the policy of sending the blind to St Dunstan's and, at least initially, sending amputation cases to be fitted with limbs at the British orthopaedic centre at Roehampton.

32 Canadian pension regulations, like their British originals, automatically classified those dead or disabled in training in a category lower than those who were killed or wounded in action. On care of the sick, see Morton, *The Canadian General*, pp. 211–12.

33 See resolution, minutes of MHC, 29 April 1916, RG 38, vol. 226, f. 8610. One key change in the MHC's authority in October 1915 was the extension of its mandate to all members of the CEF, returned or not. In Winnipeg, Rowley warned that the 'returned men' had no desire to share the new Deer Lodge hospital with either the IODE or the 'CEF men.' The latter were both left in the Immigration Hall. Rowley to Scammell, 16 June 1916, RG 38, vol. 198, f. 6091.

34 Reid to Carson, 5 June 1916; RG 9, III A 1, ser. 8, vol. 37, f. 8-2-10; Carson to Hughes, 7 June 1916, ibid.; on the unfit, see Maj. W.F. Kemp to adjutant-general, CEF, 31 October 1916; RG 9 III, vol. 90, f. 10-12-15; Report to Diretor of Recruiting and Organization, 14 September 1916, PAC, Babtie Papers, vol. 3; Lloyd Harris to Lougheed, 29 November 1916, RG 38, vol. 226, f. 8640 reported the proportion – 17.7 per cent unfit – according to a Major Kirkby, sent to co-ordinate the transfer of convalescents from England. For MHC views, see minutes, 13 March 1916, RG 38, vol. 225, f. 8-62.

35 On tuberculosis, see Katharine McCuaig, 'From Social Reform to Social Ser-

vice.' See also Chadwick and Pope, *Modern Attack on Tuberculosis* and Shryock, *National Tuberculosis Association*.

36 Scammell, 'Canadian Practice,' p. 240. On policy, see *Special Committee, 1917*, pp. 40–50, 214–22, 258–60, 746–7, 951–60; minutes of MHC, 29 April 1916, RG 38, vol. 225, f. 3506.
37 *Special Committee, 1917*, pp. 458–60 (testimony of Dr J.R. Byers)
38 Ibid., pp. 746–7; Gage to Hughes, 1 February 1916, Borden Papers, vol. 53, f. OC 238 (2)(a), p. 25523; Gage to Marlow, 25 August 1916; RG 24, vol. 4292, f. 34-1-54-8
39 On Minnewaska, see *Special Committee, 1917*, pp. 215–21; 965–6; minutes of MHC, 29 April 1916, RG 38, vol. 225, f. 3506; Scammell to Lougheed, 10 August 1916, RG 38, vol. 232, f. 2308.
40 On enhancement of tuberculosis facilities, see McCuaig, 'Anti-Tuberculosis,' pp. 485–7; *Report of the Board of Tuberculosis Consultants, December 1920*, pp. 10–12.
41 On the insane, see Borden Papers, vol. 98, f. OC 493, p. 52730.
42 Borden to Lougheed, 22 January 1916, ibid., vol. 53, f. OC 238 (1)(b), p. 25500, reporting the complaint of W.F. Cockshutt MP that soldiers should be sent where there were 'cheerful influences' and every chance for recovery. 'These conditions, in his view, do not obtain in the ordinary Asylum.'
43 On Cobourg, see minutes of MHC, 8 September 1916, RG 38, vol. 226, f. 8610.
44 Scammell to Rowley, 5 December 1915, RG 38, vol. 198, f. 6091
45 *Report of the MHC, 1917*, pp. 17–32
46 Minutes of MHC, 29 April 1916, RG 38, vol. 225, f. 3506
47 See Thompson testimony, *Special Committee, 1917*, pp. 42–3. See also report by Maj. S.A. Smith, 26 July 1916, RG 38, vol. 182, f. 8564.
48 On prostheses, see E.W. von Eberts, 'Functional Education and Vocational Training of Soldiers Disabled in War,' paper delivered to the Montreal Medical-Chirurgical Society, 6 December 1916, *Canadian Medical Association Journal* (March 1917), pp. 6–8.
49 See C.S. Chesley to Borden, 3 November 1915, RG 38, vol. 130, f. 8545; C.S. Chesley to H.B. Tremain MP, 27 April, 1916, Borden Papers, vol. 53, f. OC 238 (2)(a), pp. 25624–5.
50 See, for example, J.P. Prescott to Military Hospitals Commission, Ottawa, 27 January 1917, RG 38, vol. 130, f. 8548. The British supplied Carnes Arms to bilateral amputees 'or in cases in which they are regarded as likely to be specially useful' (Maj. C.E. Doherty to DMS, 22 October 1915, RG 9, III B 2, vol. 3585, f. 22-5-2, part 1).
51 See Doherty to DMS, 27 November 1915, ibid.
52 Minutes of MHC, 13 March 1916, RG 38, vol. 225, f. 3506; Report of the Secretary, 29 April 1916, Annex B, ibid. A full account of Dobell's findings in England and Europe was published in Military Hospitals Commission, *Special Bulletin*, April 1916, pp. 11–28.
53 Minutes of MHC, 13 March 1916, RG 38, vol. 225, Annex D
54 Minutes of the Orthopaedic Specialists' Committee, 1 December 1916, RG 38, vol. 182, f. 8864; PC 2039, 22 August 1918. See also W.E. Gallie to Capt. W.W. Chipman, 30 April 1917. Pressure also came from the new Pension Board: see J.L. Todd to Thompson, 14 December 1916, ibid.

55 *Special Committee on Pensions, 1916*, p. 113; *Special Committee, 1917*, pp. 681-90, 1005-7
56 Gwatkin memorandum, 3 June 1916, RG 38, vol. 156. See also Macphail, *Medical Services*, p. 325.
57 T.B. Kidner to Lougheed, 29 June 1916, ibid.; minutes of MHC, 13 June 1916, 8 September 1916, RG 38, vol. 226, f. 8610; *Special Committee, 1917*, pp. 94-5; Sexton to Scammell, 29 June 1917, RG 38, vol. 204, f. 15-2Q, part 3. Estimates of the number of Jamaicans involved ranged from 14 to 100. The nominal role of those who received prostheses contained seventeen names; eight of those sustained bilateral below-knee amputations. See *Report*, Superintendent Orthopaedic and Surgical Appliances Branch, 8 January 1919, RG 38, vol. 156.
58 On the blind, see *Special Committee, 1917*, pp. 109-10, 559-60; Segsworth, *Retraining*, chapter 10: J.S. McLennan and Maj. R.T. MacKeen, *Inter-Allied Conference*, pp. 12-30; *Report of the MHC*, 1917, pp. 47-8. On Pearson, see Dark, *Sir Arthur Pearson*, especially pp. 154-94. On St Dunstan's from a participant's perspective, see Rawlinson, *St Dunstan's*, and Campbell, *No Compromise*, pp. 9-13 and passim. See also Pearson to Borden, 12 August 1915, Borden Papers, vol. 52, f. OC 237 (2)(a), pp. 25124-5.
59 Kidner to S.C. Swift, PAC, Records of the CNIB, MG 28 I 233, vol. 7
60 Segsworth, *Retraining*, pp. 129-30; Pearson to Sir Edward Kemp, 8 March 1918, Borden Papers, vol. 92, f. OC 460, p. 48285; Scammell to Yates, 20 March 1918, ibid., p. 48290. On the CNIB, see Campbell, *No Compromise*.
61 Borden to Lougheed, 13 November 1915, Borden Papers, vol. 52, OC 237 (2)(B), p. 25298 (on McLennan). McLennan launched the MHC's *Special Bulletin* in April 1916 with a series of articles publicizing views compatible with the commission's philosophy.
62 McLennan memorandum, 27 March 1916, ibid., f. OC 238 (2)(a). Reprinted with approval in an article by J. Saxon Mills in the London *Daily Chronicle*, 4 October 1916, as an example for Britain to imitate; the article was reprinted in turn by an ecstatic MHC and excerpted on every possible occasion.
63 Scammell, *Provision of Employment*, p. 9
64 See ibid. and Segsworth, *Retraining*, p. 10.
65 For example, the Manitoba *Free Press*, 1 April 1916, condemned an MP (R.B. Bennett) for criticizing technical education for the soldiers. See Sexton to Scammell, 29 June 1917, RG 38, vol. 204, f. 15-2-Q, part 3.
66 Saint John *Telegraph*, 19 April 1916, in RG 38, vol. 204, f. 15-2-Q, part 1; Sexton to Scammell, 29 June 1917, ibid., part 3.
67 Von Eberts, 'Functional Re-education,' pp. 6-8
68 On Kidner's background, see *Special Committee, 1917*, p. 91.
69 See Scammell testimony, ibid., 1917, p. 971 et seq. on machine-gun money. Gwatkin to Christie, 19 November 1915, PAC, W.G. Gwatkin Papers, vol. 1, file 1.
70 Kidner's ideas are reflected in the McLennan memorandum, 27 March 1916, and in *Special Committee, 1917*, pp. 91ff.
71 See *Special Committee, 1917*, pp. 122-37 and Segsworth, *Retraining*, pp. 10-11.
72 *Special Committee, 1917*, pp. 418-20. (Another building, renovated by the

St George's Society, was available by mid-1917.) On facilities, see Halifax *Chronicle*, 13 April 1916.
73 Clarence Smith to Lougheed, 23 May 1916, RG 38, vol. 158, f. 14-7-Q, part 1; Sexton to Kidner, 11 June 1916, and reply, 13 June 1916, RG 38, vol. 204, f. 15-2-Q, part 1. On pay for trainees, see Kidner to Sexton, 14 June 1916, ibid. On policy, see Hunt, *Nova Scotia's Part*, pp. 333–4.
74 PC 1472, 29 June 1916. (McLennan had insisted that $8.00 a month was as much as any hospital patient should have.) See also Borden Papers, f. OC 238 (2)(a), pp. 25576–7. On the delay, see McLennan to Clarence Smith, 25 May 1916, RG 38, vol. 158, f. 14-7-Q, part 1.
75 Harris, *Redemption of the Disabled*, p. 126, citing Kidner and praising Canada's eminently 'practical' approach in contrast to that of its allies
76 Minutes of the MHC, 13 March 1916, RG 38, vol. 225, f. 3506
77 *Special Committee, 1917*, pp. 95–8; Kidner to McPherson, 30 May 1916, RG 38, vol. 232, f. 2308
78 PC 2566, 20 October 1916; McPherson to Lougheed, 9 August 1916, RG 38, vol. 232, f. 2308; J.J. Warwick to Kidner, 23 September 1916, ibid. On Ontario experience in vocational education, see Dupré et al., *Federalism and Policy Development*, pp. 55ff (though, for good reasons or bad, ignoring the wartime contribution and controversy).
79 T.B. Kidner, 'Vocational Work of the Invalided Soldiers' Commission,' p. 145
80 Scammell to Blount, 14 October 1915, Borden Papers, vol. 52, f. OC 237 (2)(b), p. 25228
81 See, for example, Toronto *Telegram*, 10 April 1916 'Some Loaded with Liquor.' See also Scammell to AAG-1, 15 April 1916, RG 38, vol. 137, f. 7-12; Gage to Hughes, 31 December 1915, Borden Papers, vol. 53, f. OC 238 (2)(a), p. 25523; testimony of Dr J.R. Byers, *Special Committee, 1917*, p. 460.
82 Lougheed to Scammell, 1 December 1915, RG 38, vol. 137, f. 7-12.
83 Scammell to AAG-1, 3 May 1916, ibid., adjutant-general's circular, HQ 644-1-6, 11 May 1916, ibid. Unfortunately, the certificate was printed on flimsy paper and there usually was no copy. Soldiers with bad conduct entries could find an easy solution to their problem.
84 McLennan report, 27 March 1916, Borden Papers, vol. 53, f. OC 238 (2)(a), pp. 25572–3
85 Minutes of the MHC, 29 April 1916, 13 June 1916, RG 38, vol. 225, f. 3506
86 PC 1472, 29 June 1916. See also RG 38, vol. 226, f. 8610, part 2
87 See Kidner to Sexton, 14 August 1916, RG 38, vol. 204, f. 15-2-Q, part 2. Returned men who qualified as projectionists in Calgary had promptly been hired as strike-breakers.
88 See *Special Committee, 1917*, table, p. 808; lack of direct leadership was noted by Douglas C. McMurtrie, 'Vocational Training,' p. 312. So 'professional' had the MHC become that in 1916 commission officials even opposed a YMCA bid to post one of its staff to the discharge depot at Quebec.
89 On Hughes and the Overseas Ministry, see Morton, *A Peculiar Kind of Politics*, chapter 5; Vince, 'The Resignation of Sir Sam Hughes.'
90 Col. H.A. Bruce, *Report on the Canadian Army Medical Service* (London 1916), reprinted in Bruce, *Politics and the CAMC*. On Bruce, see his autobiography, *Varied Operations*.

91 See Morton, *Peculiar Politics*, pp. 94–5.
92 On casualties during the Somme, see Nicholson, *CEF*, p. 198; RG 24, vol. 1883a, f. 27.
93 See J.S. McLennan, *What the Military Hospitals Commission Is Doing as at 1 January 1918* (Ottawa 1918), pp. 2–3, 8–9. Anxiety over excess capacity is apparent in Scammell's testimony, *Special Committee, 1917*, passim.
94 Perley to prime minister, 16 November 1916, Borden Papers, vol. 84, f. OC 410, pp. 43196–8; adjutant-general, OMFC to Military Hospitals Commission, 26 November 1916, ibid., p. 43228. See also Scammell to Mrs G. Webster, 4 December 1916, RG 38, vol. 152, f. 8470.
95 Lloyd Harris to Lougheed, 29 November 1916, RG 38, vol. 226, f. 8640
96 Loughead to Perley, 27 November 1916, Borden Papers, OC 410, p. 43229; Lougheed to Borden, 23 December 1916, ibid., p. 43210
97 *Who's Who and Why*, 1921, p. 441
98 Perley to Kemp, 16 February 1917, Borden Papers, vol. 84, f. OC 410, p. 43242; ibid., 26 February 1917; ibid., p. 43246; Perley to Lougheed, 28 February 1917, ibid., p. 43249
99 Armstrong testimony, *Special Committee, 1917*, p. 998–1004; Scammell testimony, ibid., pp. 233–8
100 The best summary of MHC construction is in *Construction*, X, 9 (September 1917), pp. 293–310.
101 *MHC Report for 1917*, pp. 45–6; see also report, Nervous and Mental Branch, MHC, RG 38, vol. 228, f. 8640.
102 On tuberculosis facilities, see *Special Committee, 1917*, pp. 951–60.
103 McLennan, *What the MHC Is Doing*, pp. 2–3, 8–9
104 *Construction*, X, 9 (September 1917), pp. 311–13
105 The MHC was now as delighted with American praise as with British. See Adam Black, 'Salvaging War's Waste,' reprinted and distributed by the commission.
106 See Segsworth, *Retraining*, p. 13. The 1917 Special Committee had nothing but praise and approval for Kidner's achievements, noting that 1,500 of 12,000 patients had accepted courses: see Report, xxiv–xxvii, and Kidner's own reports, pp. 91–133.
107 On Ontario, see Kidner to director, 4 May 1917, and table, RG 38, vol. 232, f. 2310. On Alberta, see D.C. McMurtrie, 'Reconstructing the War Cripple in Alberta,' pp. 229–36.
108 Armstrong to Lougheed, 25 April 1917, RG 38, vol. 232, f. 2310. See McPherson to Lougheed, 13 June 1917, ibid., and Nichol's testimony, *Special Committee, 1917*, pp. 693–7.
109 Kidner to Armstrong, 4 May 1917, RG 37, vol. 232, f. 2310
110 Segsworth, *Retraining*, p. 12. On the University of Saskatchewan, see Thomson, *The University of Saskatchewan*, pp. 101–2.
111 Segsworth, *Retraining*, p. 14. See Armstrong to W.F. Nickle MP, 7 August 1917, RG 38, vol. 232, f. 2311, reflecting Segsworth's influence.
112 See Segsworth, *Retraining*, pp. 8–9, and *Canada's Work*.
113 Segsworth, *Retraining*, p. 124
114 Memo for Sir James Lougheed, 25 November 1918, RG 38, vol. 232, f. 2309, reviews the history of the relationship.
115 Segsworth, *Retraining*, p. 17. See also Sexton to Kidner, 8 June 1917, RG 38, vol. 204, f. 15-2-Q, part 3; Kidner to Sexton, 13 June 1917, ibid.; W.J.

Warters to Segsworth, 19 November 1917, RG 38, vol. 157, f. 16-5-10, part 1.
116 McLennan, *What the MHC Is Doing*, pp. 4-5
117 *The Soldier's Return: How the Canadian Soldier Is Being Refitted for Industry* (Ottawa, 1919), p. 44. McLennan, *What the MHC Is Doing*, cited a two-colour poster with such slogans as 'There is no such word as "impossible" in his dictionary" and, more practically, 'That his pension cannot be reduced by his undertaking work or perfecting himself in some form of industry.'
118 *The Soldier's Return*, p. 3

Chapter 3: Avoiding the 'Pension Evil'

1 See Harris, *Disabled*, pp. 64-76.
2 On the Disablement Fund, see pp. 16-17, 194-6.
3 Griffiths-Boscawen, 'Pensions and Parliament,' pp. 390-1
4 'Minutes of Organization Meeting, Soldiers' Aid Commission,' 17 November 1915 (supplied by courtesy of the Soldiers' Aid Commission of Ontario, Ms Angela Ondruska), p. 2. See also Rowley to Scammell, n.d., RG 38, vol. 198, f. 6091.
5 CHC *Debates*, 31 January 1916, p. 441
6 Ibid., 24 January 1916, p. 215
7 See, for example, ibid., 18 May 1916, p. 4138.
8 Lt-Col. J.G. Adami, 'Memorandum upon the Civil War Pension Evil in the United States and the Means Adopted to Arrest the Evil,' Borden Papers, vol. 73, f. OC 327, p. 38316
9 Ibid., p. 38323
10 Ibid., p. 38320
11 PC 1774, 29 September 1906; Regulations Respecting Pay and Allowances, etc., 1906, ss 439-45
12 Ibid., s. 4
13 Ibid., ss 438 (a)-(d).
14 Lt-Col. C.L. Panet to W.A. Grove, 8 January 1921, RG 24, vol. 6540, f. HQ 650-30-1, part 1
15 On pre-war problems, see, for example, William Price to Borden, 23 January 1913, Borden Papers, vol. 165, f. RLB 23 (1), p. 89738.
16 Brig.-Gen. W.E. Hodgins to minister of militia and defence, 31 March 1915, RG 24, vol. 6540, f. HQ 650-30-1, part 1; Hodgins to acting minister, 23 July 1915, ibid.
17 PC 887, 29 April 1915, Borden Papers, vol. 224, f. RLB 1727; see *Special Committee, 1916*, pp. 19-20.
18 CHC *Debates*, 24 March 1915, pp. 1394 et seq.
19 See 'Pensions and Claims Board, CEF', in Canadian War Archives Survey, part 2, RG 37, vol. 353, pp. 190-7; RG 9, II B 2, vol. 3583, f. 22-4-2. On pension regulations explained, see 'What the Disabled Canadian Soldier Wants to Know,' draft notes, ibid., pp. 37-8.
20 Darling's report and letter are printed with 'Pensions, Grants and Money Allowances Made of the Canadian Expeditionary Force Since Beginning of War to February 16, 1916,' Canada, *Sessional Papers*, 185, 1916. See also pp. 58-62. On Darling, see Morgan, *Canadian Men and Women*, p. 296.

21 'Pensions, Grants, and Money Allowances,' p. 62.
22 By 16 February 1916 the government had approved pensions for 586 widows and 863 children totalling $267,835 and for 1,053 disabled men for $154,617: see ibid., pp. 8–36. For Hogg's report, see ibid., pp. 45–8; also W.D. Hogg to Borden, 7 December 1915, Borden Papers, vol. 73, f. OC 327, p. 38304. On pensions, see CHC *Debates*, 18 May 1916, pp. 4150–1.
23 Morgan, *Men and Women* (1912), pp. 15, 821
24 Ibid., p. 1104; Fialkowski, *Todd*
25 Fialkowski, *Todd*, pp. 306–7; RG 38, vol. 200, f. 8-67, parts 1–2
26 Todd to Marjory Todd, 3 October 1915, quoted in Fialkowski, *Todd*, p. 309
27 Ibid., September 1915, p. 308
28 Ibid., 8 October, 22 October 1915, pp. 312–13
29 Ibid., 7 November 1915, p. 314 (Clouston died in 1912).
30 On Canadian 'progressivism,' see Brown, *Borden*, vol. 1, pp. 129–35; Humphreys, 'Ontario "Progressive" Conservatism.'
31 Hogg to Borden, 7 December 1915, Borden Papers, vol. 73, OC 327, p. 38307
32 Todd to director of medical services, 10 November 1915, RG 9, II B 2, vol. 3585, f. 22-5-2, part 1
33 Todd to Sir Adam Beck, 15 November 1915, RG 38, vol. 200, f. 8-67, part 1
34 Ibid. (italics in original)
35 Ibid. See also Todd to Dobell, 12 April 1916, ibid.
36 'Recommendations of the Pensions and Claims Board, CEF, as to Pensions and Other Matters,' section VII, RG 9, II B 2, vol. 3583, f. 22-4-23; also in Canada, *Sessional Papers*, 185, 1916, pp. 48–56, at p. 49
37 Todd to Rosanna Todd, 18 January 1916, as quoted in Fialkowski, *Todd*, p. 321
38 'Recommendations,' p. 225 (the board proposed $360 per annum as a 'decent livelihood' for a private soldier).
39 Fialkowski, *Todd*, pp. 323–4
40 See CHC *Debates*, 31 January 1916, pp. 440ff
41 Ibid., 13 March 1916, pp. 1654ff (Borden, pp. 1660–3). The committee was announced on 14 March 1916 (p. 1704), and enlarged a week later (p. 1990).
42 Ibid., 18 May 1916 (Nickle, p. 4144)
43 *Special Committee, 1916*, p. 27. The American Army's disability pensions in 1916 were based on the specific injury, regardless of rank.
44 See J.W. Borden, 'Memorandum comparing Canadian Pensions ...,' ibid., pp. 11–13. On 'alternative pensions,' see Hodge, 'Pensions Administration,' p. 41.
45 See *Special Committee, 1916*, p. 41.
46 Ibid., pp. 42–6
47 *Special Committee, 1916*, rec. (7), p. 3
48 Ibid., rec. (9), p. 4; CHC *Debates*, 18 May 1916, p. 4135
49 *Special Committee, 1916*, rec. (9), p. 4
50 *Special Committee, 1916*, pp. 40ff; CHC *Debates*, 18 May 1916, p. 4148
51 *Special Committee, 1916*, rec. (11), p. 4
52 CHC *Debates*, 18 May 1916, p. 4147
53 *Special Committee, 1916*, rec. (17), pp. 5–6
54 CHC *Debates*, 18 May 1916, p. 4132

55 Ibid., pp. 4137–8
56 PC 1334, 3 June 1916
57 See PC 1567, 13 July 1916; PC 1881, 19 August 1916; PC 2270, 23 September 1916.
58 Morgan, *Canadian Men and Women*, pp. 973–4; Bannerman, 'The Biggest Spender,' pp. 225–30
59 On Labatt, see S.C. Mewburn to R.L. Borden, n.d., Borden Papers, vol. 243, f. RLB 2687, pp. 136056–7
60 Todd, diary, 5 September 1916, quoted in Fialkowski, *Todd*, p. 326
61 Todd to Allan, 23 February 1916, RG 9, III B 2, vol. 3583, f. 22-4-2, part 1
62 On procedures, see 'Instructions and a Table of Incapacities for the Guidance of Physicians and Surgeons, 5 February 1917,' ibid., vol. 3580 f. 22-4-0, p. 151.
63 Ibid., p. 152
64 See *Special Committee, 1917*, p. 1087.
65 Ibid.
66 'Instructions,' pp. 146ff. See also RG 38, vol. 200, f. 8-67, part 2 (Todd File).
67 'Instructions,' pp. 152–8ff; Todd to Rosanna Todd, 27 April 1917, quoted in Fialkowski, *Todd*, p. 330
68 *Special Committee, 1917*, p. 1053
69 Ibid., p. 1064
70 Todd to Beck, 15 November 1915, RG 38, vol. 200, file 8-67, part 1
71 Pensions and Claims Board, RG 9, III B 2, vol. 3583, f. 22-4-3, p. 227
72 CHC *Debates*, 18 May 1916, p. 4147
73 The 1917 Special Committee (at p. 962) was told that of the total of 13,826 men returned by the end of March 1917, 3,514 had suffered wounds, 670 were tubercular, 180 were insane, and 7,066 suffered from other diseases. Others were over or under age. A Hollerith tabulation of returned men from 1 July to 30 September 1917 found 32 per cent suffering from war wounds or injuries, compared with a variety of mental and physical disabilities present in a large majority (Borden Papers, vol. 98, f. OC 493, p. 52745).
74 *Special Committee, 1917*, pp. 1053–4
75 Todd to Marjory Todd, 10 November 1915, quoted in Fialkowski, *Todd*, p. 315
76 Todd diary, 17 March 1916, ibid., p. 324
77 Ibid., 5 September 1916, p. 327; on the MHC, see diary, 30 June 1916, p. 327.
78 J.L. Todd to Lt-Col. A.H. Thompson, 14 December 1916, RG 38, vol. 182, f. 8564
79 Todd to Scammell, 27 December 1916, ibid., vol. 200, f. 8-67, part 1
80 Todd to Rosanna Todd, 1 October 1918, quoted in Fialkowski, *Todd*, p. 344
81 ['JL Todd Major, CAMC,'], 'Returned Soldiers'; see also Todd, 'The French System,' and Todd and Kidner, 'The Re-training of Disabled Men.'
82 'Staff transferred to the Board of Pension Commissioners,' RG 24, vol. 6540, f. HQ 650-30-1
83 *Special Committee, 1917*, pp. 141, 151
84 Ibid., pp. 982–7; *Toronto Telegram*, 20 April 1917
85 *Special Committee, 1917*, pp. 1174–7

86 Ibid., p. 1196
87 Ibid., p. 1248
88 Ibid., pp. 1250–1
89 Ibid., pp. 1249–50
90 Ibid., p. 1252
91 Ibid., pp. 1070, 1076–9, 1177–80
92 On Sergeant-Major Whitton, see ibid., pp. 784–6, 1221.
93 See *Special Committee, 1917*, pp. xxix–xxx, on the Board of Pension Commissioners.
94 Ibid., pp. 1060ff
95 Ibid., pp. 785–6, 906, 922–3, and passim
96 Ibid., 1179–80 (Todd to Ames, 16 May 1917)
97 Todd diary, 27 April 1917, quoted in Fialkowski, *Todd*, p. 330

Chapter 4: Voices from the Ranks

1 Scammell, *Provision of Employment*, p. 10
2 *Special Committee, 1917*, pp. 432–4; on Montreal, see *CAR*, 1915, p. 334; Lighthall to George T. Denison, 17 December 1915, McGill University, Rare Books and Special Collections, W.D. Lighthall Papers; The Khaki League, *Report for 1915*, p. 7 and passim.
3 *Special Committee, 1917*, pp. 326–8, 330 (on Ottawa, see ibid., pp. 303, 305–6).
4 Ibid., pp. 874–5
5 On the club, see Scammell to F.W. Peters, 8 April 1916, RG 38, vol. 138, f. 14-4-A, BC, and passim; Markham to Lougheed, 20 December 1915, Borden Papers, vol. 53, f. OC 238(1), pp. 23481–3; J.R.V. Dunlop to Scammell, 15 November 1915, RG 38, vol. 138 f. 14-4-A, BC; Dunlop to Lougheed, 3 December 1915, ibid., On Markham in an earlier role, see Morton, *Ministers and Generals*, pp. 124–5, 146, 148.
6 *Special Committee, 1917*, pp. 865–73; T.S. Ewart to Sam Hughes, 8 September 1915, RG 38, vol. 137, f. 7-12, part 1; G.F. Carruthers to C.W. Rowley, 17 August 1915, ibid., vol. 198, f. 6091
7 *Special Committee, 1917*, p. 964
8 Ibid., pp. 1256–7
9 On experience in the ranks, see Winter, *Death's Men*, pp. 37–62; Bird, *Ghosts Have Warm Hands*; Kerr, *Shrieks and Crashes* and *Arms and the Maple Leaf*.
10 *Special Committee, 1917*, pp. 1162–3
11 Ibid., p. 851
12 Invalided Soldiers Commission, *Occupational Therapy and Curative Workshops*, Scammell Collection (in possession of authors)
13 Kidner, 'Vocational Work,' p. 145
14 See, for example, the arguments on social control advanced by Piven and Cloward in *Regulating the Poor*.
15 For one (admittedly untypical) soldier's attitude to his experience in the ranks, see Francis, *Frank H. Underhill*, pp. 39–42.
16 Prost, *Les Anciens Combattants*, vol. 1, p. 51. On Canadian veterans before 1914, see W.D. Otter scrapbooks passim (in possession of authors).

17 *Special Committee, 1917*, pp. 435–6 (Doble), 475–6 (Brown)
18 Ibid., pp. 441, 479, 935
19 Ibid., p. 380
20 The phrase is from R.S. Somerville, 'Canadian Celebrities, No. 69: Mr. W.D. Lighthall,' *Canadian Magazine*, XXVI (1905–6), p. 554; on Lighthall, see Morgan, *Canadian Men and Women*, p. 657, and Rutherford, ed., *Saving the Canadian City*, pp. x–xviii, 74.
21 Lighthall to general secretary, GAR, 18 June 1915, Lighthall Papers.
22 See Montreal *Star*, 17 November 1915. See also Beath, *Grand Army of the Republic*.
23 Lighthall to C.F. Winter, 3 November 1915, Lighthall Papers; Lighthall to Wilson, 15 November 1915, ibid.
24 *The Veteran*, I, 1 (December 1917), pp. 14–15
25 Lighthall to editor, *Sydney Bulletin*, 23 February 1916, Lighthall Papers.
26 On Church, see, for example, *Canadian Municipal Journal*, XIII, 12 (December 1917), p. 501; *Special Committee, 1917*, Memorandum, 20 March 1917, pp. 793–801; testimony, pp. 713–22; and Wilson, *Ontario and the First World War*, on saluting, p. xcix.
27 Cairns and Yetman, *The Veteran Movement*, vol. 1, pp. 1–2
28 *CAR*, 1917, p. 535; *Special Committee, 1917*, pp. 884, 899–900, 924–6. See W.G. Murrin to E.W. Hamber, BCRSC, 14 March, RG 38, vol. 138, f. 14-4-A, BC; Vancouver *Sun*, 22 February 1916.
29 *Special Committee, 1917*, pp. 930–1. On B.C. organizing, see *The Veteran*, IV, 10 (September 1921).
30 *Special Committee, 1917*, p. 467. For the Ottawa version, see Wilson, - *Ontario and the First World War*, p. 44, B–32.
31 Todd to Scammell, 27 December 1916, RG 38, vol. 200, f. 8-67, part 1
32 Todd to Scammell, 3 January 1917, ibid.
33 Scammell to secretaries, provincial commissions, 17 January 1917, ibid.
34 Scammell to Todd, 2 January 1917, ibid.
35 Fiset to Thomas M. Mulvey, 22 January 1917, RG 24, vol. 56, f. HQ 649-1-69
36 Doherty to Fiset, 26 January 1917, ibid.
37 CHC *Debates*, 5 February 1917, pp. 459–60
38 Ibid., 6 February 1917, p. 524; 7 February 1917, p. 587. Parliament adjourned until 22 April 1917.
39 *CAR*, 1917, p. 536 (which erroneously suggests the preliminary meeting was in Montreal)
40 *Special Committee, 1917*, pp. 577–8
41 PAC, Records of the Royal Canadian Legion; minute book of the Great War Veterans Association, pp. 1–8; Manitoba *Free Press*, 10–12 April 1917
42 Manitoba *Free Press*, 13 April 1917; *Special Committee, 1917*, p. 1212
43 *Special Committee, 1917*, pp. 1198–9
44 Palmer, *Patterns of Prejudice*, p. 42, Manitoba *Free Press*, 13 April 1917
45 Manitoba *Free Press*, 13 April 1917, and *Special Committee, 1917*, p. 1193; *CAR*, 1917, p. 536; on Purney, see pp. 13n61, 71 in connection with the Fenian Raid Bounty. On Knight, see *The Legionary* (September 1926).
46 Manitoba *Free Press*, 13 April 1917
47 *Special Committee, 1917*, p. 1196; see pp. 1201–3 on manipulation of figures.

48 Ibid., p. 1196
49 GWVA minutes, p. 23. On membership, see *CAR*, 1918, p. 585.
50 Knight to Borden, 14 June 1917, Borden Papers, vol. 221, f. RLB 1546, p. 124010; Hearst to Borden, 4 July 1917, ibid., p. 124016; Knight to Meighen, 27 March 1918, PAC, Meighen Papers, vol. 12, f. 65 (the incorporation issue was not resolved until September 1918).
51 *CAR*, 1917, pp. 537, 758, 760
52 See Morton, 'Polling the Soldier Vote,' pp. 44ff.
53 See Carrigan, *Canadian Party Platforms*, p. 77. Veterans also recalled Borden's speech before Vimy Ridge; see Bowering, *Service*, p. 3.
54 *CAR*, 1917, p. 538
55 Ibid., pp. 636-7
56 Morton, 'Polling the Soldier Vote,' pp. 51-2, 55
57 Knight to Borden, 8 March 1918, Borden Papers, vol. 241, f. RLB 2504, p. 134909
58 Knight to Borden, petition, 26 March 1918, ibid., p. 154929
59 Ibid., 8 March 1918, p. 134904
60 Minutes of conference, 28 March 1918, ibid., p. 134906. See Smith, 'Emergency Government in Canada,' pp. 437-8; Entz, 'The German-Language Press,' pp. 62-4.
61 See 7-8 George V, c. 70, 20 September 1917
62 Proceedings of the First Convention of the Army and Navy Veterans in Canada (Winnipeg 1918). See also Manitoba *Free Press*, 11-16 May 1918.
63 *Special Committee, 1918*, pp. 134-53; 'Recommendations re the Final Disposal of Cases of Neurasthenia and So-called Shell Shock,' ibid., pp. 156-7; see also Todd testimony, ibid., pp. 237-8.
64 Ibid., p. 21
65 Ibid., p. 69
66 Ibid., p. 95
67 Ibid., p. 68
68 Ibid. (Archibald), pp. 246, 258-9
69 Ibid. (on Child's case), pp. 96-7 and (W.F. Nickle) 112
70 Ibid., p. 23
71 Ibid., p. 34
72 Ibid., pp. 171-8, 229
73 Ibid., pp. 17, 28; Ottawa *Journal*, 8 May 1918; Toronto *Daily Star*, 9 May 1918; Stevens to Rowell, 23 April 1918, cited in CHC *Debates*, 15 May 1918, p. 1981
74 *Special Committee, 1918*, pp. 217-19
75 Ibid., pp. 222-5; see also Ross to Borden, 4 April 1918, Borden Papers, vol. 238, f. RLB 2366, p. 133063.
76 *Special Committee, 1918*, pp. 219, 223, 225-6
77 Ibid., pp. 285, also 274-6, 285-7; Archibald to Rowell, 10 May 1918, ibid., pp. 296-8
78 Todd to Rosanna Todd, 17 May 1918, quoted in Fialkowski, *Todd*, p. 342
79 See Mewburn, CHC *Debates*, 10 May 1918, pp. 1692-3; Toronto *Daily Star*, 10 May 1918; Mewburn to Borden, n.d., Borden Papers, vol. 243, f. RLB 2687, pp. 136056-60; Borden to Labatt, 10 May 1918, ibid., p. 136060.
80 See Ross to Rowell, 8 May 1918, *Special Committee, 1918*, p. 296. The vet-

erans were also divided on Labatt; see *The Veteran*, I, 8 (June 1918); GWVA minutes, p. 69.

81 CHC *Debates*, 23 May 1918, p. 2491

82 On Bradbury, see *Special Committee, 1918*, pp. 200–6.

83 CHC *Debates*, 23 May 1918, p. 2485; *Special Committee, 1918*, pp. x–xiv

84 Todd to Rosanna Todd, 24 February 1919, quoted in Fialkowski, *Todd*, pp. 348–9. On Ross, see Bannerman, 'Biggest Spender,' p. 225.

85 On Knight, see GWVA minutes, p. 39; on Loughnan, see H.W. Hart in *The Veteran*, IV, 10 (September 1921). On his background, see *The Veteran*, IV, 11 (October 1921), p. 7; F.W. Peters to Scammell, 8 February 1916, RG 38, vol. 138, f. 14-4-A, BC.

86 *The Veteran*, I, 1 (December 1917), p. 7. On the magazine, see minute books, *The Veteran Ltd.*, p. 25, PAC, CanVet Archives; GWVA minutes, pp. 67, 80.

87 *The Veteran*, I, 6 (May 1918), p. 7

88 *CAR*, 1918, p. 586–7

89 *British Columbia Federationist*, 2 and 9 August 1918; Robin, *Radical Politics*, p. 152

90 Toronto *Daily Star*, 1 and 9 August 1918 and passim. Varley was defeated on 19 August winning 4,297 votes to Cody's 9,135. Varley won at the Spadina Hospital by a vote of 69 to 19, but at the Base Hospital (where conscripts were treated) he lost by a vote of 17 to 11. See Toronto *Daily Star*, 20 August 1918.

91 Ibid., 30 July, 1 August 1918

92 Ibid., 3 August 1918

93 Ibid., 2 August 1918

94 Ibid., and Toronto *Globe* and Toronto *Mail and Empire*, 3 August 1918. See also Wilson, *Ontario and the First World War*, pp. lxcii, B-43.

95 'Report of the Investigation into the August Riots,' Toronto *Telegram*, 10 October 1918, Ontario Archives, T.L. Church Papers; *CAR*, 1918, p. 586

96 *Saturday Night*, 17 August 1918

97 Toronto *Daily Star*, 3 August 1918. See, in contrast, Toronto *Telegram*, 6 August 1918.

98 *The Veteran*, I, 10 (September 1918), p. 13

Chapter 5: The 'Department of Demobilization'

1 Lougheed to Sir Adam Beck, 17 December 1915, RG 38, vol. 200, f. 8-67

2 See Knight's testimony, *Special Committee, 1917*, p. 1075.

3 Lougheed's attitude was reported by F.B. McCurdy, his former parliamentary secretary. See CHC *Debates*, 5 July 1919, p. 4678 (Lougheed had apparently wanted six members, not twenty, and claimed that the commission was political and unwieldy).

4 On the provincial commissions, see minutes of provincial secretaries' meeting, 19 March 1917, RG 38, vol. 139, f. 1838.

5 On Hughes and his problems, see Bliss, *A Canadian Millionaire*, pp. 238ff, and Morton, *Peculiar Politics*, chapter 5 and passim.

6 Kemp to Borden, 8 June 1917, Kemp Papers, vol. 107, f. 1

7 On Potter, see Adami papers, RG 9, III B 2, vol. 3753, pp. 4–5; Macphail,

Medical Services, p. 316. On the Bruce report, see Col. H.A. Bruce, *Canadian Army Medical Services*; Bruce, *Politics and the CAMC*; Morton, *Peculiar Politics*, pp. 86–7, 94–5, 103–5; and Macphail, *Medical Services*, pp. 156–69.

8 On Thompson's qualifications, see *Special Committee, 1917*, 991. There were two physician-members of the MHC; Lt-Col. Thomas Walker from Saint John was seventy-seven, and Dean F.J. Shepherd of McGill University was sixty-six. See Morgan, *Canadian Men and Women*, pp. 1016, 1137.

9 See Borden Papers, vol. 53, f. OC 238, passim.

10 On medical manpower, see Macphail, *Medical Services*.

11 On Marlow, see *Canadian Who's Who*, 1920, p. 836.

12 On the report, see *Special Committee, 1917*, pp. 166–80, 182–230, 805–7; *CAR*, 1916, p. 381, and 1917, p. 533. Medical officers, as non-combatants, continued to be denied powers of command outside the medical setting, but older officers could recall a time when any authority was denied them outside the Army Medical Corps. The relative rank issue is briefly introduced by Nicholson, *Seventy Years of Service*, p. 15.

13 On Marlow's charges, see Pardee, *Special Committee, 1917*, pp. 58–9; Surgeon-General Jones to Kemp, 28 March 1917, Kemp Papers, vol. 105.

14 Kemp to Borden, 28 February 1917, Kemp Papers, vol. 107; PC 764, 20 March 1917; *CAR*, 1917, p. 533

15 Kemp to Robertson, 28 February 1917, Kemp Papers, vol. 105, f. 6

16 *Special Committee, 1917*, pp. 166–227

17 Ibid., pp. 599–600 and passim

18 Ibid., pp. 724–69; Toronto *Daily Star*, 24 March 1917

19 *Special Committee*, 1917, p. 1233

20 Ibid., p. 1233

21 Ibid., p. 1239 On Fotheringham, see Fotheringham Papers, vol. 5; Morton, 'Cadet Movement.'

22 *Special Committee, 1917*, pp. xviii–xxxviii, especially pp. xxxiv–xxxv.

23 Kemp to Borden, 8 June 1917, Borden Papers, vol. 71, f. OC 323, p. 37085; Kemp to Borden, 28 June 1917, Kemp Papers, vol. 107

24 See Fotheringham to Macphail, 1 March 1917, PAC, Macphail Papers; Fotheringham memorandum, 10 July 1917, Kemp Papers, vol. 107; Lt-Col. E.S. Ryerson to Fotheringham, 29 June 1917, PAC, Fotheringham papers, f. 15; Fotheringham to Dr J. Gordon Wilson, 28 July 1917, ibid., f. 19.

25 *Special Committee, 1917*, p. 1200.

26 See McLennan, *What the Military Hospitals Commission Is Doing*. On publicity acitivity, see *Report of the MHC*, 1917, pp. 88–9. Despite J.L. Todd's recommendation of Stephen Leacock, the commission settled for Howard A. Kennedy to manage its publicity branch.

27 McLennan, *What the MHC Is Doing*, pp. 16–20

28 Ryerson to Fotheringham, 16 August 1917, Fotheringham Papers, vol. 4, f. 15. See Fotheringham to Lt-Col. G. Grant, 3 September 1917, ibid., vol. 2, f. G; Fotheringham to Patch, 5 September 1917, ibid., f. P.

29 Armstrong to Mewburn, 6 October 1917, Kemp Papers, vol. 107, f. 1

30 Unsigned document dated 15 October 1917, ibid. The MHC had chosen an inopportune moment to ignore a wealthy contractor in awarding the construction of its new Montreal hospital to a firm run by a veteran. On the dis-

pute, see Bate McMahon to Military Hospitals Commission, 29 September 1917, Borden Papers, vol. 118, f. RLB 1930, p. 127992; R.S. Low memorandum, 22 October 1917, ibid., pp. 127994–5; Borden to Lougheed, 31 October 1917, ibid., p. 128071.

31 Mewburn report on meeting of 15 October 1917, Kemp Papers, vol. 107, f. 10

32 Minutes of the Military Hospitals Commission, 15–16 November 1917, RG 38, vol. 226, f. 8640. See also Jones to Fotheringham, 17 November 1917, Fotheringham Papers, vol. 2. f. J.

33 On the Halifax explosion, see Metson, ed., *The Halifax Explosion*, Maj. W.F. Adams to Sharples, 7 December 1917, RG 38, vol. 155, f. 899, part 1.

34 See, for example, McLennan, *What the MHC Is Doing*, p. 15.

35 R.W. Coulthard memorandum, 30 September 1919, ibid. On Chesley, see F.A. Ladd to Coulthard, 24 September 1919, ibid. See also F.S. Sexton to Scammell, 12 December 1917, RG 38, vol. 155, f. 899, part 1; Sexton to Kidner, 27 December 1917, ibid., and passim. Individual disabled civilians could be included in classes if no soldier was excluded. In fact, few applied and even fewer satisfied the Disabled Soldiers Training Board.

36 Toronto *Daily Star*, 23 January 1918; Toronto *Mail & Empire*, 24 January 1918; J.S. McLennan to Borden, 25 January 1918, Borden Papers, vol. 98, f. OC 493, p. 52633. For other reactions, see Beck to Borden, 7 February 1918, ibid., pp. 56215–2; Hector McInnes to Borden, 1 February 1918, ibid., p. 52647 (predicting an open fight in which he would support the MHC).

37 PC 3264, 29 November 1917; PC 3443, 22 December 1917. On the negotiations, see Adami Papers, RG 9, MHC file, pp. 17–24; E.C. Ashton to Cabinet War Committee, n.d., Kemp Papers, vol. 107, f. 1; Rowell to Borden, 23 January 1918, Borden Papers, vol. 98, f. OC 493, p. 52631.

38 See Clarence Smith to Borden, 29 January 1918, Borden Papers, vol. 98, f. OC 493, pp. 53642–4. Fotheringham believed that Lougheed's work in the Senate influenced the cabinet (Fotheringham to Lt-Col. F.C. McTavish, 5 February 1918, Fotheringham Papers, vol. 3, f. MC).

39 R.D. Gill to Borden, 24 January 1918, Borden Papers, vol. 98, f. OC 495.

40 On the arguments, see the Scammell paper attached to Minutes of Provincial Secretaries Meeting, 19 March 1917, RG 38, vol. 139, f. 1838.

41 Ashton memorandum, 30 January 1918, Borden Papers, vol. 53, f. OC 238, pp. 25792–4. Lt-Col. John McComb and Maj. John Russell, 'Report on the Care and Rehabilitation of the Disabled Soldier in Canada,' ibid., pp. 25796–802, underlining the dimensions of the problem Ashton presented to his minister.

42 Lougheed to Borden, 14 February 1918, Borden Papers, vol. 98, f. OC 493, p. 52659; Mewburn to Borden, 19 February 1918, Kemp Papers, vol. 107, f. 1; PC 432, 433, 434, 21 February 1918

43 Scammell to Smeaton White, 1 March 1918, RG 38, vol. 162, f. 1847 (copies sent to all MHC members)

44 G. Vankoughnet to Armstrong, n.d., RG 38, vol. 163, f. 1832

45 Sharples to Lt-Col. R.S. Wilson, 9 March 1918, ibid., f. 1847

46 Macphail, *Medical Services*, p. 322

47 Scammell to H.E. Saxby, 5 March 1918, RG 38, vol. 163, f. 1847.

48 Maj. C.V. Currie, 'History of the CAMC in MD 2,' Adami Records, RG 9, III B 2, vol. 3754, p. 5; *CAR*, 1918, p. 560; Pettigrew, *The Silent Enemy*

49 *Special Committee, 1917*, p. 453
50 On the organization of the DSCR, see *CAR*, 1923, p. 900; *Department of Soldiers' Civil Re-Establishment* (Toronto 1917) (in the Scammell Collection), p. 5; and *Reconstruction*, 1 (December 1918). On Bell, see Morgan, *Canadian Men and Women* (1912), p. 86, and *Reconstruction*, 1 (May 1918), p. 2.
51 On the ISC, see *Report of ISC* (Ottawa 1918), in Borden Papers, vol. 98, f. OC 493, pp. 52685ff, PC 445 and 446, 23 February 1918. On McCurdy, see CHC *Debates*, 5 July 1919, pp. 4676–80.
52 On Healey, see *Reconstruction*, 1 (October 1918), p. 15.
53 Lougheed to Borden, 14 February 1918, Borden Papers, vol. 98, f. OC 493, p. 52659. On prostheses, see England, *Twenty Million Veterans*, pp. 46–7, *Special Committee, 1920*, pp. 168–74, 222–30.
54 DSCR, *Invalided Soldiers Commission*, p. 19
55 McCuaig, 'From Social Reform to Social Service,' p. 486; DSCR, *Summary of Report, Board of Tuberculosis Consultants* (Ottawa, December 1920), pp. 12–13
56 DSCR, *Invalided Soldiers Commission*, p. 25
57 Segsworth, *Retraining*, p. 24; DSCR, *Invalided Soldiers Commission*, pp. 16–17
58 On the blind, see DSCR, *Invalided Soldiers Commission*, pp. 24–5; RG 38, vol. 138, file 8638.
59 Segsworth, *Retraining*, p. 164. On the 'disability line,' see RG 38, vol. 200, f. 2147 passim.
60 A.T. Jewitt to M.B. Baker, 30 July 1918, RG 38, vol. 200, f. 2147; Harold Innis to T.B. Kidner, 17 June 1918, ibid.; F.H. Riches to Segsworth, 29 June 1918 and reply, Segsworth to Riches, 4 July 1918, ibid. Admitting the legal loophole, Segsworth pleaded with Riches to keep it a secret: 'I might point out that if this were put generally into effect, the public institutions in the country would be unable to handle it and the result could be that in trying to do a large thing poorly we could not do a small thing well.' On Innis's experiences see Creighton, *Harold Adams Innis* (Innis's M.A. research for McMaster University was entitled 'The Returned Soldier.')
61 Segsworth, *Retraining*, p. 74 (see also p. 164); Hunt, *Nova Scotia's Part*, pp. 338–40
62 See W.R. Caldwell to director of vocational training, 9 September 1919, RG 38, vol. 225, f. 18-2-NB; Parkinson to Caldwell, minute, n.d., ibid.; J.V. Boate to Parkinson, 6 September 1919, ibid.
63 Segsworth to William Nickle MP, draft, 3 August 1917, RG 38, vol. 232, f. 2311 (the rude personal comments were deleted in the final draft). The history is summarized in Segsworth to Lougheed, 25 November 1918, RG 38, vol. 232, f. 2309; Macpherson to Lougheed, 13 January 1917, ibid., f. 2310.
64 Lougheed to Falconer, 4 November 1918, RG 38. vol. 232, f. 2310
65 Draft agreement between the Department of Soldiers' Civil Re-establishment and the Soldiers' Aid Commission, December 1918, ibid.
66 For example of a job survey, see Thomas Carlyle, 'Report on Prospects of Employing Disabled Soldiers as Elevator Agents, RG 38, vol. 215, f. 7259.
67 McMurtrie, 'The Canadian Publicity Campaign,' p. 150
68 *Special Committee, 1916*, p. 323
69 *Special Committee, 1917*, p. 52

70 Ibid., p. 52, 998; see the case of Wilfrid Lavelee, 'a dangerous moron,' in RG 38, vol. 218, f. 8392.
71 For a contemporary view, see Russell, 'Psychogenetic Conditions in Soldiers,' pp. 227–37; and Ames, 'Prevention of War Neuroses,' pp. 207–10. On the subject see Tom Brown, 'Shell Shock,' pp. 309–23. (The term 'shell-shock' arose from an initial erroneous assumption that the mental condition was caused by the physiological consequences of a nearby exploding shell.)
72 DSCR, *Invalided Soldiers Commission*, pp. 26–7. On Farrar, see *Special Committee, 1917*, pp. 691–2.
73 Lt-Col. John McComb and Maj. John Russell, 'Report on the Care and Rehabilitation of the Disabled Soldier in Canada,' Borden Papers, vol. 53, f. OC 238, p. 25800.
74 Minutes of meeting of provincial representatives and Military Hospitals Commission, 15 January 1919, RG 38, vol. 139, f. 8575, part 1
75 Dr C.M. Hincks to Bell, 18 November 1918, ibid., vol. 217, f. 8384 et seq.; Hincks to J. Grant Cunningham, 21 September 1918, on agreement with delegation, ibid., vol. 205, f. 8362 et seq. On the inspection, see ibid., vol. 217, f. 8384 and below at pp. 132–3. On Clarke see *Special Committee, 1916*, pp. 32–4.
76 See Brown and Cook, *Canada, 1896–1921*, pp. 198–203.
77 *CAR*, 1916, pp. 379–80; minutes of the Military Hospitals Commission, 6–7 September 1916, RG 38, vol. 226, f. 8610 (McGibbon-Gill resolution)
78 Scammell to A.F. Batty, 10 January 1917, Borden Papers, vol. 71, f. OC 323, p. 36995
79 *Special Committee, 1917*, p. 1155. On the results of the NSB questionnaire, see J.S. McLennan, 'Proposals for Future Development of the Work,' Borden Papers, vol. 98, f. OC 493, p. 52742.
80 *Special Committee, 1917*, pp. 1156–7
81 On the British system, see Graubard, 'Military Demobilization,' pp. 297ff. On British reconstruction, see Johnson, *Land Fit for Heroes*; Morgan, *Portrait of a Progressive*, pp. 68–81; Tawney, 'The Abolition of Economic Controls,' pp. 129–86; with revisionist critique by Cline, 'Winding Down the War Economy.'
82 See Carman, *The Return of the Troops*, p. 32.
83 McLennan and McKeen, *Report on the Inter-Allied Conference*, p. 17
84 McLennan, 'Proposals,' p. 52743
85 *Special Committee, 1917*, p. xviii
86 CHC *Debates*, 10 April 1918, p. 613
87 On reconstruction activities, see *CAR*, 1918, pp. 488, 556ff. The legislation is 8–9 Geo. V, c. 21 (1918). On employment offices and government policy in the reconstruction period, see Struthers, *No Fault of Their Own*, pp. 16–22; Sautter, 'Employment Service,' pp. 106–12. On post-discharge pay, see PC 1091, 18 April 1917; PC 1362, 18 May 1917; PC 2849, 11 October 1917.
88 PC 2631, 21 September 1917; PC 3262, 29 November 1917; PC 2032, 17 August 1918. See survey and commentary, A.F. Duguid Papers, vol. 2, f. 4. On U.S. reconstruction policy, see England, *Twenty Million Veterans*, pp. 19–30; Samuelson and Hagen, *After the War*, esp. pp. 1–7, and Wecter, *When Johnny Comes Marching Home*, p. 307.
89 Gourlay, *Statistical Account of Upper Canada*, vol. 1, pp. 549–50. On

Perth, see Craig, *Upper Canada: The Formative Years*, pp. 88–9, and Martin, 'The Regiment de Watteville.'

90 On soldiers as settlers, see England, 'Disbanded Soldiers,' p. 9 and passim; Morton, *History of the Canadian West*, p. 592; and Raudzens, 'A Successful Military Settlement.'

91 England, 'Disbanded Soldiers,' pp. 15–16; Martin, '*Dominion Lands Policy*' p. 166; W.J. Roche, CHC *Debates*, 7 May 1916, p. 1160

92 On the Kapuskasing development, see Morton, 'Internment Operations in Canada,' p. 30 and passim; PAC, Otter Diaries, 17–19 November 1914. On Black, see Morgan, *Canadian Men and Women*, 1912, p. 106.

93 Scammell, *Employment*, p. 9; on agriculture settlement, see pp. 7–10.

94 *A Cheerful Chat with Private Pat*, p. 3. See McMurtrie, 'Reconstructing the War Cripple in Alberta,' pp. 229ff. The prominence of agriculture in the thinking about invalids is apparent from *Reconstruction*, the MHC and DSCR magazine that appeared from November 1917 to the end of the war.

95 DSCR, *Invalided Soldiers Commission* (Ottawa 1918), p. 39

96 On Haggard's journey, see Haggard, *The After-War Settlement*. See also *CAR*, 1916, p. 380; Shultz, 'The Great War and Empire Settlement,' pp. 99–100.

97 *Report of the Commission on Agricultural Production*, pp. 18–19. See also Toronto *Mail and Empire*, 12 July 1916.

98 See E.B. Robertson and J.H. Grisdale to Roche and Burrell, 12 December 1916, Borden Papers, vol. 71, f. OC 323 (2), pp. 36959–61. The ministers were furious that Sir Thomas White and a small cabinet committee had been appointed without their knowledge to draft a bill: see Roche to Borden, 18 December 1916, ibid., p. 36970.

99 On the Ontario experience, see *Special Committee, 1917*, pp. 707–12, and Oliver, *G. Howard Ferguson*, pp. 70–1.

100 *Special Committee, 1917*, p. 507–8 (for testimony of H.W. Hart, see ibid., p. 937).

101 On the GWVA resolutions, see Manitoba *Free Press*, 13 April 1917.

102 CHC *Debates*, 7 May 1917, p. 1160; 20 July 1917, p. 3619

103 Ibid., 20 July 1917, p. 3620: Roche to Borden, 14 September 1915, Borden Papers, vol. 52, f. OC 237 (2)(b), pp. 25183–4

104 CHC *Debates*, 20 July 1917, p. 3620 (W.H. Pugsley)

105 Ibid., 25 July 1917, p. 3779

106 *The Veteran*, I, 3 (February 1918), pp. 8–9. On GWVA attitudes, see Knight to Borden, 3 October 1917, Borden Papers, vol. 255, f. RLB 1824, p. 126204; Knight to Borden, 21 January 1918, ibid., pp. 126267–8.

107 Maber to Meighen, 22 February 1918, RG 15, vol. 1126, f. 3850452

108 *SSB Report, 1921*, pp. 13, 25

109 *The Veteran*, I, 8 (July 1918), pp. 10, 27. See *CAR*, 1918, pp. 586–7, on progress.

110 See Meighen to Kemp, 5 November 1917, RG 9, III A 1, ser. 10, vol. 93, f. 10-12-44.

Chapter 6: The Year of the Bonus

1 PC 494, 20 February 1917, forbade more dependants to cross. PC 760, 1 April 1916, provided limited funds to assist their return. On policy, see J.W.

Borden to Philip Morris, 15 August 1917, RG 24, vol. 1736, f. HQ 54-11-6-50;
superintendent of immigration to private secretary, minister of militia and
defence, 30 March 1918, ibid., vol. 744, f. HQ 54-21-6-85. On problems, see
PAC, R.E.W. Turner Papers, vol. 12, f. 88.

2 Carman, *Return of the Troops*, pp. 31–6
3 *Overseas Demobilization Committee*, p. 3, Kemp Papers, vol. 137, f. D-2
and Borden Papers, vol. 196, f. OC 485A
3 On the results of the questionnaire, see Carman, *Return of the Troops*,
p. 145.
5 Ibid., pp. 18–21; *General Survey*, pp. 14–16.
6 *General Survey*, p. 4.
7 *CAR*, 1918, p. 557 (speech on 15 September 1918)
8 See Prang, *N.W. Rowell*, p. 269. Though Rowell played a prominant role in
re-establishment and reconstruction questions, those issues are not dealt with
in his biography; see p. 296.
9 On the progress of soldier settlement, see *Canadian Official Record*, 12 June
1919. On figures, see *CAR*, 1918, p. 586; on Crothers, see ibid., p. 491.
10 PC 2823, 15 November 1918
11 *General Survey*, pp. 9–12; GWVA minutes, 1–3 December 1918, pp. 91, 105,
109
12 On Daly, see Greene, *Who's Who and Why, 1921*, p. 446; Daly's presidency
of the Home Bank gave him a more substantial brush with Canadian history.
His loans of over a million dollars from his own bank contributed to the
crash of the bank in the summer of 1923. Thousands of depositors, many of
them fellow Catholics, were ruined by the bank's collapse. Daly and some of
his fellow bank directors, including the MHC's Clarence Smith, were charged.
Daly died before the trial, but Smith and others were sentenced to peni-
tentiary only to be rescued on appeal by the judicial conclusion that bank
directors could not be expected to know that the documents they signed or
the reports they approved were false. See *CAR*, 1923, pp. 284–6, and ibid.,
1924–5, pp. 582–7.
13 *General Survey*, p. 6
14 Ibid., pp. 6–7
15 On the IMB, see Bliss, *Flavelle*, pp. 382–8.
16 *General Survey*, pp. 36–8
17 Carman, *Return of the Troops*, pp. 144–8; *General Survey*, pp. 39–40;
'Memorandum on the Information and Service Branch,' 12 March 1919,
RG 38, vol. 171, f. 2374
18 White to Borden, 8 December 1918, Kemp Papers, vol. 137, f. D-2; Carman,
Return of the Troops, pp. 12–16, 76–7
19 See Gilbert, *Winston S. Churchill*, vol. 4, chapter 10, pp. 181–96; Graubard,
'Military Demobilization,' pp. 300–1.
20 GWVA minutes, executive committee, 4 December 1918, p. 124; White to
Borden, 5 December 1918, with resolution, Kemp Papers, vol. 137, f. D-2a;
Harris Turner's Weekly, 14 December 1918. On Canadian demobilization,
see Swettenham, *The End of the War*, and Nicholson, *CEF*, pp. 530–1.
21 Currie to E.H. Macklin, 4 October 1918, PAC, Currie Papers, vol. 2, f. 3;
Currie to Kemp, 6 November 1918, Kemp Papers, vol. 137, f. D-2a, no. 8;
Nicholson, *CEF*, p. 528

22 Currie to Kemp, 18 December 1918, Kemp Papers, vol. 137, f. D-2a, no. 8. Kemp to Borden, 11 November 1918, ibid. A dissenting voice was heard in an undated petition bearing eighty-nine signatures of members of the 44th Battalion, addressed to Sir George Perley, ibid., vol. 135, f. C-63.

23 Currie to Kemp, 23 November 1918, ibid., vol. 137, f. D-2. For civilian apprehensions, see Mewburn, CHC *Debates*, 10 March 1919, p. 326. (Currie overlooked the fact that the Australians split their units on the basis of length of service, reducing a grievance that helped cause the Kinmel mutiny. See the text accompanying note 35.)

24 On procedures, see *Demobilization Instructions*, esp. 26–8; Carman, *Return of the Troops*, chapter 1 and passim; Nicholson, *CEF*, pp. 528–30; on married men, Borden to White, 18 December 1919, Kemp Papers, vol. 137, f. D-2; Currie Diary 17, 21, 23 January 1919.

25 Bishop, *The YMCA in the Great War*, pp. 342–3; *Report of the Ministry of Overseas Military Forces of Canada, 1918*, p. 478; Carman, *Return of the Troops*, p. 25

26 Carman, *Return of the Troops*, pp. 48–55; Corbett, *Henry Marshall Tory*, pp. 138–58

27 Mowat, *Britain between the Wars*, pp. 22–4. A list of British disturbances was compiled by the Overseas Ministry; see Col. Thomas Gibson, 'Canadian Troops Overseas and the British Press,' 30 July 1919, Borden Papers, vol. 114, f. OC 567, pp. 62615ff.

28 On the disturbances, see Desmond Morton, ' "Kicking and Complaining," ' pp. 338–9; A.F. Duguid, 'Disturbances in Canadian Camps and Areas, 1918–1919,' RG 24, vol. 1841, GAQ 10-39F; PAC, Sir Edward Kemp Papers, vols. 155, 160, 163.

29 See *Report of the Royal Commission on the Northland*, 25 January 1919. PC 3210, 31 December 1918, authorized the formation of the commission. On the report, see Carman, *Return of the Troops*, pp. 16–17; for Kemp's response, see Kemp to White, n.d., Kemp Papers, vol. 155, f. C-6; Kemp to White, 24 February 1919, Borden Papers, vol. 102, f. OC 515, p. 55813.

30 On the *Scandinavian*, see Mewburn to Kemp, 25 January 1919, Kemp Papers, vol. 135, f. C-3; Hogarth to Kemp, 17 February 1919, ibid.; report of Mrs Yeman, n.d., ibid.; Carman, *Return of the Troops*, p. 135.

31 Carman, *Return of the Troops*, pp. 131–8; Mewburn to Kemp, 9 January 1919, Turner Papers, vol. 12, f. 91; *General Survey*, pp. 20–1; The authority for paying third-class fares for wives and for children to the age of eighteen was conferred by PC 179, 29 January 1919.

32 Lt-Col. J.O. Smith to Major Macdonald, 11 March 1919, Turner Papers, vol. 12, f. 91

33 Kemp to White, 24 February 1919, Kemp Papers, vol. 153, f. D-4

34 Kemp to Mewburn, 6 February 1919, ibid., vol. 137, f. D-2

35 On the Kinmel riot, see Morton, ' "Kicking and Complaining," ' pp. 342–52. We gratefully acknowledge the assistance of Mr Brereton Geeenhous, Mr Robert Cousins, and Mr. R.E. Henley in expanding our knowledge of the Kinmel tragedy.

36 See London *Times*, 7–8 March 1919; also *Morning Post*, *Daily Chronicle*, *Daily Telegraph*. Lamb, *Mutinies*, pp. 21–7, uses these sources.

37 On 'monster ships,' see E.J. Foley to General Hogarth, 20 January 1919,

Kemp Papers, vol. 137, f. D-3. The admiralty had been reluctant to risk its biggest ships at Halifax, where the docks were too short. Their owners also preferred to send them to New York to regain Britain's share of the transatlantic traffic. The *Olympic* made one Halifax sailing in March.

38 Kemp to Lord Cromer, n.d., draft, Turner Papers, vol. 8, f. 50, p. 5603; memorandum of War Office conference, 21 June 1919, ibid., pp. 5600–4

39 Carman, *Return of the Troops*, pp. 24–5, 154; Kemp to McBrien, 14 November 1919, PAC, McBrien Papers, vol. 1, f. 1. (McBrien reported that by the end of 1919 five hundred destitute Canadians had asked for their passages. 'Imperials' included many Canadians who had served in the RAF, rejoined regiments, or served in such British organizations as the Inland Water Transport.)

40 Memo, H.J. Daly, n.d. [September 1918], Meighen Papers, vol. 12, f. 65, p. 6731

41 PC 3165, 21 December 1918; Montreal *Gazette*, 18 December 1921. See *Handbook for the Information of Former Members*. On clothing allowance, see Duguid, report, 2 July 1940, RG 24, vol. 1846, f. GAQ 11–43B

42 Carman, *Return of the Troops*, pp. 65–75, 77–8, 102–3

43 Ibid., pp. 82–5; see Toronto *Daily Star* and Toronto *Globe*, 20–21 March 1919, and Montreal *Gazette*, 12 March 1919.

44 On the 27th Battalion, see Masters, *The Winnipeg General Strike*, p. 77.

45 On the Toronto depot, see report, PAC, B.H. Richardson Papers; Carman, *Return of the Troops*, pp. 86–8.

46 Carman, *Return of the Troops*, p. 60. See also RG 38, vol. 171, f. 2375.

47 See *Back to Mufti* I, 1 February 1919, on Montreal; *General Survey*, p. 23; Manitoba *Free Press*, 1 February 1919 and passim.

48 Manitoba *Free Press*, 11 February 1919

49 For example, J.M. Minifie, an RAF cadet, recalled his reception in *Homesteader*, pp. 203–4. On the position of 'Imperials,' see *Special Committee, 1919*, pp. 389–409.

50 Carman, *Return of the Troops*, pp. 107, 110. Names of venereal cases were reported to their provincial governments, though only Ontario compelled treatment.

51 Manitoba *Free Press*, 3 and 17 February 1919; on Manitoba's Soldiers' Taxation Relief Act, see Cairns and Yetman, *History of the Veteran Movement*, vol. 1, pp. 10–11; on provincial policies, see *CAR*, 1919, pp. 681–794, passim.

52 On the Citizens' Repatriation League, see Dr. A.H. Abbott to Currie, 27 February 1920, PAC, Currie Papers, vol. 4, f. 9.

53 Anthes report, 10 August 1919, RG 38, vol. 171, f. 1288. On employment agencies, see *Special Committee 1919*, p. 296.

54 Anthes to Robinson, 12 and 14 March 1919, 7 June 1919, RG 38, vol. 171, f. 2375

55 *DSCR Report, 1919*, p. 59

56 Carman, *Return of the Troops*, p. 152.

57 Ibid., p. 112. See PC 452, 21 February 1919.

58 Primrose, 'Presidential Address,' pp. 8–9

59 Toronto *Daily Star*, 7 February 1919

60 Béland, 'Returned Soldier,' p. 3 (based on DSCR questionnaire, 1919)

61 Wecter, *When Johnny Comes Marching Home*, p. 279. See Waller, *Veteran Comes Back*, pp. 81ff. See also Graves, *Goodbye to All That,* p. 352.
62 'People,' said Col. Cy Peck vc, 'like to go to God's Country': *Special Committee, 1920*, p. 340. *The Veteran* included a good deal of reminiscence, both fictional and purportedly factual, most of it designed to flatter British and Canadian sensibilities.
63 George Pearson, 'Fitting in the Returned Men,' pp. 27–8
64 Bell, 'Medical Services,' p. 34.
65 *Special Committee, 1917*, p. 599; *Special Committee, 1919*, p. 293
66 Van Paassen, *Days of Our Years*, p. 91
67 M.C. Molson to Brig.-Gen. Armstrong, 10 September 1919, RG 38, vol. 168, f. 8510
68 Charles Carrington, cited in Winter, *Death's Men*, p. 242
69 On inflation, see *Canada Year Book 1919*, pp. 480–3; Bercuson, *Confrontation at Winnipeg*, pp. 32–5. On attitudes, see Clifford Bowering, *Service*, pp. 4–5.
70 Private papers made available to the authors
71 Todd, 'The Meaning of Rehabilitation,' p. 5. On the re-establishment of doctors, see Williams, 'The Return of the Army Medical Officer,' and 'Editorial,' ibid. On Banting, see Bliss, *Banting*, pp. 48–50.
72 On state health insurance, see Biggar, 'State Medicine,' pp. 1013–15. A more hostile view is found in Jackson, 'The New Order,' p. 415.
73 See 'Report of Chaplain's Services, DSCR,' PAC, Beattie Papers, pp. 314–20. See *Saturday Night*, 10 May 1919, on divorce reform.
74 Palmer, *Patterns of Prejudice*, p. 55; For GWVA policy resolutions, see *The Veteran*, III, 9 (August 1919).
75 On veterans and liquor, see Gray, *Booze*, p. 196ff; Hallowell, *Prohibition in Ontario*, pp. 82ff.
76 Starr interview, Toronto *Daily Star*, 3 March 1919
77 Van Paassen, *Days of Our Years*, p. 90
78 On the Grand Army of Canada, see *CAR*, 1918, p. 588; Toronto *Evening Telegram*, 9–10 October, 1918; Toronto *Daily Star*, 18 January 1919.
79 *Special Committee, 1920*, p. 656
80 See *The Veteran*, II, 2–4 (January-April 1919); R.M. Stewart interview, Ottawa *Evening Citizen*, 30 December 1918, in Borden Papers, vol. 247, f. RLB 2869(1), p. 138614; *Back to Mufti*, I, 1 (February 1919), p. 16.
81 On MacNeil, see *Harris Turner's Weekly*, II, 4 (January 1919).
82 On the Militia Department and the GWVA, see RG 24, vol. 2571a, f. HQC 2940; chief of the general staff to Palmer, 26 August 1919, ibid., vol. 445, f. HQ 54-21-1-184. On military response to the Mayor of Edmonton's appeal for protection from potential rioting veterans, see Brig.-Gen. H.F. McDonald to Joseph Clarke, 21 February 1919, ibid., vol. 4686, f. G1A-R2 and passim.
83 *The Veteran*, II, 4 (March 1919), p. 18
84 On the Winnipeg riots, see Manitoba *Free Press*, 27–8 January, 1919; Bercuson, *Confrontation at Winnipeg*, pp. 86–7.
85 Winnipeg *Telegram*, 29 January 1919; Manitoba *Free Press*, 4 February 1919
86 Manitoba *Free Press*, 29 January 1919.
87 MacNeil to White, 6 February 1919, Borden Papers, vol. 240, f. RLB 2457,

p. 134025. On anti-Chinese riots, see Toronto *Daily Star*, 1 and 19 February 1919.

88 Toronto *Daily Star*, 8 February 1919; *The Veteran*, II, 4 (March 1919), p. 47

89 On Calgary and the Western Labour conference, see *The Veteran*, II, 5 (April 1919). Loughan offered a familiar taunt: 'Why not present the whole committee with free transportation to Russia – the land of their dreams?') On veterans and the OBU, see Bercuson, *Fools and Wise Men*, pp. 119, 135, 198–9; on the General Strike, see Bercuson, *Confrontation at Winnipeg*, pp. 142–9; Masters, *Winnipeg General Strike*, pp. 59–62. On enemy aliens and veterans, see Avery, '*Dangerous Foreigners*,' chapter 3.

90 *The Veteran*, II, 7, p. 19. Loughnan's editorials reflect the GWVA attempt to distinguish between 'legitimate' strikers and the presumably alien radicals, anarchists, and 'Bolshevists, who were the hobgoblins of official and public hysteria. See ibid. (6 May 1919), p. 16 and II, 8 (July 1919), pp. 16–17.

91 On Bray, see Bercuson, *Confrontation at Winnipeg*, p. 143.

92 Calgary *Daily Herald*, 24 February 1919. On the bonus issue, see Eayrs, *In Defence of Canada*, vol. 1, chapter 2; Morton and Wright, 'The Bonus Campaign.'

93 Calgary *Eye-Opener*, 26 July 1919; see also Edmonton *Morning Bulletin*, 2 June 1919. Many soldiers believed in a promised 'peace gift' of $2,500; the origins of this belief are a mystery. On some politicians' promises, see Robinson to Lougheed, 27 February 1919, RG 38, vol. 169, f. 8440 (Frank Carvell).

94 *The Veteran*, II, 6 (May 1919), p. 19

95 Griesbach to Lougheed, 3 June 1919, Borden Papers, vol. 240, f. RLB 2457(2)(a), p. 134074; Griesbach to Borden, 13 June 1919, ibid., p. 134088. See also Edmonton City Archives, W.A. Griesbach diary, 18 and 27 April 1919.

96 *The Khaki Call* (June 1919), p. 20

97 Main Johnson diary, 18 May 1919, Metro Toronto Library, Main Johnson Papers.

98 On the convention, see *Report of the Third GWVA Convention, The Veteran*, II, 10 (September 1919); Cairns and Yetman, *History of the Veteran Movement*, p. 5.

99 Edmonton *Morning Bulletin*, 12 July 1919

100 Resolution no. 3. See Borden Papers, vol. 247, f. RLB 2869(1), p. 138960.

101 MacNeil to Borden, 23 August 1919, ibid., p. 138750a

102 On the Liberals, see Toronto *Daily Star*, 7 August 1919. For the resolution, see Carrigan, *Party Platforms*, pp. 82–3.

103 Margeson to Mewburn, 8 August 1919, Borden Papers, vol. 247, f. RLB 2869(1), p. 138704

104 Foster to Borden, 26 August 1919, ibid., f. RLB 2869(2), pp. 138746–7; Lougheed memorandum, 22 August 1919, ibid., p. 138741

105 Borden to MacNeil, 27 August 1919, ibid., p. 138751

106 Toronto *Globe*, 6–8 September 1919; G.W. Yates memorandum, 4 September 1919, Borden Papers, vol. 247, f. RLB 2869(2), p. 138780; Foster diary, 3 September 1919, PAC, Foster Papers

107 Toronto *Globe*, 8 September 1919

108 Toronto *Globe*, Toronto *Daily Star*, and Toronto *Evening Telegram*, 8 September 1919

109 On Flynn, see Toronto *Daily Star*, 8 and 12 September 1919; Evening Telegram, 18 September 1919; Manion, *Life Is an Adventure*, p. 259; Borden, *Letters to Limbo*, p. 148.
110 Toronto *Evening Telegram*, 16 September 1919. On Turley, see ibid., 18 September 1919. The UVL was formed at Queen's Park on 20 September 1919; see Toronto *Daily Star*, 22 September 1919.
111 Church's papers are unfortunately fragmentary and consist chiefly of scrapbooks. See Toronto *Evening Telegram*, 12 and 17 September 1919. On the Union government's response to post-war crises, see English, *The Decline of Politics*, chapter 11.
112 Toronto *Evening Telegram*, 9 October 1919
113 *Special Committee, 1919*, pp. 410-56; Toronto *Daily Star*, 13 and 15 September, 1 October 1919; on reactions, see ibid., 2 October 1919, *Evening Telegram*, 2-3 October 1919, Manitoba *Free Press*, 2 and 3 October 1919; *Special Committee, 1919*, p. 928.
114 *Special Committee, 1919*, pp. 659-83; *The Veteran* II, 12 November 1919; Toronto *Daily Star*, 7 October 1919.
115 *Special Committee, 1919*, p. 983
116 Toronto *Evening Telegram*, 9 October 1919
117 *Special Committee, 1919*, p. 57
118 CHC *Debates*, 5 November 1919, p. 1749.
119 On the debate, see ibid., 6 November 1919, pp. 1784-93, and Toronto *Daily Star* and *Evening Telegram*, 7 November 1919.
120 *The Veteran*, II, 12 November 1919, p. 16. On Currie, see ibid., III, 1 December 1919; see also Toronto *Daily Star*, 29 October 1919; Toronto *Globe*, 30 October 1919. See W.D. Tait, 'The Confessions of a Near Pessimist,' *The Veteran*, III, 3 (February 1919).
121 On the War Emergency Appropriation, Canada, Senate, *Debates* (cited hereinafter as SC *Debates*), 10 May 1920, p. 393; Canadian Patriotic Fund, *Federal Emergency Appropriation Department Regulations* (n.p., n.d.) (with Scammell Collection), PC 2469, 9 December 1919. If the GWVA was alarmist, it was in excellent company. See Sir Richard Turner to Borden, 17 December 1919, Borden Papers, vol. 240, f. RLB 2457, pp. 134252-5. The *Globe* also reported desperate need: see 23 December 1919, 3 February 1920.
122 Calgary *Daily Herald*, 1 and 9 March 1920; on Woods, a future assistant deputy minister of veterans' affairs, see RG 32, C 2, vol. 257, f. 1004. On adjusted compensation, see England, *Twenty Million Veterans*, pp. 52-4; Weber and Schmeckebier, *Veterans' Administration*, p. 185; Dillingham, *Federal Aid to Veterans*, p. 154.
123 *Report of the Fourth GWVA Convention*; on the gratuity debate, see also Montreal *Gazette*, 26 and 27 March 1920; Manitoba *Free Press*, 26 March 1920; Toronto *Daily Star*, 25 March 1920.
124 *Report of the Fourth GWVA Convention*, 26 March 1920; Montreal *Gazette*, 26 March 1920
125 Foster to MacNeil, 9 April 1920, printed in *The Veteran*, III, 6 (May 1920)
126 Foster diary, vol. 9, 3 April 1920. See also Toronto *Evening Telegram*, 4 and 5 April 1920; Calgary *Daily Herald*, 5 April 1920; *Canadian Annual Review*, 1920, p. 452; King diary, 9 April 1920.
127 *CAR*, 1920, p. 453
128 *Report of the Fifth GWVA Convention*, 22 October 1921, p. 46. As late as

April 1921 the *Canadian Forum* was reporting yet another gratuity scheme fostered by G.N. Tucker and George Bayly. The editor warned: 'As the authors base it on the problematic German indemnity, it may be hoped that too many will not spend the money in advance' (p. 205). For an official GWVA view, see *The Veteran*, IV, 12 (November 1921). King's diary entries for 1920 report several meetings with veterans at which he derived satisfaction from gaining support without reiterating the bonus promise: see 29 and 30 September 1920, 7 and 11 October 1920, and 4 February 1921.

129 W.L.M. King to J.F. Marsh, 28 November 1921, Currie Papers, vol. 27, f. 3. On the Grand Army of United Veterans, see Toronto *Globe*, 4 May 1921; Toronto *Evening Telegram*, 12 November 1921.

130 Currie to McLeod, 29 May 1922, Currie Papers, vol. 37. On Meighen's reaction, see CHC *Debates*, 27 March 1922, pp. 393–6.

131 On the bonus struggle by American Veterans, see Moley, *The American Legion Story*, pp. 88–133 passim; Ross, *Preparing for Ulysses*, pp. 12–24; Mayo, *Soldiers, What Next!* pp. 83–97; Lisio, 'Bread and Butter Politics,' pp. 44–6.

Chapter 7: Re-establishment and Settlement

1 See Segsworth, *Retraining*, chapter 1; and memorandum, 22 September 1919, in *Special Committee, 1919*, pp. 178–92.

2 See *Reconstruction* (March 1918), p. 2; Toronto *Daily Star*, 4 February 1919; *DSCR Report, 1919*, pp. 15–16.

3 PC 387, 24 February 1919

4 See *Special Committee, 1919*, p. 179.

5 On drug addiction problems, see RG 38, vol. 205, f. 84091; and see Chapman, 'The Anti-drug Crusade,' pp. 99–100 on the CEF and drug problems.

6 *DSCR Report, 1919*, p. 16; *Special Committee, 1919*, p. 179

7 For the totals, see Royal Commission on Pensions, *Final Report*, p. 51. On Christian, see *Special Committee, 1920*, pp. 761–2. On amputees' concerns, see *The Veteran*, 12 August 1922.

8 England, *Twenty Million Veterans*, pp. 46–7; Col. C.L.H. Starr, testimony, *Special Committee, 1920*, pp. 223–7; *Special Committee, 1921*, pp. 305–23. On hikers, see *The Veteran*, 18 August 1923.

9 Starr testimony, *Special Committee, 1920*, pp. 225–7

10 Coulthard to deputy minister, 22 August 1919, 3 November 1919, RG 38, vol. 181, f. 8560. On veterans' resentments, see Manitoba *Free Press*, 22 February 1919, suggesting that twenty-two Winnipeg amputees had formed a club and almost all had non-Canadian limbs. On acceptance, see Saskatchewan GWVA, *Yearbook, 1922–3*. See also *DSCR Report, 1921*, pp. 37–9; *Special Committee, 1921*, pp. 305, 317–22.

11 *DSCR Report, 1920*, p. 54; *DSCR Report, 1921*, p. 33

12 *DSCR Report, 1923*, pp. 11–13; PC 963, 23 March 1921; *The Veteran*, III, 6 (May 1920), p. 26

13 *Special Committee, 1920*, pp. 732ff; testimony of W.M. Hart and Dr C.D. Parfitt, pp. 363–79. *DSCR Report, 1920*, p. 33; *DSCR Report, 1921*, pp. 42–4

14 *Report of the Board of Tuberculosis Consultants December, 1920* (Ottawa

1920), reprinted with *DSCR Report, 1920*, pp. 18ff; *Special Committee, 1921*, pp. xx–xxii.

15 On the DSCR view of the pre-enlistment origins, see DSCR *Invalided Soldiers' Commission*, p. 27; Dr E.G. Davis to Chairman, Parliamentary Special Committee on SCR, 1919 (n.d.), RG 38, vol. 168, f. 571.

16 On the visits, see RG 38, vol. 217, f. 8384. Manitoba's hospitals were the worst. Brandon had a single doctor and the crib beds; Selkirk was 'possibly the most unsatisfactory we have visited, very untidy and depressing in every sense of the word.'

17 Farrar report, 26 August 1919, RG 38, vol. 155, f. 8339

18 Unit Medical Director 'A' to DMS, November 1919, ibid.

19 *DSCR Report, 1920*, p. 13; Clarke's report is found ibid., pp. 10–13. A more critical view of the hospital – simply because it *was* pleasant – was taken by a later head of neuro-psychiatric services. See J.P.S. Cathcart to A.H. Boyes, 7 July 1922, RG 38, vol. 217, f. 6135.

20 Scammell, *Summary*, p. 12; E.G. Davis to chairman, Parliamentary Committee, 1920, n.d., RG 38, vol. 168, f. 571

21 See Russell, 'Psychogenetic Conditions in Soldiers,' pp. 227–38, and Russell, 'The Nature of War Neuroses' for a review of thought on the subject. See also Brown, 'Shell Shock,' pp. 308ff.

22 Section 29(1) of the Pension Act authorized the special treatment of neuro-psychiatric cases. See DSCR, *Invalided Soldiers' Commission*, p. 27.

23 See the report reprinted in *DSCR Report, 1919*, p. 121 (the complete report is at pp. 113–21); and see Toronto *Globe*, 23 September 1919.

24 *DSCR Report, 1919*, p. 43 et seq.

25 See Segsworth, *Retraining*, and *Special Committee, 1919*, pp. 13–16.

26 *The Veteran*, II, 4 (March 1919), p. 18. See also ibid., 5 (April 1919) on war amputees wasting their lives as pedlars when they could retrain for a new life.

27 On decisions and policies, see RG 38, vol. 200, f. 20-165, part 1.

28 Director of vocational training, memorandum, 25 March 1919, RG 38, vol. 201, f. 20-165, part 2. On universities, see *CAR*, 1919, pp. 560–1; and *Special Committee, 1919*, pp. 607–28.

29 See RG 38, vol. 200, f. 2417.

30 Memorandum, 25 March 1919, RG 38, vol. 201, f. 20-165, part 2 for earlier concerns, see Borden to Lougheed, 11 October 1919, RG 38, vol. 200, f. 20-165, part 1; Scammell memorandum, 22 October 1917, ibid.; PC 814, 16 April 1919

31 Memorandum relating to Re-establishment, 8 September 1919, Borden Papers, vol. 247, f. 2869(2), pp. 138788ff. In November 1918, 467 veterans were reported as undergoing training. New courses were cut off on 31 January, 1920.

32 For the final results, see *DSCR Report, 1922*, pp. 18–21; see also *The Veteran*, 5 May 1923. *Canada Year Book*, 1920, p. 23 summarizes the programmes.

33 *Special Committee, 1920*, pp. 438–553 passim. (Answers from Maj. Ernest Flexman, director of vocational training, pp. 554–67)

34 On the strike, see *Manitoba Free Press*, 25–31 January 1919, 18–19 and 28 February 1919; *The Veteran*, II, 7 (June 1919).

35 W.S. Woods to MacNeil, 28 April 1920, RG 38, vol. 168, f. 571
36 *The Veteran* II, 10 (September 1919), p. 16
37 Segsworth, *Retraining*, p. 68
38 *DSCR Report, 1923*, p. 19. See also Royal Commission on Pensions, *Final Report*.
39 Segsworth, *Retraining*, pp. 18, 128–34; *DSCR Report, 1919*, pp. 45–7; *DSCR Report, 1920*, p. 71; Scammell, *Summary*, pp. 26–7
40 On Baker, see Campbell, *No Compromise*. On the success of blind soldiers, see Toronto *Daily Star*, 1, 2, 5, and 6 March 1919; Scammell, *Summary*, p. 27; and *The Veteran* IV, 9 (August 1921) on James H. Rawlinson.
41 Problem cases among the blind were cited to the Royal Commission on Pensions. See *Final Report*, pp. 46–7.
42 *Special Committee, 1919*, p. 14; Biggar, 'Economic Effect of Disablement.' On Curly Christian, see *Special Committee, 1921*, p. 57; and Millar, 'The Men Who Came Back.'
43 Scammell, *Summary*, pp. 29–31. Unfortunately, detailed record-keeping and documentation ceased in 1920.
44 See Royal Commission on Pensions, *Final Report*, p. 47.
45 *Special Committee, 1920*, pp. 642–3
46 William Foran testimony, *Special Committee, 1921*, pp. 392–4, 396–400. The commission drew the line at preference for all promotions.
47 Ibid., p. 392
48 On rural postmasters, see *The Veteran*, 18 February 1922, and 7, 21 October 1922; *Special Committees, 1921*, p. 401 (Charles Bland testimony).
49 PC 2944, 31 August 1922; Scammell, *Summary*, p. 24
50 *Special Committee, 1919*, p. 54; Scammell, *Summary*, p. 25; *Canada Year Book*, 1920, p. 29; *DSCR Report, 1921*, p. 22
51 PC 4432, 12 December 1921; *The Veteran*, 18 January 1922; *Special Committee, 1920*, p. 16; Scammell, *Summary*, p. 26
52 *Special Committee, 1917*, p. 1056
53 Foster to Borden, 26 August 1919, Borden Papers, vol. 247, f. RLB 2869(1), p. 138748; *The Veteran*, III, 2 (January 1920), p. 16
54 *Special Committee, 1920*, pp. 15–16. On details, see testimony, ibid., pp. 382–437, 483–504.
55 SC, *Debates*, 25 June 1920, p. 735
56 *Special Committee, 1920*, p. 389
57 *Special Committee, 1921*, ix–x; *CAR*, 1923, p. 907; Scammell, *Summary*, 47–8; 'Pension and Other Post-war Benefits to Ex-members,' 15 June 1935, RG 38, vol. 195, f. 7261
58 SC, *Debates*, 29 June 1923, p. 1264 (in 1928, RSI was reopened for applicants and remained open until 1933).
59 *Canada Year Book*, 1920, p. 28; 1924, p. 922; *DSCR Report, 1921*, pp. 68–70; PC 43, 10 January 1921
60 *Special Committee, 1920*, p. 188
61 Scammell, *Summary*, p. 35; on employing the tubercular, see *Report of the BTC*, 1920, pp. 19–21 and passim. See also the BTC's confidential report, *The Care and Employment of the Tuberculous Ex-service Man after Discharge from the Sanatorium* (Ottawa 1920).
62 *Special Committee, 1920*, p. 20; *Special Committee*, Thomas Adams submission, 10 December 1920, pp. 557ff; testimony, pp. 439–51

63 C.B. Wace testimony, *Special Committee, 1920*, p. 181
64 *Special Committee, 1921*, p. xxii
65 *Canada Year Book*, 1924, p. 923; 1925, p. 958; PC 2328, 21 November 1919; Scammell, *Summary*, pp. 35–7. A summary of 'problem cases' as seen in 1920 is given in *Special Committee, 1920*, pp. 756–8.
66 *DSCR Report, 1919*, pp. 75–6. See also RG 9, III B 2, vol. 3570, f. 22-4-0 on Canadians in England. On imperial veterans, see RG 38, vol. 195, f. 7261; Toronto *Daily Star*, 1 October, 1919. On Canadians in the United States, see RG 38, vol. 224, f. 8479. The Militia Department reported that there had been 768 officers, 63 nursing sisters, and 34,998 other ranks in the CEF who claimed a US birthplace.
67 PC 2025, 30 September 1919; *DSCR Report, 1919*, pp. 99–121
68 *DSCR Report, 1919*, pp. 122–8; PC 1342, 1 July 1919; PC 424, 3 March 1919; HR 8778, approved 24 December 1919, was the U.S. counterpart. On problems later, see RG 38, vol. 224, f. 8433.
69 *DSCR Report, 1923*, p. 16. On the rights of Canadian and British veterans living in the United States, see *Handbook for the Information of Former Members*.
70 For example, see DSCR '*Why We Train*' (Ottawa 1919), p. 7.
71 Stanley Frost, 'Where Veterans Fell among Friends'
72 Toronto *Evening Telegram*, 10 October 1919
73 Millar, 'Men Who Came Back'
74 On the limb factory strike, see Toronto *Daily Star*, 5–6 February 1919.
75 McKelvey Bell to Borden, 6 June 1919, Borden Papers, vol. 142, f. OCA 122, p. 75489 et seq. For sidelights to the Bell resignation, see Dr G.R. Johnson to J.G. Cunningham, 19 June 1919, Glenbow-Alberta Institute, Johnson Papers, f. 7; Fotheringham to Col. J.L. Potter, 13 June 1919, Fotheringham Papers, f. 'P.' On DSCR staffing, see *DSCR Report, 1919*, pp. 9–10.
76 *The Veteran*, II, 8 (July 1919), p. 17, and II, 9 (August 1919), pp. 15–16. On Robinson, see Loughnan testimony, *Special Committee, 1919*, pp. 937–40.
77 For resolution, see *The Veteran*, II, 8 (July 1919), pp. 17–18. On the Lougheed criticism, see *The Veteran*, II, 4 (March 1919), pp. 17–18.
78 See, for example, Read, *The Great War and Canadian Society*, pp. 189–90.
79 In 1919 MacNeil had sought aid for funerals, claiming that the influenza epidemic had almost bankrupted the GWVA (*Special Committee on Pensions, 1919*, p. 15); on the Last Post Fund, see *Special Committee, 1921*, pp. 426–7. The government granted the fund $10,000 a year, and later increased that figure.
80 MacNeil testimony, *Special Committee, 1921*, pp. 262–3. The GWVA did favour the Canadian National Committee on Mental Hygiene making inspections and denounced Robinson for allegedly calling the committee 'a fad.' See *The Veteran*, III, 4 (March 1920), p. 16.
81 *Special Committee, 1921*, pp. 258, 280–1
82 Ibid., pp. 460–1
83 On unemployment estimates, see ibid., p. 281; and *The Veteran*, 12 (August 1922).
84 On recommendations, see MacNeil's testimony, *Special Committee, 1921*, pp. 257–91; *The Veteran*, IV, 6 (May 1921).
85 For Parkinson's testimony, see *Special Committee, 1921*, pp. 296–303; on loans, see p. 300; and see *DSCR Report, 1921*, pp. iv–v.

86 *Special Committee, 1921*, p. xvi; Udo Sautter, 'Measuring Unemployment in Canada,' pp. 476-9; Struthers, *No Fault of Their Own*, pp. 30-7
87 *Report of the Commissioner of the Ontario Provincial Police, 1922*, Ontario, *Sessional Papers*, 84, 1923, pp. 29-31
88 *Special Committee, 1921*, p. xvii; on German policy, see McMurtrie, 'Influence of Pension,' pp. 362-4; and *The Veteran*, 2 (September 1922).
89 *Canada Year Book*, 1915, p. 187; 1921, p. 214
90 See Graham, *Arthur Meighen*, vol. 1, p. 246. The DSCR survey in 1919 showed farming as by far the most popular option for CEF members planning to switch occupations. Only 4,716 wanted to leave the land; 20,269 wanted to take up farming; and 67,502 intended to stick with agriculture. See Béland, 'The Returned Soldier.'
91 *Harris Turner's Weekly*, II, 2 (January 1919), p. 1
92 *CAR*, 1919, p. 429; Toronto *Globe*, 20 and 21 November 1919. On the conference, see *SSB Report, 1921*, p. 26; *CAR*, 1919, pp. 420, 605-6. 'Memorandum as to Soldier Settlement,' RG 10, vol. 7530, f. 26001-1, part 1, pp. 63-5.
93 On provincial pressure, see, for example, 'Report of the Returned Soldiers Commission for Nova Scotia, 1918,' cited in Hunt, *Nova Scotia's Part*, pp. 328-9.
94 Meighen to Borden, 11 December 1918, Borden Papers, vol. 244, f. RLB 2772, vol. 224; *Back to Mufti*, I, 1 (February 1919), p. 23
95 PC 229, 11 February 1919. See SSB, *First Report*, p. 26; Scammell, *Summary*, p. 66; CHC *Debates*, 23 June 1919, p. 3849
96 SC *Debates*, 1 July 1919, p. 769. See also CHC *Debates*, 23 June 1919, pp. 3971-2 for the comments of the acting Liberal leader, D.D. McKenzie.
97 CHC *Debates*, p. 3863; Graham, *Meighen*, vol. 1 p. 248. The act was 9-10 Geo. V, c. 71.
98 SSB, *First Report*, pp. 26-7; *CAR*, 1919, p. 599
99 See *The Veteran*, II, 3 (February 1919) on imperial veterans' rights. Major Ashton and SSB officials went to England in the winter of 1919 but their primary purpose was to inform CEF members of their prospects.
100 CHC *Debates*, 23 June 1919, p. 3873; see also pp. 3864, 3870; L.L. Anthes to Miss Laurie Coates, 18 February 1919, RG 38, vol. 225, f. 6672; and SC *Debates*, 7 May 1920, p. 382, on Bill 68.
101 On progress, see *CAR*, 1919, p. 600 (as of 15 December 1919). *The Veteran* launched a monthly column on farming in 1920 and reported success stories with some acidity. See Barnett testimony, *Special Committee, 1921*, p. 359.
102 *Special Committee, 1919*, testimony of Samuel Maber, pp. 215-16. Also see Meighen, CHC *Debates*, 23 June 1919, pp. 3850-1.
103 See Toronto *Daily Star*, 1 May 1919 and 29 May 1919 on training and pay. After GWVA protests, the monthly allowance was doubled to twenty dollars plus wages. See CHC *Debates*, 23 June 1919, p. 3853.
104 SSB, *First Report*, p. 9.
105 On Kapuskasing, see Schull, *Ontario Since 1967*, pp. 228-9; Toronto *Globe*, 19 March 1920; *The Veteran*, IV, 7 (June 1920).
106 On the Porcupine reserve and other Park Belt settlement, see McDonald, 'Soldiers Settlement,' pp. 38ff. On British Columbia, see Koroscil, 'Soldiers, Settlement and Development,' pp. 63ff.

107 SSB, *First Report*, p. 10

108 *Canada Year Book*, 1921, p. 31; SSB, *First Report*, p. 7

109 *Special Committee, 1921*, p. 360

110 On savings, see Meighen, CHC *Debates*, 23 June 1919, pp. 3855–7.

111 Ibid., p. 3860; *Canada Year Book*, 1921, p. 32

112 For the GWVA resolutions, 1919, see Borden Papers, vol. 247, f. RLB 2869(1) p. 138691.

113 On Indians and soldier settlement, see SSB, *Third Report*, 31 December 1924 (Ottawa 1925); the board reported that 224 native veterans had borrowed $399,199. See also *Canada Year Book*, 1927, pp. 991–2. An otherwise useful article, which makes little reference to surrenders and none to the impact of soldier settlement among Indians themselves, is Cuthand's 'The Native People of the Prairie Province.' On the surrenders, see D.C. Scott to Meighen, 9 December 1918, RG 10, vol. 7530, f. 26001-1, part 1.

114 CHC *Debates*, 23 June 1919, p. 3877

115 SSB, *First Report*, p. 12; CHC *Debates* 25 June 1919, p. 4013. Meighen was blunt in reply to H.M. Mowat, one of the enthusiasts: 'Notwithstanding persistent and repeated pressure we have consistently resisted any inroads upon that principle. We will not accept communal responsibility.' See also *Special Committee, 1920*, p. 459.

116 *Special Committee, 1921*, p. 384; see also pp. 363, 382.

117 Black's testimony is in *Special Committee, 1920*, pp. 468–70. See a summary of the arguments in Royal Commission on Pensions, *Second Report*, pp. 69–73.

118 SSB, *First Report*, p. 12

119 Ibid., p. 17

120 On the Home Service see CHC *Debates*, 23 June 1919, p. 3861; *Manitoba Free Press*, 26 September 1919; *Special Committee, 1921*, pp. 4419–20.

121 Laut, 'Making Good'

122 CHC *Debates*, 23 June 1919, p. 3852; *CAR*, 1919, p. 600; 1920, p. 460; SSB, *First Report*, pp. 7, 20.

123 Barnett, who practiced law and farmed at Innisfail until 1916, later served as Saskatchewan's first deputy minister of lands and resources, oversaw rural relief in the province, and became Ontario manager for Crédit-Foncier. He was also a president of the Ontario Historical Society. Black soon moved on to become the CNR's director of colonization.

124 *CAR*, 1920, p. 459

125 For example, see "Gunner," *Compensation for Ex-Members of the CEF*, p. 10; *The Veteran*, III, 7 (June 1919).

126 The GWVA proposed using the SSB to distribute loans to help soldiers buy urban lots. See Loughnan articles, *The Veteran*, IV, 3–4 (February–March 1920); *Special Committee, 1921*, pp. 244, 439–51, appendices, pp. 557–86. On the aid to fishermen, see *Special Committee, 1920*, pp. 578–605, 650–2.

127 *Special Committee, 1920*, p. 17

128 SSB, *First Report*, p. 8. In Parliament, Meighen had explicitly insisted that the Soldier Settlement Act was neither a gratuity nor a reward; see CHC *Debates*, 23 June 1919, p. 3863

129 CHC *Debates*, 23 June 1919, p. 3876

130 Cairns and Yetman, *History of the Veteran Movement*, vol. 1, pp. 9–10

131 Laut, 'Making Good'
132 *Special Committee, 1920*, on the Marshall Case, pp. 461–5; 716–20
133 Ibid., p. 454
134 Ibid., pp. 467–73
135 *Special Committee, 1921*, p. 357
136 *Special Committee, 1920*, p. 475
137 Laut, 'Making Good'
138 *Special Committee, 1920*, p. 26. On salvage cases, see John Barnett to Lougheed, 28 October 1921, PAC, Meighen Papers, vol. 54, f. 225, p. 30171: it was claimed in autumn of 1921 that 94.5 per cent of the loans were salvaged, with a profit on sale of $7,000.
139 See Thompson and Seager, *Canada, 1922–1939*, p. 96; see also Thompson, *Harvests of War*, pp. 43–72, on the impact of the war on agriculture. On prices and yields, see *Canada Year Book*, 1915–21.
140 CHC *Debates*, 23 June 1919, p. 3867
141 *CAR*, 1921, pp. 344–5. On crops, see *Canada Year Book*, 1920, p. 185
142 *Canada Year Book*, 1921, p. 210, 236; 1922–3, p. 260
143 Fay, 'Diminishing Returns in Agriculture,' p. 96
144 *SSB Report, 1923*, pp. 9, 27
145 On Nicoaman Island, see Royal Commission on Pensions, *Second Report*, p. 68.
146 *Proceedings of the Fifth GWVA Convention, Alberta Command*, pp. 3, 16–7. See also *The Veteran* (January 1922).
147 Currie to McLeod, 23 May 1922, Currie Papers, vol. 27, f. 3
148 *The Veteran*, 18 (March 1922)
149 *Special Committee, 1922*, p. 187
150 *SSB Report, 1923*, pp. 16–19; CHC *Debates*, 21 June 1922, p. 3300
151 *SSB Report, 1923*, p. 9
152 *Saskatchewan GWVA, Yearbook*, 1922–3, pp. 36–7. On savings, see *SSB Report, 1931*, p. 13.
153 See SSB, *Third Report*, 1924, pp. 8, 11 on the British family scheme. On the significance of the depression, see ibid., p. 9.
154 Struthers, 'Prelude to Depression,' p. 282
155 See ibid., p. 278, citing testimony to the Mather commission at p. 455. On relief, see *DSCR Report, 1921*, pp. 68–9; and *Canada Year Book*, 1922–3, p. 934.
156 See chapter 2.
157 Struthers, *No Fault of Their Own*, pp. 26–9

Chapter 8: The Ralston Commission

1 Todd to Sir Adam Beck, 15 November 1915, RG 38, vol. 200, f. 8-67, part 1
2 Todd, 'The Duty of the War Pension,' p. 499
3 See Scammell, *Summary*, pp. 40–1; *Canada Year Book*, 1920, pp. 680–1; *CAR*, 1920, pp. 40–1.
4 On methods of rating, see testimony, Maj. W.A. Burgess, *Special Committee, 1921*, pp. 455–6; see, on Christian, Scammell to Nesbitt, 15 June 1920, *Special Committee, 1920*, pp. 761–2. In comparison, see Ontario Workmen's Compensation Board reports. In 1920 a railway brakeman who lost both legs

got $790.10 per year; a boy who lost both hands was awarded $390 a year. The board reported that the disabled 'rehabilitated themselves quickly.'

5 The attitude is reflected, perhaps justifiably, in the Garwood case: *Special Committee, 1920*, 283; see *Special Committee, 1921*, pp. 471-2 for the views of Dr H.A. Rawlings.

6 Board of Pension Commissioners, *Annual Reports* (Ottawa 1920, 1921); *Canada Year Book*, 1927, p. 990

7 CHC *Debates*, 27 June 1919, p. 4174

8 Ibid., 22 June 1922, p. 3441

9 The subject is conspicuously absent from the rather meagre historiography of Canadian social policy. See, for example, Guest, *Social Security in Canada*. The Board of Pension Commissioners, a notable example, never features in the literature on regulatory agencies. See Baggaley, *The Emergence of the Regulatory State*, or Risk, 'Lawyers, Courts and the Rise of the Regulatory State.' On the pension burden, see Morton, ' "Noblest and Best," ' p. 75, n. 1.

10 See *Special Committee on Pensions, 1919*, esp. pp. iv–v and the testimony of MacNeil, Margeson, and Ahern.

11 CHC *Debates*, 28 June 1919, p. 4209; ibid., 30 June 1919, p. 4277 (The debate had reached section 42 of the act, bypassing the earlier reference in section 32.)

12 Ibid., 30 June 1919, pp. 4282-3

13 Ibid., p. 4290. Section 32(3) of the Pension Act (9–10 Geo. V, c. 43) continued to use the offending phrase, which was of British origin.

14 SC *Debates*, 3 July 1919, p. 871

15 CHC *Debates*, 27 June 1919, p. 4179

16 Pension Act, ss 11(1)-(2)

17 Ibid., s. 12; CHC *Debates*, 27 June 1919, p. 4180

18 Pension Act, s. 15

19 Ibid., ss 25, 18

20 Pension Act, s. 25(3); Rowell, CHC *Debates*, 27 June 1919, p. 4174. See also Lougheed, SC *Debates*, 26 June 1922, p. 676.

21 The problems posed by soldiers on small pensions resulted largely from 'aggravation' cases. They were the recurrent feature of pension grievances. See 'Instruction and a Table of Disabilities for the Guidance of Physicians and Surgeons,' *Special Committee, 1919*, pp. 163-76. See, however, Biggar, 'The Pensionability of the Disabled Soldier,' explaining the BPC policy.

22 *Special Committee, 1920*, pp. 218-20. On the Lockwood case, see Toronto *Telegram*, 1 October 1919.

23 CHC *Debates*, 25 June 1919, p. 4026

24 Ibid., 25 June 1919, p. 4031; see *Special Committee, 1919*, pp. 178-81 on Mrs B.H. Vidal; p. 238 on Mrs W.H. Cotton.

25 CHC *Debates*, 23 June 1920, p. 4042 (George Nicholson)

26 Pension Act, s. 22

27 See *Special Committee, 1928*, p. 409.

28 S.B. Coristine memorandum cited by Archibald, *Special Committee, 1919*, 108-9. On Knight, see *Special Committe, 1921*, p. 461.

29 See *The Veteran*, October 1921 (on Ball's reappearance, see ibid., 18 February 1921). On Mrs Astles, see ibid., 4 August 1923.

30 Pension Act, s. 40; see CHC *Debates*, 5 May 1925, pp. 2855–61; and Royal Commission on Pensions, *Final Report*, pp. 100–1.

31 *Special Committee, 1920*, pp. 343, 348–63; *CAR*, 1920, p. 458. Sergeant-Major MacNamara, an Ontario MLA, could denounce 'the contemptible utterance of a man who has degraded the dignity and honour of his military profession' for McLean's alleged 'servant girl' remark. See Toronto *Daily Star*, 7 May 1920; Manitoba *Free Press*, 7 May 1920.

32 Pension Act, s. 32, On the U.S. example, see Archibald testimony, *Special Committee, 1919*, pp. 56–7; CHC *Debates*, 25 June 1919, p. 4176; 22 June 1922, p. 3447; SC *Debates*, 26 June 1922, pp. 674–5.

33 Mrs G.N. Warmington testimony, *Special Committee, 1919*, p. 44

34 See, for example, *The Veteran*, 10 February 1923.

35 The BPC membership is listed in Royal Commission on Pensions, *Report on the First Part of the Investigation*, 1923, no 3, p. 6. On Thompson, see Waite, *The Man from Halifax*, p. 443; Harold Daly Papers, vol. 1, 'Gwatkin and Cochrane.' On Margeson, see *Canadian Who's Who*, 1921, p. 910; *The Veteran* IV, 8 (July 1920), p. 21, and II, 10 (September 1920), p. 18.

36 *Special Committee, 1920*, p. 43. Thompson's chief concern was to reassure members that the liability would not grow. See ibid., pp. 43–5.

37 Ibid., p. 10. See also, on commutation, *Special Committee, 1921*, pp. 63–4 and passim.

38 *Special Committee, 1920*, pp. 60–1, 324; cited by Royal Commission on Pensions, *First Report*, p. 21

39 On Cronyn's views, see CHC *Debates*, 23 June 1920, pp. 4042–3 and passim; *Special Committee, 1920*, pp. 57–67.

40 Pension Act, 1921 (11–12 Geo. V, c. 45, s. 1.) See CHC *Debates*, 2 June 1921, pp. 4365–6, and SC *Debates*, 3 June 1921, p. 776. Whatever members might later claim, the significance of annulling the 'insurance principle' was clear in 1921, though it was not mentioned in either House in 1920.

41 CHC *Debates*, 2 June 1921, p. 4366. See also *Special Committee, 1921*, pp. xi–xiii.

42 Toronto *Telegram*, 14 November 1921; W.L.M. King Papers, Diary, 4 February 1921. See also *The Veteran*, October–November 1921, passim, especially 26 November 1921.

43 On the Tory appeal, see *The Veteran*, 26 November 1921. Leon Ladner reminded King of the effusive phrases he used at Cobalt on 20 November 1921; see CHC *Debates*, 11 June 1923, p. 3718.

44 *The Veteran*, 13 January 1923, described the GWVA bureau.

45 On the state of the GWVA in 1921, see ibid., passim.

46 Ibid., 21 October 1921. On U.S. influence, see 'Memorandum on the Legislative and Adjustment Service" (C.G. MacNeil, n.d.), Currie Papers, vol. 17, f. 3.

47 *The Veteran*, 28 October 1921, 27 November 1921

48 King Diary, 28 and 29 December 1921; on Béland, see *The Veteran*, 17 March 1922, acclaiming him as a man 'who knew his subject.'

49 See Struthers, *'No Fault of Their Own,'* pp. 29–33; CHC *Debates*, 2 February 1923, pp. 35–6; and W.S. Fielding to King and others, 9 January 1922, King Papers, J-1, vol. 73, pp. 61821–3.

50 *Special Committee, 1922*. See Toronto *Daily Star*, 17–22 June 1922; *The*

Veteran, 24 June 1922; CHC *Debates*, 22 June 1922, pp. 344–9. On veterans' influence, see *The Veteran*, 21 January 1922, 17 February 1922.

51 CHC *Debates*, 21 June 1922, p. 3290. See Ladner amendment, ibid., 22 June 1922, pp. 3453–5. On MacNeil's frustration, see *The Veteran*, 20 May 1922; expressed to Dominion Veterans' Alliance, ibid., 4 November 1922.

52 Pension concerns are seen in *The Veteran*, 4 March 1922, 22 May 1922.

53 On the course of events, see *The Veteran*, 24 June 1922, 9 September 1922; Royal Commission on Pensions, *First Report*, pp. 123–4; and Maxwell statement in *Saskatchewan GWVA Yearbook*, 1922–3 (Regina 1923).

54 Royal Commission on Pensions and Re-establishment, *Report on the First Part of the Investigation*, p. 5

55 SC *Debates*, 26 June 1922, p. 674 and passim

56 Parkinson to Scammell, 22 June 1922, RG 38, vol. 169, f. 1451

57 PC 1525, 22 June 1922. On members, see *The Veteran*, 19 August 1922. On Bowler, see ibid., 26 September 1922.

58 Royal Commission on Pensions and Re-establishment, *First Report*, p. 21. Belton's successor had no doubt of the animus: 'Do you think that Colonel Belton would accept my opinion as a medical opinion?' Dr Arnold asked McKeown; 'Not in a thousand years.' See *The Veteran*, 30 September 1922.

59 Ibid., 4 November 1922. See reports in *The Veteran*, 9 September–11 November 1922.

60 Ibid., 16 September 1922.

61 Ibid., 11 November, 1922. See also ibid., 4, 18 November 1922.

62 The two issues are explored in Royal Commission on Pensions, *First Report*, pp. 44–6, 80–91, 107–9. See also *The Veteran*, 14 and 21 October 1922.

63 *The Veteran*, 9 December 1922

64 Royal Commission on Pensions and Re-establishment, *First Report*, p. 126

65 For criticisms, see ibid., passim, especially pp. 47, 48, 107–8, and 119.

66 Ibid., p. 129

67 On procedures, see Royal Commission on Pensions and Re-establishment, *Final Report*, pp. 9–10; *The Veteran*, 4 November 1922.

68 *Final Report*, p. 11; *The Veteran*, 23 March 1923

69 Lunden to Scammell, 6 January 1923, RG 38, vol. 169, f. 1451 (and reply, 9 January 1923, ibid.)

70 Hewitt to director of medical services, 14 February 1923, ibid.; H. Despard Twigg to Major C.A. Bell, 25 January 1923, ibid., f. 1452; A.F. Macaulay to Hewitt, 14 March 1923, ibid.; *The Veteran*, 24 March 1923.

71 *The Veteran*, 10 February 1923–12 May 1923, reported in detail on the meetings. See also the reports in RG 38, vol. 169, f. 1452. Witnesses included local *DSCR* officials and representatives of the Soldier Settlement Board and the Board of Pension Commissioners. See Royal Commission on Pensions and Re-establishment, *Final Report*, pp. 155–9. On Mrs Bland, see *The Veteran*, 21 August 1923; Mrs L[esten], ibid., 1 September 1923.

72 Scammell to Parkinson, 1 March 1923, RG 38, vol. 169, f. 1452

73 Royal Commission on Pensions and Re-establishment, *First Interim Report on the Second Part*, pp. 23–6

74 Ibid., p. 12; see also pp. 14–15.

75 Ibid., pp. 16–17. Sam Hughes had urged that 'some man or woman ... be

appointed to an official position, who would properly present these claims.'
Rowell had promised to consider the idea: CHC *Debates*, 23 May 1918,
p. 2481.

76 *Special Committee, 1922*, p. xi
77 *The Veteran*, 19 May 1923; On the Medical Advisory Board, see PC 1526, 22
   July 1922; J.L. Biggar memorandum 24 January 1923, RG 38, vol. 239,
   f. 8-9810-1; *The Veteran*, 12 August 1922; *Renseignements Utiles* (Ottawa
   1922), pp. 6–7, 10–11.
78 CHC *Debates*, 13 June 1923, pp. 3856ff
79 Ibid., p. 3875
80 *The Veteran*, 4 August 1923. MacNeil had to miss the sixth GWVA convention to fight the Senate battle.
81 In the Senate, see SC *Debates*, 29 June 1923, pp. 1258ff for Griesbach;
   p. 1268 for Power; and see ibid., 26 June 1920, p. 750.
82 Ibid., 29 June 1923, esp. pp. 1261, 1275–8
83 Pension Act, 1924 (14–15 Geo. V, c. 60). To be fair, the Senate also
   approved pensions for imprisoned men as Ralston had urged, cleaned up the
   apparent problem with 'meritorious cases,' and adopted Ralston's proposals
   for remarried widows. On the GWVA's sour conclusion about Senate-BPC col-
   lusion, see *The Veteran*, 18 August 1923.
84 Royal Commission on Pensions and Reestablishment, *Final Report*,
   pp. 10–11. See also *Second Interim Report on Second Part of Investigation*,
   pp. 6–7.
85 Ibid., p. 12.
86 Ibid., p. 30; see also pp. 23–31. At commission hearings Colonel McKeown
   had echoed the usual fears of fraud when veterans at Calgary and Regina
   urged the cause of widows who had married the disabled. See *The Veteran*,
   31 March, 1923.
87 *Second Interim Report on Second Part of Investigation*, p. 39
88 *Special Committee on Pensions, 1924*, testimony of Reilly and Topp, pp.
   223–81; for statistics on FAB appeals, see pp. 212–16.
89 Ibid., pp. 150–2
90 Ibid., p. 430
91 CHC *Debates*, 16 July 1923, pp. 4590–4603
92 SC *Debates*, 18 July 1924, p. 890
93 Ibid., p. 910
94 CHC *Debates*, 18–19, July, 1924, pp. 4860–9
95 Royal Commission on Pensions, *Final Report*, pp. 103–9
96 Ibid., p. 94
97 Ibid., p. 101
98 Ibid., p. 57; see also pp. 58–74.
99 Ibid., pp. 44–5
100 Ibid., p. 11
101 Ibid., p. 118
102 See *The Veteran* for January–April 1923, passim, on meetings with the
    Ralston Commission, especially at Vancouver and Winnipeg, 21 April 1923.
103 Royal Commission on Pensions, *Second Interim Report*, p. 51
104 Ibid., p. 73
105 *Final Report*, p. 83
106 Ibid., p. 24

107 Ibid., pp. 21–2
108 Ibid., p. 37

Chapter 9: Veterans' Unity

1 *The Veteran*, II, 4 (March 1919)
2 See Kristianson, *The Politics of Patriotism*, pp. 5–11. Kristianson's account of the Returned Soldiers' and Sailors' Imperial League of Australia underlines the remarkable parallels in the growth, decline, and problems of post-1918 veterans' movements.
3 On the American Legion, see Jones, *A History of the American Legion*; Moley, *The American Legion Story*, chapter 1. On John Taylor and the Legion, see Culp, 'American Legion,' pp. 3–14; Duffield, 'The American Legion in Politics,' p. 259.
4 On 'adjusted compensation,' see Weber and Schmeckebier, *Veterans' Administration*, p. 185; Moley, *American Legion*, pp. 88, 113–33; Ross, *Preparing for Ulysses*, pp. 12–14, 20–21; Dillingham, *Federal Aid to Veterans*, p. 154; Mayo, *Soldiers, What Next!* pp. 70–80, 83–97; Lisio, 'Bread and Butter Politics', pp. 42–3.
5 Culp, 'American Legion,' p. 5; Mayo, *Soldiers, What Next!* pp. 109–12
6 On membership, see Culp, 'American Legion,' p. ii; Gellerman, *The American Legion as Educator*.
7 On the British veteran, see Wooton, *British Legion*, pp. 1–7; and Wooton, *The Politics of Influence*, pp. 66–7.
8 Wooton, *The Politics of Influence*, pp. 66–7; Wooton, *British Legion*, pp. 10–11; Williams, *Byng of Vimy*, pp. 263–4
9 Cooper, *Haig*, vol. 2, pp. 421–5; Wooton, *British Legion*, pp. 14–15
10 On the Cape Town meeting, see Cooper, *Haig*, vol. 2, p. 427; *The Veteran*, III, 12 (November 1920), p. 18; IV, 6 (May 1921); MacNeil to Currie, 13 January 1921, Currie Papers, vol. 27, f. 2. On the search for public subsidy, see MacNeil to Meighen, 22 December 1920, Meighen Papers, vol. 55, f. 229, pp. 30595–6; Meighen to MacNeil, 8 February 1921, ibid., p. 30604.
11 On FIDAC, see Wooton, *British Legion*, pp. 70–74, 118–19.
12 On the Grand Army, see *CAR*, 1918, p. 588; Toronto *Daily Star*, 17 March 1919 and 5 September 1919; Andrew MacDuff to Borden, 11 August 1919, Borden Papers, vol. 240, f. RLB 2457, p. 134168; for a hostile view from the GWVA, see Combe, 'Veterans, Politics, and Class-Conciousness,' p. 14.
13 Loughnan in *The Veteran*, IV, 11 (October 1921)
14 Gwatkin to Lt-Col. H.G. Henderson, 21 October 1920, RG 24, vol. 444, f. HQ 54-21-1-163
15 *Proceedings of the Third ANV Convention*, p. 29
16 Ibid., p. 152; *CAR*, 1921, p. 349; 1922, p. 875
17 *Special Committee, 1920*, p. 659
18 *The Veteran*, III, 3 (February 1920) pp. 10, 38
19 MacNeil to Scammell, 13 August 1920, RG 38, vol. 173, f. 8382
20 *The Veteran*, IV, 1 (December 1920), p. 8
21 *Manitoba Free Press*, 18 October 1921
22 On the finances of the GWVA, see *Special Committee on the Canteen Fund*, pp. 196–7.
23 On the 'open door' debate, see Montreal *Gazette*, 27 March 1920.

24 *The Veteran*, VII, 22 (November 1924); see also ibid., III, 8 (July 1920), on the debate in the British Columbia GWVA.
25 *Special Committee on the Canteen Fund*, p. 190
26 See *The Veteran* IV, 8 (August 1921) and IV, 9 (September 1921); on Fourandex, see *CAR*, 1922, p. 876; *Saskatchewan GWVA Yearbook*, 1922–3.
27 *Proceedings of the Third ANV Convention*, pp. 147–8
28 *Manitoba Free Press*, 4–5 May, 1921; Toronto *Mail and Empire*, 5 May 1921
29 Toronto *Mail and Empire*, 4 May 1921; *The Globe*, 4 May 1921.
30 On Flynn and amalgamation, see Toronto *Daily Star*, 2 December 1919.
31 *CAR*, 1921, p. 349; *Manitoba Free Press*, 16 June 1921; *The Globe*, 16 June 1921
32 On attitudes to Flynn, see Combe in *The Veteran*, III, 11 (October 1920); Borden, ed., *Letters to Limbo*, p. 148. A memorandum prepared by the Department of National Defence for Earl Haig in 1925 recalled that early in his career the GAUV was 'in a bad odour because of a secretary who ended in jail.' RG 24, vol. 5939, HQ 293–78, part 2. In 1925 Currie told Haig that Flynn had been deported.
33 *CAR*, 1922, p. 874
34 See *Proceedings of the Fifth GWVA Convention, 1921*; *The Veteran*, IV, 9 (August 1921).
35 Cairns and Yetman, *History of the Veteran Movement*, vol. 1, p. 8; *Manitoba Free Press*, 17 June 1921
36 *The Globe*, 23 June, 1921; *Mail and Empire*, 12 June 1921
37 *Mail and Empire*, 22 June 1921. A.M. Hunter, an ANV executive member, made the claim and the argument.
38 'Spud,' in *The Veteran*, IV, 9 (August 1921); Loughnan, ibid., IV, 11 (October 1921), accused the GAUV of re-creating itself.
39 *The Veteran*, IV, 8 (July 1921). At the banquet for Maxwell at the Chateau Laurier, both Commodore Hose and General MacBrien, Canada's service chiefs, were among the guests.
40 *The Veteran*, IV, 9 (August 1921); *CAR*, 1921, pp. 349–50; *Manitoba Free Press*, 6 July 1921
41 *Mail and Empire*, 7 August 1921
42 *The Globe*, 26 September 1921; *CAR*, 1921, p. 349; testimony, Col. F.F. Clarke, *Special Committee on the Canteen Fund*, pp. 110–11
43 Currie to T.W. Kinder, 4 October 1921, Currie Papers, vol. 27, f. 3.
44 MacNeil to Currie, 4 October 1921, ibid.; Currie to MacNeil, 7 October 1921, ibid.,
45 J.H. Craig to Currie, 27 September 1921, ibid., f. 7
46 Currie to Maj.-Gen. R. Rennie, 10 October 1921; 17 October 1921, ibid., vol. 13, f. 39. See *CAR*, 1921, p. 349 for a partial list.
47 *The Globe*, 1 October 1921
48 On the Amputations Association, see ibid., 2 September 1921, 29 and 30 September, 1 October 1921; *The Veteran* IV, 12 (November 1921).
49 *Manitoba Free Press*, 18 October 1921
50 Ibid., 20 October 1921; *Proceedings of the Fifth GWVA Convention*. On the weekend meeting, see Port Arthur *Daily Times*, 17 October 1921.
51 Port Arthur *Daily Times*, 19 October 1921
52 *Manitoba Free Press*, 22 October 1921; *The Veteran*, 26 November, 3

December 1921, 21 February 1922; *Saskatchewan GWVA Yearbook*, 1922–3, pp. 58–9

53 On the conference, see *CAR*, 1922, p. 671; *The Veteran*, 7 January 1922, 14 January 1922.

54 'Report of the Amalgamation Conference Held in the Parliament Buildings, Winnipeg, Manitoba, commencing Monday, February 6, 1922,' CanVet Papers, p. 146

55 Ibid., p. 153

56 Ibid., pp. 280ff

57 *CAR*, 1922, p. 672

58 On the November 1922 DVA meeting, see *The Veteran*, 4–11 November 1922.

59 Ibid., 5 May 1923, 2 July 1923, 4 August 1923, 17 November 1923

60 *Special Committee on the Canteen Fund*, p. 1; *Proceedings of the Third ANV Convention*, p. 150

61 See *The Veteran*, III, 3 (February 1920) and passim.

62 *Special Committee, 1921*, pp. 403–8 (testimony of Lt-Col. J.L. Regan). 'Military institutes' were expected to be run for the benefit of their customers. Profits from the Navy and Army Canteen Board (which ran canteens in England) and from the Expeditionary Force Canteen Committee (which ran them in France) took considerable ingenuity to distribute. Canada's share, as of 18 June 1924, was $1,687,928.14 plus $55,554.99 in accrued interest. Regimental funds from the CEF, largely from units broken up in England, contributed $347,493.53 plus $51,269.87 in accrued interest. The War Office Cinematographic Fund, earned by showing war films to the public, contributed a Canadian share of $51,269.87 in capital and interest. RG 38, vol. 149, f. 8460, 'Minutes of the Canteen Fund Disposal Committee'; Royal Commission on Pensions, *Final Report*, 1924, pp. 144–5.

63 *Special Committee, 1921*, p. xxiv

64 MacNeil to Doherty, 29 June 1921, RG 38, vol. 148, f. 8461

65 PC 2378, 5 July 1921

66 PC 3647, PC 3648, 24 September 1921; see PC 3519, 21 September 1921 and PC 3887, 12 October 1921 for the smaller organizations. See Special Report on the Canteen Fund, *Journals of the Senate*, vol. 62, p. 352.

67 Board of Trustees, minutes, 27 September 1921, RG 38, vol. 148, f. 8462

68 See statements ibid., f. 8463.

69 A. Ross to Minister of Militia, 1 December 1921, ibid., f. 8461; secretary, Disabled Veterans' Association to Lougheed, 28 October 1921, and reply, 31 October 1921, ibid.

70 Parkinson to Lougheed, 16 September 1921, ibid.

71 On auditing the GWVA account, see T.O. Cox testimony, *Special Committee on the Canteen Fund*, pp. 161–4. On other associations, see Hugh McLeod to Parkinson, 29 May 1925, RG 38, vol. 148, f. 8462; E. Browne-Wilkinson to Parkinson, 5 June 1926, ibid., f. 8463.

72 King Diary, 2 September 1921

73 On the GWVA accounts, see *Special Committee on the Canteen Fund*, exhibit 23, p. 223.

74 Dominion Veterans Alliance, *Report of Amalgamation Conference*, 1922, p. 152

75 *The Veteran*, 24 December 1921 and passim, November 1921–January 1922

76 On the role of the DVA, see Royal Commission on Pensions, *First Interim Report on Second Part of Investigation*, p. 7; *Final Report*, p. 10.
77 Royal Commission on Pensions, *Final Report*, pp. 143–9
78 CHC *Debates*, 16 July 1924, p. 4868
79 *CAR*, 1922, p. 874; *The Veteran*, 26 November 1921
80 *The Veteran*, 11 November 1922
81 *Special Committee on the Canteen Fund*, p. 196; 'Report on the Canteen Fund,' in *Journals of the Senate*, 1925, vol. 62, p. 360.
82 In 1922 the profit paid two months' expenses for the dominion command. In 1923 MacNeil reported a profit of $1,926 and $1,529 in 1924: *Special Committee on the Canteen Fund*, p. 12. The GWVA's casual way of assigning 'administrative expenses' to Poppy Day probably concealed more gains than MacNeil admitted: see ibid., pp. 172–5 and passim.
83 PC 1565, 14 August 1923
84 *The Veteran*, 21 June 1923.
85 Ibid., 21 July 1923, 4 August 1923; on Sharpe, see 21 June 1923.
86 *Special Committee on the Canteen Fund*, p. 60; on the crisis, see ibid., p. 196; *The Veteran*, 3 November 1923; MacNeil to Currie, 2 May 1923, Currie Papers, vol. 27, f. 3.
87 Currie Papers, vol. 27, f. 3
88 Currie to MacNeil, 8 May 1923, ibid., f. 2
89 Currie to King, 7 May 1923, ibid.
90 Béland to Currie, 17 May 1923, ibid.
91 On the arrangement, see Scammell to Béland, 7 March 1923, RG 38, fol. 153, f. 6954 (a briefing on the history and operation of the fund to the end of 1924).
92 MacNeil to Currie, 18 June 1923, Currie Papers, vol. 27, f. 3
93 On the fund, see RG 38, vol. 139, f. 1838; Robinson to W.G. Radford, 29 September 1919, ibid., vol. 152, f. 8470; memorandum on the Disablement Fund, 16 February 1937, ibid., vol. 153, f. 6954; Carruthers to Scammell, 12 June 1923, cited in Scammell to Béland, 7 March 1925, ibid.
94 *Special Committee on the Canteen Fund*, p. 142
95 See ibid., pp. 79–80, 139–43, 146–8, 205–6; PC 1596, 16 September 1924; Scammell to Béland, 7 March 1925.
96 *Special Committee on the Canteen Fund*, p. 207
97 CHC *Debates*, 5 March 1925, pp. 777–95
98 Montreal *Star*, 6 March 1925
99 Taylor to DVA members, 17 April 1925 (copy to Hind, RG 24, vol. 5939, f. HQ 293-78, part 1). On Griesbach's prior knowledge, see Griesbach to Meighen 25 February 1925, Meighen Papers, vol. 137, pp. 82741–2.
100 SC *Debates*, 7 May 1925, pp. 243–6ff
101 *Special Committee on the Canteen Fund*, pp. 16–31
102 Ibid., pp. 123, 133ff
103 Ibid., p. 116
104 Ibid., p. 103
105 Ibid., pp. 6–12; *Journals of the Senate*, 18 June 1925, vol. 22, pp. 352–62
106 *The Globe*, 25 June 1925
107 *Special Committee on the Canteen Fund*, pp. 124–33, 138–9; Hind to Currie,

27 April 1925, Currie Papers, vol. 27, f. 4; Hind to Major-General Mac-
Brien, 19 June 1925, RG 24, vol. 5939, f. HQ 293-78, part 1; *The Globe*, 26
June 1925
108 Lighthall to MacNeil, 22 May 1925, in Currie Papers, vol. 27, f. 4
109 Currie to Lighthall, 28 May 1925, ibid., Currie to Haig, 27 April 1925, ibid.,
vol. 10, f. 10
110 *The Globe*, 26 June 1925
111 *Special Committee on the Canteen Fund*, p. 112
112 On Steacy, see Borden, ed., *Letters to Limbo*, p. 148; Morton, *Peculiar
Politics*, pp. 114-16.
113 *CAR*, 1925-6, pp. 640-2; *The Globe*, 30 June to 3 July 1925
114 Montreal *Star*, 28 July 1925; Cairns and Yetman, *The Veteran Movement*,
vol. 1, p. 81
115 Canadian Legion of Veterans, 'Record of the Preliminary Meeting of
Ontario Veterans' Associations,' (n.p., n.d.), Lighthall Papers
116 Canadian Legion, *Proceedings of Unity Conference*, pp. 1-10
117 Ibid., pp. 2-5; *Manitoba Free Press*, 24 and 25 November 1925
118 On Moore, see *The Legionary*, X, 1 (January 1935). On officers, see *Proceedings of Unity Conference*, p. 10.
119 *Proceedings of Unity Conference*, pp. 11-13
120 *CAR*, 1926-27, p. 638; *The Legionary*, I, 1 (15 May 1926)
121 Lake to Currie, 6 August 1926, Currie Papers, vol. 26, f. 7
122 Currie to Griesbach, 15 December, 1925, ibid.
123 Griesbach to Currie, 21 December, 1925, ibid.
124 *CAR*, 1927-8, p. 665, *The Legionary*, III, 2 (July 1928); III, 5 (October 1928)
125 Information supplied by friends of the authors.

Chapter 10: The Department of Pensions and National Health

1 Scammell to minister, 9 July 1920, RG 38, vol. 225, f. 8611
2 Todd to Scammell, 13 June 1922, ibid., vol. 200, f. 8-67, part 2
3 Statistics on departmental staff, institutions, and patient loads are found in
the DSCR's annual reports, 1919-27.
4 In 1929, for example, expenditure on veterans was $50 million, compared
with $122 million for the national debt. Transportation cost more, but was
shared by several departments. See *Historical Statistics*, H-20, H-29; *Canada
Year Book*, 1930. By 1934, federal welfare spending surpassed the cost of
veterans' programs.
5 Neatby, *William Lyon Mackenzie King*, vol. 2, pp. 67-8, 165, 172. On J.H.
King, see *Who's Who in Canada*, 1936-37, p. 867.
6 On the background to the Hunter Commission, see RG 38, vol. 167, f. 8623;
on political allegations, see Frank G.J. McDonagh to W.L.M. King, 7 June
1927, King Papers, J 2, vol. 2, f. D-5000, DSCR; H. Wray-King, 23 October
1927, ibid.
7 Royal Commission on Political Partisanship, *Report*, p. 4
8 Ibid., p. 12
9 On response, see Toronto *Globe*, 25 February 1928; Vancouver *Daily Province*, 21 February 1928; Regina *Leader*, 1 March 1928; Woodstock *Sentinel*

Star, 1 March 1928; and Charles Bishop report, n.d., in RG 38, vol. 167, f. 8623; Dr A.P. Proctor to Col. W.W. Foster, n.d., PAC, R.B. Bennett Papers, reel 1260, p. 321109.

10 *DSCR Report, 1927*. On Scott, see *Canadian Who's Who*, 1930, p. 975; on his report, Toronto *Daily Star*, 21 February 1928; Toronto *Globe*, 22 February 1928; Windsor *Star*, 20 January 1928. On Scott's subsequent career and death, see Bothwell and Kilbourn, *C.D. Howe*, pp. 10–11.

11 *The Legionary*, II, 10 (March 1928)

12 Ottawa *Journal*, 14 December 1927. On the new department, see 18–19 Geo. V, c. 39, 11 June 1928; on Scammell, see RG 32, C 2, vol. 233; on officials, see RG 38, vol. 153, f. 6954.

13 *Special Committee, 1924*, pp. 19–21, 22–5, 66–8; SSB, *Second Report*, p. 8.

14 *The Veteran*, 8 March 1924; 22 March 1924; 12 April 1924; Cairns and Yetman, *History of the Veteran Movement*, pp. 19–20

15 *Special Committee, 1924*, p. 234

16 Ibid., pp. 63–5. In the Senate, Griesbach urged revaluation. See SC *Debates*, 8 May 1924, p. 187. So did the Progressives: Carrigan, *Party Platforms*, p. 105. On GWVA pressure in 1925, see Saskatoon *Star Phoenix*, 18–19 March 1925; J.A. McAra to Meighen, 20 March 1925, Meighen Papers, vol. 137, f. 179(2), p. 82764.

17 On Legion policies, see *The Legionary*, 15 February 1927; Bowering, *Service*, pp. 60–1.

18 *The Legionary*, 1 March 1927, pp. 4, 13

19 On revaluation, see *CAR*, 1928–9, p. 178; *SSB Report, 1927*, pp. 18–20; *SSB Report, 1929*, pp. 10–14; *The Legionary*, 15 March 1927, p. 13.

20 *Report of Federal Appeal Board, 1923–1925*; RG 38, vol. 231, f. 8622. On relations between the boards, see Scammell to deputy minister of justice, 26 February 1926, ibid.; Scammell to minister of pensions and national health, 16 June 1930, ibid.; *Special Committee, 1928*, pp. 309–60 passim.

21 SC *Debates*, 12 May 1925, p. 601

22 CHC *Debates*, 4 May 1925, pp. 2842ff; SC *Debates*, 25 June 1925, p. 699. By 1927, the original twenty pages of the Pension Act had swollen to thirty.

23 CHC *Debates*, 7 April 1927, pp. 2046–93

24 Ibid., 12 April 1927, pp. 2430–7; *CAR*, 1926–7, p. 108. On the significance of the presumptive clause in the United States, see Weber and Schmeckebier, *Veterans' Administration*, p. 228.

25 *The Legionary*, II, 10 (March 1928)

26 See 'Memorandum on Pension Legislation Submitted by Canadian Legion, British Empire Service League,' RG 38, vol. 232, f. 8475.

27 *Special Committee, 1928*, p. 73

28 Ibid., p. 72

29 SC *Debates*, 1 June 1928, pp. 634 and passim; citation on p. 636

30 On the Pension Act, see *The Legionary*, III, 3 (August 1928), p. 15.

31 *Special Committee, 1928*, p. 309; Scammell to minister, 15 June 1930, RG 38, vol. 231, f. 8622; Col. A.J. Hunter, 'Cruel Nonsense in Pension Procedure,' *Saturday Night*, 29 March 1930

32 The Hyndman Committee in 1935 estimated the average age of veterans at forty-seven and the disabled at forty-one; *The Legionary*, X, 3 (March 1935), p. 4.

33 On 'burn-out,' see England, *Discharged*, p. 29; *Special Committee, 1921*, p. 460. Butler, *Australian Army Medical Services*, vol. 3, p. 816, attributes the term to Canada.

34 *The Legionary*, IV, 7 (December 1929); 'President's Message,' 26 November 1928, Currie Papers, vol. 26. On Currie, see Dancocks, *Sir Arthur Currie*, pp. 264–5 and passim; Montreal *Daily Star*, 21 April 1927.

35 On pressure, see, for example, M.M. Brotherhood to W.L.M. King, 7 March 1930, King Papers, J 2, vol. 2, f. D-5000. King's views are cited in Currie to J.B. Mitchell, 21 January 1930, Currie Papers.

36 *The Legionary*, IV, 11 (April 1930)

37 Ibid.; *Special Committee on Pensions, 1930*, p. 11. On La Flèche, see *The Legionary*, IV, 8 (January 1930).

38 *Special Committee on Pensions, 1930*, pp. xii–xiii

39 Ibid., p. xvii; 20–21 Geo. V, c. 35, s. 14 (includes text of s. 73); *Canadian Annual Review*, 1928–9, p. 76. On Power's role, see *The Legionary*, IV, 11 (April 1930); CHC *Debates*, 20 May 1930, pp. 2297–2307.

40 SC *Debates*, 27 May 1930, p. 330; CHC *Debates*, 28 May 1930, pp. 2297–2307

41 Canadian Legion, *Proceedings of Third Dominion Convention*, p. 210

42 *Special Committee, 1930*, p. 498; *CAR*, 1928–9, p. 178

43 *Special Committee, 1920*, p. 55; Department of Pensions and National Health, 'Pensions and Other Post-war Benefits,' June 1935, pp. 28–31, RG 38, vol. 195, f. 7261

44 'Pensions and Other Post-war Benefits,' p. 19, RG 38, vol. 195, f. 7261; *Canada Year Book*, 1932, pp. 1056–7; for details, see Senator Laird, SC *Debates*, 15 May 1930, pp. 210–11.

45 CHC *Debates*, 4 March 1930, pp. 267, 270

46 Currie to W.L.M. King, 28 May 1930, Currie Papers

47 See 'Life with R.B.,' ms, p. 116, PAC, R.K. Finlayson Papers. On Bennett and veterans, see Bennett papers, reels M-1258-M-1265, vols. 511–28 passim.

48 Woods, *The Men Who Came Back*, pp. 95–6; PC 2280, 30 September 1930, with J.R. Bowler added as an unpaid member

49 On FAB members, see J.A. Amyot to deputy minister of justice, 6 July 1931, RG 38, vol. 230, f. 8629; SC *Debates*, 16 May 1933, p. 533 passim

50 The tribunal was formed by PC 2265, 27 September 1930. On applications, see Bennett Papers, reel M-1261, pp. 321290ff.

51 Bennett to Hyndman, 17 January 1931, ibid., p. 321591. On others see ibid., p. 321485; Currie to Bennett, 3 December 1930, ibid., pp. 321571–2.

52 PC 2264, 27 September 1930. To match Olmsted's $4,400 salary, Topp took a cut in his FAB rate of $6,000. See PC 2263, 30 September 1930.

53 Board of Pension Commissioners, memorandum, 1 March 1932, Bennett Papers, reel M-1261, p. 321829; Department of Pensions and National Health, *Report*, 1932–3, *Canada Year Book*, 1932, p. 944. On desperation, see Bennett Papers, reel M-1262 passim. See, for example, Mrs Sabrina Harris to Bennett, 22 May 1931, telling of her helpless husband and her children without shoes or warm clothes; or see Mrs F.V. Beers to Bennett, 3 July 1934; 'I know money can't buy the love of God But it can pay Bills and taxes and food and cloths [*sic*]' (p. 323358).

54 Pension advocate to minister of pensions and national health, 28 February 1931, ibid., reel M-1258, p. 317455–7

55 See PAC, J.H. Hyndman Papers, vols. 2–5. Cases were decided in ten to thirty minutes.

56 J.S. Roper to Bennett, 4 June 1931, Bennett Papers, reel M-1261, pp. 321653–4. On disaffection, see Bowering, *Service*, pp. 69–70.

57 21–22 Geo. V, c. 44, 3 August 1931; *CAR*, 1931, p. 93. Sir Richard Turner was added on the plea that he was 'hard hit by the depression.' See R.L. Borden to Bennett, 10 July 1931, Bennett Papers, reel M-1261, p. 321709.

58 *The Canadian Veteran* (Ottawa), I, 2 (1 November 1932)

59 Currie to J.S. Roper, 28 May 1931, cited by *The Legionary*, VI, July 1931. See also Bennett to Currie, 31 December 1931, Bennett Papers, reel M-1261, p. 322039.

60 Canadian Legion Minute Books, book 2, pp. 100, 116 in PAC, MG 28 I, 298, vol. 1, file 4

61 *Canadian Veteran*, 1 November 1932. On appeals, see Scammell to Bowler, 10 January 1934, PAC, Ralston Papers, vol. 153. On the Associated Veterans, see Bowering, *Service*, pp. 71–2.

62 *Pension Act Committee, 1933*, pp. 5–10. See also CHC Debates, 10 October 1932, pp. 24, 48–9; *CAR*, 1933, p. 113

63 Thompson to Bennett, 16 February 1933, Bennett Papers, reel M-1261, pp. 321903–9

64 *Pension Act Committee, 1933*, pp. 34–5; Canadian Legion Minute Books, book 2, 8 January 1933, pp. 130–1. On Ross's findings, see Hyndman to Bennett, 8 February 1933, Bennett Papers, reel M-1261, pp. 321895–6.

65 CHC *Debates*, 20 April 1933, pp. 4093–4 and passim

66 See *Special Committee on Pensions, 1933*; CHC *Debates*, 12 May 1933, pp. 4932–7; SC *Debates*, 16 May 1933, pp. 533–4.

67 Cited by one of the tribunal members, Maj. Leo Warde, to Bennett, 12 March 1934, Bennett Papers, reel M-1261, pp. 321967–8, and not denied in the reply. See also Brig.-Gen. Alex Ross to Bennett, 22 March 1934, and reply, 27 April 1934, ibid., pp. 322048–9.

68 *The Legionary*, VIII, 9 (September 1933); VIII 11, (November 1933). On pension review, see MacLaren to Ralston, 27 March 1934, Ralston Papers, vol. 153; T.G. Harding to W.L.M. King, 24 June 1934, ibid.

69 *The Legionary*, IX, 4 (April 1934); Maritime Pensioners' Protective Association, Quebec Command, resolution, 15 March 1934, Ralston Papers, vol. 153

70 *CAR*, 1934, p. 122. On the post-1933 procedure, see chart, Ralston Papers, vol. 154.

71 On veterans and the depression in Canada, *Unemployment of Ex-Service Men*, pp. 5–6 and passim; England, *Discharged*, pp. 31–2.

72 On relief camps, see James Eayrs, *In Defence of Canada*, vol. 1, pp. 124–48; J.A. Swettenham, *McNaughton*, vol. 1, pp. 269–81.

73 On veterans' relief, see RG 38, vol. 195, f. 7261, 'Pensions and Other Postwar Benefits,' p. 18: *Canada Year Book*, 1933, p. 1048; 1936, p. 1055.

74 On cases, see CHC *Debates*, 12 May 1933, pp. 4930–1 passim (esp. G.G. Coote).

75 On the War Veterans' Allowances, see RG 38, vol. 195, f. 7291. On the terms, see Scammell to James Bleasdale, 21 March 1931, ibid., vol. 223, f. 8479; H.D. Pickworth to Mrs E. Sullivan, 16 July 1931, Bennett Papers, reel M-1263, p. 324423.

76 Dave McIntosh, 'Where We've Been ...,' *Legion* (January 1986), p. 20
77 CHC *Debates*, 23 April 1933, pp. 4930–1; *The Legionary* IX, 5 (May 1934)
78 On veterans elsewhere, see Ward, *The War Generation*, esp. pp. 5–7, 31–5; Kristianson, *The Politics of Patriotism*, pp. 49–69; Whalen, *Bitter Wounds*; and Wooton, *British Legion*.
79 Weber and Schmeckebier, *Veterans' Administration*, pp. 249–52; Ross, *Preparing for Ulysses*, pp. 25–9. See Culp, 'The American Legion,' Mayo, *Veterans What Next!* and Burlingame, *Peace Veterans*.
80 See Canadian Legion Minute Books, book 2, 13 August 1931, pp. 80ff, and 16 March 1934, p. 164.
81 McIntosh, 'Where We've Been ...,' pp. 20, 22; *The Legionary*, VIII, 11 (November 1933); Canadian Legion Minute Books, book 2, 8 January 1933, p. 135; on the problems of *The Legionary* see RG 38, vol. 182, f. 8525.
82 J.S. Roper to MacLaren, 7 December 1931, RG 38, vol. 153, f. 6754: Scammell circularized unit administrators to prove how useful the fund was. Several who found it a nuisance were not included in his ensuing report. M.A. Macaulay-Scammell, 21 September 1931, insisted that the fund caused extra work, supported a small core of men who often arrived drunk and demanding, and should be cancelled.
83 Canadian Legion Minute Books, book 2, 10 January 1932, p. 127
84 *The Legionary*, VIII, 9 (September 1933), pp. 3–4
85 Canadian Legion Minute Books, book 2, 9 March 1934, p. 149; 10 March 1934, p. 155
86 *The Legionary* IX, 4 (April 1934); Ottawa *Citizen*, 10–13 March 1934. MacNeil's report is in the *Citizen* of 14 March 1934.
87 Cited in Bowering, *Service*, pp. 75–6. A monthly column in *The Legionary* recorded Ross's travels and his views.
88 *The Legionary*, IX, 7 June 1934
89 Ibid., X, 3 (March 1935); *Committee on Unemployment of Ex-Service Men*, p. 3
90 *Committee on Unemployment of Ex-Service Men*, p. 13; estimate of unemployment, ibid., p. 5; *The Legionary*, X, 6 (June 1935).
91 *Committee on Unemployment of Ex-Service Men*, pp. 15–16; *The Legionary*, XI, 7 (July 1935)
92 Ross in *The Legionary*, XI, 2 (August 1935). The magazine was careful to indicate that political advertisements were paid for at regular rates: see ibid., IX, 9 (September 1934).
93 Ibid., XI, 5 (December 1935)
94 1 Edw. VIII, c. 47, 21 June 1936; PC 1862, 7 July 1936. See Bowering, *Service*, p. 80.
95 On activities, see RG 38, vol. 226, f. 5861; on commissionaires, see PC 56, 18 January 1937; and the Winnipeg *Free Press*, 28 December, 1937 on the first report.
96 J.G. Rattray to Dr Wodehouse, 31 August 1937, RG 38, vol. 226, f. 8636
97 *The Legionary*, XI, 8 (March 1936); *CAR*, 1935–6, 122; C.G. MacNeil to Legion presidents, 17 June 1936, PAC, J.S. Woodsworth Papers, vol. 14, f. 57. See also *Special Committee, 1936*; 'Memorandum Regarding Legislation Introduced by the Hon. C.G. Power ...' RG 38, vol. 226, f. 58–61; 1 Edw. VIII, c. 44, 23 June 1936.

98 Power to Macphail, 28 June 1939, and brief of the Canadian Non-pensioned Widows' Association, n.d., Woodsworth Papers, vol. 179, f. 8511.

99 'Memorandum Regarding Legislation ...'; 1 Edw. VIII, c. 48, 23 June 1936. *Canada Year Book*, 1940, pp. 1066–7. On War Veteran's Allowance, see Hyndman, *Report*, pp. 10–12.

100 On Vimy, see Bowering, *Service*; Canadian Legion Executive minutes, book 2, 8 January 1933, p. 138, and 27 November 1934, p. 186.

101 *The Legionary*, 1935–6, especially XI, 3 (September 1935); XI, 8 (March 1936); Murray, *The Epic of Vimy*; Bowering, *Service*, pp. 83–102; *CAR*, 1935–6, pp. 186–90; Woods, *The Men Who Came Back*, pp. 106–16; Woods modestly forgot that he was in charge of arrangements.

102 *Canada Year Book*, 1976–7, p. 300, table 6.14

103 On veterans' policies during the Second World War, see Woods, *Rehabilitation*; England, *Discharged* and *Twenty Million Veterans*. On the Veterans Land Act, see RG 38, vol. 225, f. 7269; Woods, *The Men Who Came Back*, pp. 86–9.

104 Weber and Schmeckebier, *Veterans' Administration*, p. 448; *Canada Year Book*, 1933, p. 1040

Bibliography

Primary Sources – Public Archives of Canada

PRIVATE PAPERS AND RECORDS

Sir William Baptie Papers (MG 30 E3)
Rev. Wm. Beattie Papers (MG 30 E4)
R.B. Bennett Papers (MG 26 K)
Sir Robert Borden Papers (MG 26 H)
Canadian National Institute for the Blind Records (MG 28 I233)
Francis A. Carman Papers (MG 30 E7)
Sir Adolphe Caron Papers (MG 27 I D 3)
Brooke Claxton Papers (MG 32 B5)
Sir Arthur Currie Papers (MG 30 E100)
Harold M. Daly Papers (MG 27 III F9)
A.F. Duguid Papers (MG 30 E12)
R.K. Finlayson Papers (MG 30 E143)
Sir George Foster Papers (MG 27 II D7)
Maj.-Gen. John Fotheringham Papers (MG 30 E53)
Sir Willoughby Gwatkin Papers (MG 30 E51)
Hon. J.D. Hyndman Papers (MG 30 E182)
Sir Edward Kemp Papers (MG 27 II D9)
Rt Hon. W.L.M. King Papers (MG 26 J)
J.H. McBrien Papers (MG 30 E63)
Sir Andrew Macphail Papers (MG 30 D150)
C.A. Magrath Papers (MG 30 E82)
Rt Hon. Arthur Meighen Papers (MG 26 I)
Sir William Otter Papers (MG 30 E242)
Sir George Perley Papers (MG 27 II D12)
J.L. Ralston Papers (MG 27 III B11)
B.H. Richardson Papers (MG 30 E187)
Royal Canadian Legion Records (MG 28 I298)
R.E.W. Turner Papers (MG 30 E46)
J.S. Woodsworth Papers (MG 27 III C7)

GOVERNMENT RECORDS

Civil Service Commission (RG 32)
Department of Indian Affairs (RG 10)
Department of the Interior (RG 15)
Department of Militia and Defence (RG 9)
Department of National Defence (RG 24)
Department of Veterans' Affairs (RG 38)
Governor-General's Office (RG 7)
Privy Council Office (RG 2)
Public Archives of Canada (RG 37)

Primary Sources – Other Archives

Canadian Patriotic Fund Records   McGill University Library
T.L. Church Papers   Ontario Archives
W.A. Griesbach Papers   Edmonton City Archives
Dr G.R. Johnson Papers   Glenbow-Alberta Institute
Main Johnson Papers   Metropolitan Toronto Public Library
W.D. Lighthall Papers   McGill University Library

Government Publications

AUSTRALIA

Repatriation Department, *Interim Report upon the Organization and Activities of the Australian Repatriation Department, 21 August 1919* (Melbourne, 1919)

BRITISH COLUMBIA

Returned Soldiers' Aid Commission, *Report* (Victoria, 1916)

CANADA

Auditor General, *Annual Reports*, 1915–1930 (cited as *BPC Report*)
Board of Pension Commissioners, *Annual Reports*, 1921–1930
Board of Pension Commissioners, *Instructions and a Table of Incapacities for the Guidance of Physicians and Surgeons Making Medical Examinations for Pension Purposes* (Ottawa, 1917, 1918).
Canadian Patriotic Fund, *Federal Emergency Appropriation Department Regulations* (n.d., n.p. [1919])
Commission to Investigate Methods of Stimulating Agricultural Production, *Report* (Ottawa, 1916)
Invalided Soldiers' Commission, *Some Facts about Occupational Therapy and Curative Workshops* (Toronto, 1919)
– *Report of the Invalided Soldiers' Commission* (Ottawa, 1918)
Military Hospitals Commission, *The Soldier's Return: From 'Down and Out' to 'Up and In Again': A Little Chat with Private Pat* (Ottawa, 1917)
– *Special Bulletin* (Ottawa, 1916)

Overseas Military Forces of Canada, Ministry of, Overseas Demobilization Committee, *First Interim Report*, 22 July 1918 (London, 1918)
- *Report*, 1918 (London, 1918), cited as *Report of the Ministry of Overseas Military Forces of Canada*
Militia and Defence, Department of, *Regulations and Orders for the Militia of Canada* (Ottawa, 1883, 1887, 1906), cited as *Regulations and Orders*
- *Report of the Board of Enquiry Relating to the Claims of Applicants for Fenian Raid Volunteer Bounty in the Province of Nova Scotia* (Ottawa, 1913)
Parliament, House of Commons, *Debates*, 1915–35; cited as CHC *Debates*
- Senate, *Debates*, 1915–35; cited as SC *Debates*
- Senate, *Journals*, 1925
- *Proceedings of the Special Committee Appointed to Consider and Report upon the Rates of Pensions to be Paid to Disabled Soldiers and the Establishment of a Permanent Pensions Board* (Ottawa, May 1916), cited as *Special Committee, 1916*
- *Proceedings of the Special Committee Appointed to Consider, Inquire into, and Report upon the Reception, Treatment, Care, Training and Re-education of the Wounded, Disabled and Convalescent who have served in the Canadian Expeditionary Force ... 1917* (Ottawa, 1918), cited as *Special Committee, 1917*
- *Proceedings of the Special Committee Appointed to Consider and Report upon the Pension Board, the Pension Regulations, and the sufficiency or otherwise of the relief afforded thereunder ... 20 May 1918* (Ottawa, 1918), cited as *Special Committee, 1918*
- *Proceedings of the Special Committee appointed to consider the questions of Pensions and Pension Regulations, and all matters pertaining thereto and to prepare a Bill Dealing with Pensions for the consideration of the House, 7 May, 1919* (Ottawa, 1919), cited as *Special Committee on Pensions, 1919*
- *Proceedings of the Special Committee appointed by Resolution of the House of Commons on the 18th of September, 1919, and to whom was referred Bill No. 10, An Act to amend the Department of Soldier's Civil Re-establishment Act ... 21 October 1919* (Ottawa, 1919), cited as *Special Committee, 1919*
- *Proceedings of the Special Committee appointed by Resolution of the House of Commons to consider the question of continuing the War Bonus to Pensioners, and any Amendments to the Pension Law which may be proposed ... 18 June 1920* (Ottawa, 1921), cited as *Special Committee, 1920*
- *Proceedings of the Special Committee appointed by Resolution of the House of Commons on the 10th of March, 1921, to consider questions relating to the Pensions, Insurance and Re-establishment of Returned Soldiers ... May 26th, 1921*, (Ottawa, 1921), cited as *Special Committee, 1921*
- *Report and Proceedings of the Special Committee Appointed by Resolution of the House of Commons of Canada on the 30th March 1922 to consider Questions Relating to Pensions, Insurance and Re-establishment of Returned Soldiers ...* (Ottawa, 1922), cited as *Special Committee, 1922*
- *Proceedings of the Special Committee Appointed to Consider Questions Relating to the Pensions, Insurance and Re-establishment of Returned Soldiers, 1924* (Ottawa, 1924), cited as *Special Committee, 1924*
- *Reports, Proceedings and Evidence of the Special Committee on Pensions and Returned Soldiers' Problems, 1928* (Ottawa, 1928), cited as *Special Committee, 1928*

- *Reports, Proceedings and Evidence of the Special Committee on Pensions and Returned Soldiers' Problems, comprising amendments to the Pension Act, Soldiers' Insurance Act, Land Settlement Act, the establishment of a Pension Tribunal and a Pension Appeal Court for War Veterans, 23 May 1930* (Ottawa, 1931), cited as *Special Committee, 1931*
- Senate of Canada, *Reports and Proceedings of the Special Committee Appointed to Inquire into the Administration of the Canteen Fund and the Disablement Fund and the Manufacture and Sale of Paper Poppies* (Ottawa, 1925), cited as *Special Committee on the Canteen Fund*
- *Report of the Special Committee on Pensions and Returned Soldiers' Problems* (Ottawa, 1933), cited as *Special Committee, 1933*
Pensions and National Health, Department of, *Annual Reports, 1928–39*
- *Report of the Committee Appointed to Investigate into the Administration of the Pension Act* (Ottawa, 1933), cited as *Pension Act Committee, 1933*
- *Report of the Committee Appointed to carry out an Investigation into the Existing Facilities in Connection with the Unemployment of Ex-Service Men and their Care and Maintenance While Unemployed* (Ottawa, 1935), cited as *Committee on Unemployment of Ex-Service Men*
Repatriation Committee, *War to Peace: The Programme of the Canadian Government Regarding the Returned Soldiers and Readjustment to Industrial Conditions* (Ottawa, 1919)
- *General Survey of Canada's Repatriation Plans, 15 February 1919* (Ottawa, 1919)
- *Returned Soldiers' Hand Book* (Ottawa, 1919)
- *Repatriation Speakers' Handbook* (Ottawa, 1919)
Royal Commission on Industrial Training and Technical Education, *Report*, vol. 1 (Ottawa, 1914)
Royal Commission to Inquire into and Report as to the Treatment of the men of the Canadian Expeditionary Force while on Board the Transport *Northland* on her voyage from Liverpool to Halifax, *Report* (Ottawa, 1919), cited as *Report of the Royal Commission on the Northland*
Royal Commission on Pensions and Re-establishment, *Report on the First Part of the Investigation* (Ottawa, 1923)
- *First Interim Report on Second Part of Investigation* (Ottawa, 1923)
- *Second Interim Report on Second Part of Investigation* (Ottawa, 1924)
- *Final Report* (Ottawa, 1924)
Royal Commission to Investigate Charges of Political Partisanship in the Department of Soldiers' Civil Re-establishment, *Report* (Ottawa, 1928)
Soldiers' Civil Re-establishment, Department of, *Report of the Work of the Invalided Soldiers' Commission* (Ottawa, 1918)
- *Invalided Soldiers' Commission* (Ottawa, 1919)
- *Annual Reports, 1919–27* (Ottawa, 1920–8), cited as *DSCR Report*
- *Report on the Inter-Allied Conference on the After-Care of Disabled Men* (Ottawa, 1919)
- *Reconstruction Bulletin* (Ottawa, 1917–18)
- *Back to Mufti*, vol. 1, no. 1 (Ottawa, 1919)
- *The Soldier's Return: How the Canadian Soldier Is Being Refitted for Industry* (Ottawa, 1919)
- (W.E. Segsworth) *Canada's Work for Disabled Soldiers* (Ottawa, 1919)

- *Handbook for the Information of Former Members of the Canadian and British Forces Resident in the United States of America* (Ottawa, 1920)
- *Summary of Report, Board of Tuberculosis Consultants* (Ottawa, 1921)
- *The Care and Employment of the Tuberculous Ex-Service Man after Discharge from the Sanatorium* (Ottawa, 1920)
- Soldier Settlement Board, *Annual Reports*, 1921–31, cited as *SSB Report*

GREAT BRITAIN

Disabled Sailors and Soldiers Compensation Committee, *Report ... on compensation for disabled sailors and soldiers under the Workmen's Compensation Act, 1906* (London, 1918)
Ministry of Pensions, *Comparative Tables Showing the Weekly Rates of War Pensions and Allowances ...* (London, 1919)
War Office, *Funds, Associations, Societies etc. for the assisting of serving and ex-service officers, men, women and their dependants* (London, 1920)

NOVA SCOTIA

Returned Soldiers Employment Committee (after 1918, Commission), *Reports, 1917–20* (Halifax, 1917–20)
- Sub-department of Technical Education, *Reports, 1916–20* (Halifax, 1916–20)

ONTARIO

Soldiers' Aid Commission, *Minutes of the Organizational Meeting, 17 November, 1915*
- Workmen's Compensation Board, *Reports, 1915–1921* (Toronto, 1916–21)
- Ontario Provincial Police, *Report of the Commissioner, 1922* (Toronto, 1923)

Secondary Sources

BOOKS AND THESES

Adami, Lt-Col. J.G., *Memorandum upon the Civil War Pension Evil in the United States and the Means Adopted to Arrest the Evil ...* (Ottawa, 1915)
Ames, H.B., *The City below the Hill* (Montreal: Bishop Engraving 1897)
- *The Housing of the Working Class* (Montreal, 1907)
Army and Navy Veterans, *Proceedings of the First Convention of the Army and Navy Veterans in Canada* (1918)
- *Proceedings of the Third Convention of the Army and Navy Veterans in Canada, Victoria, 11–15 October 1920* (Victoria, 1920)
Artibise, Alan J., *Winnipeg: An Illustrated History* (Toronto: James Lorimer, 1977)
Avery, Donald, *'Dangerous Foreigners': European Immigrant Workers and Labour Radicalism in Canada, 1896–1932* (Toronto: McClelland and Stewart, 1979)
Baggaley, Carman, *The Emergence of the Regulatory State in Canada, 1867–1939* (Ottawa: Economic Council of Canada, 1981)

Baker, Roscoe, *The American Legion and American Foreign Policy* (New York: Bookman Associates, 1954)

Beath, Robert B., *History of the Grand Army of the Republic* (New York: Bryan, Taylor and Co., 1889)

Bercuson, David J., *Confrontation at Winnipeg: Labour, Industrial Relations, and the General Strike* (Montreal: McGill-Queen's University Press, 1974)

- *Fools and Wise Men: The Rise and Fall of the One Big Union* (Toronto: McGraw-Hill Ryerson, 1976)

Bird, Thomas Baldwin, *The Function of Psychology in the Rehabilitation of Disabled Soldiers* (Iowa City, 1920)

Bird, Will R., *Ghosts Have Warm Hands*, 2nd ed. (Toronto: Clarke, Irwin, 1968)

Bishop, C.W., *The Canadian YMCA in the Great War* (Toronto: The YMCA, 1924)

Bliss, Michael, *A Canadian Millionaire: The Life and Business Times of Sir Joseph Flavelle, Bart* (Toronto: Macmillan 1978)

- *Banting: A Biography* (Toronto: McClelland and Stewart, 1984)

Borden, Henry, ed., *Letters to Limbo* (Toronto: University of Toronto Press, 1971)

Borden, R.L., *Memoirs*, 2 vols (Toronto: Macmillan, 1938)

Bothwell, Robert, and William Kilbourn, *C.D. Howe: A Biography* (Toronto: McClelland and Stewart, 1979)

Bowering, Clifford, *Service: The Story of the Canadian Legion, 1925–1960* (Ottawa: Legion House, 1960)

Brown, R.C., and G.R. Cook, *Canada, 1896–1921: A Nation Transformed* (Toronto: McClelland and Stewart, 1974)

- *Robert Laird Borden: A Biography*, 2 vols (Toronto: Macmillan, 1975 and 1980)

Bruce, H.A., *Report on the Canadian Army Medical Services* (London, 1916)

- *Politics and the CAMC* (Toronto: Wm. Briggs, 1919)

- *Varied Operations* (Toronto: Longmans, Green, 1958)

Bryce, James, *The American Commonwealth*, 2nd ed. (New York: Macmillan, 1910)

Burlingame, Roger, *Peace Veterans: The Story of a Racket and a Plea for Economy* (New York: Minton, Balch, 1932)

Butler, A.G., *The Australian Army Medical Services in the War of 1914–1918*, vol. 3: *Special Problems and Services* (Canberra: Australian War Memorial, 1943)

Cairns, Alex, and A.H. Yetman, *The History of the Veteran Movement, 1916 to 1925 and of the Canadian Legion, 1926 to 1935*, 2 vols (Winnipeg: Manitoba Veteran, 1961?)

Campbell, Marjorie Wilkins, *No Compromise: The Story of Colonel Baker and the CNIB* (Toronto: McClelland and Stewart, 1965)

Camus, Jean, *Physical and Occupational Re-education of the Maimed* (London: Baillière, Tindall, and Cox, 1918)

Canada Year Book, 1915–32

Canadian Annual Review, 1914–30

Canadian Legion, BESL, *Proceedings of the National Unity Conference and Draft Constitution* (Calgary, 1925)

- *Proceedings of the Third Dominion Convention, Regina, Saskatchewan, 25–28 November 1929* (Regina, 1930)
- *Proceedings of the Fifth Dominion Convention, Ottawa, Ontario, 1933* (Ottawa, 1933)
- *The Legionary* (Ottawa, 1926–39)

Canadian Legion of Veterans, *Record of a Preliminary Meeting of Ontario Veterans' Associations held in Toronto* ... (n.p., n.d.)

Carman, Francis, *The Return of the Troops: A Plain Account of the Demobilization of the Canadian Expeditionary Force* (Ottawa: King's Printer, 1920)

Carrigan, Owen, *Canadian Party Platforms* (Toronto: 1968)

Chadwick, H.D., and A.S. Pope, *The Modern Attack on Tuberculosis* (New York: The Commonwealth Fund, 1946)

Cole, G.D.H., *Labour in Wartime* (London: G. Bell and Sons, 1915)

Cooper, Duff, *Haig*, vol. 2 (London: Faber and Faber, 1936)

Corbett, E.A., *Henry Marshall Tory: Beloved Canadian* (Toronto: Ryerson Press, 1954)

Craig, Gerald M., *Upper Canada: The Formative Years, 1794–1841* (Toronto: McClelland and Stewart, 1963)

Creighton, D.G., *Harold Adams Innis: Portrait of a Scholar* (Toronto: University of Toronto, 1957)

Culp, Dorothy, 'The American Legion: A Study in Pressure Politics' (PH D dissertation, University of Chicago, 1939)

Cumming, Hugh, S., *The Work of the Public Health Service in the Care of Disabled Veterans of the World War* (Washington: U.S. Public Health Service, 1921)

Dancocks, Daniel, *Sir Arthur Currie: A Biography* (Toronto: Methuen, 1985)

Dark, Sydney, *The Life of Sir Arthur Pearson* (London: Hodder and Stoughton, c. 1922)

Darling, Frank, *Report of a Committee of the Council of the Toronto and York County Patriotic Fund Association* (Toronto, 1915)

Dearing, Mary R., *Veterans in Politics: The Story of the Grand Army of the Republic* (Westport, Conn.: Greenwood Press, 1974)

Dillingham, W.P., *Federal Aid to Veterans, 1917–1941* (Gainsville: University of Florida Press, 1952)

Dominion Veterans' Alliance, *Report of Amalgamation Conference* (Winnipeg, 1922)

Duffield, Marcus, *King Legion* (New York: J. Cape and H. Smith, 1931)

Duguid, A.F., *Official History of the Canadian Forces in the Great War, 1914–1919*, vol. 1 (Ottawa: King's Printer, 1938)

Dupré, J. Stefan, David M. Cameron, Graeme McKechnie, and Theodore Rotenberg, *Federalism and Policy Development: The Case of Adult Occupational Training in Ontario* (Toronto: University of Toronto Press, 1973)

Durkin, Douglas, *The Magpie* (Toronto: University of Toronto Press, 1974)

Eayrs, James, *In Defence of Canada*, vol. 1: *From the Great War to the Great Depression* (Toronto: University of Toronto Press, 1964)

English, John, *The Decline of Politics: The Conservatives and the Party System* (Toronto: University of Toronto Press, 1977)

England, Robert, *Discharged: A Commentary on Civil Re-establishment of Veterans in Canada* (Toronto: Macmillan 1943)
- *Twenty Million World War Veterans* (Toronto: Oxford University Press, 1950)
- *Living, Learning, Remembering: Memoirs of Robert England* (Vancouver: University of British Columbia Centre for Continuing Education, 1980)
Fialkowski, Bridget, *John L. Todd, 1876–1949: Letters* (Senneville, Que., 1977)
Fitzpatrick, Hon. Col. W., *The Repatriation of the Soldier: Vocational Training, Employment, Afforestation, Land Settlement* (Melbourne, 1917)
Francis, R.D., *Frank A. Underhill: Intellectual Provocateur* (Toronto: University of Toronto Press, 1986)
Fraser, Dawn, *Echoes from Labour's War* (Toronto: New Hogtown Press, 1976)
Gammage, Bill, *The Broken Years: Australian Soldiers in the Great War* (Canberra: Australian National University Press, 1974)
Gellermann, William, *The American Legion as Educator* (New York: Columbia University Teachers' College, 1938)
Gibbs, Philip, *Now It Can Be Told* (New York: Harper and Bros., 1920)
Gilbert, Martin, *Winston S. Churchill*, vol. 4: *1917–1922* (London, 1975)
Gordon, C.W., *Postscript to Adventure: The Autobiography of Ralph Connor* (Toronto: 1975)
Gourlay, Robert, *Statistical Account of Upper Canada*, vol. 1 (London, 1822)
Graham, Roger S., *Arthur Meighen*, vol. 1: *The Door of Opportunity* (Toronto: Clarke, Irwin, 1960)
Graves, Robert, *Goodbye to All That* (London: J. Cape, 1929)
Gray, James H., *Booze: The Impact of Whiskey on the Prairie West* (Toronto: Macmillan, 1972)
Gray, Justin, and Victor H. Bernstein, *The Inside Story of the Legion* (New York: Boni and Gaer, 1948)
Great War Veterans' Association, *Report of the First Convention, Winnipeg, Manitoba* (Winnipeg, 1917)
- *Report of the Second Convention, Toronto, Ontario* (Ottawa, 1918)
- *Report of the Third Convention of the Great War Veterans' Association, Vancouver, B.C.* (Ottawa, 1919)
- *Report of the Fourth Convention, Montreal, Quebec* (Ottawa, 1920)
- *Proceedings of the Fifth Convention, Great War Veterans' Association, Port Arthur, Ontario, 17–20 October 1921* (Port Arthur, 1921)
- *Proceedings of the Fifth Annual Convention, Alberta Command, Great War Veterans' Association, Calgary. 15–21 December 1921*
- *The Veteran* (Ottawa and Toronto, 1917–26)
Guest, Dennis, *The Emergence of Social Security in Canada* (Vancouver: University of British Columbia Press, 1981)
'Gunner,' *Compensation for Ex-Members of the CEF* (Toronto, 1920)
Haggard, Sir Henry Rider, *The After-War Settlement and Employment of Ex-Service Men in the Overseas Dominions: Report to the Royal Colonial Institute* (London, 1916)
Hallowell, Gerald A., *Prohibition in Ontario, 1919–1923* (Toronto: Ontario Historical Society, 1972)
Harris, Garrard, *The Redemption of the Disabled: A Study of Programmes of Rehabilitation for the Disabled of War and Industry* (Toronto: McClelland and Stewart, 1919)

Harris Turner's Weekly, 1918–20

Hopkins, J. Castell, *The Province of Ontario in the War* (Toronto: Warwick Bros. and Rutter, 1919)

Howe, Frederic Clemson, *The Land and the Soldier* (New York: Scribner's, 1919)

Hunt, M. Stuart, *Nova Scotia's Part in the Great War* (Halifax: Nova Scotia Veteran Publishing Co., 1920)

Hutt, C.W., *The Future of the Disabled Soldier* (London: Bale, 1917)

James, Marquis, *A History of the American Legion* (New York: W. Green, 1923)

Johnson, Paul B., *Land Fit for Heroes: The Planning of British Reconstruction 1916–1919* (Chicago: University of Chicago Press, 1968)

Jones, Richard Seelye, *A History of the American Legion* (Indianapolis: Bobbs-Merrill, 1946)

Kehey, Carl, ed., *Rehabilitation of the Wounded* (Philadelphia, 1918)

Kerr, W.D.B., *Shrieks and Crashes* (Toronto: Hunter Rose, 1929)

– *Arms and the Maple Leaf* (Seaforth, Ont.: Huron Expositor, 1943)

Khaki League (Montreal), *Report for 1915*

Knocker, Douglas, *Accidents in the Medico-Legal Aspect* (London, 1912)

Krawchuk, P., *The Ukrainians in Winnipeg's First Century* (Toronto: Kobzar Publishing, 1974)

Kristianson, G.L., *The Politics of Patriotism: The Pressure Group Activities of the Returned Servicemen's League* (Canberra, 1966)

Lamb, Dave, *Mutinies, 1917–1920* (Oxford and Cambridge, n.d.)

Leacy, F.H., ed., *Historical Statistics of Canada*, 2d ed. (Ottawa: Statistics Canada, 1983)

McEwan, Lt-Col. Robert D., *From Trench to Bench: A Glasgow Scheme Put Forward for Consideration, Suggestion, and Criticism* (Edinburgh, 1917)

McLennan, J.S., *What the Military Hospitals Commission Is Doing* (Ottawa, 1918)

McLennan, J.D., and Maj. R.T. MacKeen, *Report on the Inter-Allied Conference on the After-Care of Disabled Men, London, 1918* (Ottawa, 1919)

McMurtrie, Douglas, C., *The Disabled Soldier* (New York: Macmillan, 1919)

Macphail, Sir Andrew, *Official History of the Canadian Forces in the Great War, 1914–1919: The Medical Services* (Ottawa: King's Printer, 1925)

Manion, R.J., *Life Is an Adventure* (Toronto: Ryerson Press, 1936)

Martin, Chester, *'Dominion Lands' Policy* (Toronto: McClelland and Stewart, 1973, reprint)

Masters, D.C., *The Winnipeg General Strike* (Toronto: University of Toronto Press, 1950)

Mayo, Katherine, *Soldiers, What Next!* (Boston: Houghton Mifflin, 1934)

Mee, Arthur, *The Fiddlers: How Long Will You Go on Fiddling Till We Starve?* (Westerville, Ohio, 1917)

Metson, Graham, ed., *The Halifax Explosion: December 6, 1917* (Toronto: McGraw-Hill, Ryerson, 1978)

Minifie, James M., *Homesteader: A Prairie Boyhood Recalled* (Toronto: Macmillan, 1972)

Moley, Raymond Jr, *The American Legion Story* (New York: Duell, Sloan, and Pearce, 1966)

Morgan, Henry, ed., *Canadian Men and Women of the Time* (Toronto, 1912)

Morgan, Kenneth, and Jane Morgan, *Portrait of a Progressive: The Political Career of Christopher, Viscount Addison* (Oxford, 1980)

Morris, Philip H., *The Canadian Patriotic Fund: A Record of Its Activities from 1914 to 1919* (n.p., 1920)

Morton, Arthur S., *A History of the Canadian West*, rev. ed. (Toronto: University of Toronto Press, 1973)

Morton, Desmond, *Ministers and Generals: Politics and the Canadian Militia, 1868-1904* (Toronto: University of Toronto, 1970)

– *The Canadian General: Sir William Otter* (Toronto: Hakkert Press, 1974)

– *A Peculiar Kind of Politics: Canada's Overseas Ministry in the First World War* (Toronto: University of Toronto Press, 1982)

Mowat, C.L., *Britain between the Wars, 1918-1940* (Boston: Beacon Press, 1971)

Murray, W.W., *The Epic of Vimy* (Ottawa: The Legionary, 1936)

Neatby, Blair, *William Lyon Mackenzie King*, vol. 2: *The Lonely Heights* (Toronto: University of Toronto Press, 1964)

Nicholson, G.W.L., *The Canadian Expeditionary Force, 1914-1919: The Official History of the Canadian Army in the First World War* (Ottawa: Queen's Printer, 1962)

– *Canada's Nursing Sisters* (Toronto: S. Stevens, Hakkert, 1975)

– *Seventy Years of Service: A History of the Royal Canadian Army Medical Corps* (Ottawa: Borealis Press, 1977)

Oliver, Peter, *Howard Ferguson: Ontario Tory* (Toronto: University of Toronto Press, 1977)

Palmer, Howard, *Patterns of Prejudice* (Toronto: McClelland and Stewart, 1982)

Pettigrew, Eileen, *The Silent Enemy: Canada and the Deadly Flu of 1918* (Saskatoon: Western Producer, 1983)

Piven, Frances Fox, and Richard A. Cloward, *Regulating the Poor: The Functions of Public Welfare* (London: Tavistock Publications, 1971)

Prang, Margaret, *N.W. Rowell: Ontario Nationalist* (Toronto: University of Toronto Press, 1975)

Prost, Antoine, *Les Anciens Combattants* (Paris, 1977)

Rawlinson, James H., *Through St Dunstan's to Light* (Toronto: Thomas Allen, 1919)

Read, Daphne, ed., *The Great War and Canadian Society: An Oral History* (Toronto: New Hogtown Press, 1978)

Robin, Martin, *Radical Politics and Canadian Labour, 1880-1930* (Kingston: Industrial Relations Centre, Queen's University, 1968)

Robinson, Catherine Beverley, *Soldier Citizens* (Toronto, 1918)

Romain, Jules, *Men of Good Will*, vol. 8: *Verdun* (New York, 1940)

Ross, David R.B., *Preparing for Ulysses: Politics and Veterans during World War II* (New York: Columbia University Press, 1969)

Rutherford, Paul, ed., *Saving the Canadian City* (Toronto: 1974)

Saskatchewan GWVA, *Yearbook, 1922-1923*

Samuelson, Paul A., *After the War 1918-1920: Military and Economic Demobilization of the United States: Its Effects upon Employment and Income* (Washington: U.S. Government Printing Office, 1943)

Scammell, Ernest, *The Provision of Employment for Members of the Canadian Expeditionary Force on Their Return to Canada and the Re-education of Those*

Who Are Unable to Follow Their Previous Occupations Because of Disability (Ottawa, 1916), cited as Scammell, *Provision of Employment*
- *Summary of Activities of the Government of Canada in Connection with the Demobilization and Re-establishment of Members of the Canadian Expeditionary Force to 31st December 1923* (Ottawa, 1924), cited as Scammell, *Summary*

Schull, Joseph, *Ontario since 1867* (Toronto: McClelland and Stewart, 1978)
Segsworth, Walter E., *Retraining Canada's Disabled Soldiers* (Ottawa: King's Printer, 1920)
Shryock, Richard H., *National Tuberculosis Association, 1904–1954* (New York: National Tuberculosis Association, 1968)
Smith, G. Oswald, *University of Toronto Roll of Service, 1914–1918* (Toronto: University of Toronto Press, 1921)
Struthers, James, *No Fault of Their Own: Unemployment and the Canadian Welfare State, 1914–1941* (Toronto: University of Toronto Press, 1983)
Swettenham, John, *McNaughton*, vol. 1 (Toronto: Ryerson Press, 1968)
- *The End of the War* (Ottawa: Department of National Defence, Directorate of History, n.d.)
Thompson, John H., *The Harvests of War: The Prairie West, 1914–1918* (Toronto: McClelland and Stewart, 1978)
Thompson, John H., and Allan Seager, *Canada, 1922–1939: Decades of Discord* (Toronto: McClelland and Stewart, 1985)
Thomson, W.P., *The University of Saskatchewan: A Personal History* (Toronto: 1970)
Trattner, Walter I, ed., *Social Welfare and Social Control: Some Historical Reflections on Regulating the Poor* (Knoxville: University of Tennessee Press, 1983)
United States, Bureau of Reclamation, *Farms for Returned Soldiers* (Washington, 1918)
Van Paasen, Pierre, *Days of Our Years* (New York: Dial Press, 1946)
Wade, Mason, *The French Canadians*, vol. 2, rev. ed. (Toronto: Macmillan, 1968)
Waite, Peter B., *The Man from Halifax: Sir John Thompson* (Toronto: University of Toronto Press, 1985)
Waller, Willard, *The Veteran Comes Back* (New York: Dryden Press, 1944)
Ward, Stephen R., ed., *The War Generation: Veterans of the First World War* (Port Washington, NY: Kennikat Press, 1975)
Warner, William Howard, *The Soldier Colonists: A Plea for Group Organization* (London, 1918)
Weber, Gustavus, *The Bureau of Pensions: Its History, Activities, and Organization* (Baltimore: Johns Hopkins University Press, 1923)
Weber, Gustavus, and Laurence F. Schmeckebier, *The Veterans' Administration: Its History, Activities, and Organization* (Washington: Brookings Institution, 1934)
Wecter, Dixon, *When Johnny Comes Marching Home* (Boston: Houghton Mifflin, 1944)
Werner, Morris R., *Privileged Characters* (New York: Arno Press, 1974)
Whalen, Robert W., *Bitter Wounds: German Victims of the Great War, 1914–1919* (Ithaca: Cornell University Press, 1984)

Who's Who in Canada, 1922–31 (Toronto, 1922–31)

Who's Who and Why, 1915–21 (Toronto, 1915–21)

Willenz, June A., *Women Veterans: America's Forgotten Heroines* (New York, 1983)

Williams, Jeffery, *Byng of Vimy* (London: Secker and Warburg, 1983)

Wilson, Barbara, *Ontario and the First World War* (Toronto: The Champlain Society, 1977)

Winter, C.F., *Lt-Gen. the Hon. Sir Sam Hughes* (Toronto: Macmillan, 1931)

Winter, Denis, *Death's Men: Soldiers of the Great War* (London: Allen Lane, 1978)

Wood, H.F., and J.A. Swettenham, *Silent Witnesses* (Toronto: Hakkert 1974)

Woods, Walter S., *Rehabilitation: A Combined Operation* (Ottawa: Queen's Printer, 1953)

– *The Men Who Came Back* (Toronto: Ryerson Press, 1956)

Wooton, Graham, *The Politics of Influence: British Ex-Servicemen, Cabinet Decisions and Cultural Change (1917–1957)* (London: Routledge and Kegan Paul, 1963)

– *The Official History of the British Legion* (London: Macdonald and Evans, 1956)

ARTICLES

Ames, T.H., 'The Prevention of War Neuroses,' *Canadian Medical Week* (Toronto: 1918)

Armstrong, George E., 'The Influence of the War on Surgery, Civil and Military,' *Canadian Medical Association Journal*, 9, 5 (May 1919)

Ashton, E.J., 'Soldier Settlement in Canada,' *Quarterly Journal of Economics* (May 1925)

Bannerman, James, 'The Biggest Spender We Ever Had,' in L.F. Hannon, ed., *Maclean's Canada: Portrait of a Country* (Toronto, 1960)

Bates, Gordon, 'Some Broader Aspects of the Venereal Disease Problem,' *Canadian Public Health Journal*, 10 (1918)

– 'Venereal Diseases from the Preventive Aspects,' *Canadian Medical Association Journal*, 9 (September 1919)

Béland, H.S., 'The Returned Soldier,' *Annals of the American Academy of Political Science*, 107 (May 1923)

Bell, Lt-Col. F. McKelvey, 'Medical Services of the Department of Soldiers' Civil Re-establishment,' *Canadian Medical Association Journal*, 9, 1 (January 1919)

Biggar, J.L., 'The Pensionability of the Disabled Soldier,' *Canadian Medical Association Journal*, 9, 1 (January 1919)

– 'The Economic Effects of Disablement,' *Canadian Medical Association Journal*, 9, 2 (March 1919)

– 'State Medicine and Rehabilitation,' *Canadian Medical Association Journal*, 9, 11 (November 1919)

Black, Adam, 'Salvaging War's Waste: The System Successfully Employed by the Military Hospitals Commission of Canada,' *Red Cross Magazine* (October 1917)

Boate, G.A., 'The Relation of the Short Intensive Industrial Survey to the Problems of Soldier Re-education,' *Red Cross Institute for Disabled Men*, 1, 10, (6 May 1918)

Bothwell, Robert S., and John R. English, 'Pragmatic Physicians, Canadian Medicine and Health-Care Insurance, 1910-1945,' in S.E.D. Shortt, ed., *Medicine in Canadian Society: Historical Perspectives* (Montreal, 1981)

Bresil, J., 'The Vocational School for Disabled Soldiers at Rouen, France,' *American Journal of Care for Cripples*, 6 (1918)

Broster, C.J., 'The Guelph Military Convalescent Hospital, 1917-1921,' address, Guelph Civic Museum, 8 November 1984

Brown, Tom, 'Shell-Shock in the Canadian Expeditionary Force, 1914-1918: Canadian Psychiatry in the Great War,' in Charles G. Roland, ed. *Health, Disease, and Medicine: Essays in Canadian History* (Hamilton, 1984)

Bruce, Herbert A., 'Surgical Efficiency in an Army Medical Service,' *Canadian Medical Association Journal*, 9, 11 (November 1919)

Buckley, Suzann, 'The Failure to Resolve the Problems of Venereal Disease among the Troops in Britain during World War I,' in Brian Bond and I. Roy, *War and Society: A Yearbook of Military History* (New York, 1977)

Buckley, Suzann, and Janice Dickin McGinnis, 'Venereal Disease and Public Health Reform in Canada,' *Canadian Historical Review*, 63, 3 (September 1982)

Cameron, Col. Irving, 'Surgical Observations with Especial Reference to Orthopaedics,' in *Canadian Medical Week* (Toronto 1918)

Cathcart, J.P.S., 'The Neuro-Psychiatric Branch of the Department of Soldiers' Civil Re-establishment,' *Ontario Journal of Neuro-Psychiatry* (May 1928)

Chapman, T.L., 'The Anti-drug Crusade in Western Canada, 1885-1925,' in D.J. Bercuson and L.A. Knafla, eds., *Law and Society in Canada in Historical Perspective* (Calgary, 1979)

Cline, Peter, 'Winding down the War Economy: British Plans for Peacetime Recovery, 1916-19,' in Kathleen Burk, ed., *War and the State: The Transformation of British Government, 1914-1919* (London, 1982)

Combe, C.V., 'Veterans, Politics and Class-Consciousness,' *The Veteran*, 3, 11 (October 1920)

Corry, J.A., 'The Growth of Government Activities in Canada, 1914-1921,' *Historical Papers* (1940)

Craig, Hamilton, 'The Loyal and Patriotic Society of Upper Canada,' *Ontario History*, 52, 1 (March 1960)

Cuthand, Stan, 'The Native People of the Prairie Provinces,' in Ian A.L. Getty and Donald B. Smith, eds., *One Century Later: Western Canadian Reserve Indians since Treaty 7* (Vancouver, 1978)

Dennis, J.S., 'Provision for Crippled Soldiers by the Military Hospitals Commission of Canada,' *American Journal of Care for Cripples*, 5, 1 (1917)

Dunn, Timothy A., 'Teaching the Meaning of Work: Vocational Education in British Columbia, 1900-1929,' in David C. Jones, Nancy M. Sheehan, and Robert M. Stamp, eds., *Shaping the Schools of the Canadian West* (Calgary 1979)

Eaton, Ralph M., 'The Social Unrest of the Soldier,' *International Journal of Ethics*, 21, 2 (April 1921)

England, Robert, 'Disbanded and Discharged Soldiers in Canada Prior to 1914,' *Canadian Historical Review*, 27, 1 (March 1946)

Englander, David, and James Osborne, 'Jack, Tommy, and Henry Dubb: The Armed Forces and the Working Class,' *The Historical Journal*, 21, 3 (September 1978)

Entz, W., 'The Suppression of the German-Language Press in September, 1918 (With Special Reference to the Secular German-Language Press in Western Canada),' *Canadian Ethnic Studies*, 8, 2 (1976)

Farrar, Clarence B., 'War and Neurosis: With Some Observations of the Canadian Expeditionary Force,' *American Journal of Insanity*, 76, 1 (July 1917)

– 'Rehabilitation in Nervous and Mental Cases among Ex-Soldiers,' *American Journal of Insanity*, 76, 2 (October 1919)

Fay, C.R., 'Diminishing Returns in Agriculture,' *Journal of the Canadian Bankers' Association*, 32, 1 (January 1924)

Frost, Stanley, 'Where Veterans Fell among Friends,' *The Outlook*, 135, 6 (10 October 1923)

Gadsby, H.F., 'The Government Leader in the Senate', *Canadian Liberal Monthly*, 1, 11 (July 1914)

Graubard, S.R., 'Military Demobilization in Great Britain following the First World War,' *Journal of Modern History*, 19, 4 (December 1947)

Griffiths-Boscawen, Lt-Col. Arthur, 'Pensions and Parliament,' *Reveille*, 3 (Winter 1919)

Gunn, Jean, 'The Services of Canadian Nurses and Voluntary Aides during the War,' *The Canadian Nurse and Hospital Review*, 15, 9 (September 1919)

Haultain, H.E.T., 'Industrial Rehabilitation,' *The Canadian Medical Week* (1918)

Hill, H.W., 'The Future Function of Modern Medicine,' *Canadian Medical Association Journal*, 11 (1921)

Hodge, John, 'Pensions Administration,' *Reveille*, 1 (August 1919)

Horrall, S.W., 'The Royal North-West Mounted Police and Labour Unrest in Western Canada, 1919,' *Canadian Historical Review*, 61, 2 (June 1980)

Humphries, Charles W., 'The Sources of Ontario "Progressive Conservatism," ' *Historical Papers* (1967)

Hunter, Col. A.J., 'Cruel Nonsense in Pension Procedures,' *Saturday Night*, 29 March 1930

Jackson, Gilbert, 'The New Order,' *Canadian Medical Association Journal*, 12 (1922)

Kennedy, Howard Angus, 'Reconstructing in Canada,' *Reveille*, 3 (Winter 1919)

Kidner, Thomas B., 'Vocational Re-education of Disabled Soldiers,' in National Education Association, *Addresses and Proceedings* (1918)

– 'Vocational Work of the Invalided Soldiers' Commission of Canada,' *Annals of the American Academy of Political and Social Science*, 80 (November 1918)

Kohn, Richard L, 'The Social History of the American Soldier: Review and Prospects for Research,' *American Historical Review*, 86, 3 (June 1981)

Koroscil, Paul M., 'Soldiers, Settlement, and Development in British Columbia, 1915–1930,' *BC Studies*, 54 (Summer 1982)

Laut, Agnes, C., 'Soldier Settlement Making Good,' *Maclean's Magazine*, 15 (February 1921)

– 'Little Bundles of Pluck,' *Maclean's Magazine*, 15 March 1921

Levitas, Arnold (pseud.), 'Training for Disabled Soldiers and Sailors,' *Educational Review*, 57, 4 (April 1919)

Lisio, Donald J., 'United States: Bread and Butter Politics,' in Stephen J. Ward, ed., *The War Generation: Veterans of the First World War* (Washington, NY, 1975)

McCallum, Margaret, 'Nova Scotia and the Returned Soldier, 1915–1923,' ms

- 'Canadian Pensions in Politics and Law,' ms
McCuaig, Katherine, 'From Social Reform to Social Service: The Changing Role of Volunteers: The Anti-Tuberculosis Campaign, 1900–1930,' *Canadian Historical Review*, 61, 4 (December 1980)
McDonald, John, 'Soldier Settlement and Depression Settlement in the Forest Fringe of Saskatchewan,' *Prairie Forum*, 6, 1 (1981)
Mackintosh, Dave, 'Where We've Been,' *Legion* (January 1986)
Macleod, Donald, 'Practicality Ascendant: The Origins and Establishment of Technical Education in Nova Scotia,' *Acadiensis*, 15, 2 (Spring 1986)
McMurtrie, Douglas C., 'The Canadian Publicity Campaign in the Interests of Crippled Soldiers, Their Re-education and Employment,' *American Journal of Care for Cripples*, 5, 1 (1917)
- 'Reconstructing the War Cripple in Alberta,' *American Journal of Care for Cripples*, 5, 2 (1917)
- 'Vocational Training for the Canadian War Cripple: Evidence Presented before the Parliamentary Committee on Returned Soldiers,' *American Journal of Care for Cripples*, 5, 2 (1917)
- 'Care of Crippled Soldiers and Sailors,' *New York Evening Post*, 31 August 1917
- 'Rehabilitation of the War Cripple,' *New York Red Cross Institute for Crippled and Disabled Men* (New York, 1918)
- 'The Rehabilitation of Disabled Soldiers,' *Western Medical Times* (October 1918)
- 'The Influence of Pension or Compensation Administration on the Rehabilitation of Disabled Soldiers,' *American Medicine* (June 1919)
Martin, John D.P., 'The Regiment de Watteville: Its Settlement and Service in Upper Canada,' *Ontario History*, 52, 1 (March 1960)
Millar, G.C., 'The Men Who Came Back,' *MacLean's Magazine*, 1 December 1921
Morton, Desmond, 'Sir William Otter and Internment Operations in Canada During the First World War,' *Canadian Historical Review*, 55, 1 (March 1974)
- 'Polling the Soldier Vote: The Overseas Campaign in the Canadian General Election of 1917,' *Journal of Canadian Studies*, 10, 4 (Autumn 1975)
- The Cadet Movement in the Moment of Canadian Militarism, 1909–1914,' *Journal of Canadian Studies*, 13, 2 (Summer 1978)
- ' "Kicking and Complaining": Postwar Demobilization Riots in the Canadian Expeditionary Force, 1918–1919,' *Canadian Historical Review*, 61, 3 (September 1980)
- ' "Noblest and Best": Retraining Canada's War Disabled, 1915–1923,' *Journal of Canadian Studies*, 16, 3–4 (Autumn–Winter 1981)
Morton, Desmond, and Glenn Wright, 'The Bonus Campaign, 1919–1921: Veterans and the Campaign for Re-establishment,' *Canadian Historical Review*, 64, 2 (June 1983)
Morton, John P., 'Medicine and Democracy,' *Canadian Medical Week* (1918)
Patch, Lt-Col. F.S., 'The Military Aspect of the Venereal Disease Problem in Canada,' *Canadian Public Health Journal*, 8 (1917)
Pearson, George, 'Fitting in the Returned Men,' *Maclean's Magazine*, 32 (March 1919)
Pelletier, F., 'La ré-éducation des mutilés de guerre,' *Reforme Sociale*, 1 (1916)

Percy, Alde, 'What France Is Doing for Her Disabled Soldiers and Sailors,' *Progress*, 12 (1917)

Piven, Francis Fox, and Richard A. Cloward, 'Humanitarianism in History: A Response to the Critics,' in Walter I. Trattner, ed., *Social Welfare or Social Control: Some Historical Reflections on Regulating the Poor* (Knoxville 1983)

Primrose, Col. A., 'Presidential Address,' *Canadian Medical Association Journal*, 9, 1 (January 1919)

Raudzens, George, 'A Successful Military Settlement: Earl Grey's Enrolled Pensioners of 1846 in Canada,' *Canadian Historical Review*, 52, 4 (December 1971)

Remond, René, 'Les anciens combattants et la politique,' *Revue française de la science politique*, 5, 2 (avril–juin 1955)

Risk, R.C.B., 'Lawyers, Courts, and the Rise of the Regulatory State,' *Dalhousie Law Review*, 9, 4 (November 1984)

Roland, Charles G., 'War Amputations in Upper Canada,' *Archivaria*, 10, 2 (Summer 1980)

Russell, Colin K., 'A Study of Certain Psychogenetic Conditions among Soldiers,' *Canadian Medical Association Journal*, 7, 8 (August 1917)

– 'Psychogenetic Conditions in Soldiers: Their Aetiology, Treatment, and Final Disposal,' *Canadian Medical Week* (1918), and *Canadian Medical Association Journal*, 8, 8 (August 1918)

– 'The Nature of War Neuroses,' *Canadian Medical Association Journal*, 61, 12 (December 1939)

Sautter, Udo, 'The Origins of the Employment Service of Canada, 1900–1920,' *Labour/le Travailleur* 6 (1980)

– 'Measuring Unemployment in Canada: First Efforts Before World War II,' *Histoire sociale/Social History*, 15, 30 (1982)

Scammell, Ernest H., 'Canadian Practice in Dealing with Crippled Soldiers,' *American Journal of Care for Cripples*, 5, 2 (1917)

Sexton, F.H., 'Education for Industry in Nova Scotia,' *Dalhousie Review*, 1, 1 (March 1921)

Shultz, John, 'Finding Homes Fit for Heroes: The Great War and Empire Settlement,' *Canadian Journal of History*, 18, 1 (April 1983)

Sidebothom, H., 'The Employment of the War-Disabled,' *Contemporary Review*, 115 (June 1919)

Smith, David E., 'Emergency Government in Canada,' *Canadian Historical Review*, 50, 4 (December 1969)

Somerville, R.S., 'Canadian Celebrities, No. 69: Mr. W.D. Lighthall,' *Canadian Magazine*, 26 (1905–6)

Stacey, C.P., 'The War of 1812 in Canadian History,' in Morris Zaslow, ed., *The Defended Border: Upper Canada and the War of 1812* (Toronto 1964)

Struthers, James, 'Prelude to Depression: The Federal Government and Unemployment, 1918–1929,' *Canadian Historical Review*, 58, 3 (September 1977)

Swettenham, J.A., 'The End of the War,' ms, Directorate of History, National Defense Headquarters

Tawney, R.H., 'The Abolition of Economic Controls, 1918–1921, in Winter, J.M., ed., *History and Society: Essays by R.H. Tawney* (London 1978)

Todd, Maj. J.L., 'The French System of Return to Civil Life of Crippled and Discharged Soldiers,' *American Journal of Care for Cripples*, 5, 1 1917

– 'Major, CAMC,' 'Returned Soldiers and the Medical Profession,' *Canadian Medical Association Journal*, 7, 4 (April 1917)

- 'The Meaning of Rehabilitation,' *Annals of the American Academy of Political and Social Science*, 80 (November 1918)
- 'The Duty of the War Pension,' *North American Review*, 210, 767 (October 1919)
Todd, Maj. J.L., and Thomas B. Kidner, 'The Re-training of Disabled Men,' *American Medicine* (Spring 1917)
Verma, Dhirendra, 'Frederick H. Sexton: Canadian Dean of Vocational Education,' *Journal of Education*, 3, 1 (1979)
Vince, D.M.A.R., 'The Acting Overseas Sub-militia Council and the Resignation of Sir Sam Hughes,' *Canadian Historical Review*, 31, 1 (March 1950)
Von Eberts, E.M., 'Functional Re-education and Vocational Training of Soldiers Disabled in War,' *Canadian Medical Association Journal*, 8, 3 (March 1917)
Wade, C.G., 'The Problem of the Demobilized Soldier,' *Empire Review*, 31, 80 (1917)
Ward, Stephen R., 'Great Britain: Land Fit for Heroes Lost,' in Stephen Ward, ed., *The War Generation: Veterans of the First World War* (Washington, NY, 1975)
Williams, E.J., 'The Return of the Army Medical Officer,' *Canadian Medical Association Journal*, 9, 3 (March 1919)
Woodhouse, Chase G., 'Returning the Soldier to Civilian Life,' *South Atlantic Quarterly* 5, 17 (October 1918)

Picture Credits

Unless otherwise noted below, all photographs are from the Department of Veterans' Affairs.

James Collection, City of Toronto Archives: Toronto veterans at Fenian Raid memorial; Toronto veterans on the march after the war

From *Puck*: The 'Pension Evil' cartoon

From *Canadian Construction*, May 1917: MHC meets tuberculosis consultants

Public Archives of Canada: The Wounded Soldier's Return C95286; Mewburn, Borden, and Kemp PA5725; 3rd Battalion waiting to embark on *Olympic* PA6155; *Olympic* at Halifax PA22996; discharged soldiers at Saint John PA23002

Scammell Collection, in possession of one of the authors: 'Private Pat'

Canadian War Museum: three photos of Kinmel's 'Tin Town' riots

From the *Mail and Empire*: That First Civie Collar

Foote Collection, Manitoba Archives: A suitable home for a soldier settler; a demonstration by unemployed veterans in Winnipeg

Index